THE DEADLIEST WOMAN
IN THE WEST

MOTHER NATURE ON THE PRAIRIES AND PLAINS
1800 - 1900

THE DEADLIEST WOMAN IN THE WEST

MOTHER NATURE ON THE PRAIRIES AND PLAINS
1800 - 1900

ROD BEEMER

CAXTON PRESS
Caldwell, Idaho
2006

Library of Congress Cataloging-in-Publication Data

Beemer, Rod, 1941-
  The deadliest woman in the West : mother nature on the prairies
and plains / Rod Beemer.
       p. cm.
  Includes bibliographical references (p.   ) and index.
  ISBN 0-87004-455-9
  1. Natural disasters—West (U.S.)—History. I. Title.

GB5010.B44 2006
363.34097809034—dc22

                                        2006001018

Cover design by
Chuck Beemer

Lithographed and bound in the United States of America

CAXTON PRESS
Caldwell, Idaho
173552

For Dawn Ellen

TABLE OF CONTENTS

ILLUSTRATIONS

Maps

ACKNOWLEDGMENTS

No book finds its way into this world by the efforts of one individual alone. Therefore, grateful appreciation and thanks are extended to the many who helped this one find its way:

My wife, Dawn, who read and reread innumerable drafts. Her proofreading skill, her suggestions, and her support have been without measure. My sons, Chuck, Nathan, and David, who guided their technology-challenged dad through the baffling world of computers, email, and the Internet. An additional thanks to Chuck for his graphic design skills that handled selecting and processing the images for the book.

Tom and Deb Goodrich who were the first to encourage me to write this book. Also for the material for my book that they found while doing research for their own books.

Friends and fellow writers, Judy Lilly, Joyce Pearson, Larry Uri, Therese Uri, Victoria Page and Sherida Warner for their critiques and encouragement.

Susan Marchant, director of the Kansas Center for the Book, 1987-2005, and champion of all Kansas authors; thanks for your encouragement.

Friend and author, Charles Durham, for the many hours we talked about writing and for reading the MS and suggesting many changes that made it a better work.

Friend and former New York editor, Pat LaBrutto, for reading parts of the MS, for encouragement, and for publishing suggestions.

Ben Peek and Paul Keene for reading the relevant chapter and verifying insights into their family tree.

Don Rowlison, Site Curator, Cottonwood Ranch, Kansas State Historical Society for critiquing the MS and suggesting many improvements.

Harry Spohn, retired Director of the North Platte Federal Weather Office, for reading the entire MS and offering some helpful changes.

Shelly Henley Kelly, University Archivist, Neumann Library, University of Houston-Clear Lake, for reading the last chapter and saving me from committing several errors.

Patt Murphy, "Ich^é pi," proprietor of the American Indian Art Center in Abilene, Kansas, for reading the MS and pointing out a newcomer's errors.

Librarians at the Salina Public Library who deserve special thanks are: Judy Lilly for handling countless microform requests and Linda Grieve (1947-2005) for the many, many interlibrary loans she processed. Also thanks to Connie Hocking who stepped in to fill Linda's shoes during, and after her bout with cancer.

A special thanks also to these employees, librarians, archivists, and curators at the following institutions: Betsy Crawford-Gore, Santa Fe Trail Center, Larned, Kansas; Rosalie Gardner, Fort Kearny State Historical Park, Kearny, Nebraska; Connie Childers, Fort McPherson National Cemetery, Maxwell, Nebraska; Ken R. Stewart and Matthew T. Reitzel, South Dakota State Historical Society, Pierre, South Dakota; Peterson "Pete" Brink and Carmella Orosco, Special Collections, Love Library, University of Nebraska Lincoln, Lincoln, Nebraska; Sarah M. Polak, Mari Sandoz High Plains Heritage Center, Chadron State College, Chadron, Nebraska; Anita Middleton, Graham County Historical Society, Hill City, Kansas; Mary Ann Thompson, Hays Public Library, Hays, Kansas; Diane B. Jacob and Mary Laura Kludy, Virginia Military Institute, Lexington, Virginia; Chris Moore, Prairie Museum of Art and History, Thomas County Historical Society, Colby, Kansas; Dot Halstead, New Madrid Historical Museum, New Madrid, Missouri; Reginald B. Murray, Nicodemus National Historic Site, Bogue, Kansas; staff at the Missouri History Museum and Research Center, Missouri Historical Society, St. Louis, Missouri; Mary Allen, Graham County Public Library, Hill City, Kansas; Casey Edward Greene, Rosenberg Library, Galveston, Texas; Sarah Higgins, The Library of Virginia, Richmond, Virginia; Douglas Weiskopf, Texas Room, Houston Public Library-Houston Metropolitan Research Center, Houston, Texas; Karen Smith, Temple Public Library, Temple, Texas; staff, Goodall City Library, Ogallala, Nebraska; staff, North Platte Public Library, North Platte, Nebraska; staff, Texas State Library and Archives, Austin, Texas; staff, The Center for American History, University of Texas at Austin, Austin, Texas; Nancy Sherbert, staff, Kansas State Historical Society Archives, Topeka, Kansas; Jeannette E. Pierce, The Sheridan Libraries of Johns Hopkins University, Baltimore, Maryland; Sharon Silengo, State Historical Society of North Dakota, Bismarck, North Dakota; Christopher Kortlander, Custer Battlefield

Museum, Gerryowen, Montana; Ann Marie Donoghue, Buffalo Bill Historical Center, Cody, Wyoming; Christine Montgomery, State Historical Society of Missouri, Columbia, Missouri; Mary-Jo Miller, Nebraska State Historical Society, Lincoln, Nebraska; Carol Barnett, The Royal Meteorological Society, Reading, Berkshire, United Kingdom.

I would be remiss if I failed to express my gratitude to editor Wayne Cornell whose interest and patience have been more than any writer could hope for.

The fear of errors in the text is exceeded only by the fear that I've made an error, or an omission in acknowledging and thanking the many people who helped this book become reality. To anyone I've overlooked, I offer my apologizes and my thanks.

Any errors are, without exception, mine alone.

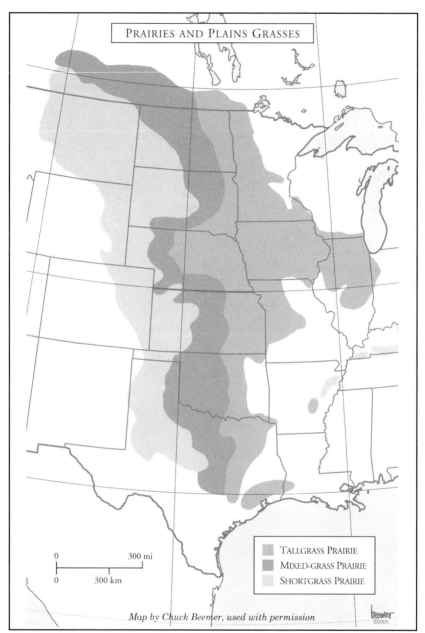

PRAIRIES AND PLAINS GRASSES

0   300 mi

0   300 km

TALLGRASS PRAIRIE
MIXED-GRASS PRAIRIE
SHORTGRASS PRAIRIE

Map by Chuck Beemer, used with permission

Humans, animals, and plants that survived in the grassland corridor between the Mississippi River and the Rocky Mountains had to adapt to Mother Nature's extremes. Rainfall can vary from 45 inches in the eastern tallgrass area to 10 inches on the western high plains. And temperatures can vary as much as 130 degrees Fahrenheit from winter to summer.

INTRODUCTION

Unknown land, or *pays inconnu*, was how early French traders described the trans-Mississippi prairies and plains.

In 1803 Thomas Jefferson lamented to Congress that this trans-Mississippi territory and its inhabitants "are not as well known as is rendered desirable." So, motivated by intellectual curiosity and national concerns, Jefferson determined to explore this unknown land.

He wasted little time and in 1804 obtained a modest amount of congressional funding and, as soon as preparation could be made, dispatched Lewis and Clark on their epic journey.

In so doing, Jefferson opened the door for America's love affair with this mysterious land. However, just five short years after Lewis and Clark's triumphant return, Mother Nature served notice that the honeymoon was over. She rolled the mighty Mississippi River backwards, swallowed entire towns, and reshaped the river valley. Nearly 800 miles away in Washington, Jefferson's successor, President James Madison and First Lady Dolley Madison, were awakened by the shock.

The New Madrid earthquakes had begun.

It was December 1811.

During the next five months more than 2,000 aftershocks agitated the North American continent from the Rocky Mountains to the Atlantic Seaboard. These quakes were a portent that the following century with Mother Nature would be a violent and stormy affair.

Between the Mississippi River and the Rocky Mountains lies the Great Plains corridor, unique to the world's topography and weather patterns. Upon this huge stage, particularly during the nineteenth century, was played out some of the planet's most intense weather events. Then as now, unimpeded by east-west mountain ranges, frigid Arctic air masses swept down from the north to collide with warm, moist air surging inland from the Gulf of Mexico.

Mighty thunderstorms rumbled across these prairies and plains accosting man and beast with tornadoes, hail, and floods. Lightning struck men dead; or it ignited prairie fires capable of overtaking the swiftest horse and rider.

On 27 May 1896, a violent thunderstorm unleashed a tornado that ripped through St. Louis, Missouri, killing more people than Lieutenant Colonel George A. Custer lost at the Little Big Horn. On 25 June 1876, companies C, E, F, I, and L of the Seventh Cavalry suffered 225 casualties. The tornado claimed 255 lives.

On the other hand, some years the thunderstorms failed to bring rain, and drought transformed the sky into fiery brass and the ground into iron. Crops withered and died. Rivers, streams, and lakes became only dusty scars upon the land; life-threatening famine overshadowed all creation.

Abruptly things could change again and the mythical Cold Maker, sweeping in from the north on a white horse, turned thunderstorms into blizzards. The howling wind and paralyzing cold froze to death thousands upon thousands of animals and scores of men, women, and children.

The Plains Indians had lived with violent storms for centuries, weaving many aspects of weather into their tribal lore and their religion. Those new to the land looked to their own religion for an explanation of catastrophic events. During the New Madrid earthquakes, some newcomers speculated that the earth and moon had collided. Others believed the great comet had struck the western mountains. Such heavenly events were interpreted as signs ushering in the day of the Lord. Both saints and sinners rushed to churches in a desperate effort to pacify their God.

Equally bizarre was the belief that flourished during the devastating drought of the early 1890s. Settlers living in the Nebraska Panhandle believed that the tall church steeples split the clouds and spoiled the rain. Therefore those new to the prairies and plains viewed one cataclysmic event as a manifestation of too little religion and the other as a result of too much religion.

After nearly 100 years of romance, Mother Nature dealt the love affair a blow that resulted in this nation's deadliest natural disaster; the 1900 Galveston Storm stunned the nation and the world. Yet, even this did not lessen people's fascination with the prairies and plains or with Mother Nature.

It isn't the intent of this work to verify or disprove any accounts since they reflect the actual feelings, recollections and opinions of those who lived through these traumatic events.

Nor will spelling variants or misspelled words be noted or corrected in any quoted material. Because, wherever it's possible, their words should be used to tell their story.

The word "newcomer" will be used to denote all non-Indians, be they European, African, Asian, or mixed blood. Not all were explorers, not all were settlers, not all were immigrants, but the one thing they all had in common when they ventured west of the Mississippi River was being new to the land.

The trans-Mississippi states, or parts of states, considered prairies and plains for the purpose of this work include those west of the Mississippi River and east of the Rocky Mountains.

Then as now, neither Indian nor newcomer could control Mother Nature, but the story of their struggle with such a powerful, unpredictable force is worthy of telling. It's a story of unspeakable hardship, unbearable heartache, and yet, ultimately, unprecedented triumph.

Here then, is the story of the Indian's and newcomer's encounter with Mother Nature in the *pays inconnu*, or unknown land of the trans-Mississippi West's prairies and plains.

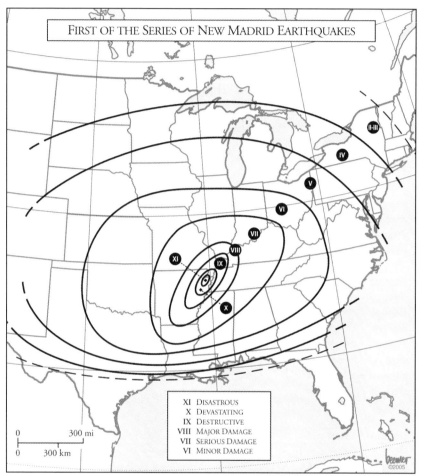

FIRST OF THE SERIES OF NEW MADRID EARTHQUAKES

XI DISASTROUS
X DEVASTATING
IX DESTRUCTIVE
VIII MAJOR DAMAGE
VII SERIOUS DAMAGE
VI MINOR DAMAGE

0   300 mi

0   300 km

Map by Chuck Beemer; used with permission

The New Madrid earthquakes of 1811-1812 remain the largest in recorded history to rock the contiguous United States. They were felt from the Rocky Mountains to the Atlantic seaboard and from Canada to the Gulf of Mexico.

Chapter One

ANGRY EARTH

Civilization exists by geologic consent, subject to change without notice.

—Will Durant, *Nature on the Rampage*

George Roddell was jolted awake in the early morning hours of 6 December 1811. The house shuddered and groaned as it swayed like a reed in the wind. Household furniture, even the bed he was in, skidded and bounced across the floor. Seconds later the chimney collapsed sending bricks crashing into the cabin's interior.

He struggled to stand and understand.

Slowly he realized that it wasn't God or a demon shaking his world. It was an earthquake. Checking his own fears, he began calming his terrified family. He managed to light a candle and by its dim light saw that his family was unhurt except for a few cuts and bruises. The inside of the cabin was wrecked.

The mantel clock had stopped but his pocket watch told him it was two o'clock in the morning. Minutes later the earth's shaking subsided enough for him to dress and step outside where he entered an equally altered world. A ghostly fog rose from the ground wrapping everything in a soft darkness that could be felt. Intermittently, strange lights flashed in the heavens and the ground itself emitted an eerie glow.[1] Beneath his feet, subterranean thunder rumbled and rolled; around him the atmosphere reeked of sulfur and brimstone.

Although the shocks were becoming less and less violent, all of nature seemed to bode ill. Roddell worried that his mill might be damaged but decided the inspection could wait until daylight; for the moment, he would remain by his house and family.

1

Roddell made a mental tally of eight or nine shocks since the first quake had rousted him and his family from their beds. He couldn't help but wonder if this was the final culmination of so many unusual events that had occurred since the beginning of the year. Spring flooding on the Mississippi River and its tributaries had been the worst in decades. Sickness, also the worst in years, followed the floods. And one couldn't ignore the two-tailed comet that was visible every clear night since early September. Then on 17 September the sun disappeared and plunged the world into darkness at noontime.

Even more unusual were the stories river boatman told of an endless moving ribbon of squirrels leaving Kentucky and moving tirelessly west. Thousands upon thousands of the creatures drowned when their path intersected the Ohio River.[2]

There were the rumors afoot that another war with Great Britain was almost a sure thing. Could this be the beginning of the final judgment? It was not a comforting thought.

As dawn began devouring the night shadows, Roddell's attention turned to more present and pressing concerns. How many hours, he wondered, would it take to repair the cabin? More importantly, was his mill still standing? Was it damaged? If so, how badly?

He started toward the mill just as a violent shock sank the bayou as far as he could see up and down the bank. It upset his mill and threatened to swallow his home. Stunned, he watched as the swamp and the dry land changed roles; swamp became dry land and dry land became a flooded swamp. In those chaotic seconds his family fled from the house towards the timber but their flight was halted by large fissures splitting open in their path. Roddell ran to join his family and reached them just as the next shock opened more crevasses around them.

Immediately water began rising from these fissures until it was waist deep. Beneath the water the earth continued to open and close sending water, mud, sand, and stone coal shooting skyward as high as the tree tops.

Roddell gathered all his courage, plus a few household items they could carry, and began leading his family away from the river and toward, what he hoped, was still higher ground to the

State Historical Society of Missouri, Columbia

Photography was still years in the future when the 1811-1812 New Madrid Earthquakes struck the North American continent. One of the few illustrations of the event was published in 1851 in *The Great West*, by Henry Howe.

west. Although to the west as far as he could see was now a lake. A lake of muddy, warm water "of a temperature of 100-degress, or over blood heat, at times of a warmth to be uncomfortable."[3] It hid chasms into which they stumbled and fallen trees over

3

which they tripped. Joining the human exodus to high ground were coyotes, wolves, bears, possums, raccoons, rabbits, squirrels, cattle, dogs, horses—all the region's quadrupeds plus countless snakes.

Roddell (sometimes Ruddell) feared for his family, feared for his friends, and feared for his fellow citizens of Little Prairie, Territory of Missouri. He led his family onward, wondering if a next step would suck them all into a watery netherworld of boiling brimstone.

The settlement of Little Prairie was located on the Mississippi River about 190 land-miles below St. Louis, Missouri. It was described as a "small river town a day's float downstream from New Madrid and a mile upstream from Island #16. It had been founded around 1800 by Francois LeSeiur—a co-founder of New Madrid seventeen years earlier. There were between 100 and 200 inhabitants."[4]

Little Prairie was mostly a French settlement located on the west bank of the Mississippi River and therefore part of the Louisiana Purchase which President Jefferson bought from France.

Prior to this, ownership had passed back and forth between France and Spain. Great Britain, from time to time, also cast a covetous eye on this trans-Mississippi land. For this reason, in 1762, France secretly ceded the Louisiana Territory to Spain thus preventing the British from gaining possession.

The Revolutionary War officially ended with the signing of the Treaty of Paris in 1783. This established, on paper at least, the Mississippi River as the western boundary of the new nation. While across the Father of Waters to the west, Spain's flag proclaimed to all newcomers that this land was part of the Spanish empire.

At the close of the Revolutionary War very few Americans had established permanent settlements between the Appalachian Mountains and the Mississippi River. Knowing that unoccupied land is difficult land to hold, the United States encouraged settlers to move west. But Spain hadn't totally given up the idea of retaining power and control of some land east of the

Mississippi, so it was encouraging settlers to ally themselves with Spain instead of the fledgling new United States.

Title to land west of the Mississippi was proving a slippery thing; in 1800 Spain and France entered a secret agreement by which Spain ceded "Louisiana" back to France. A year later President Jefferson learned of the impending transfer of control to France. Immediately he realized this could disrupt vital U.S. commerce moving on the Mississippi River.

Considering Napoleon's aggressiveness, Jefferson's concerns were valid. Luckily, problems in other parts of Napoleon's empire convinced the French leader to sell Louisiana to the United States. The purchase for $15 million was finalized in the spring of 1803 and the 827,192 square miles of new land, in effect, doubled the territory claimed by the United States.

Just a few miles westward into this new territory was the epicenter of the New Madrid earthquakes. Approximately thirty miles west of, and running nearly parallel with the Mississippi River is the St. Francis River that forms the western boundary of the Missouri bootheel. The St. Francis River is born just west of present day Farmington, Missouri, and joins the Mississippi River at Helena, Arkansas.

Men who knew the region referred to this land as sunk country. "A region 150 mi. long and 40 mi. broad, later called the 'Sunken Country,' sank from 3 to 9 ft., and river water rushed in."[5]

Timothy Dudley, who experienced the earthquake while living in New Madrid, provides a graphic description of the area's topography.

> On the west bank of the Mississippi river, sixty-five miles below the mouth of the Ohio, by the winding of the river, and about twenty miles in a direct line, stands an old Spanish town called New Madrid. The southern boundary line of Kentucky is the famous political line of 36°30' north latitude, constituting also the southern boundary line of Missouri, crossing the Mississippi river a short distance below New Madrid. Thirty miles below was an old French village called Little Prairie, and south and west of this village is a long cypress

swamp extending north and south a distance of one hundred and twenty miles, and in breadth east and west twenty-five or thirty miles, which was called fifty years since the St. Francis swamps.

I have been thus particular in locating these old towns and lowlands from the fact that evidence is continually accumulating which goes to prove that all the commotions which have disturbed the earth's surface for the last half century in the western States have had their origins in the St. Francis swamps.[6]

James Fletcher fled Little Prairie during the first hard shocks of the quake. His recollections were later published in the *Pittsburgh (Pennsylvania) Gazette*.

From Mr. James Fletcher, in whose statement we place the utmost reliance we have received the following narrative: At Little Prairie, (a beautiful spot on the west side of the Mississippi river about 30 miles from New-Madrid), on the 16th of December last, about 2 o'clock, A. M. we felt a severe concussion of the earth, which we supposed to be occasioned by a distant earthquake, and did not apprehend much danger. Between that time and day we felt several other slighter shocks; about sunrise another very severe one came on, attended with a perpendicular bouncing that caused the earth to open in many places—some eight and ten feet wide, numbers of less width, and of considerable length—some parts have sunk much lower than others; where one of these large openings are, one side remains as high as before the shock and the other is sunk; some more, some less; but the deepest I saw was about twelve feet . . . As if by instinct, we flew as soon as we could from the river, dreading most danger there—but after rambling about two or three hours, about two hundred gathered at Capt. Francis Lescuer's, where we encamped, until we heard that the upper country was not damaged, when I left the camp (after staying there twelve days) to look for some other place, and was three days getting about thirty miles, from being obliged to travel around those chasms.[7]

It was fortuitous that residents abandoned Little Prairie for the Mississippi, like a hungry predator, stalked the beleaguered town.

> Three months after Little Prairie was evacuated, in March 1812, a merchant, James McBride, came down the river with two flatboats heavily laden with flour, whiskey, and pork. He tied up on the Missouri side a mile or two above Island #16, only to realize that he was moored over part of what had been a portion of Little Prairie—"now the bed of the Mississippi River." He observed coffins projecting from the adjacent bank, the remains of a graveyard carried off by the flood. Not all of the town was under water . . .Of those that had not disappeared completly, not a single house remained standing.
>
> According to McBride's journal . . . "The surface of the ground was cracked in almost every direction," he recounts "But what particularly attracted my attention were circular holes in the earth from five or six to thirty feet in diameter, the depth corresponding with the diameters so as to be about half as deep as wide, and surrounded with a circle of sand two or three feet deep and a black substance like stone coal . . . All nature appeared in ruins," he continued, "and seemed to mourn in solitude over her melancholy fate . . . Suddenly," he said, "I was overcome with dread and hastily returned to my boat."[8]

A year later a few former residents returned to Little Prairie and attempted to rebuild the town. They renamed the new settlement Lost Village which proved all too prophetic. Within a single decade the mighty Mississippi forced the townspeople to leave the site a second time, finally abandoning it forever to the relentless encroachment of the river.

The winter of 1811 just wasn't a good time to have "Prairie" in the name of your town. Big Prairie, located near the present site of Helena, Arkansas, was founded in 1797. In December 1811 it housed about twenty families with a collective population of nearly 100 souls.

Unfortunately, "When the great quakes of 16 December hit Big Prairie, the sandy sediments upon which it stood began to liquify and sink. Everyone successfully escaped, but the town of Big Prairie was never seen again. Its former site is now occupied by the river."[9]

Today, these 1811-1812 earthquakes are referred to as the "New Madrid earthquake," a phrase that contains two erroneous concepts about the event. First, the settlement of New Madrid was not the epicenter of the first quake. Secondly, there wasn't just one earthquake but a series of at least 1,874 shocks during the following several months.

The epicenter of the initial shock on 16 December was located approximately sixty-five land-miles south and a little west of New Madrid. The site is just west of present day Blytheville, Arkansas. This was the shock that awakened George Roddell, his family, and his neighbors.

About ten miles closer to New Madrid, near present day Steele, Missouri, was the epicenter of the second violent shock. This is the quake that occurred near sunup and the one responsible for toppling Roddell's mill.

Each following shock's epicenter was moving from southwest to northeast on a line roughly parallel to today's Interstate 55. This line, called the *Bootheel Lineament*, is located halfway between I-55 and the St. Francis River.

A third major jolt struck about eleven o'clock that morning with its epicenter approximately ten miles further northeast along the Lineament. Ground zero for this mega tremor was Little Prairie. Today Caruthersville, Missouri, is near the old site of Little Prairie.

Between 16 December 1811, and 22 January 1812, the violent quakes took a holiday even though small shocks were felt almost daily. Some witnesses reported that slight tremors visited the region hourly.

Then on 23 January 1812, at nine o'clock in the morning, a violent quake rocked the area. Its epicenter was, once more, about ten miles farther northeast along the Bootheel

Lineament. The site was on the Missouri side of the Mississippi River across from today's Tiptonville, Tennessee.

It took two weeks for the epicenter to move the next ten miles to a location near Pleasant Point and Marston, Missouri. On 7 February 1812, another violent quake, dubbed the "hard shock," hit at about a quarter after three in the morning. This was the shock responsible for the legend of the Mississippi River reversing itself and flowing backwards.

When studying the New Madrid earthquakes, it is difficult to grasp the huge geographical area affected by the quakes. Nonetheless, records make it clear. Between 16 December 1811, and 7 February 1812, the most violent shocks were felt in the southeast, in the middle seaboard states, in New England, in Detroit, in Canada's Province of Quebec, far up the Missouri River, and in New Orleans. The area within which tremors could be felt without the aid of instruments approached one million square miles.[10]

The editor of the *(St. Louis) Louisiana Gazette* informed readers that

> from what we have read on that subject, we cannot find an instant, where the earth's vibration has extended to such a vast portion of country as of the last two months concussion: travelers say that that it has been felt in New York, Pennsylvania and Virginia: In Kentucky and the state of Ohio its effects were more distinctive to buildings than in Louisiana. Hunters from the west, three or four hundred miles from this place, aver that the shock felt on the 16th of Dec. was extremely violent in the headwaters of the White river.[11]

Saying something is "extremely violent" can mean different things to different people. Because of this, seismologists developed the Modified Mercalli Intensity Scale to establish standards by which to judge the severity of an earthquake. With this scale, the intensity of a quake is assigned a rating expressed as a Roman numeral from I through XII. The low end is I and the high end is XII.

For nearly two centuries seismologists have studied the New Madrid quakes and assigned various intensity ratings. They concluded that the shocks that awakened President James Madison and First Lady Dolly Madison "were of intensity IV on the above [Mercalli] scale in Washington, D.C., 800 miles away. They were felt in Canada and on the Gulf coast and as far away as the headwaters of the Missouri and the Arkansas rivers."[12]

The headwaters of the Missouri and the Arkansas rivers are located in the Rocky Mountains of Montana and Colorado respectively. These locations haven't been rated on the Mercalli scale but it is remarkable that the few individuals who were in the area at the time remembered the event.

Washington, D.C.'s rating of IV on the Mercalli scale causes hanging objects to swing; it makes windows, dishes, and doors rattle. Vibrations like passing trucks or the sensation of a heavy ball striking walls can be felt. And frame houses can creak. Washington, D.C. wasn't an isolated incident.

From the *Louisiana Gazette* issue of 22 February 1812, is an article stating

> the Earthquake noticed in our last has been felt in various parts of the country. The papers from Richmond, Edenton, Wilmington, Charleston and Savannah mention the phenomonon—In Charleston, six distinct shocks were felt; the first and most violent about 3 o'clock, and one minute and a half in duration. It was very severe and alarming; indeed the vibration was so great as to set some of the church bells ringing— the penduloms of the cloks stopped the picture glasses in many houses were broken.

Eyewitnesses all remembered not just one shock but a series of greater or lesser shocks continuing for several months. Unfortunately few of these individuals had the presence of mind, or the intellectual curiosity, to count and record the actual number of quakes.

J. Brooks of Louisville, Kentucky, was one of the few who did and his record is accepted by most authorities as valid. Between 16 December 1811, and 15 March 1812, he counted and recorded 1,874 shocks.

Brooks even created a rating system by which he attributed an intensity rating to each quake. His system began with "first-rate" for the most severe to "sixth-rate" for the least severe.

He explained the first-rate as "most tremendous, so as to threaten the destruction of the town . . . buildings oscillate largely and irregularly and grind against each other, the walls split and begin to yield . . . break in various directions and topple to the ground."

On the other end of the scale he described the sixth-rate as "although often causing a strange sort of sensation, absence, and sometimes giddiness, the motion is not to be ascertained positively; but by the vibrations or other objects placed for that purpose, or accidentally."

Eight shocks were judged by Brooks to be first-rate while 1,667 were judged to be of the sixth-rate variety. The balance of 199 shocks were somewhere in between the two extremes. Brooks recorded the shocks as they were felt in Louisville, Kentucky.[13]

William Leigh Pierce experienced the quakes much closer to the epicenters since he was on the Mississippi River "about 116 miles from the mouth of the Ohio." His recorded observations didn't continue as long as Brooks' but they are considered of great importance due to his proximity to the epicenters.

On 11 February 1812, the *New York Evening Post* published a letter Pierce had penned from Big Prairie "(on the Mississippi, 761 miles from N. Orleans,)" on 25 December 1811. Pierce reported counting "eighty-nine shocks" between "16th December" and "23rd December." Pierce's ratings for these shocks included "severe . . . very severe . . . violent . . . long and violent . . . great and awful . . . long and dreadful."[14]

Brooks and Pierce were perhaps the first to study the earthquakes and deserve much credit for their remarkable job of counting and describing the shocks. Still, the enormity of these earthquakes didn't snap into sharp focus until Richter scale magnitudes were applied.

Richter scales and seismographs obviously weren't available in 1811 and 1812, but seismologists have documented enough geological data to arrive at scale magnitudes. These various studies fail to agree 100 percent, yet one constant has emerged: these events were big.

The hard shocks of 16 December 1811, were rated as 8.0 to 8.6 on the Richter scale. The most severe shock of 23 January 1812, was assigned a value of 8.4 on the Richter. The "hard shock of 7 February 1812, weighed in at 8.8.[15] As a benchmark for comparison, the devastating San Francisco earthquake of 4 March 1906, registered only 7.8.

Indians and newcomers alike experienced the largest recorded earthquakes ever to occur in the contiguous United States. While many struggled for their lives upon a trembling land, other souls were cast adrift on a mighty river gone mad.

Rivers were the highways of the era but conventional flatboats, barges, and keel boats were slow. They were slow enough going downstream but a trip upstream against the current proved even slower and extremely labor-intensive.

A vessel that could overcome the current and travel upriver fast and easy would turn the rivers into superhighways. Such a miracle vessel could dominate the river freight and passenger trade; monetary rewards would be enormous.

Nicholas Roosevelt, a great-uncle of President Theodore Roosevelt, married Lydia Latrobe in 1809. Lydia was the daughter of architect Benjamin Latrobe who directed the building of vessels for Robert Livingston and Robert Fulton.

Roosevelt convinced these entrepreneurs that steamboats could become such miracle vessels on western rivers. As a result, the steamboat *New Orleans* was constructed at Pittsburgh during 1810-1811 with the purpose of plying the Mississippi River between New Orleans and Natchez.

On 20 October 1811, the *New Orleans* left Pittsburgh and paddle-wheeled its way down the Ohio and Mississippi rivers and into the history books of the American West. Its journey coincided with another historical event that threatened to sink the boat's designer and builder, his wife and two children, and the steamboat's crew—plus a large Newfoundland dog.

Roosevelt, his pregnant wife Lydia, and their young daughter were all aboard the *New Orleans* when it steamed out of Pittsburgh. Their friends considered it unwise at best, and insane at worst, for Lydia to accompany her husband on this journey. She could not be dissuaded.

A portent of trouble was encountered when the *New Orleans* made a midnight stop at Louisville on 1 October 1811. This harbinger of the industrial revolution came chugging, puffing, and hissing out of the night, frightening residents of Louisville into reasoning that *the* comet had fallen into the Ohio River.[16]

The comet or *the great comet* had spawned wild conjecture and religious superstition for millennium upon millennium. American pioneers were not immune to these feelings and viewed all comets with some fear and anxiety. It was obvious this wasn't your everyday comet. Initial calculations set its orbital period as 3,757 years but this was later adjusted to 3,065 years. Prior to 1811, humans last gazed upon its heavenly splendor sometime around the year 1,254 B.C. and mankind will have to wait until 4,876 A.D. for its next appearance.

During 1811 the comet was first observed in March where it became visible over parts of Europe. It was described as "spectacular," reaching peak brilliance during September and October and visible in the United States from September until January 1812. Napoleon, observed the comet while planning his upcoming campaign and view it as a good omen. If it was an omen, it didn't favor Napoleon who got mauled by the Russians when he executed his war plans.

Omens and superstition aside, the Ohio River was too low for the *New Orleans* to safely negotiate the falls below the town. Roosevelt and his miracle vessel were forced to wait for higher water. It was during this wait that Mrs. Roosevelt gave birth to a son who was probably the first child born aboard a steamboat on the Ohio River.

Low water lingered until the last week of November when the Ohio finally rose just enough to allow the *New Orleans* to successfully negotiate the falls.[17] After a long delay, the falls were finally behind them, the Roosevelt baby was fine, and the comet hadn't fallen into the river.

The *New Orleans* and crew soon encountered more challenges when the earthquake grabbed hold of the Mississippi River. "The first shock that was observed was felt on board the *New Orleans* while she lay at anchor after passing the falls. The effect was as though the vessel had been in motion and had suddenly grounded. The cable shook and trembled, and many on board experienced for the moment a nausea resembling sea sickness. It was a little while before they could realize the presence of the dread visitor."[18]

Fuel for the *New Orleans'* fire box dictated that the vessel make frequent stops to cut and load firewood. One of these stops was made at New Madrid where the Roosevelts and crew viewed the damage done to the town. Many "terror stricken people had begged to be taken on board," a request that was denied due to limited space and provisions.

The Roosevelt's dog, Tiger, prowled the deck "moaning and growling" when he sensed an impending quake. At such time he would place his head on Mrs. Roosevelt's lap, a sign that quakes were imminent. This premonition of more quakes was in itself enough to unnerve the crew, but the greatest alarm came when the pilot acknowledged that because of the caving in of the river banks and the changing of the river channels, he was lost and hadn't the slightest notion of the correct course to steer to avoid the snags and sucks of the perilous river.

The *New Orleans'* plight was shared by many other vessels on the Mississippi River. William Leigh Pierce, mentioned earlier, was aboard a flat bottom boat when the 16 December quake struck. His experiences were later published and provide one of the best accounts of what it was like on the river during the earthquakes. "Proceeding on a tour from Pittsburgh to New Orleans, I entered the Mississippi, when it receives the waters of the Ohio, on Friday the 13th day of this month, and on the 15th, in the evening, landed on the left bank of this river, about 116 miles from the mouth of the Ohio."

Assuming Pierce was counting in river miles, his location was somewhere near, or perhaps just below, present day Blytheville, Arkansas. This places him very near the epicenter of the first hard shock. He remembered that "the night was extremely dark and cloudy, not a star appeared in the heavens, and there was every appearance of a severe rain—for the last days, indeed, the sky had been continually overcast, and the weather unusually thick and hazy."

Pierce was obviously a keen observer and was very exact in pinpointing times and places during the quakes.

Precisely at 2 o'clock on Monday morning the 16th instant, we were all alarmed by the violent and convulsive agitation of the boats, accompanied by a noise similar to that which would have been produced by running over a sand bar . . . Upon examination, however, we discovered we were yet safely and securely moored. The idea of an Earthquake then suggested itself to my mind, and this idea was confirmed by a second shock, and two others in immediate succession . . . A few yards from the spot where we lay, the body of a large oak was snapped in two, and the falling part precipitated to the margin of the river; the trees in the forest shook like rushes; the alarming clattering of their branches may be compared to the affect which would be produced by a severe wind passing through a large cane brake.

. . . At the dawn of day I went on shore to examine the effects of the shock . . . fearing, however, to remain longer where we were, it was thought much advisable to leave our landing as expeditiously as possible; this was immediately done—at a few rods distance from the shore, we experienced a fifth shock, more severe than either of the preceding. I had expected this from the lowering appearance of the weather; it was indeed most providential that we had started, for such was the strength of the this last shock, that the bank to which we were (but a few moments since) attached, was rent and fell into the river, whilst the trees rushed from the forest, precipitating themselves into the water with a force sufficient to have dashed us into a thousand atoms.

. . . near our boat a spout of confined air, breaking its way thro' the waters, burst forth and with a loud report discharged mud, stick, &c. from the river's bed, at least 30 feet above the surface. These spoutings were frequent, and in many places appeared to rise to the very heavens . . .

During the day there was with very little in
termission, a continued series of shocks . . . the bed of the
river was incessantly disturbed, and the water boiled
severely in every part . . . our ears were continually
assailed with the crashing of timber . . . whilst their
heads were whipped together with a quick and rapid
motion; many were torn from their native soil, and
hurled with tremendous force into the river; one of
these whose huge trunk (at least 3 feet in diameter)
had been much shattered, was thrown better than an
hundred yards from the bank, where it is planted into
the bed of the river, there to stand, a terror to future
navigators.

. . . we passed thousands of acres of land which
had been cleft from the main shore and tumbled into
the water, leaving their growth waving above the
surface.[19]

Roosevelt's *New Orleans* and Pierce's flatboat were not alone
on the river. Probably hundreds of boats were caught on the
Mississippi during the earthquakes but how many perished
and how many lives were lost will never be known.

The task before Roosevelt and Pierce was to navigate the
turbulent Mississippi River now choked with many thousands
of new planters and sawyers. Equally important was avoiding
the sucks that were strong enough to swallow boats and crews.
Being capsized or buried by falling banks was the penalty
for steering, or being forced, too close to the banks. It was a
daunting task on a roguish river a mile wide and seven stories
deep.

The Father of Waters, however, isn't a threat to anyone or
anything at Lake Itasca, Minnesota. Here, at its headwaters,
it enjoys some aimless meandering before setting a 2,350-mile
course almost due south through the middle of the United
States. From the west it is fed by the Missouri River; from the
east the Ohio River adds its waters.

The Red, Arkansas, Kansas, and Platte are additional major
rivers of the western basin. Besides the Ohio, the eastern basin
includes the Kentucky, Green, Cumberland, and Tennessee
rivers.

Approximately 1.2 million square miles make up the giant Mississippi watershed covering one-eighth of the North American continent. All, or parts, of thirty-one U.S. states and two Canadian provinces are found within this huge expanse.

Indians called the river by many different names including *Mischipi*, *Messipi*, *Meschasip*, or *Misisipi* all of which mean Big Water or Father of Waters. It was both larder and highway to Indian tribes living along its banks.

Thinking in terms of owning the Father of Waters was inconceivable to them because they considered rivers as part of Mother Earth's gift to all people. Newcomers quickly changed this perception and the Indians soon learned that ownership was a high priority with the strange bearded men who now plied the river.

In May 1541 the Spanish explorer Hernando de Soto was one of the first. He was followed in 1673 by the French government agent, Louis Jolliet, who made his way from Canada via the Fox and Wisconsin rivers.

The next decade brought another French party who pioneered an overland route from the Great Lakes to the Illinois River and onto the Mississippi. When this Frenchman, Lord de La Salle, reached the delta he claimed the river and all its tributaries— the entire Mississippi basin—for France.

Claiming is one thing, holding is quite another.

Within a generation, the Mississippi was a vital link between France's Gulf of Mexico settlements and Canada, and La Salle's claim was vaguely designated as "Louisiana."

But France's grasp on the Mississippi was never firm. French traders settled the upper river, establishing towns like St. Louis and Prairie du Chien (now in Wisconsin), whose names survive to this day. But the lower river passed into Spanish hands in 1769; the Treaty of Paris (1783) optimistically declared the river as the western boundary of the United States; and republican France reacquired the much-bartered stream only long enough to sell it to the United States as part of the Louisiana Purchase (1803). This last move recognized what had been obvious for a quarter of a century—growing domination of the river by the Americans.[20]

Newcomers confidently declared they owned the Mississippi River. It's doubtful, however, that either George Roddell and the refugees from Little Prairie, or the Roosevelts and crew aboard the *New Orleans* could see any indication that the river recognized such ownership. Governmental decree has no meaning to the Mississippi River.

Occasionally, as if to emphasize the point, the river engages in behavior that appears to defy even the laws of nature; the New Madrid earthquakes were one such occasion. Witnesses insisted that the Mississippi River flowed backward following the hard shock of 7 February 1812.

Concurrent with, or the causation of, this retro current was the creation of two sets of falls, or rapids, on the river. The first set of falls was a few miles above the town of New Madrid; the second set was several miles below the town.

Mathias Speed was aboard a boat descending the river on 7 February 1812. That evening they reached the head of the ninth island below the mouth of the Ohio. At this point they decided to spend the night and tied to a willow bar on the west bank of the river.

When the hard shock jolted the land, this willow bar began to sink which forced the crew to cut loose and move out into the river. "After getting out so far as to be out of danger from the trees which were falling in from the bank—the swells in the river was so great as to threaten the sinking of the boat every moment. We stopped the outholes with blankets to keep out the water . . . At day light we perceived the head of the tenth island."

The Mississippi River had been charted for navigation and the islands were then numbered starting with island No.1 that is just below the mouth of the Ohio River. Island No. 9 is approximately forty river miles below the confluence of the two rivers.

Speed, in careful detail, continues his account:

> During all this time we had made only about four
> miles down the river—from which circumstance, and

from that of an immense quantity of water rushing
into the river from the woods—it is evident that the
earth at this place, or below, had been raised so high
as to stop the progress of the river, and caused it to
overflow its banks—We took the right hand channel
of the river at this island, and having reached within
about a half mile of the lower end of the town [?], we
were affrightened with the appearance of a dreadful
rapid of falls in the river just below us; we were so far
in the suck that it was impossible now to land—all
hopes of surviving was now lost and certain destruction
appeared to await us! We having passed the rapids
without injury, keeping our bow foremost, both boats
being still lashed together.

As we passed the point on the left hand below the
island, the bank and trees were rapidly falling in.
From the state of alarm I was in at this time, I cannot
pretend to be correct as to the length or height of the
falls; but my impression is, that they were about equal
to the rapids of the Ohio . . .

. . . During my stay at new Madrid there were
upwards of twenty boats landed, all of whom spoke of
the rapids above, and conceived of it as I had done.

Several persons, who came up the river in a small
barge, represented that there were other falls in
the Mississippi, about 7 miles below New Madrid,
principally on the eastern side—more dangerous than
those above—and that some boats had certainly been
lost in attempting to pass them.[21]

Eyewitness writings have, to a limited degree, succeed in
capturing the high level of drama created by the quakes. Even
so, sometimes mere words are surely inadequate, such as the
chilling scene described here.

During the various shocks, the banks of the
Mississippi caved in by whole acres at a time. Large
trees disappeared under the ground or were cast with
frightful violence into the river. At times, the waters of
the Mississippi were seen to rise up like a wall in the

middle of the stream, and then suddenly rolling back would beat against either bank with terrific force. Boats of considerable size were often cast 'high and dry' upon the shores of the river . . .

. . . A man who was on the river in a boat at the time of one of the shocks, declares that he saw the mighty Mississippi *cut in twain*, while the waters poured down a vast chasm into the bowels of the earth. A moment more, and the chasm was filled, but the boat which contained this witness was crushed in the tumultuous efforts of the flood to regain its former level.[22]

The perception that the river actually reversed its flow begs some explanation that would harmonize the laws of nature with the numerous accounts of this event. To reverse the flow, apart from some local phenomenon, would require that the entire river's drainage basin above New Madrid had suddenly become lower than the Mississippi River bed. Obviously this didn't happen.

As noted previously, the Mississippi from its headwater to its mouth is 2,350 miles and during that journey it drops 1,475 feet—640 feet of this drop occurs before it leaves its birthright state of Minnesota.[23]

That leaves a drop of only 835 feet over the remaining approximately 1,895 miles. These are river miles as taken from *Lloyd's Steamboat Directory* published in 1856. Mother Nature and the Army Corp of Engineers have both been altering the river's course by whim and by design, so the miles and figures are approximate. Nevertheless, the Mississippi River trough is very flat and the rate of drop below the Minnesota line only averages .44 of a foot per mile. The closer to the Gulf you get the less the drop.

As a comparison, some people perceive the state of Kansas as "flatter than a pancake" and a trip across the state on I-70 does little to change their minds. From border to border—west to east—the elevation drops 2,693 feet over 424 miles. This is an average of 6.35 feet of drop per mile—over fourteen times greater than the Mississippi River Valley.

Mathias Speed spoke of the falls on the Mississippi River above New Madrid as being about the same as the falls on the

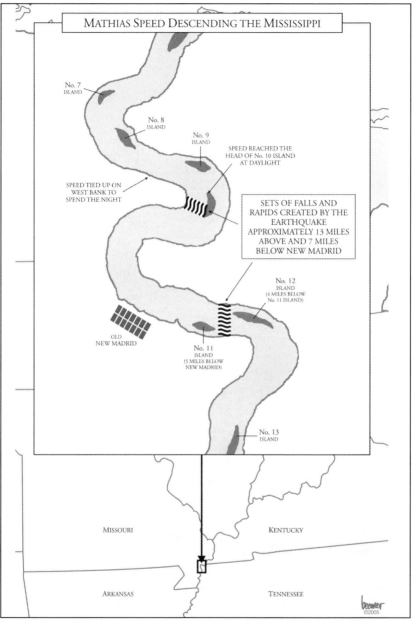

MATHIAS SPEED DESCENDING THE MISSISSIPPI

No. 7
ISLAND

No. 8
ISLAND

No. 9
ISLAND

SPEED REACHED THE
HEAD OF No. 10 ISLAND
AT DAYLIGHT

SPEED TIED UP ON
WEST BANK TO
SPEND THE NIGHT

SETS OF FALLS AND
RAPIDS CREATED BY THE
EARTHQUAKE
APPROXIMATELY 13 MILES
ABOVE AND 7 MILES
BELOW NEW MADRID

No. 12
ISLAND
(4 MILES BELOW
No. 11 ISLAND)

OLD
NEW MADRID

No. 11
ISLAND
(5 MILES BELOW
NEW MADRID)

No. 13
ISLAND

MISSOURI

KENTUCKY

ARKANSAS

TENNESSEE

Map by Chuck Beemer; used with permission

Mathias Speed, descending the Mississippi River on 7 February 1812, witnessed the reverse flow of the river and survived a quake-created falls thirteen miles above New Madrid. There also was a second falls about seven miles below the town.

Ohio River. Others agreed, so the river bed probably rose some twenty feet both above and below New Madrid.

Because the river trough is so flat, an upward tilt of twenty feet across the Mississippi could conceivably roll back the water and cause wide-spread flooding. Once the river had overcome the obstacle, the water would flow back into the river channel accounting for the "immense quantity of water rushing into the river from the woods" that Speed witnessed.

The hard shock struck at about three o'clock in the morning and Speed estimated they had traveled only three or four miles by sunup. Normally the current runs five to seven miles per hour so in three hours he should have traveled fifteen to twenty-one miles down stream.[24]

Providing his figures are correct, the restriction to the river lasted at least three hours. Under normal circumstances the volume of water flowing down the Mississippi River is 600,000 cubic feet per second. Three hours at such a rate is indeed an immense quantity of water.

Other witnesses also spoke of this devastating movement of water out of and back into the river channel.

> There were several shocks of a day, but lighter than those already mentioned until the 23d of January, 1812, when one occurred as violent as the severest of the former ones, accompanied by the same phenomena as the former. From this time until the 4th of February the earth was in continual agitation, visibly waving as a gentle sea . . . At first the Mississippi seemed to recede from its banks, and its waters gathering up like a mountain, leaving for a moment many boats, which were here on their way to New Orleans, on the bare sand, in which time the poor sailors made their escape from them. It then rising fifteen to twenty feet perpendicularly, and expanding, as it were, at the same moment, the banks were overflowed with the retrograde current, rapid as a torrent—the boats which before had been left on the sand were now torn from their moorings, and suddenly driven up a little creek, at the mouth of which they laid, to the distance in some instances, of nearly a quarter of a

mile. The river falling immediately, as rapid as it had risen, receded in its banks again with such violence, that it took with it whole groves of young cotton-wood trees, which ledged its borders. They were broken off with such regularity, in some instances, that persons who had not witnessed the fact, would be difficultly persuaded, that it has not been the work of art. A great many fish were left on the banks, being unable to keep pace with the water.[25]

The length of time the river seemingly ran backward was described as "for a few minutes" to "for several hours." The latter being supported by Speed's account of being on the river but making little, if any, downstream progress during the early morning of 7 February 1812.

It might not be technically correct to say the mighty Mississippi flowed backwards but many eyewitness accounts of a retrograde current have survived. These accounts leave no doubt that for some time on 7 February 1812, the waters of the Mississippi River at New Madrid moved from south to north.

New Madrid's ultimate demise was closely tied to this hard shock of February. However, these events were still weeks into the future when George Roddell and his charges arrived at the town.

James Fletcher, as we know, was in Little Prairie on 16 December 1811, when the first shock occurred. Fletcher noted that the entire population of Little Prairie fled with the exception of "an old negro man, probably too infirm to fly." The *Pennsylvania Gazette* of 26 February 1812, credits "Capt. George Ruddell" with leading the refugees to New Madrid. Ruddell was, according to the account, "a worthy and respectable old gentleman, and who had been the father of that neighboarhood, made good his retreat to this place, with about 200 souls."

The town that George Roddell and fellow travelers found when they struggled into New Madrid on 24 December 1811, offered little relief or encouragement to the weary and frightened refugees from Little Prairie. In fact this settlement, like Little Prairie, would also be appropriated by the Mississippi River.

Mathias Speed's description of New Madrid on 7 February 1812, suggests the town was being slowly leveled and sunk by the quakes. A sad demise for a town that briefly shared the same distinction as St. Louis.

> We landed at New Madrid about breakfast time without having experienced any injury. The appearance of the town, and the situation of the inhabitants, were such as to afford but little relief to our minds. The former elevation of the bank on which the town stood was estimated by the inhabitants at about 25 feet above common water; when we reached it the elevation was only about 12 or 13 feet- There was scarcely a house left entire—some wholly prostrated, others unroofed and not a chimney standing—the people all having deserted their habitations, where in camps and tents back of the town, and their little waterr crafts, such as skiffs, boats and canoes, hauled out of the water to their camps, that they might be ready in case the country should sink.[26]

Their concerns were well founded given that New Madrid, Missouri, was built on a ridge of sand and clay. The original town site was located on the west bank of the Mississippi River some seventy miles below the confluence of the Ohio and Mississippi.

It's strategic location earned it short-lived fame as the gateway to the trans-Mississippi west because of a natural harbor nearby. The New Madrid town site was established about 1783 as an Indian trading post. In 1789 Colonel George Morgan of New Jersey arrived after securing a large land grant from the Spanish government. Morgan's plans for a town on the west bank of the river complemented Spain's hope of attracting settlers to its side of the river. Morgan's real motive was to amass a fortune from land speculation. Both parties were soon disappointed.

Morgan laid out his original town site on the west bank of a horseshoe bend in the Mississippi. The bend was twenty-five miles in length and the current sweeping along the outside curve continually nibbled away at the soft riverbank in front of the town. During the spring floods the river didn't just nibble but took huge bites out of the bank. Consequently, the bank was eroding back at a yearly rate of 100 to 200 yards.

By 1810 the river channel was literally on the doorstep, actually consuming doorsteps, of the town's eastern-most streets. This proximity of the river coupled with the sinking of the town after the hard shock of 7 February 1812, sounded the death knell of the original town site. When the 1812 spring floods rolled down the Mississippi, the old New Madrid sank forever beneath the river's muddy waters.

Counting the number of towns and settlements that fell victim to the river and to the earthquakes is easy. Counting human victims is another matter. Fortunately the loss of life was comparatively low because the area that experienced the most severe shocks was thinly populated—with newcomers.

Nonetheless, these were killer quakes.

On land was the deadliest arena for Indians; the greatest killing field for newcomers was on the river.

William Leigh Pierce, writing about the shocks on 16 December 1811, believed that "many poor fellows are undoubtedly wrecked, or buried under the ruin of the Banks. Of the loss of four boats I am certain."[27]

Another river traveler, John Bradbury, departed St. Louis on 5 December 1811, bound for New Orleans. He commented on the many trees that had fallen into the river and the hazards they created for boats.

Along many banks the trees grew right down to the river and fell into the river as the banks eroded. Bradbury wrote that the Mississippi River harbored thousands of such trees. Some were completely hidden underwater and others were only partially submerged.

> As in most instances a large body of earth is attached to the roots of the trees, it sinks that part to the bottom of the river, whilst the upper part, more buoyant, rises to the surface in an inclined posture, generally with the head of the tree pointing down river. Some of these are firmly fixed and immoveable, and are therefore termed planters. Others, although they do not remove

25

from where they are placed, are constantly in motion, the whole tree is sometimes entirely submerged by the pressure of the stream, and carried to a greater depth by its momentum than the stream can maintain. On rising, its momentum in the opposite direction causes many of its huge limbs to be lifted above the surface of the river. The period of this oscillatory motion is sometimes of several minutes duration. These are the sawyers, which are much more dangerous than the planters . . . From these and other risks, it is common for those carrying lead, to have a canoe with them, in which they may save themselves in case of any accident happening to the boat.[28]

Accidents happened.

Bradbury reached New Madrid on 14 December 1811, and departed the next morning. He recorded passing "no fewer than thirteen arks, or Kentucky boats, going with produce to Orleans; all these we left a considerable distance behind." He mentioned that at least one of the boats carried a cargo of lead. As darkness approached, Bradbury tied up to a small island above a stretch of river known by Americans as the *Devil's Channel*.

With the coming of daylight, Bradbury and crew were able to survey the earthquake's damage. His account recorded that "two canoes floated down the river, in one of which we could perceive some Indian corn and some clothes. We considered this as a melancholy proof that some of the boats we passed the preceding day had perished. Our conjectures were afterwards confirmed, as we learned three had been overwhelmed, and that all on board had perished."[29]

New Madrid resident Eliza Bryan wrote that "the river was literally covered with the wrecks of boats, and 'tis said that one was wrecked in which there was a lady and six children, all of whom were lost."

Another loss mentioned in various accounts concerns the death of a young boy searching for a cow in the sunk country.

A family of the name of Curran were moving from New Madrid to an old French town on the Arkansas river,

Courtesy U.S. Geological Survey

The New Madrid earthquake was part of the process that resulted in this tree's double roots. The overflowing Mississippi River removed the sand from the roots and left the tree elevated. Later the tree was buried, new roots formed and then the sand was washed away again. The trees are near the south end of Reelfoot Lake in Lake County, Tennessee.

called the Port; had passed the St. Francis swamps and found some of their cattle missing; Le Roy, the youngest son, took an Indian pony, rode back to hunt for them, and was in the swamp when the first shock took place, was never seen afterwards, and was supposed to have been lost in some of those fearful chasms.[30]

Mathias Speed and companions were among the fortunate boatmen who survived the 7 February hard shock. After an almost miraculous descent over the new falls, which had been created upstream from New Madrid, they landed and spent some time ashore.

What he witnessed happening on the river was traumatic and some boats weren't able to safely negotiate the new fall but perished in the maelstrom.

##

When Americans took possession of the Louisiana Purchase in 1803 the newcomer population was only 43,000. They were primarily French as only about 6,000 considered themselves Americans.[31] Regardless of whether they were French, American, or another brand of newcomer, they were outnumbered by the Indians who considered this their home.

By 1811, when Mother Nature grabbed hold of the continent's watery backbone and commenced to shake, the Indian tribes traditionally located between the Atlantic seaboard and the Mississippi River were being inexorably nudged westward. What befell the newcomers on 16 December 1811, also befell the Indians.

Being on land didn't guarantee safety for the Indians. "A gentleman who was near the Arkansas river, at the time of the first shock in Dec. last, states, that certain Indians had arrived near the mouth of the river, who had seen a large lake or sea, where many of their brothers had resided, and had perished in the general wreck."[32]

Fletcher, who was at the town of Little Prairie reported that, "We heard of no lives being lost, except seven Indians, who were shaken into the Mississippi. This we learned from one who escaped."[33]

At least one Indian, perhaps the one mentioned above, experienced a dramatic escape according to a newspaper article. "I have heard of no white person being lost as yet—Seven Indians were swallowed up; one of them escaped; he says he was taken into the ground the depth of two trees in length; that the water came under him and threw him out again—he had to wade and swim four miles before he reached dry land."[34]

Such stories are the yarn from which legends are woven and the New Madrid earthquakes provided enough yarn for several tapestries. Reelfoot Lake, a few miles downriver from New Madrid, and situated just across the Mississippi River in Tennessee, received its name from a most unusual story.

A Chickasaw Indian chief was named Reelfoot because of his club foot and unsteady gait. Wanting a wife, and doing what Indians sometimes did, he stole a wife from a different tribe—a beautiful princess from the Choctaws. Reelfoot was so smitten with love that he stole the lovely maiden despite a warning from

Photo by author

Part of Reelfoot Lake as it appears today. The many dead Bald Cypress trees that still stand in the lake were living trees when the New Madrid earthquakes formed the lake in 1811-1812.

the Great Spirit that if he did marry the Choctaw maiden the earth would tremble in rage. It wasn't an idle threat because during the wedding ceremony the ground began to shake, the village sank and the Mississippi River flooded the site and drowned everyone.

Another legend involved a Shawnee chief named Tecumseh and his brother, Tenskwatawa, a religious leader called the Prophet. These two brothers started a political-military, religious-cultural movement to halt the influx of newcomers onto Indian land.

Tecumseh envisioned a confederacy of Indian tribes to resist, with force, the encroachment of whites. At the Creek village Tuckhabatchee, near the present site of Montgomery, Alabama, another legend was born.

When the tribe was gathered to hear the important visitor, Tecumseh made an impassioned plea for the Creeks to join the Seminoles in fighting alongside the British against the Americans. The tribe's chief, Big Warrior, accepted Tecumseh's gifts of wampum, a war ax, and a bundle of sticks. The bundle of sticks held a stick for each day until the planned battle. The "Indian practice is, to throw away a stick every morning" so there is no mistaking the appointed day of battle.

Tecumseh was an eloquent orator but Big Warrior wasn't convinced, a fact that didn't go unnoticed by Tecumseh who confronted the chief and said

> Your blood is white! You accept into your ears but not into your heart the words I bring you. You, like many of the others, have accepted the sticks and the wampum and you have even touched the hatchet at your belt, yet I know you do not mean to fight and I know the reason: you do not believe I have been sent by the Great Spirit. But you shall know. When the time comes for all these things to come together, then will I stamp my foot to the ground and awaken our great mother earth . . . and your ears will be filled with the rumble and roar of her anger. She will cause your houses to fall to the ground and the bones of every man to tremble with the trembling of the ground. Your

water jugs will crack and fall apart and great trees
will lean and fall, though there be no wind.[35]

Not surprisingly, when the New Madrid earthquakes
rumbled through the Indian villages, the event was attributed
to Tecumseh's prophecy and became part of the lore associated
with the quakes.

Not exactly legend but fitting more into the phenomenon
category, like rivers running backwards, would be the many
accounts of river islands disappearing during the earthquakes—
simply vanishing.

In 1801 a Pittsburgh printer and bookbinder named Zadok
Cramer began publishing a river guide to the Monongahela,
Allegheny, Ohio, and Mississippi rivers. Titled *The Navigator*,
the work contained information on settlements, harbors, and
distances between points. Charts showing islands, channels,
and hazards were of immense value to river boatmen. Twelve
editions were published between 1801 and 1824.

Cramer's work began numbering the Mississippi River
islands from the junction of the Ohio and the Mississippi with
island No.1 being the first one below the junction.

The edition published after the earthquakes did document
two missing islands. The first island was No. 32 which Cramer
simply noted was "destroyed by the earthquake."[36] About island
No. 94 he writes that it "has been sunk by the earthquake or
swept off by the floods."[37]

Eyewitness accounts offer additional compelling evidence
that some islands did indeed disappear beneath the turbulent
Mississippi currents. One of those accounts involved the
steamship *New Orleans*. It is possible, however, that this is the
same island as island No. 32.

The *New Orleans* continued downriver after stopping briefly
at New Madrid, and to prevent being crushed by falling river
banks adopted the habit of tying up for the night on the downstream side of an island with sloping shores. On one such
occasion Mrs. Roosevelt hoped for a quiet and restful night
since no shocks had been felt during the day.

In this, however, she was disappointed. All night long
she was disturbed by the jar and noise produced by

hard objects grating against the planking outside the boat. At times severe blows were struck that caused the vessel to tremble through its entire length. Then there would follow a continuous scratching mingled with the gurgling sound of water. Drift wood had caused sounds of the same sort before, and it was thought that drift wood was again busy in producing them. With morning, however, came the true explanation. The island had disappeared; and it was the disintegrated fragments sweeping down the river . . . At first, it was supposed, that the New Orleans had been borne along by the current: but the pilot pointed to land marks on the banks which proved that it was the island that had disappeared while the steamboat had kept its place. Where the island had been, there was now a broad reach of the river; and when the hawser was cut, for it was found impossible otherwise to free the vessel, the pilot was utterly at a loss which way to steer.[38]

Another account of a disappearing island was written by an eyewitness to the quakes but the gentleman didn't record his memories until almost fifty years after the event. It is possible that this account is also referring to Island No. 32. "In the Mississippi river, about five miles above what was then called the first Chickasaw Bluff, but in later times Plum Point, was an island about three miles long, covered with a heavy growth of timber, which sank in one of these shocks to the tops of the trees, which made the navigation extremely dangerous in a low stage of the river."[39]

Island No. 94 had acquired a rather unsavory reputation due to the thieves and robbers who frequented the island. These pirates had chosen the island as a base of operation for river piracy.

Captain Sarpy of St. Louis, planning to spend the night on the island, tied up his boat and went ashore. Upon discovering a band of river pirates already camped on the island, he quickly and quietly moved his vessel further down the river.

He described the effects of the earthquake thus: "In the night the earthquake came and next morning when the accompanying haziness disappeared the island could no longer be seen. It had been utterly destroyed as well as its pirate inhabitants."[40]

##

Today the American Psychiatric Association considers survivors of an earthquake to be at risk to develop post-traumatic stress disorder (PTSD). Almost two centuries ago it didn't take a psychiatrist to recognize signs of PTSD during the New Madrid earthquakes.

Eliza Bryan (sometimes Bryant) was a resident of New Madrid during the quakes and in March 1816 she penned an account of her remembrances. Apparently she retained a degree of composure that escaped her neighbors. "The screams of the affrighted inhabitants running to and fro, not knowing where to go, or what to do . . . formed a scene truly horrible . . . The inhabitants fled in every direction to the country, supposing (if it can be admitted that their minds can be exercised at all) that there was less danger at a distance from, than near to the river. In one person, a female, the alarm was so great that she fainted, and could not be recovered."[41]

The following is an anonymous writing by a New Madrid resident who experienced the December shocks. It was part of a newspaper article written in February 1812.

> I never before thought the passion of fear so strong as I find it here among the people . . . some so agitated that they cannot speak—others cannot hold their tongues—some cannot sit still, but must be in constant motion, while others cannot walk. Several men, I am informed, on the night of the first shock deserted their families, and have not been heard of since.[42]

Perhaps the threat of being devoured by the splitting earth drove them to such reprehensible acts. Indeed, few aspects of an earthquake terrified people like the fear of plummeting into the jaws of an opening fissure.

Documented instances of people being swallowed by a fissure during the quakes are rare. However it did apparently happen to a man who managed to reach an island after abandoning a boat before it went over the falls. During a violent shock he was clinging to a tree when the earth opened up and the tree, with him still holding on, was sunk in a fissure "so deep as to put it out of his power to get out at that place—he made his way along the fissure until a sloping side offered him an opportunity of crawling out."[43]

A white man captured by Indians as a child and living among the Osage when the quakes struck commented in his memoirs on the Indians' reactions.

> Indians were filled with great terror, on account of the repeated occurrences of violent tremors and oscillations of the earth; the trees and wigwams shook exceedingly; the ice which skirted the margin of the Arkansas river was broken in pieces; and most of the Indians thought that the Great Spirit, angry with the human race, was about to destroy the world.[44]

Pierce recorded that

> The few Indians who were on the Banks of the river, have been excessively alarmed and terrified. All nature indeed seemed to sympathize in the commotion which agitated the earth. The sun rarely shot a ray thro' the heavens. The sky was clouded, and a dreary darkness brooded over the whole face of creation, the stars were encircled with a pale light, and the comet appeared hazy and dim.[45]

There were enough of these signs and wonders during 1811 to capture the attention, and concern, of both Indians and newcomers.

Domestic animals and their wild kin began exhibiting some very strange behavior both before and after the quakes. All indications are that animals and birds were as much affected by the earthquakes as were humans.

The Mississippi River Valley is within the central flyway of migratory birds as well as being home to dozens of local species. Once again Bradbury proved to be a keen observer of events during the quakes and noted that "the screaming of the geese,

Another artist's rendition of the New Madrid earthquakes entitled "Scene of the Great Earthquake in the West." It appeared in the 1877 as an illustration in *Our First Century: One Hundred Great and Memorable Events.*

and other wild fowl, produced an idea that all nature was in a state of dissolution."[46]

Penick, in his *The New Madrid Earthquakes*, cites additional observances of this behaivor, "Ducks, geese, 'and various other kinds of wild fowl' settled on the boats, often blanketing an entire canopy. On shore smaller birds, 'retreated to the bosoms of men,' landed on heads and shoulders, and crowded about the 'fires of those who had left their dwelling' seeking the company of known enemies rather than face the terror of the unknown alone."[47]

Wild animals, the hunter and the hunted, put aside their natural instincts and mingled together like domestic barnyard stock according to another witness who "'beheld great wild animals in his [sic] yard and garden. There were bears, panthers, wolves, foxes, etc. side by side with a number of wild deer, with their red tongues hanging out of their mouths. There was no sign of enmity, but all seemed animated by a common danger . . . nor did they seem to fear man.'"[48]

All of nature was exhibiting abnormal behavior when the appearance of the comet ratcheted human's apprehension up a couple of notches. Then the eclipse of the sun wound some people right up to the edge.

Neither Indians nor newcomers considered any of these signs as harbingers of good tidings. Consequently, the earthquakes were like dropping a match in a powder magazine.

Psychiatrists weren't available; psychologists weren't to be found. There were no SRS counseling centers. Religion, it seems, proved to be the one place both Indians and newcomers could seek comfort.

These omens of ill tidings caused Indians to start purifying ceremonies to get right with their God. In some cases, because of the many signs, these rituals began even before the quakes began.

The newcomers reacted after the fact. A giant ground swell of religious revival followed hard on the heels of the earthquakes. Preachers and evangelists of all faiths were drawn to the scene like flies to carrion. They came to save the many saints and sinners of the realm and found willing sinners aplenty.

> Many hardened sinners fell "like those slain in battle." During the shocks grown men were known to fall to the floor groaning and pass out from terror . . . They "fled into the streets, clinging one to another, and crying for mercy." When a shock had passed, people raised their voices in "grateful thanks to the Supreme Ruler of Nature" for their preservation. But the return of shocks, even during a sermon, sent them shrieking and running for the outdoors. "It was a time of great terror to sinners . . ."
>
> "Earth-quake Christian" was a phrase embittered preachers reserved for those whose devotions were more enthusiastic during the course of the shocks than before and after.[49]

The *great comet* was generally visible in the United States from 6 September 1811, through 16 January 1812, providing skies were clear. Historically, comets have been associated with impending disaster so it isn't surprising this twice-tailed heavenly visitor excited hysteria in some souls. They found no difficulty linking the comet with the earthquakes. Sometimes, however, the two were joined together in strange ways.

Bradbury left New Madrid and put ashore near the fourth Chickasaw Bluffs where, he said,

> more than twenty people came out as soon as they discovered us . . . I found them almost distracted with fear, and that they were composed of several families, who had collected to pray together . . . One of the men, who appeared to be considered as possessing more knowledge than the rest, entered into an explanation of the cause, and attributed it to the comet that had appeared a few months before, which he described as having two horns, over one of which the earth had rolled, and was now lodged betwixt them: that the shocks were occasioned by the attempts made by the earth to surmount the other horn. If this should be accomplished, all would be well, if otherwise, inevitable destruction to the world would follow.[50]

One newspaper editor tried applying the balm of humor to the comet's appearance by suggesting that because it was moving to the west, "perhaps it has touched the mountains of California, that has given a small shake to this side of the globe."

His next remarks suggest that despite the humor he was leaving the door open for a cause-and-effect connection with a higher power. Natchez was the object of his continuing editorial, wondering if

> the shake which the Natchezians have felt may be a mysterious visitation from the Author of all nature, on them for their sins—wickedness and the want of good faith have long prevailed in that territory.
>
> Sodom and Gomorrah would have been saved had three righteous persons been found in it—we therefore hope that Natchez has been saved on the same principle.[51]

Following the first shocks of December, a New Madrid resident explained that he believed the cause was due to "this world and the moon coming in contact, and the frequent repetition of the shocks is owing to their rebounding."[52]

##

Pioneers who settled in the earthquake zone weren't expecting government relief which was just as well because three years passed before Washington decided relief was due. Congress responded by issuing New Madrid Certificates entitling land owners in the zone to acquire equal parcels of unclaimed land in Missouri Territory—now the states of Missouri and Arkansas.

The claim couldn't exceed 640 acres but it did allow some legitimate land owners to relocate. Sorry to say, Congress's good intentions became a con man's dream. The resulting scams bilked many earthquake victims out of their rightful aid.

Hopefully George Roddell and his family didn't fall victims to any con artists. If not, it's possible that Roddell used his New Madrid Certificate to relocate his family away from the sunk country.

Or, perhaps he stayed in the New Madrid area and helped rebuild the town. This, though, is unlikely because "of the 1,000 people living there when the quakes struck, less than two dozen remained. Many simply abandoned their holdings, never to return again, not even to claim a certificate."[53]

Today the new town of New Madrid stands on the same horseshoe bend but now is secure behind a levee constructed by the Army Corp of Engineers.

##

Roosevelt, his wife, and crew aboard the *New Orleans* cruised safely into port at New Orleans on 10 January 1812. Latrobe's account adds an interesting footnote to that first steamboat journey.

> Although forming no part of the story of the voyage proper, yet, as this has been called a Romance, and all romances end, or should end in a marriage, the incident was not wanting here: for the Captain of the boat, falling in love with Mrs. Roosevelt's maid, prosecuted his suit so successfully as to find himself

an accepted lover when the New Orleans reached Natchez; and a clergyman being sent for, a wedding marked the arrival of the boat at the chief city of the Mississippi.[54]

The historic journey ended happily for all concerned for the *New Orleans* had successfully pioneered the way for steamboat travel on western rivers. By 1850 steamboat travelers reported that they were almost always in sight of at least one other steamer churning along on the mighty Mississippi River.

##

Some events that were reported to have happened during an earthquake seem to belong in a believe-it-or-not category. The New Madrid quakes were no exception. There were no NBC, CBS, or CNN news teams streaming real-time footage of these quakes thus digitally validating every account. Therefore readers can decide for themselves if these reports are fact or fiction.

"In a violent earthquake the vertical motion shoots objects into the air. Large stones bounce up and down like peas on a drum and potatoes have been seen jumping out of the ground."[55] Dug, stone-lined wells have been observed jumping out of the ground as high as ten feet above the surface before breaking into fragments.

Trees were mentioned repeatedly in the accounts of eyewitnesses. This isn't surprising considering the amount of timber growing throughout the earthquake zone. Trees were snapped off and hurled into the river. One observer wondered how the many dead trees that were dislodged from the river bottom could now float on the river's surface because "it must be obvious to every person that those trees must have become specifically heavier than the water before they sunk, and of course after being immersed in the mud must have increased in weight. We therefore submit the question to the Philosophical Society."[56]

Curious changes to the zone's topography was the subject of several writings. Eyewitnesses told of several incidents where the bottoms of the lakes were elevated higher than the surrounding ground and instead of water the lake bed was now "filled with a beautiful white sand . . . a little river called

Pemisece, that empties into the St. Francis . . . is filled also with sand."[57]

The Pemisece River referred to above is likely a variant spelling of the Pemiscot River that was the subject of another remarkable change to the earth's surface.

A family by the name of Culbertson settled along the Pemiscot River about ten miles below Little Prairie. Like the town of New Madrid, Culbertson built his cabin on a bend in the river; unlike New Madrid he built on the inside of the bend. Between his house and the river was "about an acre of ground . . . and in this space was situated the well and smokehouse."

This family was apparently made of stern stuff for when other people were abandoning towns, leaving homes, and fleeing in terror, the Culbertsons were hungry. At sunup on 16 December , after the second hard shock, "Mrs. Culbertson started to the well for water and to the smokehouse for breakfast meat, when, to her great astonishment, no well or smokehouse was to be seen. Upon further search, they were both found on the opposite side of the river, and a canoe was necessary to reach them."[58]

One of the hard shocks of that morning had opened a fissure completely across the Culbertsons' yard between the house and the well and smokehouse. The fissure was deep enough and wide enough to permit the river to adopt the fissure as its new channel.

After 1812, the New Madrid zone slumbered, stirring only occasionally. That all changed on 31 October 1895, when Mother Nature rousted herself and decided to go trick or treating. This earthquake's epicenter was near Charleston, Missouri. It registered 6.2 magnitude and produced shocks felt in western Kansas, in eastern Colorado, and on the eastern seaboard from New York state to Georgia.

##

Mother Nature may rest but she never relinquishes her right of visitation.

Chapter One notes

[1] David Stewart and Ray Knox, *The Earthquake America Forgot* (Maple Hill, Missouri: Gutenberg-Richter Publications, 1995),

[2] J.H.B. Latrobe, *The First Steamboat Voyage on the Western Waters* (Baltimore: Maryland Historical Society, 1871), 22.

[3] House of Representatives. *Annual Report of the Board of Regents of the Smithsonian Institution, Showing the Operations, Expenditures, and Condition of the Institution for the Year 1858.* Timothy Dudley, "The Earthquake of 1811 at New Madrid, Missouri." 35th Congress, 2d Session, Mis. Doc. No. 57. 422. Washington: GPO, 1859.

[4] David Stewart and Ray Knox, *The Earthquake America Forgot* (Maple Hill, Missouri: Gutenberg-Richter Publications, 1995),

[5] *Encyclopedia Britannica*, 1962 ed., s.v. "Earthquakes."

[6] House of Representatives. Annual Report of the Board of Regents of the Smithsonian Institution, Showing the Operations, Expenditures, and Condition of the Institution for the Year 1858. Timothy Dudley, "The Earthquake of 1811 at New Madrid, Missouri." 35th Congress, 2d Session, Mis. Doc. No. 57. 421-424. Washington: Government Printing Office, 1859.

[7] James Fletcher, "Earthquake," *Pittsburgh (Pennsylvania) Gazette*, 14 February 1812.

[8] David Stewart and Ray Knox, *The Earthquake America Forgot* (Maple Hill, Missouri: Gutenberg-Richter Publications, 1995), 151.

[9] Ibid., 143.

[10] Myron L. Fuller, *The New Madrid Earthquake* (1912; reprint, Cape Girardeau, Missouri: Ramfre Press, n.d.), 17.

[11] Editor, (St. Louis) *Louisiana Gazette,* 15 February 1812.

[12] *Encyclopedia Britannica*, 1962 ed., s.v. "Earthquakes."

[13] H. (Henry) McMurtrie, *Sketches of Louisville and Its Environs* (Louisville: S. Penn, 1819), 255. The table of shocks containing these numbers and the descriptions is contained in the appendix which McMurtrie "extracted principally from the papers of the late J. Brooks, Esq."

[14] William Leigh Pierce, "Earthquake," *New York Evening Post*, 11 February 1812.

[15] David Stewart, foreword to *The New Madrid Earthquake* by Myron L. Fuller (1912; reprint, Cape Girardeau, Missouri: Center for Earthquake Studies, Southeast Missouri State University),

[16] J.H.B. Latrobe, *The First Steamboat Voyage on the Western Waters* (Baltimore: Maryland Historical Society, 1871), 16-17.

[17] Ibid., 20.

[18] Ibid., 22-23.

[19] William Leigh Pierce, "Earthquake," *New York Evening Post*, 11 February 1812.

[20] *Encyclopedia Britannica*, 1999-2000 ed., s.v. "Mississippi River."

[21] Mathias M. Speed, "Earthquake," (Philadelphia) *Pennsylvania Gazette*, 15 April 1812.

[22] James T. Lloyd, *Lloyd's Steamboat Directory and Disasters on the Western Waters* (Cincinnati: James T. Lloyd & Co., 1856), 325-326.

[23] Andrew H. Malcolm, *Mississippi Currents* (New York: William Morrow and Company, Inc., 1996), 42.

[24] Charles Ellet, Jr., *The Mississippi and Ohio Rivers: Containing Plans for the Protection of the Delta from Inundation* (Philadelphia: Lippincott, Grambo, and Co., 1853), 36.

[25] Lorenzo Dow, *History of Cosmopolite; or, the Four Volumes of Lorenzo Dow's Journal,* 4th ed. (Washington, O.: Joshua Martin, 1848), 344-345.

[26] Mathias M. Speed, "Earthquake," (Philadelphia) *Pennsylvania Gazette*, 15 April 1812.

[27] William Leigh Pierce, "Earthquake," *New York Evening Post*, 11 February 1812.

[28] Reuben Gold Thwaites, ed., *Early Western Travels, 1748-1846*, vol. 5: *Bradbury's Travels in the Interior of America, 1809-1811*(1817; reprint, Cleveland, OH: Arthur H. Clark Company, 1904), 200-201.

[29] Ibid., 206.

[30] House of Representatives. *Annual Report of the Board of Regents of the Smithsonian Institution, Showing the Operations, Expenditures, and Condition of the Institution for the Year 1858.* Timothy Dudley, "The Earthquake of 1811 at New Madrid, Missouri." 35th Congress, 2d Session, Mis. Doc. No. 57. 422. Washington: GPO, 1859.

[31] Marilyn Miller and Marian Faux, eds., *The New York Public Library American History Desk Reference* (New York: Stonesong Press, 1997), 94.

[32] (Philadelphia) *Pennsylvania Gazette*, 11 March 1812.

[33] James Fletcher, "Earthquake," *The Pittsburgh (Pennsylvania) Gazette*, 14 February 1812.

[34] "Earthquake," (Philadelphia) *Pennsylvania Gazette*, 26 February 1812.

[35] Allan W. Eckert, *A Sorrow in Our Heart: The Life of Tecumseh* (New York: Bantam Books, 1992), 550.

[36] Zadok Cramer, *The Navigator* (1814; reprint, Utica, KY: McDowell Publications, 1979), 182.

[37] Ibid., 203.

[38] J.H.B. Latrobe, *The First Steamboat Voyage on the Western Waters* (Baltimore: Maryland Historical Society, 1871), 29-30.

[39] House of Representatives. *Annual Report of the Board of Regents of the Smithsonian Institution, Showing the Operations, Expenditures, and Condition of the Institution for the Year 1858.* Timothy Dudley, "The Earthquake of 1811 at New Madrid, Missouri." 35th Congress, 2d Session, Mis. Doc. No. 57. 423. GPO 1859.

[40] Myron L. Fuller, *The New Madrid Earthquake* (1912; reprint, Gape Girardeau, Missouri: Ramfre Press, n.d.), 43.

[41] Lorenzo Dow, *History of Cosmopolite; or, the Four Volumes of Lorenzo Dow's Journal,* 4th ed. (Washington: Joshua Martin, 1848), 344.

[42] "The Earthquake," (Philadelphia) *Pennsylvania Gazette*, 26 February 1812.

[43] Mathias M. Speed, "Earthquake," (Philadelphia) *Pennsylvania Gazette,* 15 April 1812.

[44] John D. Hunter, *Memoirs of a Captivity Among the Indians of North America* (London: Longman, Hurst, Rees, Orme, Brown, and Green, 1824), 39.

[45] William Leigh Pierce, "Earthquake," *New York Evening Post*, 11 February 1812.

[46] Reuben Gold Thwaites, ed., *Early Western Travels, 1748-1846*, vol. 5: *Bradbury's Travels in the Interior of America, 1809-1811*(1904; reprint, Bowie, MD: Heritage Books, Inc., 2000), 208.

[47] James Lal Penick, Jr., *The New Madrid Earthquakes,* rev. ed. (Columbia: University of Missouri Press, 1981), 103.

[48] Ibid., 105-106.

[49] Ibid., 116-118.

[50] Reuben Gold Thwaites, ed., *Early Western Travels, 1748-1846*, vol. 5: *Bradbury's Travels in the Interior of America, 1809-1811*(1817; reprint, Cleveland, OH: Arthur H. Clark Company, 1904), 209.

[51] (New Orleans) *Louisiana Gazette and Daily Advertiser*, 21 December 1811. From Chad Richards' website giving transcripts of period newspaper accounts. This site must be accessed through a web search of the Arkansas Memory Project. The URL will not access the site.

[52] "The Earthquake," (Philadelphia) *Pennsylvania Gazette*, 26 February 1812.

[53] David Stewart and Ray Knox, *The Earthquake America Forgot* (Maple Hill, Missouri: Gutenberg-Richter Publications, 1995), 262.

[54] J.H.B. Latrobe, *The First Steamboat Voyage on the Western Waters* (Baltimore: Maryland Historical Society, 1871), 32n.

[55] Frank W. Lane, *The Elements Rage* (Philadelphia: Chilton Books, 1965), 213.

[56] (New Orleans) *Louisiana Gazette and Daily Advertiser*, 21 December 1811. From Chad Richards' website giving transcripts of period newspaper accounts. This site must be accessed through a web search of the Arkansas Memory Project. The URL will not access the site.

[57] *The Pittsburgh* (PA) *Gazette*, 14 February 1812.

[58] *History of Southeast Missouri* (Chicago: Goodspeed Publishing Co., 1888), 307, quoted in James Lal Penick, Jr., *The New Madrid Earthquakes,* rev. ed. (Columbia: University of Missouri Press, 1981), 95-96.

Chapter Two

WHITE DEATH

Of all the elements, cold remains our deadliest enemy.   And with the cold comes death.

—John Lynch, *The Weather*

Fourteen year-old William J. Lewis was glaringly out of place when he arrived in the Texas Panhandle during the spring of 1885. At age fourteen many Panhandle born-and-reared youth were a bit rough around the edges; in contrast Lewis look sissified in his knickerbockers, black stockings, frilly shirt, and ribbon bedecked sailor hat. What made him fashionable back east in Maryland branded him a rank tenderfoot in Texas.

William's father, Charles Lewis, had succumbed to the siren song of the beef bonanza and purchased interest in a Panhandle ranch. The Lewis family soon moved to Clarendon, Texas, even though the elder Lewis knew nothing about ranching.

Charles Lewis' contribution to the partnership was maintaining the company books and, hopefully, learning something worthwhile about the cattle business. He was to be a silent partner and the family didn't plan to remain in Texas once their investment was secure.

The ranch, the Half Circle K, was a neighbor to Charles Goodnight's JA spread that was located to the west and south, the Diamond F to the north, with the Quarter Circle Heart, the Spade, the RO, and the Rocking Chair brands located to the east.

Palo Duro Canyon, Adobe Walls, Red River, and the XIT Ranch were all famous landmarks of the Panhandle where the saga of Indians, soldiers, and ruthless cattlemen unfolded while a growing tide of newcomers elbowed its way westward.

The Panhandle was an expanse of endless prairies that hosted some vicious weather extremes. It could be swept by a blistering south wind that licked up all remnants of moisture or by a deadly norther that screamed down out of the Arctic. During spring and fall, a body could swelter at noonday in 100-degree heat and by sundown be shivering in a blinding blizzard; the temperature was capable of dropping a degree a minute when a blue norther ripped across the Panhandle.

Occasionally, however, the wind tiptoed instead of stomped, the air became free of dust, sleet, or snow and the grass grew lush with the temperature hovering in the perfect range. Most of the time it was excellent cattle country.

William Lewis saw this new land through the trifocals of youthful enthusiasm, high adventure, and boundless opportunity. He embraced it all and after buying an appropriate change of clothes set out to become a cowboy and if luck smiled on him, eventually a rancher. In pursuit of these goals, unfortunately, both humans and Mother Nature conspired to discourage him and send him packing back east.

The following summer, at age fifteen, young Lewis went to work on a survey crew to earn some money but the foreman refused to pay the "kid" his wages. The foreman justified his theft by telling Lewis that the experience was worth far more than money.

Undaunted, Lewis earned a $50 reward by searching for and recovering a lost mule team. Lewis invested the reward money in several cows that soon died from the Texas fever brought in by a herd of Texas Longhorns. Stubbornly he followed his dream by going to work at the Half Circle K where, because he was one of the owner's kids, the foreman gave him every rotten job around the ranch.

He endured these unpleasant tasks but the next trial to come his way was devastating for the Half Circle K. This event nearly snuffed out any hopes he held of becoming a cowboy, much less a rancher. The disaster was ushered in by a chilling omen—the death and burial of William's infant cousin.

It was 7 January 1886, and the day was as sunny and warm as a day in spring. Not one cloud broke the wide expanse of blue sky. It was late afternoon before

W. H. D Koerner's painting *The Snow Eddied and Whirled About the Men*, is a graphic portrait of the cowboy's woes during a blizzard. They couldn't take a personal day off work or not show up. Many stayed on the job until succumbing to the cold, giving their lives for the brand.

Cooper began the Lord's Prayer. During the service an ominous dark bank arose on the northern horizon. A wind from the same direction blew in a few scattered clouds, then subsided as quickly as it had come, leaving the atmosphere sultry and still, as still as if the earth had stopped moving. Before the minister finished his prayer, the norther struck. By the time the grave was filled, the sky was completely overcast; it was as dark as late dusk, and the sudden, cold wind had turned into a freezing gale. It was night when the family reached home, and the air was filled with stinging and whirling particles of ice and snow.

All night the wind raged, and the house creaked as if it would collapse under the next blast. Steadily, until the following afternoon, the snow continued to fall, so thick and fast that it was impossible to see two feet ahead. William sat up, wrapped in blankets, to assure the stove's being kept red hot. It was the onset of the worst blizzard in the history of the Panhandle.[1]

##

Extreme weather is normal weather for those living and working on the prairies and plains. It becomes as much a part of the individual's makeup as the color of their hair or the tone of their voice. It shapes and bends the mind every bit as effectively as books and school learning.

Consequently, plains dwellers adopted some pet names for these storms that roar down from the north. The term norther was descriptive but it wasn't colorful enough. To these folks such storms were a blue norther, a blew-tailed norther, a blue whistler, a blue darter, or a blue blizzard.[2] The word blizzard, as applied to weather, can make a strong case for originating on the prairies and plains.

> The blizzard is the grizzly of the Plains . . . the word may have been derived from the German word *blitzartig*, which means "lightning-like," and applied to the weather phenomenon that it now describes. It seems, however, that "blizzard" was used long before the Germans, or others, took up their abode in the open country. It was used by David Crockett to denote a blast, a devastating volley, either of shot or of words, a blazing away. It was first applied to a weather phenomenon by O. C. Bates, the erratic editor of an Iowa newspaper, in reference to the storm of March 14, 1870.[3]

Frontiersman Billy Dixon spent his life on the Great Plains as scout, buffalo hunter, Indian fighter, and teamster. A lifetime of enduring Mother Nature's tough hospitality prompted Dixon to write that

> in civilized surroundings a Plains blizzard is bad enough; in a wild country, a blizzard is more appalling than a tornado, for the latter may be dodged, but the blizzard is every where and sets its teeth into a man's vitals, wherever he may be. A blizzard brings a feeling

of terror that even the strongest man can hardly resist. I have seen men moaning and trembling in a blizzard, as if the last drop of courage had oozed from their bodies. They were not cowards. Their distress was due to an instinctive, animal-like feeling that death was everywhere about them, invisible, dread and mysterious.[4]

Robert Service wasn't a cowboy, rancher, or plainsman but was born half a world away in Liverpool, England, in 1874. He was a banker-turned-poet who wrote some of the most-memorized poems in the English language. Service, who spent years in the Yukon, wrote about cold as only those can who have experienced severe, killing cold.

Service's poem, "Lost," wasn't yet written at the time of the Great White Ruin and the Big Die-Up but, had they read it, surely those folks would have felt they inspired the following stanza.

> The cold's got an edge like a jackknife—
>   it must be forty below;
> Leastways that's what it seems like—
>   it cuts so fierce to the bone.
> The wind's getting real ferocious;
>   it's heaving and whirling the snow;
> It shrieks with a howl of fury,
>   it dies away to a moan;
> Its arms sweep round like a banshee's,
>   swift and icily white,
> And buffet and blind and beat me.
>   Lord! it's a hell of a night.

Colonel Richard Dodge would have surely said, "Amen" to Service's poem. Colonel Dodge was stationed in the West before and after serving as a Union officer in the Civil War. Following Lee's surrender at Appomattox, Dodge was dispatched to the West where he saw duty during the Indian Wars. While stationed at Fort Dodge, Kansas, he gathered a stockpile of experience with blizzards.

An exposure to the full force and fury of a violent "plains Norther" would be certain death to any indigenous animal. Buffalo and antelope fly before it, and seek protection in the deepest and most wooded cañons. Near Julesburg, I once saw the snow dotted with the bodies of a great number of snow-birds frozen to death in a storm of a few days before. Men suffer more than animals. Lacking the instinct of the latter, which enables them to presage the coming storm, men new to plains life, misled by the mildness of the ordinary winter weather, expose themselves possibly in light clothing on the plains, are caught in a storm, and perish miserably in a few hours.

A gentleman, competent and in a position to form a correct estimate, once told me that at least 100 buffalo-hunters had perished from cold in the country, within 100 miles of the Arkansas River, in two years. During the winter of 1872-3 I was in command at Fort Dodge, Kansas. At least seventy capital amputations were preformed by the post surgeon on citizens who were buffalo-hunters or railroad employés, whilst a much greater number of frozen men were sent East for treatment. I think it safe to say that over 200 men in that vicinity lost hands or feet, or parts of them . . .

The cold itself is not intolerable. The danger is from the sharp wind, which drives the cold like icy daggers through the body. Great suffering can always be avoided, if it be possible to get out of the wind . . .

The army frequently suffers greatly from these storms . . . At other times some military necessity . . . requires the movement of troops in mid-winter. The amount of suffering in all such cases can hardly be exaggerated . . .

In the winter of 1865-6 a considerable command was caught on the Cimarron, and barely escaped total destruction. An officer who was with it describes the sufferings as most fearful. Many men were more or less frosted, and about 600 animals frozen or starved to death.[5]

Indians and newcomers living on the prairies and plains felt the sting of blizzards to a far greater degree than the present generation. There were no electric blankets, no central heat, no heated automobiles, no heated trucks, no heated tractors, no insulated underwear, no cell phones, no GPS, and no EMS.

In some locations on the high plains, firewood was simply unavailable. Once the buffalo were gone the plain's primary fuel source, buffalo chips, was also gone. If a settler was fortunate enough to have a corn crop in storage he could burn his corn, corncobs, and corn stalks. When those were consumed he began burning fence posts and fence rails—if they were lucky enough to have any. In a prolonged blizzard many turned to burning furniture and sometimes even parts of their dwelling.

Getting caught away from shelter during a blizzard was life threatening. During the winter of 1848, freighters traveling on the Santa Fe Trail were overtaken by a severe winter storm. Part of the story was reported by a newspaper correspondent at Independence, Missouri, on 11 December.

> Smith, Brown & Co., who undertook a large Government contract for freight to Santa Fe last Summer, are losing great numbers of cattle, by the severe weather on the Plains, and no doubt many of their hands are suffering severely, for they are not near all in.

On 27 December 1848, a follow-up report from Fort Leavenworth said "a Santa Fe party with the oxen for the government contractors—they lost one man who perished in the snow; and 1,600 oxen died on the way."

Mules didn't fare any better than oxen during the same winter according to a letter from Big Timbers on 3 December 1848, Lieutenant E. F. Beale wrote, "a trader who passed some sixty miles to the southward of me lost in one snowstorm *ninety* mules frozen to death in a single night. I counted in one day myself, seventy-two animals dead and dying, belonging to a large company returning to the United States."[6]

Loss of oxen and mules occasionally started a domino effect that led to some rather bizarre events at remote outposts. During the winter of 1865, supply trains from Salt Lake were caught in Beaver Canyon by a winter storm. The train, carrying mostly flour, became stranded when all the oxen perished in the storm. Consequently Virginia City, Montana, had flour shortages that sent prices skyrocketing. Flour prices rose and then rose again until on 28 February, it hit $150.00 per hundred weight forcing some families onto a "meat straight" diet.

In April, 500 heavily armed men invaded Virginia City. With military precision they proceeded to search all premises for flour and "if flour was found it was packed off without ceremony; an account being kept and a promise to pay for all at the rate of $27.00 per cwt. for Salt Lake flour and $36.00 for states flour. A notice was handed to the *Montana Post* ordering all flour to be sold from $27.00 to $30.00 for the future."[7]

The Flour Vigilantes, it seems, were successful in restoring fair flour prices to Virginia City. Granville Stuart, who recorded the incident, didn't identify the armed men other than that they were from "Montana."

Blue northers favor the High Plains, but states bordering the west bank of the Mississippi can also feel the sting of numbing cold and killer blizzards.

The winter of 1855-1856 was recorded as one of the most severe on record at Fort Snelling, Fort Ripley, and Lakeland, Minnesota, with temperatures from six to eleven degrees below normal for four months.

On 6 January at Fort Snelling the thermometer dropped below zero °F and stayed there for 140 hours; at Fort Ripley it stayed at sub-zero readings for 230 hours—almost ten straight days and nights. At Dubuque, Iowa, the mercury stayed below freezing from 21 December to 15 February.

The December storm of 1856 was the first killer blizzard faced by many newcomers as they moved onto the prairies of Iowa, Kansas, Nebraska, and Minnesota. Even old-timers succumbed to the Great Storm, as it was called, and "that December day claimed many human lives."[8]

It happened again on New Year's Day in 1864 when an Arctic air mass dropped south and took up squatters rights from the Rockies to the Appalachians. It was, up to that time, "the greatest combination of cold, snow, and blow in the region's recorded meteorological history."

An unidentified pioneer family somewhere in the Dakotas after a blizzard practically buried their home. The family appears well-clothed so perhaps didn't suffer like many early homesteaders did during blizzards.

The Iowa prairies got hammered where "In Muscatine County horticulturist Suel Foster related that 100 head of cattle had been lost locally, with many sheep frozen and more smothered from huddling together to escape the penetrating cold. From Sterling a correspondent of the *Country Gentlemen* told of pigs, sheep, calves, quail, and prairie chickens being frozen to death in considerable numbers."[9]

Any winter could bring tragedy on the prairies and plains if nature wasn't given due respect. The 3 February 1866 issue of the *Loyal Georgian*, an Augusta newspaper, carried this article: "A man who was noticed to be driving quite slowly, near Boonsboro, Iowa, the other night, was found, though tightly grasping his reins, to be frozen to death."

Just as the beef industry was hitting its stride up the Chisholm Trail, it experienced one of many industry-altering blizzards. During the summer of 1871 approximately 600,000 cattle arrived on the central plains of Kansas. Supply far outstripped the demand and rather than sell at depressed prices, many drovers opted to winter the herds in central or western Kansas. Some trailed herds west into Colorado or north into Wyoming or Nebraska. Still other herds were turned around and pushed back south to Indian Territory for the winter. Stockmen were all hoping for better markets come next spring.

What they got instead was an unusually severe winter in 1871-1872. The early snows and intense cold killed an estimated 300,000 Texas cattle being wintered on the central plains.

Joseph McCoy opened an eastern market for Texas cattle by building and promoting shipping facilities at the Kansas Pacific railhead in Abilene, Kansas. In his writings he recorded a firsthand account of the 1871-1872 winter kill.

> Before the herds had scarce arrived at their destined wintering ranges, a great rain storm set in and a keen cold wind sprung up at a brisk rate from the northwest, freezing the water into ice soon after reaching the ground. The whole surface of the earth had become thus encased to the thickness of two or three inches, covering and freezing the short buffalo grass up solid with sheets of ice. Then the furious gale of piercing wind continued, accompanied with sleet and snow, and lasted for three days and nights. Men and horses froze to death; and as for the cattle, they perished by the thousands, or it might be truly said, tens of thousands.[10]

Many of the cattle that lived through the storm suffered frozen legs that would eventually break off. Some critters tried to get around on the stumps before collapsing and dying. It was enough to touch even the worst stoic on the range.

Ten thousand dead cattle were counted between Garden City, Kansas, and the White Woman River. And "cowboys reported that a man could walk from Kingsley, Kansas, to the Colorado line using cattle carcasses as a path and never touch the ground."[11]

After the weather moderated, some owners tried to recoup a small pittance of their investment by selling the hides. McCoy estimated that "perhaps one-third to one-half of the dead animals were skinned, after the storm abated and the weather moderated . . . At one railway station twenty thousand, at another thirty-five thousand, at another near fifty thousand hides were collected and shipped east . . . It has been estimated that fully two hundred and fifty thousand cattle, and many hundred cow ponies perished."[12]

Billy Dixon called this same November storm "one of the worst in memory." The storm caught the Snuffer's bull train returning to Hays City from Camp Supply. It had taken on a load of cordwood at Walnut Creek and had just gone into camp at Five Mile Hollow, five miles outside of Hays City. The stock had been unhitched and turned loose. Then, without warning, the blizzard howled into their camp.

Stock immediately began drifting with the storm and the men trying to hold them became lost in the blinding snowstorm. All but one man was eventually found alive by searchers from Hays City but unfortunately "there was hardly a man in this ill-fated outfit who didn't not suffer the loss of a hand, a foot, or a limb."[13]

The oxen all froze to death as did the cook who had found his way back to the camp. He was found in the wagon, frozen stiff. It was obvious to the search party that he'd tried to build a fire in the bottom of the wagon using the wagon end gate as kindling. "The wind blew with such terrific force that the fire was blown away in all directions. Though surrounded with enormous quantities of wood, all within easy reach, the poor fellow perished for want of fire."[14]

At Fort Dodge, during this same blizzard, thousands of buffalo sought shelter around the walls of the post and on the lee side of buildings. At regular intervals artillery pieces were fired in an effort to keep the buffalo from crowding against and pushing down all the fort's buildings and corrals.[15]

Buffalo hunters caught away from adequate shelter by this storm found themselves in serious trouble. The thermometer fell to twenty below zero °F and the wind was howling at sixty miles an hour. A hunter named Happy Jack and his outfit were camped near Five Mile Hollow when the blizzard struck. "Every man in the outfit froze to death that night; and there was also a big Newfoundland dog froze to death lying on the bed."[16]

Longhorns, like buffalo, earned a reputation for being incredibly tough critters. Even so, they often died during brutal winters after being pushed onto northern ranges too late in the year. Sometimes the results were a real dream killer.

Just about every cowboy that ever forked a pony dreamed of having his own brand. Some, through hard work and luck, achieved that goal. Drover Dick Pincham was one of the lucky ones—for a short time. In 1879 he bought 4,500 Texas steers and trailed them up into Dakota Territory to fatten on free grass. That winter "a five-day blizzard hit, and in the spring, Pincham found that only 123 of his steers had survived."[17]

Texas stock arriving in Montana Territory late in the summer of 1880 fared no better. One rancher trailed in 5,000 head that fall and next spring only 135 head could be found still alive. Consequently, "the cowboys with the outfit were never paid their wages."[18]

The 1880s were ten years of "removal and replacement;" a decade of change that recast the prairies and plains forever. During these years the northern buffalo were nearly exterminated and the Army removed the Indians to make way for the cattlemen; Longhorns were giving way to short horns, and many cattlemen were being elbowed aside by the sodbuster.

The winters of 1885-86, 1886-87, and 1887-88 were some of the severest winters on record and played a major role in bringing about this change.

Despite all the change, a few years during the 1880s were the best times for the free range cattle industry. Some years the price for beef on the hoof was good, grass was always free—if ranchers could find and hold it, and profits were occasionally spectacular.

Books like James Brisbin's *Beef Bonanza* and Reginald Aldridge's *Life on a Ranch* romanticized ranching as not only an ideal way of life but capable of 30, 40, and even 50 percent net profit annually.

Harper"s Weekly, 27 February 1886; Charles Graham
Open prairies, blizzards, and fences claimed thousands of cattle during the
nineteenth century ranching boom. Cattle instinctively drifted with the
storm, seeking shelter. A fence halted the drift and left them without hope.

In 1879 the Montana Territory Legislature published
a booklet, authored by Robert E. Strahorn, under the title
*Resources of Montana Territory and Attractions of Yellowstone
Park.* Author Strahorn painted a glowing testament to the
cattle business by writing that "in this vast free pasturage, no
one need really own an acre of land and thus far, few have
cared to." Strahorn included a statement from a local banker
that informed readers that concerning risk, there really wasn't
any.[19]

Like thirsty cattle catching the scent of water, banks and
private investors stampeded to invest millions of dollars in
this sure bet. Ranching syndicates, local and foreign, couldn't
wait to throw their hats, stuffed with money, into the ring.
Even members of Congress, along with foreign lords and ladies
galloped hard to stake a claim on the free grass of the great
American West.

Some of the historical brands funded by foreign money,
in these cases Scottish money, were the Hansford Land and
Cattle Company; The Matador Cattle Company; The Prairie

Cattle Company; The Texas Land and Cattle Company; The Western Land and Cattle Company; and The Wyoming Cattle Ranch Company.[20] The Prairie Cattle Company, fairly typical of the corporate mega ranches, reportedly ran 150,000 head of cattle on its ranges in Colorado, New Mexico, and Texas.

Already entrenched were the cattlemen who had done it the old fashioned way, historical legends like Charles Goodnight, Conrad Kohrs, John Ilif, Granville Stuart, and Richard King. Men who had built ranching empires by personally saddling up and working cattle.

The new money, however, gave birth to the heady era of cattle kings, or bovine kings, who often had a lot more money than cow sense. But ranchers were riding high, so to speak, and before long the rich and powerful cattlemen were building private clubs that stood like feudal castles on the wide, lonesome plains. It seemed that every territory had its club: the Cheyenne Club, the Montana Club, the Colorado Club, and others. Here, at these islands of opulence, cattle barons, powerful politicians, and foreign investors gathered to wine and dine, wheel and deal, and toast and boast while promoting the beef business.

All of this attention and promotion was literally "overkill."

Granville Stuart, age fifty-two in the fall of 1886, was an old-timer in Montana Territory. Stuart had left the Iowa farm fields for the California gold fields back in 1852 when he was seventeen years old. He abandoned the California diggings in 1857 and moved to Montana's Beaverhead Valley. Here Stuart tried his hand at road ranching, tried his hand at blacksmithing, tried his luck as a merchant, and tried his skills as a bank accountant. Stuart hadn't found much money or satisfaction at any of these pursuits so he decided to try ranching.

Montana Territory became a great cattle state but not all the Territory was great for cattle. In April 1880 he "left Helena for a trip to the Yellowstone country to look for a good cattle range."[21]

He traveled southeast to Bozeman and worked his way to Fort Custer and then on to Miles City. He did pronounce some country as "well grassed" but frequently noted that water was scarce or that the streams and rivers were muddy and deep with a miry bottom. The miry bottom problem was pointed out again and again. "A good range for one thousand to fifteen hundred cattle but it wouldn't do at all for they would all mire in the Rosebud."

Or, "a good grazing country where plenty of hay could be cut all along, but there is no accessible water and therefore it won't do for cattle." His evaluation continued, noting that some locations had "water in all these ravines and coulees but is probably not permanent . . . Do not like the country north and east of McDonald creek. Too much sage."

He eventually selected Ford Creek near the Judith Mountains as the right location for the ranch headquarters.

The Pioneer Cattle Company, with Stuart as manager, was originally founded in 1879 as a partnership between Davis, Hauser, and Stuart. At this date the country was wide open and unsettled. Buffalo numbered in the tens of thousands and deer, elk, and antelope were in sight at almost any point of the compass.

Once the partnership with Davis and Hauser was finalized, Stuart gathered a crew and "by the first of October we had our buildings completed, some range cabins built, and five thousand head of cattle on the range and sixty head of horses."

Shortly after Stuart found the ideal location for the ranch headquarters, the army decided it, too, liked the area. Just days later Captain Dangerfield Park established Fort Maginnis on the north end of Stuart's hay meadow. Others were already crowding in on Stuart's DHS Ranch.

Actually, the crowding began years earlier in 1866 when Nelson Story proved that Longhorns could be driven from Texas to Montana Territory. It wasn't long before Longhorns were streaming up the Texas trail in staggering numbers.

In addition to the Texas herds, Western, or pilgrim, shorthorn cattle were being trailed onto the high plains from the west coast. These rivers of cattle spread out like a flood over the range land of Montana Territory, Wyoming Territory, Dakota Territory, Colorado, Nebraska, and Kansas.

But the cattle, rattling hocks and horns, just kept on coming to the northern range. Almost overnight Stuart witnessed the Montana range fill up faster than whiskey glasses in a cow town saloon; the buffalo hunters and the cattlemen changed it all in just three short years. By 1883 the enormous northern buffalo herds were reduced to a sea of bleached bones and rotting carcasses. In their place was an "estimated six hundred thousand head of cattle."

Worried cattlemen tried to stem the tide by posting notices and warnings to new arrivals that certain range was off limits to any new herds. Even without law to support these claims some ranchers continued to publish notices and warnings.

It didn't work.

Stuart looked around and observed that "by the fall of 1885 the Montana ranges were crowded. A hard winter or a dry summer would certainly bring disaster." Ranching was now, according to Stuart, "no longer a reasonably safe business; it was from this time on a 'gamble' with the trump cards in the hands of the elements."

The rancher followed the old Indian's gaze and watched a white owl winging overhead. The Gros Ventre warrior told Stuart that he had not seen the white owls this far south since he had been a very small boy. The old Indian pulled his robe close and grunted, "Heap Cold!"

It was summer, 1886.

Nonetheless cattle continued to arrive until "in the fall of 1886 there were more than one million head of cattle on the Montana ranges." There was also just shy of one million head of sheep bleating and eating their way across the same Montana ranges.[22]

Stuart, who was married to a Shoshoni Indian woman, had spent thirty years in Montana Territory and could read sign almost as well as the natives. And all the sign told Stuart that a rough winter was set to blow in on the heels of the summer's severe drought.

Another Montana Territory pioneer and friend of Stuart, Conrad Kohrs, bought out the Davis brothers in 1883 and the DHS Ranch name became Stuart, Kohrs, and Co. Then in the spring of 1885 it was incorporated as the Pioneer Cattle Company.

Conrad Kohrs of Deer Lodge, Montana Territory served as president, and Granville Stuart, Fort Maginnis, Montana

Territory, was superintendent and manager. The brand remained the DHS.

In the fall of 1886 Stuart watched the white owls riding the high rivers of air down into Montana Territory. These Arctic messengers told him it was time to make "what preparations we could" to protect the ranch's 18,880 head of cattle and meet a severe winter "with as little suffering to the stock and loss to ourselves as possible."[23] Finding some better grass along the foot of the Little Rockies north of the Missouri River, Stuart began moving cattle to the new range.

Meanwhile Kohrs, friend and now partner with Stuart, telegraphed him saying that he'd leased some better grass across the border in Canada. Stuart, however, didn't agree with this eleventh-hour remedy saying,

> I was not in favor of taking the herd north of the British line because of the severe blizzards that swept the open treeless plains that afforded no shelter for stock and was too far north to get the warm Chinook winds. It was too late in the season to move cattle a great distance. It always injures range cattle more or less to move them and it would never do to throw them on a strange range too late in the season.[24]

The fall rains didn't come and Stuart's fears of a hard winter or a dry summer were already half fulfilled; the last half was only a few short months away.

The story and conditions were the same in Wyoming Territory. The Wyoming Stockgrowers Association's 1885 report listed 435 members with 2,000,000 head of cattle on the open range.[25] Things were getting crowded and ranchers realized the grass couldn't carry any additional cattle and sheep.

But they just kept coming.

And so did the white owls circling on silent wings above, more subtle signs that caused a feeling of impending doom. "Wild geese, ducks and songbirds started south early, and white arctic owls appeared on the range for the first time since a dire cold season long past. Beavers piled up huge quantities of willow saplings for winter food. Muskrats built their lodges twice as large and thick as usual and their hair grew long and heavy."[26]

##

The endless influx of cattle on the range had old-time cattlemen howling something fierce about the intrusion of foreign investors. They eventually made enough noise that in 1886 congress agreed to take a look at the free-grass ranching industry.

The Committee on Public Lands in the United States House of Representatives responded to complaints of foreign monopolies by sponsoring a bill forbidding alien owership of land in territories of the United States. In this manner the legislators proposed to prevent landlordism from swamping America's free institutions . . . In 1887 Congress passed, with President Cleveland's approval, a law prohibiting alien ownership in land in the territories of the United States except by inheritance or in collection of debts.[27]

The investigation didn't change ranching all that much but much change was at the door.

##

Longhorn cattle are weather savvy critters and their behavior before a storm was often the first clue cattlemen had of approaching blizzards. "They would stand with heads pointed to the north, sensing expectantly; they would low and bawl and look off south; they would be bunching up or sifting down from the uplands to sheltering breaks, their routine of grazing, watering and sleeping entirely upset."[28]

This instinctive nature led to the great drifts where Longhorns transplanted on northern ranges "often preceded a storm in their travel south, stringing out in long, thin lines."[29] It wasn't unusual for cattle from Kansas, Nebraska, and farther north to drift all the way to Texas, that is if they didn't encounter a deep gully, or a sheer cliff, or an impassable river, or a drift fence.

A blizzard in 1884 swept across Kansas and the Oklahoma Strip setting range cattle drifting south, driven and pushed by the howling norther. Cowboys on the XIT range in the Texas Panhandle watched their arrival as "the gaunt cattle, marching in rapid tread, paraded like gray ghosts across the Capitol

Lands, icicles hanging from their muzzles, eyes, and ears. Any number of the loudest cussing cowpunchers in Texas couldn't have turned them."[30]

But there was something that had just been developed that could stop them. Barbed wire, which debuted in Texas about 1875, was eventually adopted as a solution to the drift problem.

> Though there was not a long unbroken fence line, though the slender strands whistling in the wind off the prairie looked frail and insubstantial—and very much out of place—they nevertheless formed a wall of wire which proved to be a sufficient barrier in the path of cattle moving from north to south. Sections built in 1881-82 were so effective that additional sections were put up the following year, and by 1885 barbed-wire drift fences had been erected across the entire Texas Panhandle, from Indian Territory on the east to New Mexico [Territory] on the west, and beyond.[31]

Man's attempt to outthink nature has, it seems, more often than not produced disastrous results. After the 7 January 1886 Panhandle blizzard, young William Lewis, who dreamed of being a rancher, and the Half Circle R cowboys examined the grisly results of the drift fence.

> On the first day that the ground was passable, Koogle and William's father drove out upon the plains to estimate the damage. Because the buckboard, which they used in preference to the heavier hack, seated only two comfortably, William, who was eager to go along, rode Tex. Sickening sights greeted them. For the entire length of one drift fence, cattle lay in piles so high it would have been possible to walk for a long distance on top of them without touching a foot to the ground. Instinct had forced the dumb creatures to move away from the wind, and they had drifted until stopped by the barrier of barbed wire. Presumably, they had huddled there in bewilderment, bellowing mournfully until they froze stiff. Koogle and William's

father knew that the same conditions existed at the other fences even though they did not drive that far. The few cattle that survived were those which were in the canyons where snow-covered brush and mesquite trees had not only protected them in a measure from the cold, but also had provided them with temporary fodder until the snow disappeared from the grass.

The catastrophe left the smaller ranchmen bankrupt. They had no herds, only a few horses for which they no longer had any use. The large companies were severely injured. The Quarter Circle Heart lost over five hundred cattle in one corner west of town. Many steers, in an effort to reach brush, had stepped off into snow-filled crevices of the cap rock. It was a crippling blow for the three partners of the Half Circle K.[32]

This blizzard proved a tragic test case for barbed wire drift fences; the drift fences didn't turn any cattle back but it did stop them dead in their tracks.

The Great White Ruin, as it came to be called, did ruin nearly all of the small outfits while many of the larger ranchers struggled to remain solvent. Spring thaw found the Half Circle K owners facing bleak financial prospects.

William Lewis's grim task, assigned by the foreman, was dragging dead cattle from the Salt Fork of the Red River. Both jobs were highly unpleasant and both were doomed to failure. Williams dreams seemed as lifeless as the bloated, stinking carcasses that frequently made him vomit.

A similar storm swept across the western Kansas plains on 1 January 1886, and was tagged the "Blizzard of '86." It took a heavy toll in human and animal lives. Snow piled up six feet deep and the temperature plummeted well below zero °F. Trains were stalled, telegraph wires were down, and "two men frozen to death, found nine miles from Dodge City clasped in each others arms; one entire family, father, mother, and three children frozen . . . Reported thirty-five people frozen near Garden City, including whole family of seven. Not confirmed for no wires in operation west of Larned. Six hundred telegraph wires down between Larned and Dodge City mostly."[33]

Frederic Remington, Thirty Below and a Blizzard Raging

It was tough duty for the cavalry when it's *Thirty Below and a Blizzard Raging* as depicted in the Frederic Remington painting. Finding shelter was probably foremost in the minds of both men and mounts. Such marches were necessary because the best time to strike hostile Indian camps was in the dead of winter.

During this blizzard Indians begged Wichita, Kansas, residents to allow them inside their homes. It was reported that newcomers viewed this request as an "annoyance."[34]

Another casualty of this storm was discovered when a stagecoach, pulled by a six-horse hitch, staggered into the station at Fort Camp Supply, Indian Territory. Inside the coach three men and a woman passenger were almost frozen to death but survived. Up top, on the box, Ol' Charlie had driven his last run—the driver was frozen stiff.

The storm finally blew itself out, permitting Les Cator, a Panhandle rancher, to ride out and check his stock. On the windswept plains he stumbled upon a settler's wagon. The team, still in the harness, was dead and inside the wagon an entire family—father, mother, and three small children were huddled together in frozen death.[35]

The killer winter of 1885-1886 was followed by a scorching summer drought that seared the range grass dead brown.

Unfortunately during the following winter, 1886-1887, another blizzard pushed drift cattle into the Panhandle fences for a ruinous encore. Cattle piled up and froze to death by the tens of thousands. Ranchers estimated losses to their herds as high as 75 percent. "John Hollicot, manager of the LX Ranch in the Texas Panhandle, and his men skinned two hundred and fifty cattle to the mile for thirty-five miles along the fence."[36]

This double-barreled calamity proved to be a dress rehearsal for another engagement at a northern theater the following winter. As they were tallying up their losses down south, up north in Montana, Wyoming, and Dakota Territories Mother Nature was already setting the stage.

As mentioned, the year 1886 was a year of "toos" on the northern plains: too many cattle, too many sheep, too little rain, and too little grass. This was followed by another stretch of toos: too much snow, too much ice, too much wind, and too much cold.

In November the curtain rose on what was to become the worst winter kill on record. The script read pretty much like the Great White Ruin. On the sixteenth a severe storm dropped the temperature to two °F below zero and during the next two days eighteen inches of snow fell.

Early in December another storm dropped four inches of snow and pushed the temperature to twelve below. This storm was followed by a three day blizzard in mid-December. After this storm blew itself out the weather remained normal until 9 January 1887. Stuart later wrote that

> on that day a cold wind blew from the north. It began to snow and snowed steadily for sixteen hours, in which sixteen inches of snow fell on a level. The thermometer dropped to twenty-two degrees below zero, then twenty-seven degrees, then thirty degrees, and on the night of January 15 stood at forty-six degrees below zero, and there were sixteen inches of snow on the level. It was as though the Arctic regions had pushed down and enveloped us. Everything was white. Not a point of bare ground was visible in any direction. This storm lasted ten days without abating.[37]

Stuart's recollections refer to conditions on the DHS range but other parts of the territory were also suffering. On the last day of January 1887 a howling blizzard swept into southwestern Montana dropping the mercury to thirty-two below for four days. The Dillon and Bannack area was hit on 9 February by a storm that again pushed the thermometer below zero.

Anywhere east of the mountains with their protected valleys the stock had less shelter and the ranchers had put up little or no winter feed for their range cattle.

Chinook winds promised relief and cheered the cattlemen but proved a cruel, false hope. Suddenly the wind switched and came howling out of the north. Sub-zero temperatures froze the melted snow into a mantel of ice that locked away what little graze was left. Neither horses nor cattle could break through the ice to forage. The critter's efforts to penetrate the frozen armor bloodied their nostrils, hocks, and legs. Weak and emaciated, the doomed creatures drifted across the snow and ice leaving trails of crimson in their wake.[38]

Stuart had read sign correctly.

Wyoming Territory ranchers shared the same fate as their Montana neighbors. "For two months, the wind blew from sun-up to sun-down. Ranch employees were found frozen to death near Sundance, Evanston and Stinking Water, according to reports in the Laramie *Boomerang*."[39]

Everything and everybody suffered during the Big Die-Up. Crow Indians were barely existing on winter killed beef and Fort Benton was dangerously low on food and fuel.

The Indians said they couldn't remember a winter as severe and in some areas they lost half of their horse herd when Cold Maker visited their winter lodges.[40]

It's impossible to know just how many lives, animal and human, were lost but the loss was staggering. If, however, there was a bright side of the Big Die-Up it was because so many cattle drifted and died it was impossible to get a correct tally on herds. Mother Nature had provided a much-needed adjustment to many ranch manager's books.

Some of the absentee owners and investors were never told the real extent of yearly losses to predators, Indians, and winter kill. And these owners naively expected a 100 percent calf crop every year—all heifers. Consequently many herds were far short of actual stock when compared to the numbers on the books. After the Die-Up it no longer mattered and it almost certainly saved some manager's reputations—deservedly so or not.

By spring thaw the stench of ruin fouled the warming winds; free grass ranching and the beef bonanza died side-by-side with cattle, sheep, horse, oxen, mules, Indians, and newcomers.

Ranchers realized that "for the first time in Wyoming's history, so far as anybody knew, there were flocks of buzzards hovering over the plains, lured from distant areas by the immensity of the fetid harvest."[41]

First news reports and gossip regarding a major disaster are generally understated or overstated. The Big Die-Up was no exception; since the actual losses can never be determined, considerable weight must be given to the accounts recorded at that time.

A Fort Laramie pioneer estimated a loss of about 15 percent of the cattle in Wyoming. In Laramie County 227,792 cattle were assessed in 1887 while in 1888 the figure had dropped to 183,437; in Johnson County the count dropped from 141,286 to 91,740. Both of the previous numbers indicate a loss far greater than 15 percent.

Ranchers simply refused to believe how bad the loss was until spring roundup removed all doubt. First estimates on the losses suffered by newly arrived "through" cattle were thought to be less than 50 percent. It was soon discovered that in actuality it was nearly 100 percent in some instances. It wasn't unusual for herds of 5,000 to be reduced to only 100 survivors.[42]

Some stock drifted so far and wide that it was a year before they were collected in some distant roundup. A number of cattlemen never even attempted to gather the remains of their stock but quietly abandoned ranching for a less risky business.

As expected, the eastern open range of Montana Territory suffered heavy losses. Even the area's old timers were stunned— Conrad Kohrs believed the loss was 50 percent while Nelson

Story put it somewhat higher at 66 2/3 percent. "One spread went from assets of $1,000,000 to liabilities of $350,000."[43]

For an illustration of just how adversely the overstocking affected the winter kill we can look at DHS losses for the first winter, 1880-1881. Stuart reported

> losses all told, this first year were thirteen per cent, five per cent from Indians, five per cent from predatory animals and three per cent from the storms. The small loss from the storms was because there were so few cattle on the range; that feed was unlimited; and the creeks, and brush, and tall rye grass furnished them dry beds and shelter equal to a good stable and our cattle were northern range stock.[44]

In 1880 there were only 250,000 head of cattle, including dairy cattle and work oxen, in the entire territory of Montana.

It was a very severe winter according to Granville Stuart.

For years western lore insisted that buffalo would move into a norther, impervious of the cold and snow. Another bit of buffalo lore was that they could horn their way through the frozen snow and ice to the lifesaving grass beneath.

According to Stuart this isn't always true. He recorded that the winter of 1880-1881 was unusually severe and,

> on December 8 eighteen inches of snow fell and the thermometer registered thirty-two degrees below zero. The storm lasted four days and from that time on until 15 May there was a series of storms with the thermometer from twenty-two to forty degrees below zero. The snow lay deep and many of the buffalo died.[45]

Yet Stuart said their cattle only suffered a 3 percent winter kill. It's difficult to draw any other conclusion than that flagrant overstocking was largely to blame for the Big Die-Up.

Theodore Roosevelt came west to mend a sorrowing spirit and a frail body. He took up ranching on the Maltese Cross and Elkhorn spreads along the Little Missouri River in Dakota

Territory. Soon there were beeves with his brands rustling for grass on the crowded range.

Roosevelt, a greenhorn *extraordinaire*, initially demanded to be addressed as "Mr. Roosevelt." The locals ignored the demand and immediately dewlapped the bespectacled easterner as "Four Eyes." Despite a not-so-promising beginning, Roosevelt became a respectable cowboy and rancher and was eventually dubbed "Old Four Eyes" by the locals—a more affectionate and respectable handle.

Mother Nature showed no partiality to a future president of the United States. Roosevelt later wrote about the Big Die-Up conditions on his ranch.

> In the thick brush the stock got some shelter and sustenance. They gnawed every twig and bough they could get at. They browsed the bitter sage brush down to where the branches were the thickness of a man's finger. When near a ranch they crowded into the outhouses and sheds to die, and fences had to be built around the windows to keep the wild-eyed, desperate beasts from thrusting their heads through the glass panes.[46]

Horses, according to Roosevelt, were not immune to the killing cold. "Even many of the horses died. An outfit near me lost half its saddle-band, the animals having been worked so hard that they were very thin when fall came."[47]

After the Big Die-Up, Teddy's enthusiasm for playing cowboys and Indians seemingly perished along with his stock. Fortunately he was able to exercise an option many other ranchers didn't have—retreat back east to the sure things of privileged money and power.

The Big Die-Up was a career changer for another famous individual who opted to stay put in the west. Charlie Russell, a cowboy with the OH outfit in the Judith Basin, passed the storm-bound days pursuing his love of painting and drawing. The ranch owners, who lived in Helena, wrote and asked foreman, Jesse Phelps, how the herd was wintering. Phelps didn't know how to break the news to the owners so Russell sketched an old brindle cow that was hanging around the building. The cow was skin and bones, her ribs resembled a washboard and her hips poked skyward like twin mountain peaks. She stood hunched backed and head down in the snow with three wolves watching and contemplating a meal.

Russell gave the sketch to Phelps and said to send it because it told the story better than words could. The sketch titled "Waiting for a Chinook" or as it was later titled, "The Last of Five Thousand," was worth a thousand heartbreaking words.[48] Charles Russell had created a fitting logo for the Big Die-Up.

In retrospect it's amazing that cattlemen, old and new, were blinded by the immensity of the land. Consequently many, if not most, ranchers failed to believe it could someday end or that someone else might want some of the range they had come to view as their own private empires.

The Homestead Act of 1862 required a total filing fee of $18 to claim 160 acres of public land. But, cattle barons no doubt reasoned, what good is ownership of 160 acres when a ranching operation requires thousands of acres? For that reason many of the large ranchers failed to even file on the ranch headquarters' site.

Doctor T. A. Larson, chairman of the history department at the University of Wyoming, studied the Big Die-Up and its effect on ranching. "The winter of 1886-7 had a terrific impact upon Wyoming. Losses were magnified by the fact that those who lost were often hard pressed by creditors and had to liquidate as best they could in a market ruinously low. Between 60,000 and 70,000 head of stock were shipped during the summer and fall of 1887."

That winter, in Larson's words, "brought Wyoming stockmen back to earth. There was one third as many cattle in the Territory in 1894 as there had been in '86."[49]

Stockmen now realized that ranching was, out of necessity, going to change. Small herds that could be provided with better shelter, better feed, and better management were needed if ranching was to be sustainable and profitable on the plains.

Another casualty of the Big Die-Up was the opulent Cheyenne Club which "defaulted on its bonds, and was to be sold for two winter-thin dimes on the dollar."

It was the beginning of the end of the free range era that had produced some of western history's most dynamic and colorful characters. The few short years of the cattle barons reigning birthed the romance and legend of cowboys and Indians, Longhorns and trail drives, gamblers and soiled doves, lawmen and outlaws, range wars and gunfighters.

##

Texas ranchers and cowboys could expound on the foraging skills, ability to do without water for long periods, and the just plain toughness of the Longhorns for hours, if not days, without pausing for breath.

Longhorns, they might explain, "would hook down the bloom stalks of the Spanish dagger, live for months on prickly pear without drinking water, and, in some grassless regions, endure for a lifetime by browsing the brush like deer."

For good measure they might mention the story about the hide and bones of a Longhorn lodged in the limbs of a tree growing beside a gulch. The rider that discovered the remains recognized the brand and the next time he saw the owner he told him about the critter in the tree. The owner exclaimed, "Great browsers, those Bar Y cattle of mine . . . Spring of the year, and that old Longhorn clumb the elm like a squirrel to eat the buds, and jest accidentally hung himself."[50]

Northern cattlemen, however, believe the Western cattle from the offspring of Shorthorn and Devon bulls, were superior and favored

> the so-called Westerns, because of their physical attributes, developed by environment and inherited traits, were better suited to the northern ranges of the great plains than were the southern imports. When moved to Montana, they did not have to become acclimated. They knew how to rustle in winter, and they had the stamina and instinct to assume more than perfunctory responsibility for their calves when it came to fighting off predators.[51]

Regardless of the romance of the old Longhorns and the trail drives, serious stockmen realized that the Longhorns needed to be retired. Recognizing this trend, the giant XIT Ranch began "a policy of controlled breeding, introducing Hereford, Shorthorn, and Angus to upgrade or replace the scrubby Texas cattle which they originally purchased or bred."[52]

Regrettably the Great White Ruin of 1885-86 and the Big Die-Up of 1886-87 was followed by another killer blizzard in January 1888.

After this storm had spent itself, the XIT ranch hands stripped the hides off of 3,500 high-dollar imported short horn beeves that had frozen to death. They never found another 1,000 that had become lost in the storm. The loss of these animals alone smeared about $100,000 of red ink on the XIT's ledger sheet.

The Lewis family who were forced off the Half Circle K by the Great White Ruin only suffered minor loss in 1888. "The shelves and shelves of preserves his mother had made during the summer had burst, and the two milk cows when finally found were still standing, but frozen stiff."[53]

Up north in Dakota Territory—present day North Dakota— this storm was considered worse than the Big Die-Up. "Perhaps the worst struck on 12 January 1888. It covered haystacks, barns, and houses with snow and brought death to nearly a hundred people."[54]

Mercifully, in the midst of all the suffering and deaths during blizzards, there did emerge some amazing accounts of survival and rescue.

An oft' told story from the buffalo country involves hide hunters caught on the plains by a norther. Within minutes, wind driven snow erased any sense of direction and any hope of finding camp. In a number of cases the resourceful hunter took a fresh skinned buffalo hide, put it down hair side up, and then rolled up in the hide. It provided excellent protection and the hunters reported they were cozy warm and soon fell asleep during the blizzard.

However, while they slept the green hides froze as stiff as an iron straight jacket. They were alive, and cozy, but trapped until rescued by others or until the sun thawed the hide enough for them to free themselves.

Out in west Texas during February 1877, a hide hunter, Jim Ennis, was surprised by a blizzard while skinning a fresh kill.

Visibility dropped to zero making it impossible for him to find the outfit's camp. So, he just rolled up in the fresh buffalo robe and hours later discovered a terrifying downside to his green-hide shelter.

> During the night a blue norther froze the hide stiff. Then lobo wolves came and began tearing bits of meat from the hide. Jim couldn't understand why they seemed to prefer those bits to the whole carcass lying near by. He yelled at them, but they kept on coming. Some bit so close that they tore his clothes.
>
> At dawn the wolves left, and about ten o'clock the sun thawed the hide enough for Jim to crawl out. When he found his way back to camp, his fellow hunter and skinners didn't recognize him. In the night his hair had turned from black to gray.[55]

When the great blizzard of 1888 blew into Nebraska, four men who were shopping at a store in the town of Chambers, Holt County, left the store to return to their boarding-house. Earlier, when they had left the boarding house to go to the store, they were not expecting a blizzard and consequently didn't dress warmly.

Their house was only a short distance from the store, but the storm was so blinding that they became lost and for two or three hours drifted before the storm like livestock. Dangerously chilled and nearly exhausted, the men happened upon "some cabbage and castor bean stalks and we knew we were close to a house. We shouted long and loud, and a dog heard us and barked, and we followed the dog who led us to a hog shed which we welcomed with open arms."

Using the last of their strength they crawled over the fence and crowded in among the hogs. The body heat of the hogs saved their lives and ten hours later the men had recovered enough to find the farm house and safety.[56]

Another survival story gives credit to the Longhorn's natural instincts which were honed to a fine edge by years of survival on the southern plains. Occasionally a human was smart enough to recognize this quality in the leggy bovine.

WHITE DEATH

Harper's Weekly, *27 January, 1883; Charles Graham*
Blizzards occassionally shut down rail travel, even when multiple engines were used to push giant snowplows. Some trains spent the entire winter snowbound. Passengers had to endure the cold until rescued or leave the train and attempt to find shelter.

Trail boss, Jack Potter, liked to name his lead steers and "John Chisum" was the name of his best and most appreciated lead Longhorn.

After the fall roundup in 1889, Potter was bound for Clayton, New Mexico, with a herd when they were caught by an early blizzard. It proved to be the worst blizzard in history in that part of the country where it froze to death thousands of sheep and cattle before subsiding.

True to form, when the storm struck, the cattle tried to turn south and drift with the wind. The drovers held them until John Chisum finally turned and followed Potter into the teeth of the storm. The trail boss figured they could find shelter in Tremperos Canyon—if he could stay on the trail in the blinding, wind-driven snow.

When Potter came to a fork in the trail, he took the branch he calculated would lead to shelter but John Chisum refused to follow. Potter had a few words with his mulish lead steer.

> "You don't seem to realize I am piloting this herd," I said to him. "I know a horse has more sense than a man. If you give a horse with any sense at all his reins on a dark night or in a snowstorm, he will take you to camp; but you've never been where you are headed, so far as I know. What right has an old, cold-blooded,

scalawag steer to be making decisions for a trail boss? If we don't find shelter before night, God knows what will become of us. Nevertheless, I'm just guessing too, and now I'm going to let you have your way."

Twenty minutes later John Chisum led the men and cattle into the Tremperos and the shelter of a ranch. Potter said if shelter had been "a mile farther off I don't believe my horse would ever have got me there." [57] Potter owed a lot to John Chisum because other herds that were caught in this same blizzard drifted and died as did the men who stayed with the cattle.

##

Charles Goodnight, ever the ruthless opportunist, quietly leased a major part of the open range used by the Half Circle K spread. By doing so he was able to force William Lewis and the other owners to sell out—to Goodnight of course.

In the end, despite such setbacks, William Lewis prevailed and fulfilled his dream of becoming a cowboy and a rancher. In her memoirs his wife explained the character traits that she credited with his success. She said he maintained,

> a stubborn Sunday-school kind of nonviolence, backed by courage instead of guns. In a country where the six-shooter was in every man's hand, he refused to wear a gun; where swearing was part of the *lingua franca*, he never swore; where no man would get on a horse without wearing high-heeled cowboy boots—to keep the foot from slipping through a stirrup and being dragged when a horse panicked and ran away—he wore low-heeled shoes and liked the Mexican *tapadero*, the slipper-like leather guard over the front of the stirrup, to avoid the risk of being dragged . . .
>
> Yet at the time a boy nowadays is about a junior in college, he was top hand—about the equivalent of a colonel in the army—of the big R.O. Ranch; at thirty was already a highly regarded cattleman who could lease a ranch of over half a million acres; and shortly thereafter he became owner of the famous R.O. Ranch he had always dreamed about. [58]

Harper's Weekly, *28 January, 1888; R. F. Zogbaum*
Getting caught in a blue norther could be as deadly for a cavalry patrol as an Indian ambush. Soldiers sometimes slapped their mounts with the flats of their sabers to keep the animals moving.

The Big Die-Up penned a much sadder epilogue to Granville Stuart's ranching endeavors. Stuart, like many others, at first disbelieved the enormity of the loss until the spring roundup when they branded only 900 calves compared to 8,000 the previous year.

Stuart, considered by his peers as the premier cattleman of Montana Territory, was appalled at what the spring thaw revealed. He was a man who could hang outlaws without losing any sleep but the devastating aftermath of the Big Die-Up caused him to abandon ranching forever. He wrote that in

> the spring of 1887 the ranges presented a tragic aspect.
> Along the streams and in the coulees everywhere were
> strewn the carcasses of dead cattle. Those that were
> alive were poor and ragged in appearance, weak and
> easily mired in the mud holes.
>
> A business that had been fascinating to me before,
> suddenly became distasteful. I wanted no more of it. I

never wanted to own again an animal that I could not feed and shelter.[59]

He turned management of the ranch over to Conrad Kohrs although, in spite of his feelings, he stayed with the stockmen and for several years remained president of the Board of Stock Commissioners of Montana.

Appointed state land agent in 1891, his job required him to select state land for schools and in 1894 Stuart was appointed envoy to the republics of Uruguay and Paraguay." For five years he traveled extensively fulfilling the duties of that office. At the time of his death on 2 October 1918, he was working on a history of Montana. He was eighty-four years old and never realized any significant monetary rewards from ranching.

Perhaps the following stories are true, perhaps they are not. Either way, they are interesting.

The Easter Storm of 1873 was responsible for the following story from near the town of Harvard in Clay County, Nebraska. L. C. Hurd and his wife were living about three miles northwest of the town of Harvard. Hurd recalled that his "stable was sod walls 30 inches thick and sod roof; my livestock a yoke of cattle (Tige and Nig) and a Texas cow with five feet ten inches from tip to tip of horns."

Hurd and his wife stopped at a neighbor's after church and were there when the storm began. Tige and Nig were stalled in the sod barn and relatively safe from the storm but his milk cow had been picketed to graze about 100 yards north of the barn. The storm continued all night and by the following afternoon Hurd was determined to check on his stock, especially the cow. Hurd remembered that

> When I reached my place the snow was banked from the eves of the stable tapering 200 yards out into the prairie, and "Glory be!" my scoop was outside. The [staked out] cow had come to the end of her rope, a ball of ice as big as a wash boiler on her tail, and her body cased in ice and a sheath over her head with a hole through which she breathed, and standing with snow halfway up her sides.

I could not untie her rope, and took a long time to undress enough to get my knife, then clear the snow away and pound the ice off her, and then she could not move. I beat her sides with flat-footed kicks, and then took her by the horns and moved her sidewise so she had to shift her feet to stand. After much exercise she could step a little as I pulled, and at last could walk a little and we got to the stable. It was cozy warm inside. I tried to get hay from the stack but couldn't carry it, and gave each some ear corn and shut the door.[60]

Another story fitting in this same category is from western Kansas. Joe N. Hulpieu and Mrs. J. F. Miller were guests at the home of Mr. and Mrs. Norton Hulpieu located six miles north of Garden City, Kansas, for an 1885 New Years Eve watch party. The blizzard struck while they were ringing in the New Year. "It was 32 below zero," Mr. Hulpieu recalls,

and the snow was so dry and fine that it went wherever air could go. There was no keeping it out. I remember how it sifted through the shingles of our new roof and piled up on the bed.

And here's something that sounds like a big lie, but it's the absolute truth: the snow blew through a keyhole and piled up on the floor as high as the keyhole itself.

He goes on to describe what he believes is the oddest thing about the storm—the durable sow. When the storm struck he turned loose the 400-pound sow that was in a pen which offered no shelter. He wanted to give the animal a chance to find whatever safe haven it could during the blizzard. After the storm passed there was no sign of the sow and it was believed it perished along with all other animals caught without sufficient protection.

Incredibly, over a month later the sow was discovered in a hollow cavern inside a large snowdrift. "Peering through the hole, he saw the lost sow, weak and so skinny that her ribs stuck out, but still alive."[61] The sow had lived thirty-three days beneath the snowdrift.

##

Mother Nature, robed in seasonal splendor, inspires love even of the stoic; alas, on a whim, she can be a cold, cold, mistress.

WHITE DEATH

Chapter Two notes

[1] Willie Newbury Lewis, *Tapadero: The Making of a Cowboy* (Austin: University of Texas Press, 1972), 67-68.

[2] The Handbook of Texas Online, "Blue Norther," http://www.tsha.utexas.edu/handbook/online/articles/view/BB/ybb1.html

[3] Walter Prescott Webb, *The Great Plains* (Waltham, MA: Blaisdell Publishing Company, 1959), 25.

[4] Olive K. Dixon, *Life of "Billy" Dixon* (1927; reprint, Austin: State House Press, 1987), 221.

[5] Richard Irving Dodge, *The Plains of the Great West* (1877; reprint, New York: Archer House, Inc., 1959), 39-41.

[6] Louise Barry, *The Beginning of the West* (Topeka: Kansas State Historical Society, 1972), 791.

[7] Granville Stuart, *Forty Years on the Frontier,* edited by Paul C. Phillips (Cleveland, OH: The Arthur H. Clark Company, 1925), 2:28-29.

[8] David M. Ludlum, *The History of American Weather: Early American Winters II 1821-1870* (Boston: American Meteorological Society, 1968), 165.

[9] Ibid., 169-171.

[10] Joseph G. McCoy, *Historic Sketches of the Cattle Trade of the West and Southwest* (Kansas City: Ramsey, Millett & Hudson, 1874), 227.

[11] Lewis Nordyke, *Great Roundup* (1955; reprint, Edison, NJ: Castle Books, 2001), 157.

[12] Joseph G. McCoy, *Historic Sketches of the Cattle Trade of the West and Southwest* (Kansas City: Ramsey, Millett & Hudson, 1874), 228.

[13] Olive K. Dixon, *Life of "Billy" Dixon* (1927; reprint, Austin: State House Press, 1987), 68.

[14] Ibid., 68.

[15] Mari Sandoz, *The Buffalo Hunters* (1954; reprint, Lincoln: University of Nebraska Press, 1978), 113.

[16] Miles Gilbert, *Getting a Stand* (Tempe, AZ: Hal Green Printing, 1986), 20.

[17] Lewis Nordyke, *Cattle Empire* (New York: William Morrow and Company, 1949), 82.

[18] Granville Stuart, *Forty Years on the Frontier,* edited by Paul C. Phillips (Cleveland, OH: The Arthur H. Clark Company, 1925), 2:150.

[19] Robert H. Fletcher, *Free Grass to Fences* (New York: University Publishers Incorporated, 1960), 44-45.

[20] Edward Everett Dale, *The Range Cattle Industry* (Norman: University of Oklahoma Press, 1960), 82n21.

[21] This and the following eight quotations are from Granville Stuart, *Forty Years on the Frontier,* edited by Paul C. Phillips (Cleveland, OH: The Arthur H. Clark Company, 1925), 2:99; and 108, 109, 133, 146, 188, 227, 227, 236 respectively.

[22] *First Annual Report of Montana Bureau of Agriculture, Labor and Industry*, 272-276, quoted in Edward Everett Dale, *The Range Cattle Industry: Ranching on the Great Plains from 1865-1925* (Norman: University of Oklahoma Press, 1960), 99.

[23] Granville Stuart, *Forty Years on the Frontier,* edited by Paul C. Phillips (Cleveland, OH: The Arthur H. Clark Company, 1925), 2:234.

[24] Ibid., 231.

[25] Robert H. Fletcher, *Free Grass to Fences* (New York: University Publishers, 1960), 54.

[26] Ogden Tanner, *The Old West: The Ranchers* (Alexandria, VA: Time-Life Books, 1985), 73.

[27] Lewis Atherton, *The Cattle Kings* (Lincoln: University of Nebraska Press, 1961), 197-198.

[28] J. Frank Dobie, *The Longhorns* (Boston: Little, Brown and Company, 1941), 196.

[29] Ibid., 196.

[30] Lewis Nordyke, *Cattle Empire* (New York: William Morrow and Company, 1950), 69.

[31] Henry D. and Frances T. McCallum, *The Wire that Fenced the West* (Norman: University of Oklahoma Press, 1969), 130-131.

[32] Willie Newbury Lewis, *Tapadero: The Making of a Cowboy* (Austin: University of Texas Press, 1972), 67-68.

[33] Ida Ellen Rath, *The Rath Trail* (Wichita: McCormick-Armstrong Co., Inc., 1961), 187-188.

[34] Kirke Mechem, ed., *The Annals of Kansas 1886-1925 In Two Volumes* (Topeka: Kansas State Historical Society, n.d.), 1:2.

[35] Lewis Nordyke, *Great Roundup* (1955; reprint, Edison, NJ: Castle Books, 2001), 154-155.

[36] Ibid., 158.

[37] Granville Stuart, *Forty Years on the Frontier,* edited by Paul C. Phillips (Cleveland, OH: The Arthur H. Clark Company, 1925), 2:235.

[38] Maurice Frink, *Cow Country Cavalcade* (Denver: The Old West Publishing Co., 1954), 58.

[39] Ibid., 57.

[40] Ibid., 57.

[41] Ibid., 58.

[42] Ibid., 58-59.

[43] Robert H. Fletcher, *Free Grass to Fences* (New York: University Publishers, 1960), 90.

[44] Granville Stuart, *Forty Years on the Frontier,* edited by Paul C. Phillips (Cleveland, OH: The Arthur H. Clark Company, 1925), 2:150.

[45] Ibid., 149.

[46] Theodore Roosevelt, *Ranch Life and the Hunting-Trail* (1888; reprint, New York: Winchester Press, 1969), 78.

[47] Ibid., 78.

[48] Robert H. Fletcher, *Free Grass to Fences* (New York: University Publishers Incorporated, 1960), 88.

[49] Maurice Frink, *Cow Country* (Denver: The Old West Publishing Co., 1954), 60.

[50] J. Frank Dobie, *The Longhorns* (Boston: Little, Brown and Company, 1941), 195.

[51] Robert H. Fletcher, *Free Grass to Fences* (New York: University Publishers, 1960), 39.

[52] Cordia Sloan Duke and Joe B. Frantz, *6,000 Miles of Fence* (Austin: University of Texas Press,

1975), 6.

[53] Willie Newbury Lewis, *Tapadero: The Making of a Cowboy* (Austin: University of Texas Press, 1972), 137-138.

[54] Elwyn B. Robinson, *History of North Dakota* (Lincoln: University of Nebraska Press, 1969), 168.

[55] Wayne Gard, *The Great Buffalo Hunt* (New York: Alfred A. Knopf, 1959), 284-285.

[56] Henry Vauck, *Blizzards: Reunion and Fiftieth Anniversary 1888-1938.* (Clay Center, Nebraska: John M. Fisher, printer, 1938), This book isn't paginated, quoted material will be found in part two.

[57] J. Frank Dobie, *The Longhorns* (Boston: Little, Brown and Company, 1941), 278-280.

[58] Willie Newbury Lewis, foreword to *Tapadero: The Making of a Cowboy* (Austin: University of Texas Press, 1972), xiii.

[59] Granville Stuart, *Forty Years on the Frontier,* edited by Paul C. Phillips (Cleveland, OH: The Arthur H. Clark Company, 1925), 2:237.

[60] Henry Vauck, *Blizzards: Reunion and Fiftieth Anniversary 1888-1938.* (Clay Center, Nebraska: John M. Fisher, printer, 1938), This book isn't paginated so reference is made to part one or part two.

[61] Esther Hulpieu Irvine, *Histories of the Jelly Family and the Hulpiau Family* (n.p., n.d.) Paper at Kansas State Historical Society, Topeka, Kansas, GL BBB H878. Internal text spells Hulpiau as Hulpieu, which is probably the correct spelling.

Chapter Three

WINDS OF TERROR

Wind in a sense is the engine of the weather, and its story is one of adventure, tragedy and surprise.

—John Lynch, *The Weather*

Carl Travers awoke, rolled over and watched his wife sleep for long moments before swinging his legs over the edge of the bed. He stretched and yawned; then tiptoed to the pallet on the floor where a child lay sleeping. Young Travers looked down at his firstborn child, said a silent prayer of thanks, then turned and walked to the kitchen area of their small house on the outskirts of St. Louis.

Pulling aside the curtain on the window he studied the sunrise blush showing along the eastern horizon. The sky gave no hint that 27 May 1896, would be anything other than a delightful late spring day. It would probably be hot and humid along the Mississippi River waterfront but that was expected by those who labored on the busy wharf.

A considerable percentage of supplies for the westward expansion flowed up and down the river and across the landings at St. Louis. Additional cargo bound for the western settlements crossed the river on the Eads Bridge that spanned the Mississippi not far from where Carl spent his working days.

Just over a year previously when his wife, Lillian, told him they were going to become parents he began planning to build a crib for their first child. Although he'd saved and scrimped, it was still months before he could afford the lumber and woodworking tools required.

Despite his diligent labor during bits of free time, the crib wasn't finished when the child was born. But now it was nearly completed. Visualizing what it would be like to put his child to bed in a crib fashioned with his own hands galvanized Carl to action. He carefully honed the plane iron and began to true up the rough oak boards from which he would fashion the crib's slats.

Thirty minutes later Lillian called him to breakfast and after finishing the meal he took the baby in his arms and lingered at the table. He talked with Lillian about her plans for a flower garden around the front porch. He promised to help her after the crib was finished; hopefully he'd have it done by Saturday. Perhaps they could start the flower garden after church on Sunday.

All too soon the sunlight slicing through a gap in the curtains reminded Carl that it was time to leave and catch the Olive Street car. He handed the baby to Lillian and kissed them both before saying goodbye.

Carl had no way of knowing that before this day was over he'd live through one of the deadliest tornadoes to ever touch down on U.S. soil.

##

The word tornado comes from the Latin word *tornare*, which means to turn or to twist. The Italian word *tornare* means to turn, as does the Spanish word *tornear*. The French word for tornado is *tornade*.

Regardless of the word's origin, more tornadoes occur in the United States than any other country. The relatively flat expanse between the Mississippi River and the Rocky Mountains allows polar air from Canada, tropical air from the Gulf of Mexico, and dry air from the Southwest to clash on the prairies and plains. These are the ingredients necessary for generating thunderstorms and the tornadoes they spawn.

It varies from year to year but, speaking in general terms, there are about 100,000 individual thunderstorm cells generated in the United States during any given year. About 10 percent, or 10,000, become severe, and of those severe cells, about 1 percent, or 1,000 give birth to tornadoes.

The months with the most tornadic activity on North America's prairies and plains are April, May, and June. "The Great Plains, stretching from the Gulf of Mexico to Canada,

A. A. Adams is credited with being the first photographer to capture a tornado on film. The twister touched down near Garnett, Kansas, on 26 April 1884. In the photo, the funnel is beginning to dissipate but it did kill one man who was caught in the open.

have more tornadoes than anywhere else on earth. The area comprising Texas, Oklahoma, Kansas, and Missouri have earned the reputations as 'Tornado alley.'"[1]

The deadliest U.S tornado of record began when it touched down about one o'clock in the afternoon near Ellington, Missouri. It traveled on a northeast heading into and across the entire state of Illinois and then into Indiana before dissipating. It had spent nearly three and a half hours on the ground traveling

219 miles at an average speed of 62 mph. It left in its wake 695 human casualties.

The deadliest nineteenth century tornado of record in the United States occurred on 6 May 1840. It touched down near the Red River about forty miles above Alexandria, Louisiana, and moved across eastern Louisiana until it struck the Mississippi River about ten miles below Natchez.

Most reports indicate its path then followed the river upstream striking Vidalia on the west bank and Natchez on the east bank. The tornado was reported to be from one to two miles wide as it followed the river causing destruction on both banks as well as on the river itself.

Witnesses said that the river rose from six to twenty feet at Natchez sinking fifty to sixty flatboats tied up at the Natchez landing. Most of the crews perished.

The Vidalia ferry sank and two other steamers, the *Prairie* and the *St. Lawrence*, were badly damaged and some accounts reported these steamers also went to the bottom. It was initially reported that the steamboat *Hinds* sank, taking most of the crew with her to the bottom of the river. But two weeks later it arrived in Baton Rouge where "fifty-one bodies had to be removed from the wreckage."[2]

Unconfirmed reports said that 200 slaves were killed by the tornado in Louisiana. Just how many lives were lost will never be known but the official toll for Vidalia, Louisiana, was one dead while across the river at Natchez, Mississippi, forty-eight were killed. Casualties on the Mississippi River were listed as 269.

Despite the Natchez calamity, tornadoes probably weren't the threat feared most by newcomers when they crossed the Mississippi River and struck out toward the setting sun.

Feared or not, tornadoes did frequently kill and injure newcomers on the trans-Mississippi prairies and plains during the nineteenth century. Author Thomas P. Grazulis spent years tracking down and investigating every recorded tornado that has occurred in the United States. The fruit of his efforts have been published in two definitive books: *Significant Tornadoes 1680-1991* and *Significant Tornadoes, 1880-1989 Volume I: Discussion and Analysis*.

These works have provided the data from which the following list is compiled. It must be remembered that the westward movement was gradual and some territories didn't become states until near the end, or in the case of Oklahoma, after the turn of the century. At the beginning of the nineteenth century, Texas was part of Mexico and it wasn't until 1845 that it became a state. Obviously, before that date tornadoes did occur in what is now Texas but were never "recorded." Compiling a comprehensive record of tornadoes during the early nineteenth century was hindered by slow communications and the low priority sometimes given to record keeping on the frontier.

The states are listed in the order in which they became part of the union. The numbers are for the entire nineteenth century.

	Killed	Injured
1812, Louisiana	360	396
1821, Missouri	499	2,332
1836, Arkansas	130	706
1845, Texas	215	1,194
1846, Iowa	534	2,125
1858, Minnesota	196	1,051
1861, Kansas	241	1,644
1867, Nebraska	51	270
1876, Colorado	0	10
1889. N. Dakota	7	53
1889, S. Dakota	46	152
1889, Montana	0	6
1890, Wyoming	0	0
1907, Oklahoma	114	450
TOTAL	2,393	10,389

This is only interesting data that tells us that newcomers did encounter killer tornadoes. The third deadliest U. S. tornado, and the one that Carl Travers experienced, occurred on 27 May 1896.

Records indicate that May 1896 was an especially potent weather-breeder that produced more than thirty-five tornadoes across the country. These storms killed 230 and injured 437—all in addition to the St. Louis tornado casualties.

Reverend Irl R. Hicks of St. Louis wasn't surprised by this outbreak of violent weather because he'd been predicting the 1896 St. Louis tornado for months. St. Louis merchants and residents, however, were preoccupied with building what they saw as the providential Great City of the West. Consequently little heed was given to his prophetic warnings which began in the summer of 1895.

In 1896 St. Louis was the fifth largest city in the United States, sprawled over approximately sixty-one square miles with nearly twenty miles of river front. Population figures were somewhere between 451,770 and 575,238—perhaps as high as 615,000 depending upon who did the counting.

Regardless of the actual number, the citizens would have done well to consider Hicks' warning of impending disaster. If some of the old-timers had paused to reflect on St. Louis' past, they may have remembered that tornadoes were no stranger to the city. Records show a tornado visited the Gateway City in 1833 and again in 1871.

Hicks tried again to warn St. Louis of impending disaster when he reiterated his prophecy of doom on 17 May 1896. This warning was only ten days before his prophecies became reality.

Hicks was reportedly studying the clouds just before the tornado touched down on 27 May and warned that "we were in the vortex of a tornado. Everybody in this office was apprised of it. The readings of the barometer were an absolute guarantee."[3]

Unfortunately, Hicks had been right all along.

Six days after the disaster, the Graf Engraving Company of St. Louis completed and offered for sale a book titled: *The Great Tornado At St. Louis.* Text was written by Martin Green and the work was illustrated with sixty-five photographs taken the morning after the storm. Green's eyewitness account describes the weather conditions as they unfolded in the hours just prior to the storm. It also provides a stirring example of the era's prose.

There was something in the air that foretold disaster . . . The clouds were giving their victims a foretaste

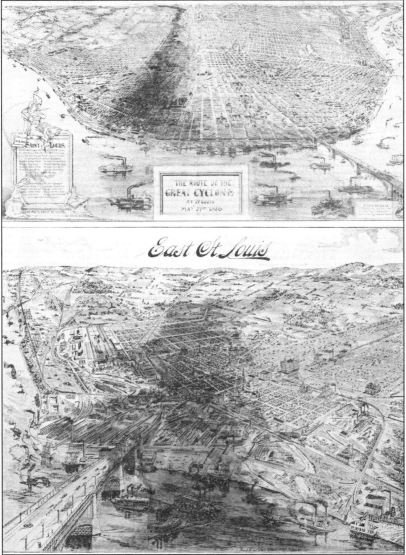

Author's collection

The dark area in the top drawing shows the path of the 1896 St. Louis tornado as it approached the Mississippi River from the west. It struck the river very near where Gateway Arch now stands. The bottom drawing shows the tornado's path of destruction through East St. Louis after crossing the river and damaging the approach to the Eads Bridge.

Trinity Lutheran Church in St. Louis suffered considerable damage in the 1896 tornado. Part of the steeple landed in the intersection at Eighth and Lafayette Avenue.

of their fury and the victims rested secure in blissful ignorance . . . Beginning at noon the barometer began to fall . . . alarming to those who observed it.

Shortly after 3 o'clock peculiar looking clouds began to float lazily across the sky . . . And the sky in the north and west began to assume a sickly green color, the color that makes the dweller on the prairies run to his storm cellar . . . A few minutes before 5 o'clock the forces of the air began to marshal for the attack on the city. Long lines of clouds in array like trained soldiers suddenly ceased shifting from place to place and took up a steady, swift procession . . . All the time the clouds were gathering in the west the wind was rising and from the Weather Observatory was obtained a view of the most brilliant electrical display ever seen in St. Louis. Against a background of various tints of green,

Photo by author
Trinity Lutheran Church in St. Louis as it appears today.

forks and sheets and luminous balls of fire, colored purple and red and blue, shot out, accompanied by roars of thunder.

At 5:05 the advancing masses of clouds came together over the western part of the city . . . across the green sky there seemed to be torn a rent of white light twisting and turning from north to south that was visible nearly 10 seconds . . . in the momentary glimpse that could be had of the attacking elements by its assistance it was seen that a long cloud shaped more like a big sausage than anything else was rapidly forming and that one end of it was descending toward the earth.

At 5:10, while darkness was swiftly settling down over the roofs of the city . . . below in the streets people could be seen scurrying to places of safety and the street cars were compelled to wait long on the corners for the crowds desiring to get aboard . . . strange blue balls began to flash along the telegraph and trolley wires.

At 5:17 a glance at the instrument showed a wind velocity of 80 miles and hour. And then from the tower the watchers saw the great battle. The Storm King and the Fire King combined in the attack on St. Louis.[4]

Eighteen minutes later the tornado had carved a festering gash through St. Louis and East St. Louis, or in Green's words "it was 5:35 when the army of the air withdrew from the assault."

During those few minutes 311 buildings were completely destroyed, 7,200 were heavily damaged, and 1,300 more sustained significant damage. Scattered among and buried beneath the rubble were 137 dead in St. Louis and another 118 dead in East St. Louis.

Property loss was tabulated at $10 million.

As appalling as the actual carnage was, it wasn't anywhere close to the reports that soon appeared in newspapers across the nation.

Virtually all the telegraph wires were down or damaged which effectively isolated, for a short period of time, St. Louis from the rest of the world. Eventually one or two lines were found to be operational and the outside world learned that a tornado had struck St. Louis. Major newspapers picked up on the story and ran specials that exaggerated the destruction and death caused by the tornado. Some papers reported that St. Louis was completely wiped from the face of the earth or "blotted off the map." Spurious casualty reports ran as high as 100,000.

When this information reached the outside world it created a blizzard of telegrams from concerned family members and friends seeking information about their loved ones in St. Louis and East St. Louis. This was in addition to the thousands of outgoing telegrams residents were trying to send to family and friends.

As expected, hundreds of newspaper correspondents from across the country rushed to St. Louis. By Friday night, despite many downed wires, "nearly 1,000,000 words of special telegrams were sent by these correspondents."[5]

The telegraph services were overwhelmed.

Residents turned to the postal service as an alternative method of outreach to family and friends. Dozens, hundreds, thousands, simply sent copies of local newspapers as the best way to convey the damage done by the storm. "The volume of this kind of matter jumped up from an average of 600 pounds per day to 10,000 and 12,000 pounds."[6]

The postal service was overwhelmed.

Human beings, responding to a deep-seated macabre curiosity, descended on the wounded city. On Sunday the railroads ran forty-five special excursion trains to St. Louis in addition to the one hundred regular scheduled passenger trains. "The greatest crowds of all were on the Sunday following the calamity, when they were dangerous in their magnitude. Over 140,000 people came in by train on that day."

Union Station Master, Jere J. Coakley, estimated that "over 150,000 passed through the Union Station to-day. This is a cyclone in travel."[7] Union Station's Midway passage, fifty feet wide and just over six hundred feet long, was jammed with thirty thousand people and raised the real possibility of a second deadly catastrophe in St. Louis. This prompted Coakley to call for fifty police patrolmen to manage the crowd.

On Sunday, according to one estimate, at least 500,000 people thronged the streets along the tornado's path of destruction.

The railroads were overwhelmed.

The economic impact was felt by every class of resident whether or not they suffered direct loss of life or property. Many thousands were without employment because there was no longer a place of employment to go to. One of the largest employers devastated by the storm was the St. Louis Refrigerator and Wooden Gutter Company located at Main and Park Avenues. The concern employed 250 workers before wind and fire completely destroyed the business.

Just prior to the storm, this company had placed an order for 100 million feet of lumber, which at the time was possibly the largest such contract ever made. An order for 100 million feet of lumber is impressive even by today's lumber industry standards.

Scores of other businesses sustained enough damage that it was necessary to lay off some, or all of the staff. Until repairs or rebuilding was completed, these employees were without jobs or paychecks. Clean-up operations did, however, offer temporary work for some of the unemployed.

Tornadoes can destroy more than life and property; they can destroy the mind. The St. Louis city hospital lay directly in the path of the tornado and the three story structure sustained severe damage. Some wards were completely destroyed while others had walls crumbled and roofs removed. Miraculously only two of the 416 patients were killed outright although many suffered injuries.

Three more died during the night from injuries other than physical. "One was Jean d'Archimbault, who crazed with fear when the partition wall of his division fell near him, jumped up and proceeded 30 feet on one sound leg and a freshly amputated limb." Four hours later he passed away from the shock.

An elderly patient, Francisca Rodriguez, "also died of fear." The third victim, a woman named Collins, died as a result "of frenzied terror at the storm."[8]

After a tornado completely destroyed a farm near Rodman, Iowa, on 13 June 1899, "the owner became a 'living madman.'"[9]

The series of storms that rumbled through Kansas, Nebraska, Missouri, and Iowa on 29 May, and 30 May 1879, were particularly violent and deadly. The town of Irving, Kansas, was struck by two tornadoes within a few minutes of each other.

These storms left dreadful memories and it took years for some lives to return to normal. "Night after night following the storms hundreds of persons never went to bed, but peered into the darkness watching for a recurrence of the scenes through which they had passed. Every dark cloud or sudden freshening of the wind filled them with foreboding which could not be allayed until every sign of supposed damage had passed."[10]

During the 1896 St. Louis tornado an entire tree was uprooted and dropped through the roof of a house behind a main residence in Clifton Heights. The elderly lady living in the house was not struck or injured in any way but was killed. "Her nervous system had been so shattered by the intensity of the storm that the additional strain was too much for her."[11]

Birds and animals are, it seems, also subject to mental stress during a tornado. Reminiscent of bird and animal behavior during the New Madrid earthquake is the story of "a snow white dove" observed during the St. Louis tornado.

People had taken shelter in the Union Trust Building and the dove, "unable to cope with the wind in its native element, equally unable to find security on any resting place exposed to the wind, blown hither and thither, in its fright entered the open doorway and flew to the shoulder of a gentleman standing there. The frightened bird seemed to know it was safe, and sat there quite and contented."[12]

Published accounts of tornadoes during the nineteenth century frequently use the word cyclone or hurricane when referring to a tornado. Misunderstanding and misinformation, plus a lack of technology to study these storms led to understandable confusion. As an example Frederick Grundy wrote an article, "Cyclones and Tornadoes," published in the

March 1883, issue of *Frank Leslie's Popular Monthly Magazine*."
One of the few things he got right in the article was that a
tornado and cyclone are different weather events.

> Many people have an idea that a tornado and a cyclone
> are one and the same thing, but that is where they
> are mistaken. A tornado has a straight forward and
> sometimes downward motion . . . They are caused
> by two winds of equal strength coming together and
> darting forward in the shape of a V, the destroying
> point rarely exceeding 150 feet in width. They travel
> with great velocity, two to ten miles, destroying
> everything in their course, then vanish as quickly as
> they formed.
> A cyclone is a powerful monster whirlwind, full of
> and largely held together by electricity. The outside
> whirls downward, exerting a tremendous pressure
> towards the inner circle, where suction more than
> equals the outside pressure . . .
> In the case of a tornado proper, the bark will be
> peeled off the trees on the side where the storm came;
> but in a genuine cyclone, it is likely to be peeled from
> the opposite side, especially if the storm is heavily
> surcharged with electricity.[13]

In spite of, or because of, this lack of understanding about
the proper meaning of the word cyclone and tornado, period
writers used them, along with hurricane, interchangeably.

Julian Curzon compiled and edited *The Great Cyclone at St.
Louis and East St. Louis, May 27, 1896*. It was published with
amazing speed and the first printing of the book is dated 10
June 1896, just three weeks and three days after the event.

Three words are used by Curzon when referring to the
storm that struck St. Louis—cyclone, hurricane, and tornado.
The National Weather Service web site gives the following
definitions of cyclone, hurricane, and tornado in its *Glossary of
Meteorology* (AMS 2000):

A tornado "is a violently rotating column of air, in contact
with the ground, either pendant from a cumuliform cloud or

State Historical Society of North Dakota A1973-1

Miles of empty prairie surround this homestead, yet a tornado zeroed in on the settler's sod buildings and reduced them to rubble. This photo was taken by J. N. Templeman after the tornado touched down on 15 July 1885, near Highmore, Dakota Territory (South Dakota).

underneath a cumuliform cloud, and often (but not always) visible as a funnel cloud."

"The terms 'hurricane' and 'typhoon' are regionally specific names for a strong 'tropical cyclone.' A tropical cyclone is the generic term for a non-frontal synoptic scale low-pressure system over tropical or sub-tropical waters with organized convection (i.e. thunderstorm activity) and definite cyclonic surface wind circulation."

Tropical cyclones with wind speeds of less than 39 mph are classified as tropical depressions. Once the winds reach 39 mph, the storm is named and becomes a tropical storm. If sustained wind speed reaches 74 mph or above and the storm is in the North Atlantic, the Northeast Pacific east of the dateline, or the South Pacific it is called a hurricane. If the storm is in the Northwest Pacific west of the dateline with sustained wind speed of 74 mph or above it is referred to as a typhoon.

Tropical cyclones, be they hurricane or typhoon, and tornadoes are both atmospheric vortices but otherwise have almost nothing in common. Tornadoes are primarily an over-land phenomena   although over-water tornadoes, or waterspouts, do occured.

In contrast, tropical cyclones are purely an oceanic phenomena - they die out over-land due to loss of a moisture source. Tropical cyclones have a lifetime that is measured in days; tornadoes usually last only ninutes."[14]

Interestingly enough, there is another reason for the confusion about the correct name for these tornadic storms. This reason has to do with government, politics, and a man named John Park Finley.

In 1849 the Smithsonian Institution inaugurated a system of weather observation that relied on a network of civilian volunteer weather observers. This system of approximately 500 "stations" was the genesis of the first thunderstorm and tornado observation and forecasting.

The Smithsonian system operated until 1872 when it was disbanded. The following year weather observing and forecasting was transferred to the War Department. This duty fell under the direction of the Chief Signal Officer of the U.S. Army Signal Corps.

Finley joined the Army in 1877 and after completing the Signal Corps schooling, began an intensive study of tornadoes. His study led to the first systematic forecasts warning people of possible tornadoes. This system contained many observations that are still valid today.

Finley's work was scrapped, along with the forecasts, in 1887 when the new chief of the Signal Corps issued "a ban on the use of the word *tornado* in any public forecast . . . The ban was based on the idea the people would panic at the first warnings, then grow complacent and ignore subsequent warnings. The ban would be in place for the next sixty-five years."[15]

Tornado damage can leave eyewitnesses and post-storm viewers at a loss for words to describe what they had experienced or what is right before their eyes. Consequently, nineteenth century writers often pushed the envelope on their prose in an effort to transfer what they were seeing to their readers.

Reports in newspapers of nineteenth century yield a gold mine of descriptive phrases relating to tornadoes such as "scattered to the four quarters of the earth," "dashed into eternity and oblivion," "crushed like an egg shell," "shattered to splinters," "reduced to fragments," "smashed into a thousand atoms," "disappeared as if by magic," "obliterated," "blown to bits," and "swept away."

Survivors and witnesses also stretched their vocabulary to describe the tornado with phrases like "blacker than the abode of Pluto," "like a column of smoke from a locomotive," "huge swaying trunk of an elephant," "like a streamer rising and falling," "a monster top," "a great auger revolving," "a giant icicle," "bounding along the prairie like a huge ball," "shaped like an hourglass and forked at the bottom," and "like water being sprayed from a large hose."

Extreme lightning and electrical phenomena often accompany a tornado and this was described by eyewitnesses as "a volume of rotating smoke with a big light in the center," "a ball of fire rolling along the ground," "black as tar with millions of sparks," "a rolling ball of fire," "a twisting and writhing black mass, like smoke with a ball of fire and luminous columns," and "the funnel had a ball of fire attached to the front."

Studies have established that "lightning discharges in connection with tornadoes are of exceedingly high voltage and are 'brighter, bluer, and more vicious than those from any other type of storm.'" It has been described as "'very bright sheet lightning' and lacework."[16]

For some survivors and witnesses, the sounds were equally unforgettable. Some said "the roar could be heard for ten miles." Others believed it sounded "like a heavily loaded train on a trestle" or "a roar like Niagara Falls." Another likened the sound to "the low rumble of a thousand bass drums."

Others remembered that it "dips to the ground with a terrific roar, often described as resembling the noise of a thousand railway trains crossing trestles or the sound of a cannon prolonged for a few minutes. Observers have also mentioned a peculiar whining sound like the buzzing of a million bees, which is usually heard when the cloud is high in the air. It is commonly drowned out by the roar when the cloud makes contact with the ground and destruction begins."[17]

The color of storm clouds can provide a hint that tornadic activity is present. "A Weather Bureau official who was an eyewitness of the St. Louis tornado of 27 May 1896," recalled that 'intensely vivid flashes of forked lightning were frequent, being outlined in green, blue, purple, and bright yellow colors against the dull yellow background of the never ceasing sheet lightning.'"[18] The color most often mentioned in eyewitness reports is a green cast to the storm clouds as they approach.

While there is no such critter as a "normal" tornado, it is commonly held that tornadoes most often travel from the southwest to the northeast following a slightly curved path that drifts off toward the north in its dying throes.

But that isn't cast in stone because every possible exception has been noted concerning tornadic thunderstorms; they can move to and from almost every point of the compass. They have also been known to remain practically stationary for up to twenty minutes. And, "have been known to make U-turns and even complete circles in their paths."[19]

Northern hemisphere tornadoes revolve in a counterclockwise direction, as a rule. Again, however, there have been exceptions—twenty-nine exceptions among 550 tornadoes that Finley studied.

The Weather Bureau didn't have any official system for counting tornadoes until 1916. Prior to that date it was a hit-or-miss effort among several government agencies.

Due to the unpredictable location of occurrence, the short duration, and the violent nature of tornadoes they do not lend themselves easily to scientific study.

Not all wind damage is the result of a true tornado although to the untrained eye a downburst that wrecks a home and kills an occupant probably gets stamped with the title tornado. Or, sometimes great damage is done but a funnel cloud wasn't observed and hence a true tornado gets recorded as a straight wind.

Tornadoes can, and have, occurred in any season or month of the year. Finley's report of 1884 listed the relative frequency.

June	101
April	96
July	97
May	82
September	49
August	42
March	37
November	22
February	19
October	15
December	9
January	7

This report also credits Kansas with the most tornadoes with sixty-two, followed by Illinois with fifty-three, and Missouri with forty-three for the top three states.[20]

Not all tornadoes are created equal and consequently the damage they cause ranges from minor to major, from non-deadly to deadly, and from four-figure damage to multi-million dollar damage. Severe-storm studies, especially tornadoes, present the meteorologist with a unique set of problems because a tornado doesn't lend itself readily to a scientific laboratory analysis.

Tornadoes destroy laboratories.

A tool employed in the study of post-storm damage is the Fujita Scale or F Scale. There are several versions but essentially they agree, except some don't include anything past the F5 rating. The ratings are:

F0 (40-72 mph): Minor damage.

F1 (73-112 mph): Moderate damage; peel surface off roofs; windows broken; trailer houses pushed or overturned; trees on soft ground uprooted; some trees snapped; moving autos pushed off the road.

F2 (113-157 mph): Considerable damage; roofs torn off frame houses leaving strong upright walls standing; weak structures or outbuildings demolished; trailer houses demolished; railroad boxcars pushed over; large trees snapped or uprooted; light-object missiles generated; cars blown off highway; block structures and walls badly damaged.

F3 (158-206 mph): Roofs and some walls torn off well-constructed frame house; some rural buildings completely demolished or flattened; trains overturned; steel framed hangar-warehouse type structures torn; cars lifted off the ground and may roll some distance; most trees in forest uprooted, snapped or leveled; block structure often leveled.

F4 (207-260 mph): Devastating damage: Well-constructed frame house leveled, leaving piles of debris; structure with weak foundation lifted, torn, and blown some distance; trees debarked by small flying debris; sandy soil eroded and gravels fly high in the wind; cars thrown some distance or rolled considerable distance finally to disintegrate; large missiles generated.

F5 (261-318 mph): Incredible damage: Strong frame houses lifted clear off foundation and carried considerable distance to disintegrate; steel-reinforced concrete structures badly damaged; automobiles-sized missiles fly through the air a distance of 100 yards or more; trees debarked completely; incredible phenomena can occur.

F6 (319-379 mph): Inconceivable damage: Large objects such as storage tanks and automobiles will fly through a long distance; home foundations ripped from the ground. Assessment of tornadoes in these categories is feasible only through detailed survey involving engineering aerodynamical calculations as well as meteorological models of tornadoes.

F7-F12 (380 mph to the Speed of Sound); not expected to occur![21]

Expected or not, meteorologists still haven't been able to determine the top wind speed created by a tornado. Tornadoes have a habit of destroying the instruments necessary to measure such velocity.

##

National Oceanic and Atmospheric Administration / Department of Commerce
A tornado's wind can make almost any object into a deadly missile. Luckily, the St. Louis tornado on May 27, 1896, embedded this shovel in a tree, not a person.

Cowboys and Indians, besides keeping a wary eye out for each other, had to keep a constant watch for a common enemy—tornadoes.

During the heyday of the Texas cattle drives, James H. Cook was one of the cowboys trailing a herd north to Kansas. At the Canadian River the drovers "had an experience with a tornado which I should not care to repeat." They were camped on the south side of the Canadian and about noon saw a bad storm brewing to the west so they staked down the chuck wagon and tied extra ropes over the wagon sheet.

Cook later wrote of the storm saying, "I had never seen such queer looking clouds before. They seemed to be rushing toward the center of the heavens, and we could hear a steady sullen roar." Everybody but the cook mounted up and rode out to hold the herd. When the storm broke with strong wind, torrential rain, and large hail the herd stampeded and lit out for parts unknown."

Once the storm blew over, the cowboys learned just how lucky they were because, according to Cook, a tornado had just missed the herd and the camp. "In the center of its pathway, which was not over a quarter of a mile from our wagon and where the timber grew along the Canadian River, great trees had been torn out by the roots and piled into tangled masses, some of them being carried several hundred feet. Many little willows growing on the river bottom were still rooted to the ground, but the bark was twisted and stripped from them."[22]

This kind of damage was not new to the Plains Indians who had lived with the tornado for millennia. As a result, the tornado eventually found a place in their tribal lore.

> A legend related by the Kiowa people says that the first twister came about when ancient tribespeople attempted to mold a horse from clay. The beast took shape, recounted one storyteller, but it was a terrible thing: "It began to writhe, slowly at first, then faster and faster until there was a great commotion everywhere. The wind grew up and carried everything away. The Kiowas were afraid of that awful thing and they went running about, talking to it. And at last it was calm." Ever after, when the black clouds began to swirl, Kiowas knew the monster was approaching: "Lightning comes from its mouth, and the tail, whipping and thrashing on the air, makes the high, hot wind." Kiowas speak to it, saying "Pass over me." And, in time it does.[23]

Considering the unpredictable nature of tornadoes, it isn't surprising that newcomers developed their own apocryphal tornado beliefs. One such belief is that, like lightning, tornadoes never strike the same place twice.

Not true; apparently some locations have an unexplained attraction for tornadoes. Oklahoma City has been struck twenty-six times between 1892 and 1975. As previously mentioned, Irving, Kansas, was struck by two tornadoes on 30 May 1879.

Grazulis mentions several examples of unusual tornado coincidences in his works. "In Logan County, Nebraska, only two homes have been leveled by a tornado in 110 years. It was the same home both times."

And, "It is very rare to have a single tornado kill people in two separate schools, and extremely rare to have teachers killed in two separate schools. That has occurred only once, on 3 May 1895, in Sioux County, Iowa. Remarkably, the two teachers, miles apart, were brother and sister.[24]

This same storm was reported to have carried school children "for up to a half mile, and many sustained injuries that would be life-long burdens."[25]

##

Ely Moore, Jr. first journeyed to Kansas Territory in the summer of 1854. It was here that the 21-year-old New Yorker encountered the untamed trans-Mississippi west. Young Moore was carrying letters from Washington to his father, Ely Moore, Sr. who was "special agent of the confederated Indian tribes, consisting of the Miamis, Weas, Peorias, Kaskaskias, and Piankeshaws."[26] The Miami mission was approximately sixty-five miles below, or south, of Westport (present Kansas City), Kansas Territory.

Moore, Jr. arrived at the Miami's mission just prior to the Indian's annual buffalo hunt to lay in a supply of buffalo meat and robes. Moore, enchanted by the land and eager for adventure, quickly accepted an invitation to accompany the tribes when they headed west.

The Miami were joined by groups from other tribes and the combined assemblage "was a strong one, able to cope with any of the hostiles on the plains. It consisted of 400 men and 50 squaws of the five tribes; 20 Shawnees and 30 Pottawatomies, all well armed. Our equipment consisted of about 100 wagons, two yoke of oxen to each, and 200 pack-ponies."[27]

The main hunting camp was established somewhere in what is now southwestern Kansas near a place the Indians called "Blind River." Here they encountered vast herds of buffalo that reached as far as the eye could see.

One morning, three weeks into the hunt, the weather turned hot and sultry. Just breathing was an effort; men and animals slipped into a state of lethargy. All of nature seemed unable to draw a breath.

About noon the Indian chief summoned the hunters into camp and Moore, curious about the interruption, sought out the chief to learn why. "The chief, in answer to my inquiry, pointed to the sun, and then I noticed millions of insects, grasshoppers, winging their way east. So dense were they that the sun was obscured for minutes at a time. The chief, with gestures of foreboding evil, further explained: 'they (grasshoppers) know. Devil wind come, kill all, maybe. Great Spirit knows best!'"

Everyone in the party worked quickly to make preparation for the arrival of the "Devil Wind." Wagons were circled and narrow trenches dug to allow each wagon wheel to be lowered to the axles and then strips of buffalo hides were cut and tied together making straps to further secure the wagons and wagon-covers against a strong wind.

All of the hunting horses were corralled within the wagon enclosure and the cattle were herded close to the camp and held by double guard. Moore recalls that it was after five o'clock when the camp was secure "and at that time could be seen in the southwest a dark, greenish-purple cloud hanging close to the horizon, revolving and bounding as it approached . . . licking up the beasts, earth, water and air to satiate the ponderous maw of this fiend of might."

Moore and his Indian companions watched the approaching storm as an eerie stillness and darkness settled over the prairie. The women sought safety in the wagons while the men stood next to their favorite hunting horse. A good hunting horse was of great value in this life and a desirable companion in the crossing-over journey.

As the clouds broke momentarily, illuminating the camp, Moore glanced at his companions. "There stood the Indians, stolid, but in an attitude of supplication to the Great Spirit.

Now the storm came on apace, descending with unmitigated violence upon the quaking, dusky forms, who seemed awaiting their doom."[28]

##

Man's fascination with tornadoes has prompted some inquisitive minds to measure, or attempt to measure, the wind speed and power generated by these mega windstorms. "Vonnegut calculates that for a tornado with a diameter of about 350 feet—a small one—its power is about 10^{18} ergs per second, or 10^8 kilowatts, which is in excess of the capacity of all the generating stations in the United States."[29] This was written in 1965 and might not hold true today. Nevertheless, then or now, it is an awesome amount of power.

Wind speeds involved in a large tornado are simply unknown but many guesses, calculations, and experiments have been offered to account for some post-tornado phenomena. Pioneer researcher Finley concluded that "theoretical velocities of over 2,000 m.p.h., based upon certain assumed atmospheric conditions, have been deduced. Such velocities are mathematically possible, but not meteorologically probable."[30]

Elias Loomis graduated from Yale University in 1830 and had an exemplary career as professor, author, and lecturer on the earth sciences. "Loomis, in a sense, was the originator of experimental as well as observational meteorology."[31]

In 1842 he examined the aftermath of a tornado and discovered a blunt-ended board driven into the turf to a depth of eighteen inches. Intrigued by the discovery he planned an experiment designed to determine the velocity required to drive a board into the earth to the same depth as the tornado.

First he gathered a number of similar boards; he then procured a six-pounder cannon. Thus armed, Loomis fired board after board into the hillside. When the smoke finally cleared, the professor "concluded that the winds must have had a velocity of 682 m.p.h.—the speed of a revolver bullet!"[32]

Another researcher, Frank H. Gigelow, also did some calculations after viewing the damage done by the St. Louis tornado of 1896. He "estimated that speeds in excess of 250 meters per second, *i.e.*, above 560 m.p.h., must have been reached."[33] Not everyone agrees with these elevated wind speeds and hasten to point out that there are other factors at work during a tornado. These must also be considered.

Cannons and calculations notwithstanding, the problem of wind speed within a tornado has yet to be solved. And, according to Howard Bluestein, professor of meteorology, University of Oklahoma, it may not be for some time. As recently as 1999 he wrote that "In terms of destructive power, tornadoes are the most violent storms on earth. Hurricanes and typhoons pack winds of 200 mph at most; the top speeds of tornadoes have been estimated at 300 mph. No instruments to measure wind speed directly has ever survived a strong tornado."[34]

An interesting and much debated phenomena observed after the passing of a tornado is fowl without feathers. Nude birds, wild and domestic, dead and alive, are frequently mentioned by witnesses. "The cause of this stripping of feathers is not definitely known but it is believed highly possible that the hollow quills of their feathers might expand suddenly or even explode in the rapid decrease of pressure within a tornado vortex."[35]

Professor Loomis, it seems, favored the six-pounder as his primary laboratory instrument for meteorological field experiments. Hence, because "He noticed that when a tornado struck chickens were often stripped of their feathers" he once again employed the artillery piece. "He conceived of a plan to determine the wind velocity in a tornado. he shot eight chickens from a cannon with different charges and therefore different muzzle velocities. The velocity that resulted in the plucking of the chicken's feathers therefore was a measure of the wind velocity in a tornado."[36]

"Exploding buildings" is another hotly debated topic among lay people and scientists. Following the St. Louis tornado of 1896 it was reasoned that the sudden drop in pressure (10 percent according to H. C. Frankenfield who was the official in charge of the local Weather Bureau office) would apparently cause enough pressure differential to account for some buildings "exploding."

Proponents of the theory state that "It has been computed that a sudden drop in pressure of the magnitude of that in the St. Louis tornado applied to the outside of a house twenty feet square with walls ten feet high would cause a lift of forty tons on the ceiling or roof and an outward pressure of twenty tons on each of the four walls, unless equalized to some extent by rapid escape of air from inside the building."[37]

Others disagree, believing most structures are sufficiently ventilated by flying debris to quickly equalize the pressure before any pressure variant "explodes" the building. Again, like with wind speeds, tornadoes can't be studied in a controlled laboratory environment so the disagreement remains unanswered.

There is however, no disagreement about the power of a tornado. A remarkable example of a tornado's tremendous energy was demonstrated at the Eads Bridge that spans the Mississippi River at St. Louis. This bridge was struck and damaged by a tornado in 1871; it was then rebuilt to be tornado proof.

Although the bridge wasn't destroyed by the 1896 tornado, it did sustain damage on the eastern approach. One particular bit of damage seems to defy the laws of physics. Nevertheless it is well documented that "a 2-inch by 10-inch white pine plank was driven through the 5/16" thick wrought iron plate. No significant damage was done to the steel span of the bridge, but this remains a remarkable example of a tornado's ability to generate missiles."[38]

Another report of the same, we believe, incident reads: "On the long East St. Louis approach to the St. Louis bridge a white pine plank, 2 by 8 inches, was driven into the south side of a steel girder with such velocity that it punched a hole in the web and remained sticking in the girder."[39]

There are two other kinds of damage that appear again and again in tornado reports: livestock killed and standing timber destroyed. Livestock was marketable income, motive power for business and farms, and transportation for the masses. Even more devastating was the loss of a food supply and in isolated areas on the frontier it could be a life-threatening loss for newcomers.

In Le Sueur County, Minnesota, a tornado touched down on 2 July 1879, and left "dead hogs, dead chickens, dead turkeys in one confused mass."[40]

Near Flat Springs, Missouri, on 12 June 1881, a tornado destroyed eighty buildings along "with great losses of livestock. About 80 head of cattle were killed on one farm, 60 sheep on another, and six horses on a third."

In Minnesota, about a month later, a "boy was killed along with the 40 cattle he was herding." This happened on 15 July 1881, in Cairo Township.[41]

On that same day, near Wellington, Minnesota, "many animals killed, some of which had pieces of timber driven through their bodies."[42]

Hundreds of livestock were destroyed on 29 September 1881, when a tornado touched down two miles northwest of Emporia, Kansas.[43]

"Hundreds of sheep, horses and cattle were killed" on the McKinney plantation near Mount Ida, Arkansas, on 8 May 1882.

South Dakota was hit by tornadoes on 28 August 1884, killing thirty head of cattle near the town of Carthage. Another thirty head were reportedly killed near Forestburg and south of Bridgewater "all livestock was killed." Then on 9 September in Clay County, thirty head of livestock, mostly hogs, were killed.

When a tornado touched down near Coon Rapids, Iowa, on 14 April 1886, it "destroyed about 70 houses and killed many hundreds of animals."

East of Aurora, South Dakota, on 15 August 1886, "Many cattle were killed by flying debris." And "Lumber from a house in Elkton was driven so deeply into the ground that a team of horses could not pull it out."

Moving on a course east-southeast, a family of tornadoes zigzagged through Iowa on 18 May 1898, where "the funnel passed near Lost Nation, Elwood, Delmar, and Riggs, with farms destroyed and livestock killed for mile after mile. Over 900 head of livestock were reported killed in the Elwood area alone, with trees debarked and farm homes leveled."

Standing timber could be translated into income as building materials or as firewood and any community with a ready supply close at hand was fortunate. When a tornado leveled a "million board feet" it was a harsh blow to the local lumber industry and those needing to rebuild their destroyed structures. Of course, most of this timber was in the area bordering the eastern part of the prairies and plains or along major waterways.

"Great quantities of timber destroyed on the Missouri river" was reported in Doniphan County, Kansas, as a tornado ripped through the area on 4 July 1860.[44]

Once a tornado has touched down and swept through an area it often "appropriates" articles and then carries them aloft for a great distance. In Iowa a clock was carried for two miles during a tornado on 11 June 1881.

An F5 tornado hit Grinnell, Iowa, on 17 June 1882, causing major damage and thirty-nine fatalities. Debris from Grinnell was found more than 100 miles to the northeast in Wisconsin.[45]

During a tornado in Missouri on 18 May 1883, a teaching certificate was carried for fifty miles.[46]

On 4 June 1890, a tornado touched down south of Chester, Iowa, and "hogs were carried for up to two miles."[47]

When a tornado passed through Edgar, Nebraska, "long sections of sidewalk were carried for a half mile, and a barrel was carried for two miles and dropped 'unharmed.'" This occurred on 31 March 1892.

On 15 May 1896, an F5 tornado touched down in Denton County, Texas, and continued on the ground until it hit Sherman, Texas. Property damage was reported at $200,000 and seventy-three people lost their lives in the tornado. "A trunk lid, with the owner's name, was carried for 35 miles."[48]

A deed from Kirksville, Missouri, was found ninety-five miles away after a tornado passed through the town on 27 April 1899. "One home was carried aloft and exploded in mid-air, as if it was detonated by explosives."[49]

##

Time and again tornadoes and the Mississippi River proved a deadly combination during the nineteenth century. A tornado's perceived affinity with rivers, and the belief that they follow rivers, is mentioned numerous times in tornado literature.

The following is from a letter written after the 1840 Natchez tornado. It was penned by a resident of Natchez to a friend who was out of town when the tornado struck. It was reproduced in the *Natchez (Mississippi) Times* on 7 May 1957. In part it said: "An extra of the *Natchez Free Trader* published the day after the catastrophe listed the dead at 481 . . . Many persons were seen blown off the bluff into the river of whom there has not been received any intelligence. It is assumed for the time being that they are dead."

A storm that lashed Iowa in June 1860 became known as "The Great Tornado of the Northwest" and cut a swath of death and destruction across eastern Iowa before intersecting the Mississippi River at the town of Camanche, Iowa, located on the west bank of the Mississippi. The *New York Herald* ran a piece on 9 June 1860, reporting that "several dwellings standing on the river bank were blown into the stream and their inmates drowned. A raft was passing at the time with twenty men on board, all of whom were carried into the stream and drowned."[50]

At Perry, Missouri, on 9 November 1864, a tornado ambushed a vessel on the Mississippi River. This time a ferryboat was hit and "all but the hull, engine and boilers were blown 'a quarter-mile, half way up the bluff . . . as were skiffs and canoes.'"[51]

The fast moving tornado of 8 March 1871, struck St. Louis and the Mississippi River at the same location as was hit in 1896. This encounter, too, was extremely destructive to the river's shipping concerns. "Ferries and steamers were torn apart on the river and fragments carried 30 miles."[52]

On 13 July 1890, it was again proven that water, water craft, and high winds are a deadly mix. It was estimated that this storm drowned between ninety-seven and 180 passengers when an excursion craft capsized in a downburst on the Lake Pepin, Minnesota, section of the Mississippi River.[53]

At the time of the 1896 St. Louis tornado, Louis Tisch's barber shop was located on the top floor of the Wainwright building. From this vantage point he watched the tornado pass through the city. "Preceding the black cloud was a dense yellow cloud that looked as though its interior was a mass of flames. From out of this cloud shot long fiery arms in every direction, and wherever one of these arms struck something went to pieces."

He watched it cross the Mississippi River until it got "nearly to the Illinois shore and started directly up the stream. In this he is borne out by the statements of others who were watching it."[54]

When it reached the wharf the damage to shipping was almost total. "There were sixteen steamers, five ferryboats, two transfer boats and six tugs blown from their moorings and completely demolished by the storm, besides six others which suffered comparatively little damage. The loss to shipping interests exceeded $1,000,000, as most of the boats have to be entirely rebuilt. Besides this, every wharfboat on the river front, except that of the Anchor Line, and those used by the city, was blown away and sunk in small fragments."[55]

Understandably, when people aboard boats saw the tornado churning toward them, they panicked. There were eleven ladies aboard the steamer *Pittsburg* that was lying just below Eads Bridge when the storm reached the river. The ladies saw the destruction caused to other boats and, fearing the *Pittsburg* would be destroyed, they attempted to jump overboard "and the Captain, James P. Boland, and the crew had all they could do to prevent them from carrying out their mad intentions."[56]

Water transportation wasn't the only form of travel molested by tornadoes. "Five people were injured as a stagecoach was overturned" near Park Rapids, Minnesota, on 14 April 1886. On that same date: "An 18-car train at Coon Rapids (Iowa), heading west (for California) was struck and derailed. The cars at the head of the train were thrown to the south, the cars to the rear (to the east) were thrown to the south. A middle car, loaded with beer, remained on the tracks."[57]

Hail frequently, but not always, accompanies tornadic activity. The resulting crop and property damage is costly and tragic in itself but occasionally hail can be as deadly as the tornado. "On July 26, 1895, Near the Djuberg School in Barnes County, South Dakota, a home was swept away and debris was carried for almost a half mile. A woman hiding in the cellar was then pelted to death with baseball size hail."[58]

Mercifully, not all tornadoes and hail result in human death, but when they touch man's homes and buildings, be it rural or urban, man's handiwork always loses. Studying old newspapers and writings leaves the impression that tens of thousands of homes, barns, and business buildings were destroyed almost as fast, it seems, as the newcomers could build more.

"The general appearance of tornado destruction—demolished and exploded buildings and trees stripped of all foliage and small limbs—is similar in many ways to that following heavy artillery bombardment."[59]

During the nineteenth century most homes and businesses in the trans-Mississippi west were heated with wood or coal and cooking was done on a stove using the same fuel. A tornado could, and did, scatter the fire and coals onto, and into, many buildings along its path.

A large percentage of the building materials, aside from stone and brick, were flammable and fire fighting equipment many times consisted of only a rain barrel and bucket. Towns or communities fortunate enough to have a well equipped fire department that survived the tornado frequently couldn't reach the fires because of debris in the streets.

Fires raged; more people died.

Thunderstorms capable of spawning tornadoes are also capable of torrential rainfall. Devastating winds might be followed by devastating fires which might be followed by devastating floods and flash floods.

More people died.

##

Sunday, following the 1896 tornado, was the day St. Louis and East St. Louis buried its dead with some 200 funerals conducted on 31 May. "All day long these mournful corteges, wending their way silently and tearfully to some peaceful cemetery, were seen in every section of the city, and on the avenues leading to the principal burying grounds one procession followed another so closely as to make it look like one long, unbroken line, miles in length."[60]

The religious communities were overwhelmed.

It's a fact that curiosity isn't the only human trait that draws people to disaster sites. Unbelievably, but predictably, gangs of thieves from Chicago, Cincinnati, and Kansas City plus several other cities descended on St. Louis to prey on those already suffering loss of loved ones and property.

St. Louis Chief of Police Desmond, with extra police and detectives, responded and the thieves "were nabbed almost before they had taken a breath of the exhilarating atmosphere common to St. Louis, and others who followed met with the same experience."[61]

Law and order was not overwhelmed.

Tornadic winds can cause some very extraordinary incidents such as what happened to a Natchez's family during the 6 May 1840, storm. "Levin Covington, Probate Judge of Adams County, and his family were seated at the dinner table in their new brick home when the tornado struck. When they could see they found themselves seated at the table, the service on it uninjured, and the roof, timbers, and walls of their home lying all around them outside and nobody hurt!"[62]

A tornado on 5 June 1854 crossed the Cedar River in Iowa and "took large stones from the bottom and carried them on land."[63]

At least three tornadoes touched down in Linn County, Iowa, on 3 June 1860, and were part of a family of tornadoes that brought death and destruction to the state. "One of the sills of the farm house, 16 feet long and 8" x 10" in cross section, was carried 30 rods (about 500 feet) to the west and buried 13 feet deep in the soil of the prairie."

During the same day "three persons were taken up bodily and vanished forever from mortal eyes." In the wake of the same storm "houses, barns, fences, and hundreds of head of dead livestock littered the fields across the northern tier of Cedar County townships.[64]

Nebraska, both the territory and the state, earned its rightful place as part of Tornado Alley because these devestating storms left in their wake some inexplicable curiosities. Who would have thought of seeking shelter in a straw stack? That's what the Bayer family did on 1 June 1899 when a tornado approached their home just east of Minden, Nebraska.

> A little after 7:00 P.M. after the clouds had twisted and turned for about a half hour, a large funnel was seen to form. It stood poised in the air for fifteen minutes or more, and then moved northeast, just missing the town.

117

Roofs were torn from houses and barns were wrecked in the country. Joe Bayer's home, a mile northeast of town was completely destroyed. The storm continued on into Adams County where a number of people were badly injured.

The Bayer's family took refuge in a straw stack and escaped without injury. Another tornado made its appearance about nine miles northeast of town on the Olof Hawkinson place. Mr. Hawkinson saw a horse, wagon, and hayrack going up. He ran to the barn and a few minutes later the horse came walking back with no injuries except a few wire cuts, the wagon and rack timbers were located nine miles away.[65]

The list of strange happenings is almost as endless as it is fascinating.

Heavy carts have been carried, free from the ground, at such a velocity, that, when they strike, the tires are bent and twisted, and the spokes are broken from the hubs. Iron chains are blown through the air . . . Children, and even men, have often been carried many feet above the ground, and sometimes dropped unhurt . . . Strange examples of the wind's strength are found in the treatment of small objects: nails are found driven head first firmly into planks; a cornstalk is shot partly through a door, recalling the firing of a candle through a board. More than this, the winds shows signs of very unequal motions in a small space: bedding and clothing are torn to rags; harness is stripped from horses. Nothing can withstand the awful violence of the tornado's centre; and yet, at a little distance one side or the other, there is not only no harm done, but there is no noticeable disturbance in the gentle winds.[66]

The tornado that struck St. Louis in 1896 also left many examples of bizarre damage. "Near the corner of Russell and California avenues the storm took the roof off one house and moved the roof of the next house over upon the first house. It was a sad misfit, however."[67]

The Carr home in St. Louis remained standing even though it suffered some strange damage. "It tore frames from doors, broke locks in half, twisted one hinge off a door and left the other on, shattered some window panes, while it scratched others in a zig-zag fashion, drove enormous boards through one side of a house in the third story, and never moved a wooden bucket from an unsheltered position in the yard."[68]

And, "As an illustration of the freaks played by the wind, a large wagon loaded with lumber, which an ordinary gust would be sufficient to overturn, was left standing in the yard uninjured, while the horses hitched to it were torn loose and whisked away."[69]

The following story supposedly occurred near St. Louis's King's Highway and New Manchester Road: "Mrs. Bredemeyer went out to the cow shed to get some bran for her cow's supper. She did not find the cow shed and it was not until she had gone around like Diogenes with a lantern that she discovered the shed up in her attic. She did not attempt to explain the trick the wind had played upon her."[70]

When the tornado struck the race track it lifted the roof off the grandstand and sent it crashing down nearby. "Women became hysterical and ran around the basement like mad while strong men were terror-stricken and speechless."

A large part of the roof fell upon a horse and buggy standing on a road next to the track. No one believed the horse could have survived but when the storm abated volunteers fell to work and, "After fifteen minutes' hard labor the roof was raised, and the horse pulled out from his position—alive, and not a scratch on him."[71]

Wherever tornadoes touch down they are capable of leaving a stranger-than-fiction legacy. In Iowa on 24 May 1896, a tornado reportedly drove a steel railroad rail fifteen feet into the ground.[72]

Several other strange incidences occurred during the tornado that touched down in central Kansas on 30 May 1879. The storm path crossed the Saline River southwest of Minneapolis,

Kansas, and dropped very large hailstones; some stones were "as large as a man's head" and weighed over six pounds.

"A Delphos man was reported to have been carried a half-mile with only minor injuries." When the tornado reached the Solomon River it "pumped it as dry as the upland."

A cat was carried a half-mile and "crushed as flat as if passed through a cider press."

Victims repeatedly mentioned that anything and everything in the tornado's path was covered with a thick coat of mud that "filled eyes, ear, mouth, and wounds with mud, chaff, straw, and bits of wood. Two weeks of washing could not clean the skin."[73]

John Park Finley investigated this family of tornadoes that swept through central Kansas and into southeast Nebraska. Some of the most devastating damage was observed near the Kansas town of Irving. This community wasn't hit by just one tornado that day but by two powerful tornadoes. The first arrived at 5:35 in the afternoon and the second followed at 6:45. Both caused great loss of life and great loss of property.

Finley was especially impressed by the tornado's power after viewing the wrecked 250-foot, 100-ton iron bridge across the Blue River. This structure was "completely twisted into shapeless ruin" and thrown into the river. Two and a half inch iron rods were "broken square in two." "This," he wrote, "was perhaps the most terrific manifestation of force recorded in any of the storms."[74]

This same storm lifted the home of Robert Reed "as easily as a feather, and without at first cracking a timber." This occurred just as Reed was "thinking it time to make good his escape." When the home was about twenty-five feet off the ground, he opened the door, stepped out, and plunged that distance to the ground, seriously injuring himself.[75]

This storm path widened to almost three miles at one point near Irving, Kansas. A resident living in a stone house near the storm's path reported that "'during the passage of the storm electricity ran over the walls of my house, throwing off sparks like an emery wheel.'"[76]

"Trees were debarked, ponds and wells were reported as being emptied of water, chickens were plucked, and some were said to be in a 'partially cooked' condition" following a tornado that touched down north of Mexico, Missouri, on 20 May 1891.[77]

A deadly tornado passed through south-central Kansas on 31 March 1892, killing four or five members of one farm family near Wellington. Their deaths were caused when "a reaper was thrown into their farm home."[78]

Compared to the loss of property or the death of adults, the accounts of children and tornadoes are especially heart rending. "Two young children died in O'Brien County," Iowa on 30 April 1898, "The father had one under each arm as he was about to enter the outside cellar entrance. The home was leveled, and both were found dead, still in the father's arms."[79]

Helping to offset the deaths are a few accounts of survival and deliverance. On 25 May 1859, a child was picked up by a tornado near Iowa City, Iowa, and carried "nearly 500 yards, thrown into a slough, but, strange to say, escaped with its life."[80]

On 20 June 1889, near Parnell, Missouri, "A six-year-old child was found a quarter mile away from the school site, alive but bruised."[81]

When the first tornado passed through the Irving, Kansas, community on 30 May 1879, it destroyed the home of a man named Fitch. His young son was plucked from the house and "carried over the tree tops and the creek, a distance of a quarter of a mile to the NW., and landed unhurt."[82]

Among the unsolved mysteries of tornadoes are numerous accounts of straws being driven into trees and other dense objects. Yet, it's just as astounding and mysterious when straw and hay remains undisturbed by a tornado's powerful winds.

Following the 1896 St. Louis tornado, some livery stable owners on the south side of the city reported that "everything but the great stacks of hay in the lofts was blown away. In one case carriages were taken half a dozen blocks and set down with little injury. The hay was not disturbed."[83]

Equally inexplicable, but infinitely more embarrassing for the victims, was the account of two young women who were riding the Fourth street cable car when the storm struck. Both women "were entirely denuded. They left the car stark naked and were cared for in a house near by."[84]

Ely Moore, Jr. and the Indian buffalo hunters, as previously noted, had taken every measure they could to prepare for the tornado that roared straight toward their camp. When the storm was almost upon them Moore recalls that

> We were literally cover-wrapped in an electric cloud. As electric sparks snapped from the tips of our horses' ears, the moaning, shivering creatures pressed close to their masters. The wheels of our wagons were circled by the electric fluid, and many bolts were drawn from our wagon-beds. Then came the wind, and with it hail of irregular shape and great size, descending with such force that many of our cattle had their eyes forced out of their sockets, and many of our ponies were badly lacerated on the back and flank, while some of our wagon-covers were tattered and torn into strips.[85]

Moore estimated the main "cyclone" to be a mile or more in length to the north and east of the circled wagons. As it bore down on them "it seemed to bound into the air some hundreds of feet." What was probably a secondary funnel (Moore called it a "drag-net" or "feeder" of the parent dragon) was about to strike the camp when he believes it was "struck by lightning, or was surcharged, for a downpour of sand, earth, grass, weeds and limbs of trees was deposited within our corral of wagons, amounting to many hundred tons. The breaking of this drag-net is all that saved us. The force was broken, and satiated its gluttonous intent by destroying a few wagons and filching some bales of robes."[86]

Homeward bound, after the hunt was finished, they came across the path of the "cyclone" where it had "stripped acres of sod and soil from the prairies. We also found two dead buffaloes completely denuded of hair, and every bone in their bodies crushed. These animals must have been picked up by the cyclone, carried to a great height, and then dashed to the earth."[87]

Ely Moore, Jr. didn't let a tornado dampen his growing enthusiasm for the prairies and plains. He expressed his newfound love for the land this way: "With these beauties and blessings before me the thought was instilled, the resolve approved, that here will I dwell; here and now do I link my fortunes with the destiny of those 'beyond the Mississippi.'"[88]

He remained true to his resolve, living and working in Kansas for the rest of his life. In 1918 Moore died at the age of 84 in Lawrence, Kansas.

##

Carl Travers was one of the lucky laborers working on the Mississippi River water front. The tornado heavily damaged the elevator where he worked but he didn't receive even a scratch—a dreadful scare but not a scratch. Now his only thought was the welfare of his wife Lillian and their baby.

Frantically he searched for a trolley, a buggy, a wagon, or any means of transportation that would take him home quickly. The streets were a tangle of rubble making travel dangerous and maddeningly slow; it was pouring down rain.

No trolleys were running because of downed power lines and wreckage on the tracks. He ducked into a telegraph office to send word to Lillian that he had been spared and to inquire about her and the child's welfare.

The operator informed him no messages could be sent or received; the lines were all down. Now, more anxious than ever, Carl resolved to run all the way home if that's what it would take to learn the fate of his family.

He was soaked to the skin by the torrential rain and nearly exhausted before he finally managed to flag down a buggy and offered the driver a week's pay to be driven home. The driver asked where home was and when told said he'd just come from there and there was absolutely no damage there. In fact, it was discovered that he lived only a few blocks from the Travers.

Relieved, Travers asked where the man was headed. The buggy driver replied that he was on his way to help with the rescue effort and suggested that Travers pitch in and help too. Travers agreed and crawled into the buggy which was soon at the Eads Bridge. After walking across the bridge they joined the rescue crews working in East St. Louis. It wasn't long before their labors were rewarded.

#

Travers and his men heard some cries for help. This was the signal for which they were waiting. With a right good will and such energy as would make their fortunes in an ordinary pursuit they attacked the wreck with vigor. Thanks to their grand labors many a poor half mangled body was dragged forth and sent to the many hospitals that had been temporarily fitted up at different places near the scene of slaughter.

Finally the wreck became so dangerous that the rescuers dared not work in it longer. They were about abandoning further search in that quarter when Travers caught sight of a white object in the wreckage and called to his companions for help. They made their way towards the body—for such it was found to be— and discovered that it was that of a woman. On her breast lay a baby but a few months old. Both were still in death. Tenderly they gathered up the remains and conveyed them out of the demolished structure. As usual the bodies were covered with dust from head to foot. The nearest relatives could not have recognized the woman in that condition, so, as was customary, the body was stretched on a bench and the face of both mother and child was carefully sponged free of the obscuring dirt.

The man who attended to this delicate matter was no other than Travers. He carefully cleaned away the dust on the forehead, then the eyes, and the cheeks and suddenly with a gasp of horror stood petrified.

"My God!" he cried, "It is Lillian and the baby!"

Poor fellow. He had carried the body of his own wife from the ruins of a house where she had been visiting a friend. His grief was most pitiful to behold.[89]

The above story is certainly representative of the suffering and heartache caused by the tornado but it requires some explanation. It did not ring quite true and therefore some effort was made to verify the account.

The *St. Louis City Directory* of 1896 did list the name, Travers. However, since the source from which the story is taken does not list the man's first name, this information was not of immediate help.

The source did say that the Travers had been married "but a little over a year and his pretty young wife and her little child were the things always uppermost in his thoughts." The child's name is not given and it isn't stated if it is a boy or a girl. And, we don't know how many months the writer meant by "a little over a year" but it would have to fall somewhere between one year and two years. This would put the marriage sometime between 27 May 1894, and 25 May 1895.

No marriage license could be found for a Travers during that time period either in St. Louis or East St. Louis. The baby was "but a few months old" according to the source but there wasn't found any birth records for a Travers during the above mentioned time period. Nor could the Travers name be found in the burial permits or the Register of Deaths for the appropriate time period.

It is possible that somehow, perhaps due to the hectic events surrounding the tornado, these documents failed to be recorded or that they were missed by a limited research effort. Nonetheless, no Travers, Lillian and/or baby, was found among necrologies published following the tornado.

These included the *St. Louis Genealogy Society Quarterly*, Vol. 8 No. 2; the *Missouri State Genealogical Association Journal*, Vol. 14 No. 2; *The Great Cyclone at St. Louis and East St. Louis, May 27, 1896*, and the *East St. Louis Daily Journal*, May 28, 29, 31, 1896.

Perhaps the story is true; perhaps it is one of those parasitical appendices that flourish in the wake of epic drama. Either way, it is a tragic story that embodies all the emotion of the event— human love, self sacrifice, and dreadful loss.

##

With the passage of time, all catastrophic events gather a satellite body of stories that fall somewhere between fact and folklore; tornadoes have a mother lode of such stories. Meteorologist, Henry Tooley, examined the destruction at Natchez after the 1840 tornado and concluded that "many houses where the rooms were closed exploded outward, because of the vacuum created by the funnel of the tornado."

A second conclusion reached by Tooley was that this same vacuum had killed any vegetation that wasn't uprooted because "the juice of the leaves, herbs, and grasses had been extracted by the pressure."[90]

Four miles outside of Natchez, J. F. H. Claiborne reported that after the tornado had passed "about one hundred bottles of French wine, of which he had sampled only moments before, became saturated with sulphur. Later in the evening it was noted that the cistern water had been affected in the same manner."[91]

A large street clock, about three feet in diameter, located on a rooftop at the corner of Park Avenue and Broadway was blown off during the 1896 St. Louis tornado. The clock was found almost in perfect condition on the street in the 1337 block of South Broadway. It was unbroken except for one curious fact. "The strange feature of the matter is the fact that the hands of the clock remain unfastened. How the wind managed to screw the dial off is peculiar in itself, but how it could remove the dial without tearing the hands off with it is inexplicable."[92]

Is the following another tall tale or the gospel truth? A respectable source records that "Milkmaids have been left with nothing but the bucket as a wind carried their cow away; and on one memorable occasion a whole herd of cattle were seen drifting off together, 'looking like gigantic birds in the sky.' It was suggested later by another meteorologist that, if the story were true, it would be 'the herd shot around the world'."[93]

Is it possible to have a house totally destroyed yet have a cupboard full of dishes carried afar and set gently down without breaking a single dish?

Can a mattress be sucked through a farmhouse window without waking the child sleeping on it?

Can a tornado really pick up a lighted kerosene lamp and carry it the length of a football field before setting it down right side up, still burning, with just a slightly smoky chimney?

Here are some oft repeated "facts" that orbit tornado material: A rooster was blown into a jug with only his head sticking out of the jug's neck.

A cast iron kettle was turned inside out without cracking the kettle.

A two-gallon jug was blown into a quart bottle without breaking either.

Water wells and ponds have been sucked dry.

Wax candles were driven into solid walls without damaging the candles.

Delicate flowers were imprinted into boards.

True or false?

Fact or fiction?

Who's to say since science is still unable to prove what a tornado is, or isn't, capable of doing.

Mother Nature, like all women, guards her secrets jealously; her ways beyond man's understanding.

Chapter Three notes

[1] Frank W. Lane, *The Elements Rage* (Philadelphia: Chilton Books, 1965), 41.

[2] R. Bruce Davis, "The Tornado of 1840 Hits Mississippi," *Journal of Mississippi History* 36, no. 1 (February 1974): 43-51.

[3] Julian Curzon, comp. and ed., *The Great Cyclone at St. Louis and East St. Louis, May 27, 1896* (St. Louis: Cyclone Publishing Company, 1896), 56.

[4] Martin Green, *The Great Tornado at St. Louis* (St. Louis: Graf Engraving Co., 1896), 1-8.

[5] Julian Curzon, comp. and ed., *The Great Cyclone at St. Louis and East St. Louis, May 27, 1896* (St. Louis: Cyclone Publishing Company, 1896), 253.

[6] Ibid., 254.

[7] Ibid., 261.

[8] Ibid., 103.

[9] Thomas P. Grazulis, *Significant Tornadoes 1680-1991* (St. Johnsbury, VT: Environmental Films, 1993), 688.

[10] Snowden D. Flora, *Tornadoes of the United States* (Norman: University of Oklahoma Press, 1953), 97.

[11] Julian Curzon, comp. and ed., *The Great Cyclone at St. Louis and East St. Louis, May 27, 1896* (St. Louis: Cyclone Publishing Company, 1896), 404.

[12] Ibid., 364.

[13] Frederick Grundy, "Cyclones and Tornadoes," *Frank Leslie's Popular Monthly* 15, no. 3 (March 1883): 279-283.

[14] American Meteorological Society "Glossary of Meteorology." http://amsglossary.allenpress.com/ glossary; Atlantic Oceanographic and Meteorological Laboratory, Hurricane Research Division, "Frequently Asked Questions." http://www.aoml.noaa.gov/hrd/tcfaq/A1.html.

[15] Thomas P. Grazulis, *The Tornado: Nature's Ultimate Windstorm* (Norman: University of Oklahoma

Press, 2001), 83 .

[16] Snowden D. Flora, *Tornadoes of the United States* (Norman: University of Oklahoma Press, 1953), 6.

[17] Ibid., 3.

[18] Ibid., 7.

[19] Ibid., 13.

[20] John P. Finley, *Character of Six Hundred Tornadoes* (Washington: Signal Office, 1884), 23.

[21] National Weather Service Forecast Office, Tulsa, Oklahoma, "The Fujita Scale." http://www.srh.noaa.gov/tsa/wcm/fujita.html. An abridged rendering.

[22] James H. Cook, *Fifty Years on the Old Frontier as a Cowboy, Hunter, Guide, Scout, and Ranchman* (New Haven, CT: Yale University Press, 1923), 74-78.

[23] Editors, *The American Indians: Tribes of the Southern Plains* (Alexandria, VA: Time-Life Books, 1995), 21.

[24] Thomas P. Grazulis, *Significant Tornadoes, 1880-1989 Volume I: Discussion and Analysis* (St. Johnsbury, VT: Environmental Films, 1991), 134.

[25] Thomas P. Grazulis, *Significant Tornadoes 1680-1991* (St. Johnsbury, VT: Environmental Films, 1993), 670.

[26] Geo. W. Martin, ed., *Transactions of the Kansas State Historical Society, 1907-1908* (Topeka: State Printing office, 1908), 10:403.

[27] Ibid., 404.

[28] Ibid., 408.

[29] Frank W. Lane, *The Elements Rage* (Philadelphia: Chilton Books, 1965), 45.

[30] Ibid., 46.

[31] Karl K. Turekian and Barbara L. Narendra, "Earth Sciences," in *Science at Yale*, edited by S. Altman, (New Haven, CT: Yale University, 2002). http://www.yale.edu/geology/graduate/history.html.

[32] Frank W. Lane, *The Elements Rage* (Philadelphia: Chilton Books, 1965), 46.

[33] Ibid., 46.

[34] Howard B. Bluestein, *Tornado Alley: Monster Storms of the Great Plains* (New York: Oxford University Press, 1999), 7.

[35] Snowden D. Flora, *Tornadoes of the United States* (Norman: University of Oklahoma Press, 1953), 81.

[36] Karl K. Turekian and Barbara L. Narendra, "Earth Sciences," in *Science at Yale*, edited by S. Altman, (New Haven, CT: Yale University, 2002). http://www.yale.edu/geology/graduate/history.html.

[37] Snowden D. Flora, *Tornadoes of the United States* (Norman: University of Oklahoma Press, 1953), 28.

[38] Thomas P. Grazulis, *Significant Tornadoes 1680-1991* (St. Johnsbury, VT: Environmental Films, 1993), 677.

[39] H. C. Frankenfield, *The Tornado of May 27, 1896, at Saint Louis, Missouri* (Washington: Weather Bureau, 1896), 4.

[40] Thomas P. Grazulis, *Significant Tornadoes 1680-1991* (St. Johnsbury, VT: Environmental Films,

1993), 604.

41 Ibid., 612.

42 John P. Finley, *Character of Six Hundred Tornadoes* (Washington: Signal Office, 1884), 20-21.

43 This and the following five quotations are from Thomas P. Grazulis, *Significant Tornadoes 1680-1991* (St. Johnsbury, VT: Environmental Films, 1993), 613; and 615, 631, 637, 641, 683 respectively.

44 John P. Finley, *Character of Six Hundred Tornadoes* (Washington: Signal Office, 1884), 4-5.

45 Thomas P. Grazulis, *Significant Tornadoes 1680-1991* (St. Johnsbury, VT: Environmental Films, 1993), 615-616.

46 Ibid., 619.

47 Ibid., 652.

48 Ibid., 674.

49 Ibid., 686.

50 David M. Ludlum, *Early American Tornadoes 1586-1870* (Boston: American Meteorological Society, 1970), 129.

51 Thomas P. Grazulis, *Significant Tornadoes 1680-1991* (St. Johnsbury, VT: Environmental Films, 1993), 568.

52 Ibid., 575.

53 Ibid., 116.

54 Julian Curzon, comp. and ed., *The Great Cyclone at St. Louis and East St. Louis, May 27, 1896* (St. Louis: Cyclone Publishing Company, 1896), 346.

55 Ibid., 44.

56 Ibid., 49.

57 Thomas P. Grazulis, *Significant Tornadoes 1680-1991* (St. Johnsbury, VT: Environmental Films, 1993), 637.

58 Thomas P. Grazulis, *Significant Tornadoes, 1880-1989 Volume I: Discussion and Analysis* (St. Johnsbury, VT: Environmental Films, 1991),114.

59 Snowden D. Flora, *Tornadoes of the United States* (Norman: University of Oklahoma Press, 1953), 4.

60 Julian Curzon, comp. and ed., *The Great Cyclone at St. Louis and East St. Louis, May 27, 1896* (St. Louis: Cyclone Publishing Company, 1896), 277.

61 Ibid., 286.

62 R. Bruce Davis, "The Tornado of 1840 Hits Mississippi," *Journal of Mississippi History* 36, no. 1 (February 1974): 50.

63 Thomas P. Grazulis, *Significant Tornadoes 1680-1991* (St. Johnsbury, VT: Environmental Films, 1993), 562.

64 Ibid., 566.

65 Roy C. Bang, *Heroes Without Medals: A Pioneer History of Kearney County Mebraska* (Minden, Nebraska: Warp Publishing Company, 1952), 84.

66 William Morris Davis, *Whirlwinds, Cyclones and Tornadoes* (Boston: Lothrop, Lee & Shepard Co., 1884), 75-76.

[67] Julian Curzon, comp. and ed., *The Great Cyclone at St. Louis and East St. Louis, May 27, 1896* (St. Louis: Cyclone Publishing Company, 1896), 82.

[68] Ibid., 134.

[69] Ibid., 176.

[70] Ibid., 182

[71] Ibid., 184, 187.

[72] Thomas P. Grazulis, *Significant Tornadoes 1680-1991* (St. Johnsbury, VT: Environmental Films, 1993), 676.

[73] Ibid., 600.

[74] J. [John] P. Finley, *Report of the Tornadoes of May 29 and 30, 1879* (Washington: GPO, 1881), 43.

[75] Ibid., 41.

[76] Ibid., 45.

[77] Thomas P. Grazulis, *Significant Tornadoes 1680-1991* (St. Johnsbury, VT: Environmental Films, 1993), 654.

[78] Ibid., 656.

[79] Ibid., 682.

[80] David M. Ludlum, *Early American Tornadoes 1586-1870* (Boston: American Meteorological Society, 1970), 120.

[81] Thomas P. Grazulis, *Significant Tornadoes 1680-1991* (St. Johnsbury, VT: Environmental Films, 1993), 646.

[82] Sergeant J. P. Finley, *Report of the Tornadoes of May 29 and 30, 1879* (Washington: GPO, 1881), 54.

[83] Julian Curzon, comp. and ed., *The Great Cyclone at St. Louis and East St. Louis, May 27, 1896* (St. Louis: Cyclone Publishing Company, 1896), 397.

[84] Ibid., 398.

[85] Geo. W. Martin, ed., *Transactions of the Kansas State Historical Society, 1907-1908* (Topeka: State Printing office, 1908), 10:408.

[86] Ibid., 408.

[87] Ibid., 409.

[88] Ibid., 402.

[89] *The St. Louis Disaster, or Broken Hearts and Homes* (Cincinnati: Barclay & Co., n.d.), 35-36.

[90] R. Bruce Davis, "The Tornado of 1840 Hits Mississippi," *Journal of Mississippi History* 36, no. 1 (February 1974): 50.

[91] Ibid., 51.

[92] Julian Curzon, comp. and ed., *The Great Cyclone at St. Louis and East St. Louis, May 27, 1896* (St. Louis: Cyclone Publishing Company, 1896), 310.

[93] Lyall Watson, *Heaven's Breath* (New York: William Morrow and Company, Inc., 1984), 52-53.

Chapter Four

EARTH ABLAZE

Nothing else, not even Indians, was dreaded as much as the plume of smoke that indicated that a prairie was on fire.
—Lewis Nordyke, *Cattle Empire*

Brigadier General Robert B. Mitchell rode south out of Camp Cottonwood, Nebraska Territory, on 15 January, 1865, at the head of 650 cavalrymen. Supporting the horse soldiers were four 12-pound howitzers, two three-inch Parrott guns, and 100 mule wagons.[1]

The general's goal was to find and punish the Cheyenne, Arapahoe, and Sioux who had sacked Julesburg on 7 January, 1865. The attack on Julesburg was only one of many Indian raids along the Platte River Road since the atrocity at Sand Creek the previous fall. Julesburg was, however, the attack that prompted General Mitchell to carry the fight to the Indians in their own territory south of the Platte River.

During the next twelve days the troops averaged a bit over thirty miles per day in bitter cold weather that inflicted enormous hardship on men, horses, and mules. Doggedly the shivering columns snaked south to the Big Timbers on the Upper Republican River and from there scouting parties were sent west and south; some going as far southward as Sappa Creek in northwestern Kansas.

Now and again these scouts observed lone Indians watching from a distant vantage point. Many recently abandoned Indian campsites promised that a large force of hostiles was close at hand. Discovering the enemy seemed imminent.

General Mitchell was a decorated, battle-tested Civil War veteran. Severely wounded at the battle of Wilson's Creek, he recovered his health and fought again at Perryville plus several other Union and Confederate clashes.

In April 1864 he was transferred to the Indian Wars theater along the Platte River Road. Here he was given command of the District of Nebraska where he quickly learned that Cheyenne, Arapahoe, and Sioux were a very different foe than Johnnie Reb.

Part of the road Mitchell and his command were to patrol paralleled the South Fork of the Platte into Colorado Territory. The Territorial Governor, John Evans, had a very succinct and simple Indian policy: "kill and destroy all hostile Indians." Another Colorado resident, Colonel John Chivington, took Evans' view one step further and moved it into the realm of righteousness. The former, and obviously re-reformed, minister of the Christian faith "believed it to be right and honorable to use any means under God's heaven to kill Indians that would kill women and children."

On 29 November 1864, Chivington and approximately 700 members of the 1st and 3rd Colorado Volunteers attacked Black Kettle's camp on Sand Creek. Of course the Indians retaliated and on 7 January, 1865, a war party of about 1,000 Cheyenne and Sioux raided Julesburg.

General Mitchell and his frost-bitten troops returned to Camp Cottonwood, Nebraska Territory, on 26 January after twelve, bleak, frustrating days. In Mitchell's own words they were "unsuccessful in meeting the enemy in battle." They had not found the enemy, much less punished him.

Captain Eugene F. Ware was part of General Mitchell's staff during his command in Nebraska. Captain Ware later published his recollections of these events in his book, *The Indian War of 1864.*

Captain Ware wrote that the day after returning to Camp Cottonwood

> General Mitchell had been revolving in his mind, and for several days planning, a big prairie-fire. He had determined that if he could not catch the Indians he could at least fire the whole country and make it a lean place for them. On the morning of 27 January, 1865, the sky was bright and clear, with a keen wind blowing

from the northwest. "Just the day I want," said the General. "I will give them ten thousand square miles of prairie-fire." He cleared the telegraph line early in the forenoon, and wired instructions up and down the river, and also requests to the officers in command of Colorado stations. The orders and requests were that fire details be sent up and down so as to connect, and that at sundown the prairies be simultaneously fired from Fort Kearney west to Denver. Instructions were sent to every ranch and post along the line. Each was to use its own methods to accomplish the purpose, but the whole country was to be set in a blaze at sunset. The order was fully carried out. The country was fired for three hundred miles . . . The wind took up the scattered beginnings; they were soon united, and they rolled as a vast confluent sheet of flames to the south. At Cottonwood Springs we rode out onto the plateau to see and watch it. The fire rolled on and on, leaving in its train only blackness and desolation.[2]

##

Newcomers were awed by prairie fires; they were beautiful, illuminating the night sky and glowing like an artificial sunrise or sunset. Early explorers and pioneers compared the prairie fire's beauty and splendor to that of an aurora borealis.

The 4 December 1858, issue of the *Nebraska City (Nebraska Territory) News* includes a fascinating portrayal of a prairie fire. The writer makes the experience sound much like today's TV entertainment.

One of the finest spectacles we have ever witnessed is a prairie on fire, and it is now visible every evening— upon all sides of us, north, south, east and west the lambent flames are licking up the prairie grass, and causing the heavens to be all aglow with their reflected brilliancy. The sight is indeed a fine one, and we love to gaze at it for hours at a time; it is one of the most beautiful objects in nature.

Artist George Catlin made several journeys into the *pays inconnu* between the years 1830 and 1836. His motivation was to make a lasting portrayal of the Plains Indians before they were exterminated or civilized. In his own words he resolved "by the aid of my brush and my pen, to rescue from oblivion so much of their primitive looks and customs" as his lifetime could accomplish.

One subject of his brush and pen was the recurrent prairie fires. He agreed that

> prairies burning form some of the most beautiful scenes that are to be witnessed in this country, and also some of the most sublime. Every acre of these vast prairies (being covered for hundreds and hundreds of miles, with a crop of grass, which dies and dries in the fall) burns over during the fall or early in the spring, leaving the ground of a black and doleful colour.
>
> . . . These scenes at night become indescribably beautiful, when their flames are seen at many miles distance, creeping over the sides and tops of the bluffs, appearing to be sparkling and brilliant chains of liquid fire (the hills being lost to the view), hanging suspended in graceful festoons from the skies.[3]

John D. Hunter was captured by Indians as a child and lived among them and learned their ways until reaching his late teens or early twenties. He then returned to the white man's world and later penned his memoirs. Hunter was a contemporary of Catlin and it is probable that the two knew each other.

In language very similar to Catlin's, Hunter describes the prairies' fires. "In the fall of the year, when the prairie grass is dry, the prairies are sometimes set on fire by accident, and at others by design. Should the wind be high on these occasions, no spectacle can surpass them in grandeur and sublimity; a space as far as the eye can reach, is seen devastated by the igneous torrent."[4]

Billy Dixon's biography paints a similar word picture of prairie fires.

> The fires on the Plains in fall and winter, after frost had cured the grass, were often a magnificent spectacle, especially at night when their radiance reddened the

Library of Congress, Prints and Photographs Division, LC-USZ6-2160

This Currier & Ives illustration entitled *Prairie Fires of the Great West* depicts the grandeur and threat of a prairie fire. Ironically, many fires were started by the cinders and ash from steam locomotives.

sky for many miles. The sky would be luminous, even though the fire was too far beyond the horizon to be seen . . .

. . . At night, when the wind was still, a fire on the Plains was a beautiful sight. In the far distance, the tongues of flames appeared so small that they looked like a red line of countless fingers, pointing with trembling motion toward the sky.[5]

Brilliant, beautiful, and magnificent they may have been, but when the grass was tall and the wind was high, most Indians and newcomers learned to respect and fear prairie fires.

Some did not.

Albert D. Richardson, in his 1867 work, *Beyond the Mississippi*, writes that "During night rides in winter, I often saw prairie fires blazing along the horizon. Though never dangerous to men or animals, as depicted in our school-geographies, they are always startling and grand. The sky is pierced with tall pyramids of flame, or covered with writhing, leaping, lurid serpents, or transformed into a broad ocean lit up by a blazing sunset. Now a whole avalanche of fire slides off into the prairie, and then opening its great, devouring jaws closes in upon the deadened grass."[6]

Richardson's comment that these fires are "never dangerous to men or animals" is certainly at odds with other accounts suggesting he didn't have first-hand knowledge of a serious prairie fire.

We find Richardson isn't alone in his opinion. Another author, Lewis Atherton, in *The Cattle Kings* proclaims that "prairie fires seldom took human lives."[7] "Seldom" is an extremely relative term making it difficult to know the author's exact intent.

Obviously Richardson and Atherton hadn't spent enough time observing or fighting major fires to appreciate their lethal potential. But, for those who fought with or escaped from a big "burn", the prairie fire was transformed into a haunting, terrifying, devouring demon.

With his pen Catlin praised the burning prairie for its beauty and then described its destructive nature. In one of his letters he writes

> There is yet another character of burning prairies, that requires another Letter, and a different pen to describe—the war, or hell of fires! where the grass is seven or eight feet high, as is often the case for many miles together, on the Missouri bottoms; and the flames are driven forward by the hurricanes, which often sweep over the vast prairies of this denuded country. There are many of these meadows on the Missouri, the Platte, and the Arkansas, of many miles in breadth, which are perfectly level, with a waving grass, so high, that we are obliged to stand erect in our stirrups, in order to look over its waving tops, as we are riding through it. The fire in these, before such a wind, travel at an immense and frightful rate, and often destroys, on their fleetest horses, parties of Indians, who are so unlucky as to be overtaken by it; not that it travels as fast as a horse at full speed, but that the high grass is filled with wild pea-vines and other impediments, which render it necessary

for the rider to guide his horse in the zig-zag paths of the deers and buffaloes, retarding his progress, until he is overtaken by the dense column of smoke that is swept before the fire—alarming the horse, which stops and stands terrified and immutable, till the burning grass which is wafted in the wind, falls about him, kindling up in a moment a thousand new fires, which are instantly wrapped in the swelling flood of smoke that is moving on like a black thunder-cloud, rolling on the earth, with its lightning's glare, and its thunder rumbling as it goes.[8]

Hunter is equally respectful of a prairie fire's dangers.

In some places the tortuous flames, comparatively lost in distance, appears to smoulder beneath impervious columns of smoke; at others, they burst into the skies with the vividness and rapidity of lightning, and seem to threaten universal desolation. Their speed is that of the winds, and destruction betides every living thing that cannot outfly its course.[9]

Billy Dixon agrees that a fire is ominous but doesn't go as far as Catlin or Hunter in describing its danger.

Once under strong headway, with the fire spread over a wide area, it was difficult to arrest its progress . . .

. . . Carried forward in the teeth of a high, boisterous wind, the fire was appalling, and there was something sinister and somber in the low roar that sent terror to the heart of wild animals. Vast clouds of smoke were carried into the heavens, until the sun lost its radiance and hung red and dull, like a copper shield, in the opaque depths. The ashes of burned vegetable sifted down hour after hour, as if a volcano were throwing out fine lava dust.[10]

While Catlin obviously has seen and painted a fire in the tallgrass prairie, he does make a distinction between those fires and the fires on the shortgrass plains.

> Over the elevated lands and prairie bluffs, where the grass is thin and short, the fire slowly creeps with a feeble flame, which one can easily step over; where the wild animals often rest in their lairs until the flames almost burn their noses, when they will reluctantly rise, and leap over it, and trot off amongst the cinders, where the fire has past and left the ground as black as jet.[11]

No one can challenge Dixon's right to be considered an experienced plainsman, yet he, like Catlin, views the threat posed by prairie fires on the plains as negligible.

Dixon maintains that "to the experienced plainsman, equipped with a flint or matches, there was no imminent danger, as he knew how to set out protective fires, and thus insure his safety. These big fires were rather terrifying, nevertheless, especially to the 'tenderfoot.'"

Dixon, too, makes a distinction between the plains and the prairie by explaining: "The danger of these fires to life in the Plains country has been exaggerated. The grass that grew in the Plains did not have the height to produce a sweeping, high-rolling fire, such as was often seen in the regions of the tall bluestem in eastern Kansas."[12]

Keeping in mind that the twenty-inch isohyet shifted with wet and dry cycles thus determining the amount of biomass available to fuel a fire. The location, hilltop or river valley, also influenced how rank the grass cover grew.

The following story illustrates how quickly prairie fires can turn tragic if conditions favor the fire. The account is taken from the *Beatrice (Nebraska) Express*, 6 November 1873, and gives details of a

> prairie fire in Brownville settlement, Saline County, Nebraska, but it only tells a part of the calamity as it falls on those acquainted with the sufferers. The papers tell us that "Mrs. Morey, seeing three of her

Frank Leslie's Illustrated Newspaper, *28 October 1882*
Sheep outnumbered cattle on some ranges and they were especially vulnerable to fires that swept the grasslands during the nineteenth century. Mounted herders try to drive a flock out of the path of an approaching fire somewhere in Texas in 1882.

children struggling for life, ran to their assistance." The truth is, she saw three of her children, three of her grand children, two nieces and one nephew struggling for life, ran to their assistance, and died with them. The three Morey's were her own children; the three Beany's were her oldest daughter's children; the Neely's were her brother's children, and Annie Berkley was a sister's child . . . Mrs. Morey was about fifty years of age, a quiet, industrious, motherly woman. She saw the children in danger and ran to their assistance; she could not save them, would not leave them, and heroically died with them.

Regrettably this wasn't an isolated tragedy but one that occurred time and again across the endless ocean of grass. Newcomers found this ocean either fascinating and promising or empty and threatening. Regardless of their viewpoint, encountering these seemingly endless grasslands was an entirely new experience for most. Unless the newcomer came from, or had been to, one of the other great grasslands of the globe such as the *pampas* of South America, the *pusztas* of Hungary, the *steppes* of Asia, or the *velds* of Southern Africa; or, as a strange contrast, had been sailors.

The prairies and plains between the Mississippi River and the Rocky Mountains are divided into three groups: tallgrass, mixed-grass, and shortgrass. These groups are not entirely exclusive of each other. There is a considerable blending of the species as the tallgrass gives way to the mixed-grass which in turn gives way to the shortgrass. This transition unfolds from east to west and is first and foremost governed by rainfall.

John Wesley Powell in his 1878 report on the arid regions of the United States choose the 100th meridian as a dividing line between the humid and arid halves of the United States. This meridian is roughly where the rainfall lessens to twenty inches per year.

Later some geographers suggested that this dividing line should fall along the line of the 98th meridian. This would have the line running through Hutchinson, Kansas, instead of Dodge City, Kansas, or about 125 miles farther east.[13]

Regardless of which meridian is favored, east of this shifting line (depending on the wet and dry cycles) is where farming could be practiced successfully without irrigation. West of this line farming without irrigation was considered impossible.

However on both sides of this line, grasses, along with diverse grassland plants, adapted to the rainfall and provided one of the largest and richest pastures of the world.

The tallgrass prairie is so called because Big Bluestem and prairie cordgrass can grow as tall as twelve feet when ample moisture is present. Where rainfall is up to thirty-plus inches per year, Big Bluestem dominates the prairie. Although it dominates it does tolerate other prairie grasses such as little bluestem, Indiangrass, cordgrass and switchgrass.

Lauren Brown, in her book *Grasslands,* describes the transition along the twenty-inch isohyet. "On its western edge, the tallgrass prairie grades into a broad north-south belt dominated by grasses of medium height—those that are approximately two to four feet tall. This area is primarily known as the mixed prairie, although it is also sometimes called the midgrass prairie, the mixed-grass prairie, the bluestem bunchgrass prairie, or the Great Plains."[14]

Little bluestem, blue grama grass, buffalo grass, and western wheatgrass along with some Big Bluestem found along waterways are the major grasses of the mixed-grass prairies. This mixed-grass prairie was a favorite grazing area for the buffalo and other herbivores that thrived here until newcomers altered these grasslands forever.

West of the mixed-grass prairie and extending all the way to the Rocky Mountains is the shortgrass plains; sometimes called the High Plains. The dominant grasses of the shortgrass plains are blue grama and buffalo grass. Growing along side these dominant species can be found Junegrass, western wheatgrass, and needle-and-thread. The arid climate also allows cacti, such as the prickly pears, as well as yucca and some species of sagebrush to flourish in the shortgrass habitat.

Originally these virgin prairies and plains stretched from the Canadian providences of Manitoba, Saskatchewan, and Alberta south into Old Mexico. At its widest point, from Wyoming back into Indiana, it was nearly one thousand miles across.

Regardless of the region—tallgrass, mixed-grass, or shortgrass—how "large" a prairie fire became depended on rainfall which determined the grassland's biomass. If the spring and summer were wet, the growth could be extremely rank covering some 1,250,000 square miles in area. That's about 800,000,000 acres of potential fuel for a prairie fire.

Each year as fall brought frost, more than ever during the green and lush years, these prairies and plains became a multi-million-acre highly flammable carpet. And each year some of this carpet burned in spectacular fires lasting for weeks as this account from Wells County, Dakota Territory attests.

> One of the worst perils to contend with in those days were the terrible prairie fires which would rage for weeks in the fall after the grass was dry enough to burn. These fires usually originated far to the north.
>
> They would burn steadily on for six weeks or more. Each day the smoke became more dense until at last the sun would be entirely obscured for days. Then at

night the reflection of the fire on the clouds could be seen, gradually drawing nearer, and the reflection on the clouds growing brighter and larger each night.

Finally after about ten days of this it would pass through, sweeping everything before it unless every possible precaution had been taken in making firebreaks. On a calm night it was a most beautiful sight to see the fires pass through and light the heavens bright as day.[15]

Given that the U.S. Army spent a great deal of time on the expanding frontier of the trans-Mississippi west, it isn't surprising that soldiers had to cope with prairie fires.

Occasionally, as in the case of General Mitchell, the army intentionally started a prairie fire as an offensive weapon against the Indians. Most of the time, however, the soldiers found themselves, for one reason or another, on the defensive end of a fire. Such was the case with Colonel Dodge who wrote that

> when a boy, fresh from 'The Point,' new to army life, and perfectly 'green' in frontier service, I was sent on my first scout after Indians, in command of a party of twenty cavalry. I had not the first dawning of an idea of the details of plains life, nor did my commanding officer think it necessary to give me any instructions ... When out about a week we went one day into camp, on a piece of ground covered with grass two feet high and very dry. The wind was blowing quite strongly.
>
> After designating the position of the squads and picket line, I ... went with my rod to the stream near by to get some fresh fish for dinner.
>
> I had just got interested in fairly good sport, when I was startled by shouts and commotion in camp . . . I ran back to find the whole camp ground in a blaze, and the flames going with great speed towards the grazing horses. Ordering some of the men to the relief of the animals, I plunged with the others into the flames to save, if possible, the arms and equipment. We had hardly got to work before the carbines (laid

across the saddles on the ground) began to go off with the heat; and this fire, added to the other, and an occasional explosion of a cartridge-box, made it so hot that we were all obliged to get out of camp and take cover. Some of the horses broke their lariat ropes and stampeded; and in five minutes from the first alarm we were reduced from a well-armed, well-mounted aggressive force, to an apparently half-armed, half-mounted, singed, and dilapidated party.[16]

This was the first of numerous "trials by fire" Colonel Dodge endured. A prairie fire in the shortgrass country was, in his opinion, "a very insignificant affair." However, he learned that "where the grass is high and vegetation of all kinds is abundant, to be caught in one is a most serious misadventure."

One such mishap was due to Dodge's own carelessness. He had shot a deer, "a splendid animal, with, I think, the most magnificent antlers I have ever seen," and while field dressing the animal paused for a smoke and after lightning his pipe blew out the match and tossed it behind him. The match wasn't completely extinguished and soon Dodge and his servant

> found the grass blazing to the height of three or four feet. We both jumped on the fire and attempted to put it out . . . finding this impossible and the fire gaining, I directed him to run for the horses. I ran for my gun, and the progress of the flames towards it was so extremely rapid that I barely secured it in time. Running off, and quartering to the wind, I fortunately found under some large trees a spot of half an acre in extent bare of grass and underbrush. Here I remained for nearly half an hour almost stifled by the smoke and heat, until the fire had passed and the burned ground got cool enough to walk over. I went back to my deer. He was literally cooked; not very artistically, as the outside was burned to a cinder, the inside being raw. The antlers and almost the whole head were burned off . . .

> This was the hottest fire I have ever seen on the plains, the flames sometimes appearing at least thirty feet high.[17]

The recollections and experiences of Colonel Dodge are representative of thousands of fires that blazed up in the grassland corridor between the Mississippi River and the Rocky Mountains.

The following accounts are of specific fires dating back to the very early years of the century. These accounts show just how quickly a fire could turn deadly—even to the Plains Indians who had centuries of experience living with, and sometimes dying in, a prairie fire.

On 29 October 1804, about thirty miles above present day Bismarck, North Dakota, Lewis and Clark witnessed a fire where Indians became victims.

> The prairie was set on fire (or caught by accident) by a young man of the Mandans; the fire went with such velocity that it burned to death a man and woman who could not get to any place of safety. One man, a woman and child much burnt and several narrowly escaped the flame. A boy, half white, was saved unhurt in the midst of the flame. Those ignorant people say this boy was saved by the Great Spirit medicine because he was white. The cause of his being saved was, a green buffalo skin was thrown over him by his mother, who perhaps had more foresight for the protection of her son and less for herself than those who escaped the flame. The fire did not burn under the skin, leaving the grass around the boy. This fire passed our camp last night about eight o'clock p.m. It went with great rapidity and looked tremendous.[18]

Famous mountain man, Jim Beckwourth, sometimes carried military dispatches for the frontier army. In December 1848 he arrived at Santa Fe and reported that "there was little snow on the prairie and grass was burned from Pawnee Forks to Council Grove," which was nearly a 150 mile stretch.[19]

Photo by author

The author's wife, Dawn, in Big Bluestem grass near Topeka, Kansas. This is an illustration of the great amount of fuel available for a fire on a tall-grass prairie. The bluestem is seven to eight feet tall and can yield perhaps four tons of fuel per acre, generating 2,500 tons of fuel per square mile.

Another deadly fire was reported in the *St. Joseph (Missouri) Gazette*, Wednesday, 24 December 1851.

Distressing.—A family by the name of Cooper, from Hickory county, returning from a visit North, encountered fire in the prairie some ten miles north of this place on Thursday last, and were greatly injured. They lost their wagon and contents, and a child was so severely burned, as to be despaired of. The father and mother were also greatly injured by the flames in their efforts to rescue the child, which it seems became frantic, and endeavored to escape through the fire. The luxuriant growth upon the prairies this season, renders fire in them alarming indeed. In many places, waves of fire will roll twenty or thirty feet.—*Osceola Independent*

During the fall of 1852, a high drama unfolded on the Santa Fe Trail when a troop of U.S. Cavalry went into camp near Diamond Springs, in what is now Kansas. In the waning hours before sundown, a party of Indians set fires on all sides of their camp. The full account was described by Colonel Percival G. Lowe.

Nothing of special interest occurred until we reached Diamond Springs, now in Morris County. The weather had been frosty at night and days sunny—a continuous Indian summer all the way—grass dry as powder . . . All day we had seen little bands of Indians a mile or two off the road traveling the same direction that we were and apparently watching us. This was the Kaw country and probably no other Indians were there, and we could hardly understand why they kept aloof and watched our progress . . . We camped on high ground a little east of Diamond Springs, on the south side of the road. We had been very careful of fire all the way in, and here we were especially careful on account of the dense growth of grass and the consequent danger of burning the camp. We had finished dinner, about two hours before sunset when, as if by one act, fire broke out in a circle all around us not more than a mile from camp. A stiff gale was blowing from the south, and when we noticed it the fire in the tall grass was roaring furiously and the flames leaping twenty feet high. Quickly we commenced firing outside our camp, whipping out the fire next to it, thereby burning a circle around it. Every man used a gunny sack or saddle blanket and worked with desperate energy. The utter destruction of the camp was imminent, and we faced the fire like men who had everything at stake. Success was ours, but the battle left scars on nearly all. I have never seen fifteen minutes of such desperate work followed by such exhaustion—scarcely a man could speak. Blinded by smoke, heat and ashes, intuitively we found our way to the creek and bathed our burned hands and faces, many of us terribly blistered. My hands and face were blistered in several places; my mustache and whiskers, the first I had ever raised, were utterly ruined; I could not wash on account of the blisters, and dipped my face and head deep down in the lovely spring of water and held my hands under to relieve the pain. My experience was that of most of the troop. We had quite a quantity of antelope tallow, which was warmed and gently applied to our sores. Undoubtedly the Kaws had set fire to burn us out.[20]

Whether fighting Indians or a prairie fire, one's odds of surviving were greatly increased by being resourceful and quick of mind.

In Dakota in 1859 one woman, caught alone at home in a terrible fire which swept the prairie and set the woods ablaze, and finding herself in imminent danger of certain death, took her child and crawled down into the well. Hardly had she gotten down into the well when everything about her was enveloped in flame. She was nearly suffocated from the heat and smoke, but held out until the danger was past and by her sheer nerve and resourcefulness, saved herself and child.[21]

Lieutenant Colonel George Armstrong Custer reported for duty at Fort Riley, Kansas, in the fall of 1866. He was accompanied by his wife Elizabeth who remained at the post while her husband led the 7th Cavalry on an Indian campaign the following spring.

Later, describing the prairies around the post, she wrote that "it is impossible to appreciate their vastness at first. The very idea was hard to realize, that from where we lived we looked on an uninterrupted horizon."

This vastness, coupled with an approaching prairie fire made quite an impression on the General's wife. "As the sky became lurid, and the blaze swept on toward us, surging to and fro in waving lines as it approached nearer and nearer, it seemed that the end of the world, when all shall be rolled together as a scroll, had really come. The whole earth appeared to be on fire."[22]

On this occasion the wind shifted, thus sparing Elizabeth Custer and the fort but, in her words left "the charred, smoke-stained earth spread as far as we could see, making more desolate the arid, treeless country upon which we looked. It was indeed a blackened and dismal desert that encircled us."

A sidebar to this story is noted on a sign next to the Fort Riley Post Cemetery explaining that some of the stone markers say simply "U.S. Soldier." These markers are replacements for wooden markers that were destroyed by a prairie fire. When the wooden markers were burned, all records of those interred were lost forever. This didn't happen during the fire that Mrs. Custer watched but probably occurred sometime in the early 1880s.

The *Annual Report of the Chief Signal-Officer to the Secretary of War for the Year 1872* included a paper, "The Great Fires of 1871 in the Northwest," by Professor I. A. Lapham.

Lapham writes that "Fires have swept more or less completely along the whole northern frontier, from the Rocky Mountains through Dakota, Minnesota, Wisconsin, and Michigan, and even into New York and Pennsylvania."

Of course, east of the Mississippi is out of the scope of this work but it does bring into focus just how wide spread and serious the prairie fire was. And when it ran into a wooded area and set forests ablaze before a strong wind, the results were catastrophic.

Lapham added that "Not only has the wild prairie region been swept by the fires of 1871, but thousands of square miles of forest have been destroyed. Many farms, with their houses, barns, stacks of hay and grain, miles of fence, &c., have been destroyed."[23]

The summer of 1871 also saw substantial fires in the central plains. Further settlement of Morris County, Kansas, was brought to a halt "in 1871 when a prairie fire swept in from the west. It was fought by all the male citizens under the leadership of Patrick Maloney, who was said to be 'the best fire fighter in the state.' The women pumped water and two small boys of the town, Will Miller and Graff Abbot, wet the sacks. A man and woman drove furiously in a buggy for 60 miles, it is said, ahead of the fire and when they stopped both horses dropped dead."[24]

No matter where professional buffalo hunters found the herds it was a hazardous business. If the Indians didn't lift a hunter's hair, a blizzard could kill or maim him. Add to this the threat of prairie fires and it's a wonder any man survived a career as a buffalo runner.

In 1875 Jack Bickerdyke was hunting in the area that later became the Oklahoma Panhandle. As luck would have it, Bickerdyke was one of those shooters that helped skin out the carcasses after the killing was done.

One afternoon on his way back to camp he came upon a crippled animal. He quickly killed it and was skinning it out when he became aware of a "prairie fire sweeping down between the Beaver [Creek] and Palo Duro Creek . . . Bickerdyke looked for his horse . . . the mount was gone."

He then bolted for the creek but the fire was moving faster than he could run. Surrounded by fire, he had only one option that would perhaps save his life. He ran back to the partly skinned buffalo . . . ripped open the carcass . . . just before the fire reached him, he crawled inside, taking his rifle and pulling the skin over him as well as he could. . . After the worst of the fire had passed . . . he pushed up the hide and crawled out"

On his way back to camp, Bickerdyke met two of his Skinners, who had come out to look for him. "Which one of you threw that match down?" he asked. "You came near cooking me alive."[25]

Eight-month-old H. J. Marshall accompanied his parents to Dakota Territory in the year 1878. The burning prairies were a memorable part of his childhood and he included the following account in his reminiscences.

> About the year of 1883 my father proved up his homestead and filed on a tree claim. We were getting along fairly well with a large range of praire for our cattle to feed on but sometimes they were out of feed on the praire as there were large praire fires that would burn the whole state. We could see the large cloud of smoke rolling ahead of the fire about two or three days before the fire really got to our territory. It would burn everything as it came . . . One time father came home a few days after a fire with the sad news that a mother and two daughters burned to death a few miles from our place. They were found about forty rods from their house that burned on a small patch of plowed ground. They had their clothes burned from their bodies and it was a terrible sight. The neighbors were all sick at heart as neighbors were few and far between and we treasured them very highly.[26]

Texas was not without its share of prairie fires, Texas sized, of course. Owning three million acres of grassland in Texas and leasing two million additional acres in Montana made the Capitol Freehold Land and Investment Company, Limited, one of the biggest outfits to ever burn a brand on a critter. Theirs was the famous XIT brand that adorned tens of thousands of cattle in the Texas Panhandle and eastern Montana during the fading decades of the Old West's cattle empires.

Colonel Amos C. Babcock, one of the four original partners, arrived in the Panhandle in 1882 to inspect the three million acres he and his associates had contracted for without ever seeing a single acre.

Accompanied by a local guide, Babcock pushed west from the small frontier town of Tascosa, Texas, and just south of

Marker at a cemetery near Fort Riley, Kansas. The original markers for some 100 soldiers, civilian workers and their dependents were made of wood and were destroyed by a prairie fire.

the Canadian River Babcock spotted green grass poking up through black sod. This was his introduction to

> the great plague of the prairie states—the prairie fire. Vivian [a guide], who had fought many a flaming prairie in his days as a cowboy, told him that the first killing frost and a few dry days made the grass as

inflammable as coal oil. A fire might break out at any time at any place, he said, and if the wind happened to be high, the fire could crackle across hundreds of thousands of acres in a night or two.[27]

This quiet verbal introduction was far from the last lesson Colonel Babcock would learn about prairie fires for "Not a single winter had the XIT escaped the loss of large areas of grass because of the fires, the origin of nearly all of them unknown."[28]

In 1885 a big burn lit up the skies over the Oklahoma Strip and roared its way toward XIT ranch headquarters at Buffalo Springs in the northwest corner of the Panhandle.

> To the north, the glow brightened and widened, and grew ever nearer. It lighted the range for miles around . . . it was a wild night at Buffalo Springs, but it was fiercer still out on the fireline.
>   . . . fighters galloped their foam-flecked horses straight to the fire. Here flames leaped, roaring and crackling, thirty feet into the turbulent air.
>   . . . there was nothing, then, they could do even to delay the fire's onward sweep. They rode back to headquarters, singed, smoked, black as . . . coal, defeated.[29]

This time the firebreak around the ranch headquarters checked the flames although "for a few eerie moments, the headquarters was surrounded by flaming prairie. Then to the north, at the limits of the protective strip, the fire went out as quickly as a candle might be snuffed. But to the south—and as far east and west as the tired men could see—the bright glow raced across the grasslands, finally to die out in draws and canyons where the grass was too thin to burn."[30]

Despite a desperate effort to control that blaze there were substantial losses according to Olive Dixon. Some of the losses were post-burn which shows the long-term effect a fire can have.

In the fall of 1885 a big prairie fire broke out and swept the country bare from the Beaver south almost to the South Canadian. We fought it with all our strength, but there were not men enough in the country to get it under control. This misfortune was followed by an early and severe winter. The company at Buffalo Springs drifted its herds out to the Canadian and to the south Plains, yet despite every precaution the loss was tremendous. I was told that only 7,000 of the 20,000 [cattle] were gathered the following spring.[31]

And there were still more and bigger burns in XIT's future; some that came close to destroying the Capitol Freehold Land and Investment Company, Limited.

Kansas, along with its other real and imagined faults, seemed especially susceptible to the prairie fire. On 10 April 1887, "A prairie fire near Nicodemus, Graham County, caused nine deaths and large property damage. The fire was driven through Rooks and Phillips counties by a 40-mile wind"[32]

In that same winter Americus, Kansas, in Lyon County, was threatened when "a big prairie fire raged on Saturday afternoon, 2 November 1887, and all day Sunday. Several Americus men were out fighting the fire. The fighting was done by backfiring, and fighting with wet gunny sacks. The fire didn't get inside the city limits but many head of cattle and horses were burned to death out on the common range, and many farmers lost all their feed and grain."[33]

Turner County, Dakota Territory, suffered a bad fire in 1889 where it was reported that "in less than a half hour after attention was attracted to a fire, one family saw seven neighbors' homes in flames. Jack rabbits, birds, and here and there a loose team, went rushing by. The closest neighbor was terribly burned while his horses were roasted with the harness on. One woman was out pouring milk on her house to save it."[34]

G. W. Rensker moved from a Dutch community in Greenleafton, Minnesota, to Campbell County, Dakota Territory, (presently South Dakota) in 1885. Here he and others came with the intent of establishing a "colony" of Hollanders. His recollections of a prairie fire show the immediate and long-term damage caused by man-made fires and those ignited by Mother Nature.

> The winter of 1891 and 1892 was mild, there scarcely being any snow. The spring opened fair and a favorable summer followed. But in the fall when threshing commenced the prairie was set afire by an engine, which swept over a large tract of country, and two persons lost their lives. The following day, while a shower passed along the south side of the colony, lightening set the prairie afire in five different places. The east wind fanned the blaze of a width of twelve miles. Suddenly at ten o'clock at night it shifted to the south and, accompanied by an electric storm, drove the blaze northward with great rapidity carrying with it destruction of grain, buildings, stock and machinery. It seemed as if the air was filled with flame. Grain and stacks were set afire three forths of a mile in advance of the oncoming blaze.
>
> This disaster affected all the settlers more or less. A few were made destitute, barely escaping with their lives. Some lost part of their grain and hay. Heaviest loss was in grain and horses. During the following severe winter a lot of the stock that had escaped the fire perished for wont of feed. People in need again were helped by those who had been assisted by eastern friends and by their more fortunate neighbors. Only one Hollander was hurt during this fire, but no lives were lost. Five dwelling houses were burned.[35]

The dug well could be considered a settler's "safe house" for it meant salvation for yet another settler in 1894. "A big prairie fire swept down on the Carl Mann home so suddenly that Sidney Manning, who was visiting . . . jumped into the well. A cow chip rick in the yard caught fire; the chips were carried aloft by the convection currents and the burning embers kept dropping down onto him in the well. He said afterwards that he had to duck under the water so often to avoid the fire that he wasn't sure but that he might drown trying to keep from burning to death."[36]

George Catlin, Prairie Meadows Burning
Buffalo and other prairie wildlife flee a fire in this Catlin painting done
sometime between 1861 and 1869.

As mentioned before, the 100th meridian is generally
considered mixed or shortgrass country where prairie fires
were tame compared to fires in tallgrass. But during wet years
there was heavy growth that provided sufficient fuel for very
destructive fires.

There was an abundance of grass over the prairies,
which easily carried the fire; with a high wind
behind it, the fire moved forward at a terrific speed,
consuming everything in its path. A speed of a mile
every two minutes was not uncommon . . . On March
12, 1893, a fire started about 10 miles south of Hill
City (Kansas) . . . in less than four hours, the fire had
crossed Graham County into Rooks. When the wind
shifted to the northwest, the blaze went toward the
southeast, "faster than a horse could run" and "burning
all the way to Salina, a strip forty miles wide and one
hundred and fifty miles long." It left eleven dead at
different points along its course. There was a great
loss of property, houses, barns, livestock, feed, and

farm implements, among people who could ill afford to lose their few belongings.[37]

Hill City, Kansas is almost due north of Dodge City which locates it just east of the 100th meridian. This account suggests that when the conditions are favorable, any grassland can support a deadly inferno.

Christie Dalager was born in Norway and only three years old when her mother died. As a young girl she came to America with her father, step-mother, and other relatives. The family initially settled in Minnesota but pushed on west to the Dakota Territory when Christie was 15 or 16 years old. She walked all the way, herding the cows along behind the wagon.

Sometime later she witnessed a prairie fire where the dug well saved her aunt's life. It was a bittersweet victory for

> when they saw the fire coming, the women got the children to a small field they had plowed and went back to the barn to get out the oxen. They were trapped. The grandmother and the oxen were so completely consumed that only one or two small fragments of bone were found . . . The aunt, being more agile, managed to reach a well and jump into it. Although terribly burned, she survived but was badly crippled for life from the effects of the burns and standing in the icy water for hours before help could be brought to get her out.[38]

Up north of the border, Canadians were beset by their share of prairie fires, many were as large and savage as any in the States.

> In the dry autumn, men might be firefighting many nights in a row, riding to help neighbouring homesteaders whose danger was advertised by the glow of fire in the distance. Hardly an autumn night passed without the red flickering light appearing in the sky. Yet their firefighting could only dabble at the edges of some gigantic blazes, which rushed across the grass at the speed of a galloping horse,

advancing on a front many miles wide. In the case of the largest fires the homesteader could hope only to use his wet sacking against the possibility of the flames jumping his fireguard. And even then he might be overwhelmed. In one account, a fire sweeping the prairie on a thirty-mile arc was said to have jumped a broad fireguard against the wind. In another, a man in southern Alberta reportedly lit his pipe carelessly, and the resulting fire burned off fifty square miles of prairie, taking scores of cattle, horses and homesteads with it. In the face of such terrors a pioneer could only gather a few possessions and run—returning later, perhaps, to the blackened acres, where neither house, crop, stock nor hay remained, to start over again.[39]

It wasn't only the people and things that suffered from a major fire. Animals, both wild and domestic, repeatedly fell victims to the flames.

From time to time explorers and hunters encountered buffalo that has been overtaken by a prairie fire. A very graphic example was recorded by Alexander Henry as he traveled across the southern plains of Manitoba, Canada in 1804. His *Journal* entry of 27 October mentions "fire in the plains in every direction." On 1 November he records "fire running all over the country." On 19 November, "Fire raging all over the plains." Then on 25 November he records,

Plains burned in every direction and blind buffalo seen every moment wandering about. The poor beasts have all the hair singed off; even the skin in many places is shriveled up and terribly burned, and their eyes swollen and closed fast. It was really pitiful to see them staggering about, sometimes running afoul of a large stone, at other times tumbling down hill and falling into creeks, not yet frozen over. In one spot we found a whole herd lying dead. The fire having passed only yesterday these animals were still good and fresh, and many of them exceedingly fat. Our road was on the summit of the Hair hills, where the open ground is uneven and intercepted by many small creeks

running eastward. The country is stony and barren.
At sunset we arrived at the Indian camp, having made
an extraordinary day's ride, and seen an incredible
number of dead and dying, blind, lame, singed, and
roasted buffalo. The fire raged all night towards the
S.W.[40]

In his memoirs, John D. Hunter recorded the same animal
behavior that eyewitnesses observed during the New Madrid
earthquakes. Instinctive animosities and aggressions are
forgotten when animals are threatened with a universally
dreaded foe. His writings explain that

the grazing herds, conscious of the threatening
calamity, fearlessly congregate with their natural
enemies; and the buffalos, elks, deer, panthers, wolves,
and bears, are seen promiscuously crowded together.
They sometimes escape to the ravines and avoid
death, but more frequently they are overwhelmed by
the resistless flames. One of these fires raged to a very
great extent a few years since, on the prairies between
the Kansas and Arkansas rivers; and it is extremely
painful on passing over them, to witness the ruin it
produced. The mass of bleached bones strewed on the
earth is astonishingly great; and no doubt remains,
that many thousands buffalos and other animals
perished at this particular period.[41]

David A. Dary in his work, *The Buffalo Book,* writes that
"still another natural enemy of the wild plains buffalo was the
prairie fire which might sweep across the open grasslands for
hundreds of miles before stopping at a river or other natural
barrier. It was not uncommon for such fires to trap buffalo and
other wild animals. The flames moved at a high rate of speed
when fanned by the wind. There was nothing to stop the fire
and it had no mercy for man or beast."[42]

For those humans and animals that survived the initial fire
there were still threatening consequences. It left the traveler
or homesteader without feed for his animals and often without

food for himself and his family. What game the fire didn't kill it drove out of the country.

Furthermore, "Prairie fires, started by lightning, malicious Indians, or a cook's carelessly left coals, often made detours necessary."[43] This, of course, added days or weeks of additional travel time with the risk of not finding water or grass for the livestock on a new and unmarked trail.

Once new grass and game was located, care was still needed because if the season was extremely dry and the ground cover parched, even a burning wad from a discharged firearm was enough to ignite a blaze.

A large percentage of motive power for the westward expansion was provided by "grass burners" or "hay burners." Without adequate fuel for oxen, horses, and mules, the wheels of progress stopped turning.

Certain Indians came to call a prairie fire the "Red Buffalo" because of the fire's voracious appetite for grass. After the Red Buffalo had grazed a large region of the country there was nothing left for animals or humans.

Don't Fence Me In makes a catchy tune and reflects a mindset linked with the frontier West; fences were a basic ingredient of the newcomer's world. And newcomers took their fences seriously. "The United States Department of Agriculture Report of 1871 estimated that where the cost of fencing in thirty-seven states had amounted to $1,747,549,091, the annual cost of repairs in the same era had reached $93,963,187, so that the expense of upkeep was in many places considered to be more than the gross intake by farmers."[44]

Before the advent of barbed wire, a landowner on the prairies and plains had few options for fence construction. If there was a supply within reasonable hauling distance, a wooden rail fence was one option. If not, the settler could plant a hedge on his property line and in about three or four years, if conditions were favorable, have a "fence."

A rock fence was another possibility and the government would pay the homesteader to lay one up. The forty cents per rod was indeed helpful to the small landowner with plenty of rocks and a family to help carry and stack them. Obviously this wasn't an option for fencing large tracts of land lacking a ready supply of rocks.

The alternative wooden rail fences or hedge rows could be, and were, destroyed by the almost annual prairie fires. Sometimes ranches, like the XIT, had hauled in (from a great distance) thousands of fence posts to string its hundreds of miles of barbed wire. In the wake of a prairie fire the ranches had to haul replacement posts and rebuild many miles of fence. Until the advent of steel posts, prairie fires just weren't fence-friendly.

##

An infant named Sarah was about to enter this world on the afternoon of 9 April 1887. Her mother was in labor and it was going to be a home delivery on the family homestead in Graham County, Kansas. Sarah's father was the attending staff of one—no doctor, no midwife, and no Lamaze coach—just Dad.

At the same moment that Sarah made her noisy entry into the human race there was another birth five miles west of the homestead; a prairie fire sprang to life and was being driven toward the family home by a howling wind.[45]

Sarah's father laid his daughter at her mother's breast and then gently cleaned the infant and tied off the umbilical cord. Her lungs were obviously fine; he counted fingers and toes, all twenty of them. While rejoicing with his wife on the birth of their healthy daughter a faint odor of smoke drifted into the bedroom.

Sarah's father stepped to the window and saw a wall of flames racing directly toward their home. It had already passed the farm's property line and was less than a half mile away. Mesmerized he watched the head fire launch burning chips in fiery arches through the dense smoke. Wherever these burning missiles landed they started additional fires. The firestorm was leap-frogging directly toward them with startling speed.

"Honey, did you leave something on the stove?"

He spun around and rushed to the bed.

"Honey, what's the matter?"

"Fire."

"Where, where's the fire?"

160

"Don't worry, it's outside."

He knew he had only precious seconds to find safety for his wife and daughter.

No time to plow a fireguard now.

No time to turn loose the team of horses tied in the stable.

No time to untie the milch cow.

No time to rescue the sow and piglets.

No time to save the hen and chicks.

No time, perhaps, to save themselves.

The couple homesteaded their quarter section of land last fall and had managed to break only about twenty acres of sod that was now ready to plant to corn. They'd come from the East where the ground was more sandy and easier to turn than the black, sticky, root-bound prairie sod. But the father had not complained. This was their land and he didn't mind working from dawn to dusk for his wife and future family. Time would bring rewards aplenty.

They were one of the fortunate ones who came west with a grubstake large enough to purchase the land outright and build with lumber instead of sod. The ground had remained frozen during much of the winter and he'd just begun to dig a root cellar for storing garden produce and for protection from the much dreaded "cyclones" of the plains.

Prairie fires had seemed a remote threat during the bitter winter days when the wind howled and snow lay on the ground. Finding enough fuel for cooking and heating was a constant struggle and on long frigid days any fire seemed a friend, not a foe. Now, ironically, here racing toward him was fire enough for a lifetime. The smoke, riding the wind ahead of the flames, engulfed the house in dark, choking waves.

Gathering the bed sheets and blankets around his wife and child, the man saw the reflection of flames in the small mirror on the family dresser they'd brought all the way from Pennsylvania.

Scooping up his wife and daughter, he kicked open the front door and ran; flames nibbled at his feet and then ignited the tangled bed covers that trailed behind them.

##

THE DEADLIEST WOMAN IN THE WEST

For a fact, in one form or another, smoking has been a health hazard for years. A thoughtless act committed by a smoker in 1865 started a prairie fire in Riley County, Kansas. A party of settlers had departed Manhattan, Kansas, for a location approximately twenty miles to the west. "They started their journey the morning of 19 June and followed Wild Cat Creek stopping for lunch at Riley Center. The sun was broiling hot and the vegetation parched and brown, and when one man lit his pipe thoughtlessly tossing the match into the dry grass, it burst into flames. The fire spread so quickly that it could not be stopped until several thousand acres of prairie grass were engulfed."[46]

Happily there was no report of death, injury, or destruction of property with this careless fire. But, even when great care was exercised to prevent fires, accidents did happen.

On the other hand, as bizarre as it seems, the uninitiated or ignorant newcomer would occasionally set the prairie afire just for the heck of it. A case in point involved an unnamed easterner who purchased, or so he thought, 20,000 acres of land in the Mexican province of Texas. In 1831 he traveled to Texas to claim this property but the Mexican Republic refused to recognize his purchase; he'd been the victim of a land swindle.

While still in Texas he and some local men were out riding one day east of Galveston Bay when the small party decided

to set the Prairie on fire. They separated from each other, and at distances of about half a mile, dismounted, struck fire, and kindled the dry grass . . . It instantly began to flame; and the fire sweeping on before the wind, cut three paths through the grass, which was then about three feet high . . . The darker the sky became, the brighter shone the light; and the two lines of fire gradually approached each other, so that they at length came near, and blazed up bright on the right and left . . .

The scene was described as very splendid and striking. Even when viewed from a distance, the effect was brilliant; and on the return of the gentlemen to Anahuac they found the people attracted by the light. Though about two miles and a half off, the fire was distinctly visible, being then spread over a great extent of the surface in a narrow band, with the dark smoke above and the prairie beneath, so that it appeared something like the bright sky at sunset, as we sometimes see it when a long cloud stretches nearly to the horizon, and leaves a single stripe of dazzling light.[47]

The chagrined investor remained in Texas for some days after which he returned to New York and published a book warning others of the land swindle. He was apparently so embarrassed by his gullibility that he published the book anonymously.

Sometimes it was Mother Nature who ignited these fires but man, Indian and newcomer were often guilty of providing the spark that touched off a prairie fire. To be sure, once the spark got a good bite on the dry grass it was Mother Nature who took control.

In Professor I. A. Lapham's paper, noted earlier, he identifies some rather obvious causes of these fires as "a small spark . . . the camp fire, the wad from a gun, a spark from a locomotive, even the remnant of a cigar, or ashes from a pipe . . . a stroke of lighting . . . The Indians are said to have purposely set them on fire to rout the deer and other game."[48]

In *The Prairie Traveler*, author Randolph B. Marcy, cautioned the novice overland traveler about fire hazards while en route across the prairies and plains. Marcy was a captain in the U.S. Army and spent twenty-five years of his lengthy military career on the western frontier. The War Department, well aware of the perils of overland travel, requested that Marcy write a guide book to help initiate the inexperienced. It was published in 1859 and became one of the most popular guide books of the era.

Common sense would seem to dictate travelers should exercise extreme caution with any type of fire when crossing an ocean of potential fuel. Considering the great number of fires caused by carelessness, caution apparently could never be stressed enough.

Marcy mentioned all of the potential sins of ignition but picked the camp fire as potentially the most dangerous. "Great caution should be taken to guard against the occurrence of such accidents, as they might prove exceedingly disastrous."

He focused the reader's attention on the volatility of grass, explaining that "When the grass is dry it will take fire like powder, and if thick and tall, with a brisk wind, the flames run like a race-horse, sweeping everything before them."[49]

George Catlin has something to add about how these fires originated. "There are many modes by which the fire is communicated to them, both by white men and by Indians— *par accident;* and yet many more where it is voluntarily done for the purpose of getting a fresh crop of grass, for the grazing of their horses, and also for easier traveling during the next summer, when there will be no old grass to lie upon the prairies, entangling the feet of man and horse, as they are passing over them."[50]

Taking into consideration how dangerous these fires were, it should be obvious that an ounce of prevention could be worth a ton of cure. And preventative methods were offered. Professor Lapham's theory of fire prevention was as idealistic as it was impracticable. He viewed these measures as "of the simplest kind . . . not only watchfulness, but the disuse, as far as possible, of all combustible materials . . . the use of kerosene in all its forms should be prohibited; no locomotive should be allowed to move without adequate means to prevent the emission of sparks . . . and no fences of wood should be built. If the farmers of France, Germany, etc., can do without fences, certainly we can do the same."[51]

Not doable.

A doable, but less-than-perfect, yet better-than-nothing fire prevention technique was a fireguard. To make such a guard two lands of turned earth, usually about six feet wide and thirty or more feet apart, were plowed around the homestead, or ranch, or town. To complete the job, the grass and other vegetation growing between the furrows was burned off on a calm day.

This fireguard, or firebreak as they were called, properly maintained, offered some protection but it wasn't fool proof. If the grass was rank and dry and the wind was high, fires often leaped these breaks as easily as a deer sailed over a rail

fence. Entire towns were just as vulnerable to the prairie fire as
were homesteads or ranches. This prompted many newspaper
editors to seasonally badger their readers to take action and
maintain a fireguard.

Some heeded, others didn't.

By virtue of its size, everything the XIT did was on a
Texas-sized scale, including firebreaks, or fireguards. It was
a loathsome job to the cowboys who hated any work that they
couldn't do from horseback.

Most assuredly it was hated.

> Plowing fireguards alone seemed like running a
> break plow around the equator. XIT cowpokes on
> that assignment opened some of the longest straight
> furrows ever turned. Two sets were plowed all around
> the ranch, the first one at the fence and the second
> thirty-five yards inside, the strip between to be
> burned off when the grass browned. Moreover, mere
> protection of the borders was not enough, and other
> guards were plowed around buildings, corrals and big
> bodies of grassland. By late in the summer, more than
> one thousand miles of guards had been finished. The
> burned-off area between the furrows, if put together in
> one patch, would have made a good-sized ranch, even
> in Texas.[52]

Although 12,730 acres wouldn't make a large Texas ranch,
it's an impressive number of acres to be included in a fireguard.
Those XIT fireguards comprised the equivalent of about twenty
sections of land.

Unfortunately, even these huge fireguards didn't always
stop a prairie fire. That being the case, in 1885 XIT ranch
manager, Barbecue Campbell, penned a booklet of *Ranch Rules*
that cowboys and other employees were expected to abide by.
There were twenty-two rules in this first booklet.

In 1888 it was updated by Abner Taylor and contained
twenty-three rules. Most rules in the new draft were essentially
the same as the first booklet except for rule number XIII which
in the new booklet read: "In case of fire on the ranch, or on lands
bordering on the same, it shall be the duty of every employee

to go to it at once and use his best endeavors to extinguish it, and any neglect to do so, without reasonable excuse, will be considered sufficient cause for dismissal."[53]

During fire seasons, ranchers kept a wagon loaded with water barrels, blankets, buckets, gunny sacks, and brooms. Hides were kept soaking in the water barrels to help make them more effective when dragging over or beating out the flames.

In the unfortunate event that smoke from a fire was noticed by someone, the horses were harnessed and as soon as the rest of the crew could saddle up, they made for the fire as fast as the horses could travel.

In the tallgrass and mixed-grass prairies it was impossible to fight the head fires that raced ahead of the main fire line. These v-shaped head fires created their own wind and updraft that fed the fire and propelled it forward at great speed. It was not only foolhardy, but impossible, to attempt to extinguish these. The only hope of containment was a well controlled backfire. But often backfires broke out of control which added a second fire to the first.

For that reason firefighters worked on the side fires that burned sideways to the headfires. These offered hope of being extinguished and thus saved lives, livestock, farms, ranches, settlements, grass, feed, and timber.

Some of the best accounts for fighting a prairie fire are given by XIT ranch hands in *6,000 Miles of Fence: Life on the XIT Ranch of Texas* by Cordia Sloan Duke and Joe B. Frantz. In this work is found Gene Elliston's account of a large fire that came roaring out of New Mexico and onto XIT range.

> A high wind from the west was blowing and continued to blow for several days. Of course the fire swept east over the staked plains. There were no streams or anything to check it until it reached the Texas line. There the XIT outfit had a fireguard seventy-five feet wide plowed and burned out. However, the wind was so high and the cow chips was [so] dry it would blow the fiery chips across the guard . . . the fire went almost to Amarillo. It burned thousands and thousands of acres of grass.[54]

Harper's Weekly, 28 February 1874; Frenzeny and Tavernier
Fighting a prairie fire was hot, dirty, exhausting work but every able-bodied man, woman, and youngster pitched in. Sometimes the motivation was self-preservation and sometimes they lost the battle.

In his book, *Cattle Empire: The Fabulous Story of the 3,000,000 Acre XIT*, Lewis Nordyke, adds detail to how these fires would jump a very wide fireguard by explaining that

> grass fires do not depend wholly upon the wind for their speed. Once they have a good start, they generate currents which sweep then forward in heads . . .
> Pushed by their own currents and the west wind, the heads leaped twenty to thirty feet into the sky. Burning cowchips sailed in great arcs and sprayed the area ahead, setting blazes in advance of the fire . . . headfires hit the XIT guards. But before that, burning embers had already shot over it as if from enemy guns and fired the grass on the ranch.[55]

From Duke and Frantz's book comes another story of a mammoth fire on the XIT ranch. This one was told by J. W. Armstrong.

> I have been in many fires, the largest being of seventy-two hours' duration, and as far as I know the largest

in the Ranch's history . . . Orders were to go to any fires within a radius of a hundred miles. Sacks, saddle blankets, brooms, or chaps were used to fight fires with till you got men and horses enough to kill a cow, split her open and turn the flesh side down and drag her on the edge of the fire line, and if you had horses enough you kill two of the cows and tie them together side by side so as to cover a wider space and drag the two of them, sixteen or twenty head of horses being required for this dragging the cows by the horns of the saddles. They soon exhaust the horses because of the rapid speed of the fire, horses often have to go in a lope. However the smoke exhausts the horse perhaps quicker, because a horse cannot stand smoke. Therefore a horse has to be changed every half mile to a mile. The heavier the cow a better job, hence often a bull is slaughtered instead of a cow, this is if there are horses enough to drag the animals. You could put out more fire in this manner than fifty men could with sacks and blanket . . .

Men were placed in relays every hundred yards, to fight out the little spots of fire left after the drag had gone by. These men had to go in a run to keep up; therefore a new man was dropped out every hundred yards . . . leaving his horse where he started for the man fighting fire to pick up and bring back to the main fire and there to drop out again when his turn came. Every man riding his own horse and taking time about, dragging the cows, dropping out again to hand-fight the remaining spots of fire, when his time came.[56]

It was hot, dangerous, and exhausting work that pushed the men's endurance to, and past, their limits. Once the battle was engaged the men didn't eat, sleep, or rest until they could not fight another step.

Returning to the account of the seventy-two hour burn on the XIT, Armstrong wrote that a second fire started in New Mexico Territory and raced toward the XIT. By the time the fire neared the ranch the exhausted boys refused to fight any further till they got something to eat . . . I went about fifteen miles to Middle Water Ranch for food . . .

When I got to the ranch R. C. Clendennin, the windmiller, was already loading prepared food into the windmill wagon . . . By the time we got back out there the boys' tongues had swollen so that they could eat only oatmeal and some couldn't even eat that. This was on the twenty-first day of March1895 . . . cattle had drifted ahead of the fire till they reached the XIT fence. There 750 of them were burned to death. Then the wind changed to the north and it snowed and the wind blew so hard it blew the fire out. That was the first time I ever knew a wind to get so high it put out a fire.[57]

Ira Aten, another XIT cowboy, pointed out that it wasn't only hard, risky work for the men but the horses used to pull the drags along the fire lines suffered too. "A horse could not stand walking over the burned stubble more than a half hour at a time without being relieved, as the ground would be so hot it would ruin his feet. Several of our horses were injured in that manner and it took just a year for their hoofs to grow off and then they would be all right."[58]

Randolph Marcy, in his *Prairie Traveler*, offers his solution for surviving a prairie fire

if escape from its track is impossible, it may be repelled in the following manner: The train and animals are parked compactly together; then several men, provided with blankets, set fire to the grass on the lee side, burning it away gradually from the train, and extinguishing it on the side next the train. This can easily be done, and the fire controlled with the blankets, or with dry sand thrown upon it, until an area large enough to give room for the train has been burned clear. Now the train moves on to this ground of safety, and the fire passes by harmless.[59]

While sound in theory, controlling the backfire as well as managing the animals caught in the path of a head fire driven by a stiff wind would be a challenge for even the most experienced plainsman.

But when the fires came, everyone, even women and children, were expected to help with the fighting. Once the fire was extinguished the effect on those involved was indelibly seared in their memory as described by a young Kansas girl.

> The darkness that follows the going out of a prairie fire is something portentous. From being the centre of a lurid glare you are suddenly plunged into the bottom of a bucket of pitch. Nothing reflects any light, and there is nothing to steer by. You don't know where you are nor where the house is; everything is black. Your throat is full of ashes and you can hardly breathe for the choking of the fluff in the air. If you call to your nearest pal on the back firing line, the chances are that he or she has moved away, and may be half a mile distant. You may feel as if you were the last survivor in a horrible world of cinders and blackness. At length a welcome shout is heard—in our case it was my father hailing us, and bidding us gather in. This we did most gladly, for he knew which way to go to reach home. And so once more the fire danger is over, and we may rest.[60]

These roaring infernos were an equal opportunity destroyer as they rode the wind across the grasslands. What was left in the fire's wake was often difficult to visualize or verbalize. "As he surveyed a smoldering, blackened range, one old-timer said, 'It shore looks like hell with the folks moved out.'"[61]

##

Did General Mitchell's fire give the Indians "ten thousand square miles of prairie-fire?"

Were the Indian "folks moved out?"

The jury's still out on that one. Some additional information must be considered before drawing any conclusion.

Captain Ware wrote that "All night the sky was lighted up. The fire swept the country clean; three days afterwards it was burning along the banks of the Arkansas River, far to the south, over which river it passed in places and ran out down in the Panhandle of Texas."[62] His account seems to be varified by Mari Sandoz in her books *The Cattlemen* and *The Buffalo Hunters.* Unfortunately Sandoz doesn't give definitive sources.

First consideration: Captain Ware did admit that some of the country was spared and that some Indians had backfired and saved themselves. He does say that the game was driven out of the country and that it "did much damage to some portions of the Kansas frontier, which was then far east of the middle of the State."[63]

Second consideration: some disagreement exists concerning whose idea the fire really was, General Mitchell's or Colonel Livingston's. Illinois State Historian, Clyde C. Walton, wrote an introduction and provided notes to the 1960 reprint of Captain Ware's book. Walton notes that "Ware not only greatly overestimates the extent and damage done by the prairie fire, but incorrectly credits General Mitchell with developing the idea. The credit should go to Colonel Livingston, for the idea was his."[64] There seems to be no disagreement, however, about who gave the orders to set the fires; all agree that it was General Mitchell.

Third consideration: of particular interest is George Bent's comment that "Although I was south of the Platte at the time and right in the way of such a fire, I did not see a sign of it, and never saw an Indian who knew anything about such a fire."[65]

Fourth consideration: on 2 February just days after the fire was set, a large war party attacked Old Julesburg for a second time.

Fifth consideration: the following report of Colonel James H. Ford from Fort Zarah, Kansas, clearly shows that many Indians south of the Platte River were alive and well in spite of General Mitchell's fire.

MAJOR: I have the honor to state, for the information of the general commanding, that since my last communication of 28 January up to the present date all is quiet throughout the district. No large parties of Indians have been discovered by our scouts along the line of the Arkansas River, and with the exception of an attack upon a fatigue party chopping wood one mile from Fort Zarah, no casualties have occurred. Upon the morning of the 1st of February a fatigue party of eight men, chopping wood on the Arkansas one mile from Fort Zarah, were fired upon by Indians; one man mortally wounded.[66]

Sixth consideration: Colonel Ford's report makes no mention of a large prairie fire, a lack of game, or any damage done by the fire. Other than the accounts of Captain Ware and Mari Sandoz, the record of this prairie fire is lacking in all the sources examined. It appears that this time Mother Nature, or the Great Spirit, thwarted the newcomers and spared the Indians.

Nevertheless, with or without a famous prairie fire, Brigadier General Robert B. Mitchell left his mark on the Great Platte River road. Mitchell Pass, Mitchell Valley, Fort Mitchell, and the town of Mitchell all derived their names from General Mitchell.

If indeed this fire had burned on a front 300 miles wide all the way down to the Canadian River in the Texas Panhandle, it would have encompassed 90,000 square miles; nine times more than Mitchell's "ten thousand square miles of prairie-fire."

All things considered, this was apparently the greatest ineffective prairie fire in history.

##

Sarah's father, carrying his wife and newborn daughter, raced toward the twenty acres of plowed field reaching the bare ground only a step ahead of the flames.

He kept running until the burning blankets reached his arms. Then he sank to his knees and laid his wife and child down and smothered the fire with handfuls of dirt.

The child was crying and his wife was weeping; he was gasping for breath. The mother's clothes did catch on fire causing some minor burns to her but the family all survived.[67]

The fire circled the plowed field and then joined again on the south side and rushed off as it had come—a wall of flames devouring all in its path.

Behind them the house and stable were engulfed in flames. A smoking heap marked the place where the milch cow was picketed. The family was alive but all their earthly possessions were lost and they were alone on a smoldering ocean of black.

A very brief account (only two column inches) of this birth during the prairie fire was found in the 14 April 1887, issue of the *Western Cyclone* published at Nicodemus, Kansas. The article provided no names of the family; neither surnames or given names. The fire burned into three counties making it impossible to pinpoint the family's homestead since it wasn't given in the newspaper article.

There are several reasons why I took the liberty to expand and include this account. Any human birth has a built-in amount of stress and drama under the most ideal circumstances. It became necessary for me to deliver one of my own sons and I can't really imagine what the stress level would have been if a prairie fire had been bearing down on our home.

I wanted to find the names of this family and perhaps some of their descendants because to me they were extraordinary individuals. Instead, to my great disappointment, no birth records for this child could be found in Graham, Rooks, or Phillips counties in Kansas. The state didn't begin requiring birth records until 1911 and the county clerks offices for these counties retain no birth records. After a reasonable search I concluded that their names are lost to us.

Not wanting to abandon the story I decided to give the child a name and a gender. I have no daughters so I decided the child would be a girl. Sarah is one of my favorite names so she became Sarah. I hope she and her father and her mother lived long and happy lives.

##

When drought parched the prairies and plains, when blizzards turned the land into a white morgue, and when grasshoppers ate them out of house and home, the one thing newcomers never lost was their humor.

Prairie fires were an exception. A bad one was hell with the roof peeled back and pure 'nough church-goin' serious. Mother Nature apparently never intended for prairie fires to be a joking matter.

Chapter Four notes

[1] George E. Hyde, *Life of George Bent Written from His Letters* (Norman: University of Oklahoma Press, 1983), 176.

[2] Eugene F. Ware, *The Indian War of 1864* (Topeka, Kansas: Crane & Company, 1911), 448-449.

[3] George Catlin, *North American Indians* (Philadelphia: Leary, Stuart and Company, 1913), 2:19.

[4] John D. Hunter, *Memoirs of a Captivity Among the Indians of North America* (London: Longman, Hurst, Rees, Orme, Brown, and Green, 1824), 146.

[5] Olive K. Dixon, *Life of "Billy" Dixon* (Austin: State House Press, 1987), 52-53.

[6] Albert D. Richardson, *Beyond the Mississippi* (Hartford, CT: American Publishing Company, 1867), 143-144.

[7] Lewis Atherton, *The Cattle Kings* (Bloomington: Indiana University Press, 1961), 154.

[8] George Catlin, *North American Indians* (Philadelphia: Leary, Stuart and Company, 1913), 2:19-20.

[9] John D. Hunter, *Memoirs of a Captivity Among the Indians of North America* (London: Longman, Hurst, Rees, Orme, Brown, and Green, 1824), 146.

[10] Olive K. Dixon, *Life of "Billy" Dixon* (Austin: State House Press, 1987), 52-53.

[11] George Catlin, *North American Indians* (Philadelphia: Leary, Stuart and Company, 1913), 2:19.

[12] Olive K. Dixon, *Life of "Billy" Dixon* (Austin: State House Press, 1987), 52-53.

[13] Donald Worster, *A River Running West: The Life of John Wesley Powell* (New York: Oxford University Press, 2001), 355.

[14] Lauren Brown, *Grasslands* (New York: Alfred A. Knopf, n.d.), 45.

[15] Walter E. Spokesfield, *The History of Wells County, North Dakota, and its Pioneers* (Valley City, ND: n.pub., 1929), 59.

[16] Richard Irving Dodge, *The Plains of the Great West* (New York: G. P. Putnam's Sons, 1877), 78-79.

[17] Ibid., 80-81.

[18] Meriwether Lewis and William Clark, *The Journals of Lewis and Clark*, abridged by Anthony Brandt (Washington: National Geographic Society, 2002), 96.

[19] Marc Simmons, *"The Santa Fe Trail . . . Highway of Commerce,"* in *Trails West,* ed. Gilbert M. Grosvenor, 28 (Washington: National Geographic Society, 1979).

[20] Percival G. Lowe, *Five Years a Dragoon ('49 to '54)* (Kansas City, Missouri: The Franklin Hudson Publishing Co., 1906), 139-140.

[21] Everett Dick, *The Sod-House Frontier 1854-1890* (Lincoln: Johnsen Publishing Company, 1954), 217.

[22] Elizabeth B. Custer, *Tenting on the Plains or General Custer in Kansas and Texas* (New York: Charles L. Webster & Company, 1887), 491-492.

[23] I. A. Lapham, "The Great Fires of 1871 in the Northwest," in *Annual Report of the Chief Signal-Officer to the Secretary of War for the Year 1872,* 187 (Washington: GPO, 1872).

[24] Daniel Fitzgerald, *Ghost Towns of Kansas* (Holton, Kansas; The Gossip Printery, 1979), 2: 107.

[25] Wayne Gard, *The Great Buffalo Hunt* (New York: Alfred A. Knopf, 1959), 288-289.

[26] H. J. Marshall, "Pioneer Days in North Dakota." MS 20053, Small Manuscripts Collection Ms 21000. State Historical Society of North Dakota, Bismarck, ND.

[27] Lewis Nordyke, *Cattle Empire* (New York: William Morrow and Company, 1949), 45.

[28] Ibid., 218.

[29] Ibid., 107.

[30] Ibid., 108.

[31] Olive K. Dixon, *Life of "Billy" Dixon* (Austin: State House Press, 1987), 103-104.

[32] Kirke Mechem, ed., *The Annals of Kansas 1886-1925* (Topeka: Kansas State Historical Society, 1972),1:35.

[33] Daniel Fitzgerald, *Ghost Towns of Kansas* Vol. I (n.p.: privately printed, 1976), 1:142.

[34] Everett Dick, *The Sod-House Frontier 1854-1890* (Lincoln: Johnsen Publishing Company, 1954), 218.

[35] Henry S. Lucas, ed., *Dutch Immigrant Memoirs and Related Writings* (Assen, Netherlands: Van Gorcum & Comp. N.V. - G. A. Hak & Dr. H. J. Prakke, 1955) 2:346.

[36] Everett Dick, *Conquering the Great American Desert* (Lincoln: Nebraska State Historical Society, 1975), 230.

[37] "Trials That Harassed the Settlers," *Hill City* (Kansas) *Times*, May 22, 1980.

[38] Percy Wollaston, *Homesteading* (New York: Penguin Books, 1999), 79.

[39] Douglas Hill, *The Opening of the Canadian West* (New York: The John Day Company, 1967), 218.

[40] Elliott Coues, ed., *New Light on the Early History of the Greater Northwest* (New York: Francis P. Harper, 1897), 1:253-254.

[41] John D. Hunter, *Memoirs of a Captivity Among the Indians of North America* (London: Longman, Hurst, Rees, Orme, Brown, and Green, 1824), 146-147.

[42] David A. Dary, *The Buffalo Book* (Chicago: Swallow Press Inc., 1974), 39.

[43] Wayne Gard, *The Chisholm Trail* (Norman: University of Oklahoma Press, 1984), 126.

[44] Henry D. and Frances T. McCallum, *The Wire That Fenced the West* (Norman: University of Oklahoma Press, 1969), 19-20.

[45] "A Big Fire," *Western Cyclone* (Nicodemus, Kansas), 14 April 1887.

[46] Daniel Fitzgerald, *Ghost Towns of Kansas* Vol. III (Holton, Kansas; Bell Graphics, 1982), 3:360.

[47] [M. Fiske?], A Visit to Texas (1834; reprint, Ann Arbor: University Microfilms, Inc., 1966), 124-125.

[48] I. A. Lapham, "The Great Fires of 1871 in the Northwest," in *Annual Report of the Chief Signal-Officer to the Secretary of War for the Year 1872* (Washington: GPO, 1872), 186-187.

[49] Randolph B. Marcy, *The Prairie Traveler: A Hand-Book for Overland Expeditions* (New York: Harper & Brothers, 1859), 159.

[50] George Catlin, *North American Indians* (1844; reprint, Philadelphia: Leary, Stuart and Company, 1913), 2:19.

[51] I. A. Lapham, "The Great Fires of 1871 in the Northwest." in *Annual Report of the Chief Signal-Officer to the Secretary of War for the Year 1872* (Washington: GPO, 1872), 188.

[52] Lewis Nordyke, *Cattle Empire* (New York: William Morrow and Company, 1949), 145-146.

[53] Ibid., 271.

[54] Cordia Sloan Duke and Joe B. Frantz, *6,000 Miles of Fence* (Austin: University of Texas Press, 1975), 45.

[55] Lewis Nordyke, *Cattle Empire* New York: William Morrow and Company, 1949), 228.

[56] Cordia Sloan Duke and Joe B. Frantz, *6,000 Miles of Fence* (Austin: University of Texas Press, 1975), 47-48.

[57] Ibid., 49.

[58] Ibid., 52.

[59] Randolph B. Marcy, *The Prairie Traveler* (New York: Harper & Brothers, 1859), 160.

[60] Mrs. Orpen, *Memories of the Old Emigrant Days in Kansas, 1862-1865: Also of a Visit to Paris in 1867*, (New York: Harper & Brothers, 1928), 72-73. Mrs. Orpen is the name given on the full title page. Author's full name is Adela Elizabeth Richards Orpen.

[61] Bart McDowell, *The American Cowboy in Life and Legend* (Washington: National Geographic Society, 1972), 109.

[62] Eugene F. Ware, *The Indian War of 1864* (Topeka, Kansas: Crane & Company, 1911), 489.

[63] Ibid., 490.

[64] Eugene F. Ware, *The Indian War of 1864* (1911; reprint, New York: St. Martin's Press, 1960), 471.

[65] George E. Hyde, *Life of George Bent Written from His Letters* (Norman: University of Oklahoma Press, 1983), 177.

[66] Official Records; series 1, vol. 48, part 1 (Powder River Expedition), http://ehistory.osu.edu./uscw/library/or/101/0796.cfm.

[67] "A Big Fire," *Western Cyclone* (Nicodemus, Kansas), 14 April 1887.

Chapter Five

EARTH OF IRON

Drought is one of the most damaging climate-related hazards to impact societies.
　　　　　—Connie A. Woodhouse and Jonathan T. Overpeck,
　　　　　　　　Bulletin of the American Meteorological Society

Jennie Ball was twelve years old when her family moved to a homestead forty miles from Topeka, Kansas. The year was 1879. Like thousands of other settlers, the Ball family looked forward to a new and better life on the prairies and plains.

Immediately after reaching the claim, all of the sunup-to-sundown hard work required to transform their dreams into reality began in earnest. Jennie and her mother prepared meals for the neighbors who came to help build the sod house. Just as soon as the soddie was completed Jennie's father and brother started breaking the prairie and planting a corn crop.

While the men worked in the fields, Jennie and her mother toiled at the myriad of women's tasks required to make a soddie a home. They planted a garden and dreamt of the produce it would provide for the coming winter. Promise lay all about them like the twilight prairie solitude.

Life was good—for awhile.

Seasonal rains failed and drought transformed their prairie paradise into a fiery purgatory where they lingered to expiate the innocent sin of hope. Jennie remembers that "with crops burned up every year, and no money, father and brother went to Phillips County to husk corn. Father was getting a soldier's pension of $20.00 a month. He left that with mother, saying 'I'll be back before the next check comes.'"[1]

The only human to come calling at the Ball doorstep in the following weeks was a child. When the youngster finally stopped crying he said "we are starving, we haven't had any food since Friday night." The boy said his father had left to find work but had become sick and couldn't send any money or food to the family.

Mrs. Ball, feeling certain of her husband's promise to "return before the next check comes," gave most of their remaining food to the boy's family.

That promise, unhappily, wasn't kept. The date for the promised return of Jennie's father and brother came and went with no sign of them, of money, or of food. Day-by-day the mother and daughter watched their remaining meager food supply dwindle. Day after day passed and still the menfolk did not return. Finally word came that Jennie's brother was very ill and couldn't travel. There was no mention made of when the men might return.

Jennie remembered that after every morsel of food was eaten and hunger gnawed at their empty stomachs "Mother went to the post master asking if the pension check had arrived. It had, but the post master refused to give it to mother, saying, 'Mr. Ball might die and it would have to be sent back to Washington.'"

After that Jennie and her mother, like scavenging animals, pawed through the drought-stricken corn for the few immature ears that had set on before the hot winds sucked the life from the stalks. One night they were only able to find three small, hard, wormy ears to feed two humans and one dog. That night as she tried to sleep, Jennie, for the first time in her life, heard her mother crying.[2]

##

The prairies and plains are a land of extremes, constantly ebbing and flowing to a rhythm millions of years in the making. This rhythm isn't understood by humans for man's lives are too brief to become truly one with the land. The best humans can do is react.

Man frequently reacts from ignorance, sometimes from arrogance, but most often from greed. Both the Indians and newcomers discovered that this vast, "empty" expanse of prairies and plains offered much to enrich their lives. Initially these riches seemed without end. From time to time, however, the land's rhythms remind man that these riches are neither without end nor without price.

Early nineteenth century explorers who traveled onto the prairies and plains proclaimed that the land west of the ninety-eighth meridian was desert—unfit for anything other than roaming bands of aborigines, nomads, and society outcasts.

Principal among the explorers who described this land as desert were Lewis and Clark (1803-6), Zebulon Pike (1806), John Bradbury (1811), and Major Stephen H. Long (1819-20).

Long's "Great American Desert" included what would become all or parts of the states of Kansas, Nebraska, Oklahoma, Colorado, Wyoming, Texas, New Mexico, and South Dakota.

Even though Long and his party traversed the prairies and plains from eastern Kansas to the Rocky Mountains, his map isn't specific concerning this desert's boundaries. Most likely he intended only the area lying east of the Rocky Mountains and west of approximately the ninety-eighth meridian to be included in his "Great American Desert."

Long's map included the following notation: "The Great Desert is frequented by roving bands of Indians who have no fixed place of residence but roam from place to place in search of game." Furthermore he declared the region "wholly unfit for cultivation and uninhabitable for those dependent on agriculture."

Considering recent research into historical droughts, it is unfair to judge Long harshly for he and his expedition endured first hand "the effects of a drought more severe than the Dust Bowl, and such occurrences are relatively common on the Plains."[3]

In subsequent years cartographers and writers located this desert much as Long did concerning east and west boundaries. The north and south limits varied from the Canadian border to the Rio Grande or various latitudes in between.

The invisible line that marks the eastern boundary of the desert was in reality, and in the minds of people, extremely fluid. Where it fell depended on Mother Nature's generosity with yearly rainfall, and where promoters felt they could entice newcomers to settle.

Twenty inches of rain annually is considered the minimum necessary for successful farming. The 100th meridian is a general, flexuous line of demarcation between twenty inches or more rainfall east of this line to twenty inches or less west of this line. It also varies from sub-humid to semi-arid along the 100th meridian.

How much is semi-arid "varies from year to year due to the large variability of the precipitation in this region. Thus, droughts are a recurrent feature of the climate of the Great Plains."[4]

Just as we are today, humans living in the nineteenth century were dependent upon rain in due season for their daily bread; the entire commerce of agriculture is a rain-based business. Irrigation, then and now, made some short term alteration to this dependency on rainfall.

Yet, the big reality across the prairies and plains remained constant: Indians lived and died according to the rainfall, newcomers lived and died according to the rainfall, and every form of prosperity for both groups rose or fell according to the rainfall. When the rains failed, drought brought the dying and failing.

Viewed in comparison, droughts are especially sinister; tornadoes kill and injure in a matter of minutes, hurricanes in a matter of hours, floods and blizzards in a matter of days but drought can linger and kill for years—even decades.

Taking into account that most of the earth's surface is covered with water, it seems inexplicable that there could ever be a shortage of water. Lyall Watson in his book, *Heaven's Breath*, offers some clarification when he points out that

> at any one time, 97 per cent of all water on Earth is in the oceans and most of the remainder is locked up in the ice sheets and glaciers on land. A mere 0.0001 per cent is held in the atmosphere, sufficient in itself for only ten days' rain. But there is a constant influx of moisture into the air as a result of evaporation from both land and sea. This moisture is released when air expands or cools sufficiently to allow condensation to take place, producing a mean annual global rainfall of eighty-six centimetres [33.858 inches]. Local

Drawing of the Flory Locust Machine for a
government publication authored by C. V. Riley

Rocky Mountain Locust swarms caused so many problems that this horse-propelled grasshopper/locust exterminator was approved by the Federal Commissioner of Agriculture.

evaporation is, however, seldom the major source of local precipitation. For example, only 6 per cent of all rain that falls in Arizona originates in that state. The rest is carried there by wind, mainly from the sea.[5]

Drought expert Norman J. Rosenberg states this dilemma, as it applies to the prairies and plains, by saying that "in western Nebraska, as in the western portion of most of the Great Plains, the atmospheric demand for water vapor far exceeds the amount of water available through precipitation . . . the Great Plains is a region of deficit water supply."[6]

Defining deficit water supply and drought proves difficult because "there is no universally applicable definition of drought." Writing to that point, Richard E. Felch, states that "drought is a meteorological phenomenon—an extended period of time with inadequate precipitation."

Carrying the definition further he cautions that "it is important to distinguish the concept of drought from the concept of aridity. Aridity is usually defined as low average rainfall or available water, and it is a permanent climatic feature of the region. Drought, on the other hand, is a temporary feature of the climate. In the context of variability, drought occurs only when rainfall deviates appreciably below normal."[7]

Humans have imposed the concept of drought on those years and those geographical regions that fail to live up to their expectations and desires. The settlement of marginal agricultural land and the introduction of humans, plants, and animals ill suited to the environment are quickly and adversely affected when the perceived normal amount of moisture is lacking.

Humans, therefore, classify drought as a negative occurrence in direct proportion to the effect it has on the ability of people to live and prosper in the affected region. Hence, drought is, in many respects, a human invention to explain what is entirely normal to Mother Nature.

Another human invention, and in all likelihood the greatest hoax of the nineteenth century, was the theory that "rain follows the plow." In hindsight it was all just hopeful thinking and promotional hype bolstered by very bad science.

Nonetheless, the belief that rain follows the plow had a "scientific" explanation provided by Samuel Aughey, "PH.D., LL.D.," who explained that

> it is the great increase in absorptive power of the soil, wrought by cultivation, that has caused, and continues to cause an increasing rainfall in the state.
>
> . . . For vast ages the prairies have been pelted by the elements and trodden by millions of buffalo and other wild animals, until the naturally rich soil became as compact as a floor. When rain falls on a primitive soil of this character, the greater part runs off into the canyons, creeks and rivers . . . After the soil is broken, the rain as it falls is absorbed by the soil like a huge sponge. The soil gives this absorbed moisture slowly back to the atmosphere by evaporation. Thus year by year as cultivation of the soil is extended, more of the rain that falls is absorbed and retained to be given off by evaporation, or to produce springs. This, of course, must give increasing moisture and rainfall.[8]

Other writers such as Mrs. M. A. Humphrey of Junction City, Kansas, were almost euphoric in their prose depicting just how fast Mother Nature was back peddling before the plow. "And so cheerfully has Mother Nature responded to the touch of the wand of labor, that our earliest planters now sit in the shade of their own vines and trees, and their children sport beneath the wide-spreading branches thereof. To the former the lone barren prairie is a memory, to the latter a myth. Twenty miles a year, it is said, we are gaining upon and wiping out the Great American Desert."[9]

This "scientific evidence" confirmed the newcomers' feelings that God was leading them into the promised land. In fact, this belief was almost hard-wired into their psyche. John L. Allen, writing in the *Great Plains Quarterly*, submits that

> from earliest colonial times, Europeans and Europeans-become-Americans had seen the land of the Atlantic seaboard settlements as a New World Garden, long kept virgin to redress the over cultivation of the Old World. It was easy to extend this myth beyond the Mississippi and to view the plains, like the seaboard of earlier times, as a land of promise, an Eden of vacant and fertile land held back by the Creator until it was needed by his chosen people.[10]

To those anxious to capitalize on this promise it began to appear that God was squarely on their side. By the middle of the nineteenth century not only was the "Great American Desert" theory getting very thin, from time to time it disappeared completely from the minds of railroad promoters, land speculators, and newcomer farmers.

During the post-Civil War westward expansion, the desert belief was replaced by an image that was much easier to profit from: a trans-Mississippi Garden of Eden. Amber waves of grain . . . across the fruited plains. This new vision dovetailed nicely into the emerging gospel of Manifest Destiny that began to take root in the 1840s as Americans turned longing eyes toward the Pacific coast.

Railroad promoters and eastern newspapers painted a glowing picture of the prairies and plains as unlimited flower gardens and "flour fields." They enticed immigrants by promising them land that was a piece of heaven-on-earth. As it turned out, sometimes it more closely resembled a piece of hell-on-earth.

The 1930s Dust Bowl and Okie Exodus are the benchmarks by which most Americans judge drought. Surprisingly, there is compelling evidence that the 1930's were matched, if not bested, by at least three different droughts during the nineteenth century.

Tree-ring analyses in Nebraska reveal several nineteenth century droughts in the desert-turned-garden. The earliest began in 1798 and lasted until 1803; a second began in 1822 and lasted for eleven years through 1832; this was followed by a nine year dry spell commencing in 1858 and ending in 1866; and the last drought period in the nineteenth century lasted for twelve years. It began in 1884 and kept the region dry and dusty through 1895.[11]

After studying the data,

> Many of the tree-ring reconstructions suggest that the droughts of the 1930s and 1950s have been equaled or, in some regions, surpassed by droughts in the past several centuries. This is illustrated . . . for grid points in eastern Montana, central Kansas, and north-central Texas . . . reconstructed annual precipitation for four regions flanking the Great Plains (centered in Iowa, Oklahoma, eastern Wyoming, and eastern Montana). Although they found the individual years of 1934, 1936, and 1939 to be among the driest 10 of 278 years investigated (1700-1977), they found several periods of widespread prolonged drought (3-10 years) that equaled or surpassed the 1930s drought in intensity and duration: the late 1750s, early 1820s, early 1860s and 1890s.[12]

##

It wasn't an empty land that newcomers "discovered" between the Mississippi River and the Rocky Mountains. This land was home to many thousands of Indians whose history spans scores, centuries, or millennia of past time. These Indians, dwelling alongside the grassland's flora and fauna, had worked out an intricate weave of living and dying that was well suited to the prairies and plains.

But to most newcomers it was mostly empty land, wilderness land, free land, unproductive land waiting to be transformed into communities and societies that mirrored the communities and societies they had left behind. They were trappers, traders, half-breeds, ranchers, dirt grubbers, city builders, industrialists, miners, dreamers and schemers.

All, it seems, were energized by unbounded greed marching under the guidon of the Old Testament's "God's chosen people" and "the right of riches" set to the tune of Manifest Destiny.

Actually this land was home to the Sioux, Arapaho, Cheyenne, Arikara, Crow, Mandan, Omaha, Ponca, Iowa, Kiowa, Kiowa Apache, Comanche, Pawnee, Oto, Missouri, Shawnee, Sauk, Fox, Potawatomi, Cherokee, Choctaw, Chickasaw, Seminole, Kickapoo, Delaware, Wyandot, Wea, Piankashaw, Peoria, Kashaskia, Miami, Quapaw, Seneca, Osage, Kansa, Creek, Plains Apache, and Wichita Indians. Some of these tribes were living on the prairies and plains by choice; others had been shoved there by force.

Regardless, it was not an empty land.

Drought did impact the Plains Indians, but unlike the newcomers' lifestyle of ownership and permanent residences, the Indians' lifestyle was structured so they could move to an area not suffering from drought. These drought-induced moves were compulsory to find graze for the horse herds, a usable water supply, and game that had fled the drought-stricken region.

This was a workable lifestyle for the Plains Indians until newcomers altered the equation. As the newcomers pushed ever westward from the Atlantic seaboard the Indian tribes were forced to retreat ever westward. When these eastern tribes began to spill across the Mississippi river they set foot on land that was an essential refuge for the buffalo and the plains tribes during drought years.

These eastern tribes were backed by newcomer "laws" and by firearms. The severe droughts of the 1850s were "a total disruption of the southern Plains trade system" and disrupted "the migration of Plains tribes east as they escaped the drought."[13]

The Plains Indians who were now prevented from following their food supply to greener pastures were faced with two possibilities. They could remain on the withered plains and starve to death quietly or they could raid newcomers and other Indian tribes to obtain the food necessary for survival.

In 1855 grasshoppers joined with drought to plunge the majority of the southern Plains Indians into desperate straits. "In the Choctaw Nation, many were faced with famine and turned to stealing from their more wealthy neighbors for sustenance."

Feed for animals dwindled as corn and other feed crops failed. In desperation, the hungry humans and animals consumed the seed supplies leaving nothing to plant for next year's crop.

In 1857 the Quapaw and Osage Indians at the Neosho Agency in southeastern Kansas Territory were suffering from low crop yields and an unsuccessful buffalo hunt. The Osage lost most of their horse herd to thieves and "by early September, men from the tribe were so desperate that they sold the few remaining horses they had kept from being stolen at reduced rates in order to purchase food to feed their children."[14]

Conditions weren't any better further west along the Arkansas River. A reserve, called Point of Rocks, was set aside for the southern Cheyenne and Arapaho Indians. This reserve was bordered on the south by the Arkansas River, on the west by the Front Range of the Rocky Mountains, and the east side of the triangle was formed by Sand Creek.

Here the Indians had little choice but to give Uncle Sam and farming a try, but unfortunately, the promised farming implements and assistance, not to mention food, was too little and too late.

The ill-administered reserve policy coupled with the drought caused an officer at Fort Lyon to write in September 1863 that Indians "must depend upon the Government and the friendship of the whites in a great measure for their support, especially the coming winter, as the buffalo have all left their accustomed ranges, owing to the unprecedented drought upon the Arkansas, the river being perfectly dry for 400 miles."

The same letter continued, "They [Indians] are very destitute, and from all reports, are suffering terribly from disease and hunger." The commanding officer at Fort Lyon, Colorado, Major Scott J. Anthony, closed his report by repeating "The Indians are all very destitute this season, and the Government will be compelled to subsist them to a great extent, or allow them to starve to death, which would probably be much the easiest way of disposing of them."[15]

At this time the future held little promise for Plains Indians. They were literally on a shrinking island of grass between the Platte and the Arkansas rivers and surrounded by ever-increasing numbers of newcomers. It would have been difficult to continue their way of life had the rains been generous. Perhaps, still, if the rains had come and the newcomers' diseases had not, another generation of Indians could have lived the hunter-warrior way of life.

Drought made this improbable.

Newcomers made it impossible

During the first three decades of the nineteenth century curiosity, national security, and trade with the Indians comprised the newcomers' interest in the prairies and plains. Then in the 1840s the nation's attention shifted to the west coast and the intoxicating yellow-dust fever. Now the prairies and plains became a vexing region newcomers were forced to cross on their pilgrimage to Oregon and California.

In 1859 the new gold rush to the Rocky Mountains was in full stride. Once again the prairies and plains were a bothersome, loathsome piece of real estate that must be crossed. Undeterred, hundreds of thousands of hopeful and determined newcomers, plus prodigious herds of their livestock, stomped across the land rutting the prairie, consuming the timber, and grazing the grass to ruin.

The northern route was the Oregon-California Trail that paralleled the Platte River; the southern route was the Santa Fe Trail that paralleled the Arkansas River. The Republican and Smoky Hill rivers also had their trails—all headed west across the homeland of the Plains Indians.

But not all newcomers were through-travelers for some chose to establish road ranches, trading posts, freight stations, and homes along these routes. Thus were added many additional people and animals needing to be sustained within the delicate weave of Plains Indians and the grassland's flora and fauna.

Even with this added burden the fabric could have perhaps held together if the rains had been generous after the 1840s. Alas, it was not to be; the rains stopped and the fabric began to fray and unravel. Recurring droughts then played a huge role in reweaving the colorful tapestry of the West.

##

The logo of the "Dirty Thirties" had to be the rolling clouds of dust that piled drifts to the rooftops of abandoned farm buildings. Granted, drought was a root cause of duststorms but these storms constitute the most visual evidence of a drought. There are few, if any, images of the nineteenth century dust bowls but as the records show, these duststorms were equal to, or worse than, the Dirty Thirties even though the prairie had never been broken.

As has been previously noted, tree-ring analyses identified three major drought periods during the nineteenth century. Other records show that droughts weren't limited to these three periods but occurred during additional years with equally disastrous results.

The first major drought period was identified as beginning in 1822 and lasting for eleven years through 1832. Early records of droughts on the prairies and plains substantiate the findings.

Dry years in Texas were noted very early when "Stephen F. Austin's first colonists were hurt by drought. In 1822 their initial food crop of corn died from lack of moisture."[16]

Isaac McCoy was an ordained Baptist minister and missionary who served among the Indian tribes in Michigan and Indiana. He was one of the first whites to advocate the removal of Eastern Indian tribes to unoccupied (by newcomers) lands in the West. The bill for removal of Eastern tribes to the country west of the Mississippi River was approved by the U.S. Congress on May 28, 1830. On 3 June 1830, McCoy was directed by the Secretary of War to survey "lands which had

Harper's Weekly, *1874*
Rocky Mountain Locust swarm around a stalled train in this *Harper's Weekly* illustration. The location was eastern Nebraska. Insects crushed under the drive wheels created a "grease" that prevented traction. Crews had to clean and sand the tracks before the locomotive could move.

been assigned by treaty to the Delawares." He departed to fulfill this commission on 16 August 1830, and returned to his family after being "absent One hundred and two days."

His journal repeatedly documents drought conditions the party encountered during their journey from Cantonment Leavenworth to near the present-day town of Cawker City, Kansas, approximately 210 miles to the west. McCoy also noted that prairie fires destroyed any remaining plant cover which led to erosion of the exposed topsoil.

According to McCoy's journal, the party "encamped on a small branch of Stranger [Creek], 26 miles from the garrison on Saturday, October 9." The garrison he mentioned is Fort Leavenworth which at the time was referred to as Cantonment Leavenworth. The diary entry also noted that "Thus far the country about the garrison and this way is very well supplied with springs of water, even at this time of great drought."

When they reached Soldier Creek, north of present-day Topeka, Kansas, on 14 October, he noted that "Grass for our horses, is every day becoming more scarce. The season is remarkably dry."[17]

Eolian activities, or dust storms, were not invented for, nor were they an exclusive phenomenon of, the 1930s Dust Bowl. As McCoy discovered, "the Great Plains is the windiest region of the country—open as it is to the free sweep of air masses from north and south." Consequently "wind erosion has been a serious problem on the Plains, probably from times well before settlement."[18]

McCoy and his survey crew repeatedly endured annoying dust storms as they worked their way west. On 18 October 1830, McCoy wrote that they "Had a little rain last night-the country is exceedingly parched with drought . . . the ashes from the recently burned prairies, and the dust and sand raised so by the wind that it annoyed us much . . . the wind blew incessantly and excessively severe."

The drought and burned prairie was beginning to take a heavy toll on the horses by 28 October when McCoy wrote in his journal that they couldn't continue until some graze was found for the horses.

Upon reaching the Republican River and Coperas Creek they found a "little green though coarse & hard, grass that had escaped the destruction occasioned by the great drought, and the ravages of the fire."

By 5 November they were 150 miles west of Fort Leavenworth when a sudden wind swept down on the party. McCoy wrote that "it was not three minutes after I had first discovered its approach, before the sun was concealed, and the darkness so great, that I could not distinguish objects more than three or four times the length of my horse. The dust, sand, & ashes, were so dense that one appeared in danger of suffocation. The wind driving into ones eyes seemed like destroying them."[19]

The second nineteenth century prairies and plains "bake out" was a nine year dry spell commencing in 1858 and ending in 1866. By 1860 the drought had deepened and that year stands as one of the driest in recorded history on the prairies and plains. Historical accounts often speak of 1860 as "the year of famine."[20]

Lettie Little Pabst's writings of her family's experiences in Lyon County, Kansas, illustrates how quickly life and fortunes could change in the Garden of Eden. "If 1859 was a bountiful year, 1860 was the opposite. That was the year of the most terrible drought. Nothing was raised. Only starvation lay ahead. More than a year passed and there was no rain in Lyon County."[21]

As it turned out it wasn't just one year of drought but years with little or no rain. "Crop production first plummeted when troops of local farmers took off for the gold fields, the ugly droughts of 1860 and 1861 devastated much of the eastern plains. As many as 30,000 stricken farmers . . . fled the area."[22]

This widespread drought was felt further west on the High Plains as a brief article in the *Lawrence (Kansas) Republican*, 30 August 1860, reported that "The drough on the Plains has had the effect of driving the buffalo eastward toward the settlements, much earlier than usual this season. They are reported quite plenty upon the east bank of the Republican, and in fine condition."

As the drought deepened dust, more dust, and most dust became unavoidable and nearly unbearable. In an address prepared by G. W. Martin, probably about 1906, but not published, he described a dust storm which he dated 11 July 1860.

> The year 1860, known as the great drought and famine year, was quite remarkable for these hot winds. At Topeka, July 11th of that year, the thermometer at 11 a.m. stood at 85 degrees, when a heavy dust cloud came from the south with great force. The air was so filled with exceedingly fine dust that a person could scarcely be seen one hundred yards. At 1 p.m. the thermometer stood at 112 degrees in Topeka; at Fort Scott 115; and at Fort Riley about the same as at Topeka. Domestic fowls and animals suffered terribly, and in some places many perished. Business in some sections was entirely suspended for from five to six hours.[23]

This dust storm made copy in newspapers throughout the region. Datelined 11 July 1860, Oskaloosa, Kansas, *The Independent* carried this news item: "On Monday afternoon last this region of Kansas was visited by so extraordinary a wind storm as to seem out of the course of nature, except on the burning deserts of Africa . . . The leaves of plants were literally parched up and killed, as if by a heavy frost."

Three long years later, according to the Leavenworth, Kansas, *Daily Times* 24 October 1863, it was still dry and dusty in Nebraska. Along the South Platte River "they had been no rain for almost a year and clouds of dust and sand arise from what was once the bed of the river."

In November things were even worse along the Platte River, "The present season is said to be the dryest ever known on the plains. Owing to the drying up of the Platte River and its tributaries, large numbers of stock have died for the want of water above Fort Kearney." So said the Leavenworth, *Daily Times*, 25 November 1863.

Dust storms were an annoying aggravation throughout this dry spell and provided newspapers with plenty of grist for the media mill. It's inconceivable that the newspapers felt any local person needed to be informed of the dust storms.

Drought and wind continued through the fall of 1864 but in the spring of 1865 the tide began to turn and good spring rains were reported over much of eastern Kansas.

Years with, what newcomers called, normal precipitation followed until 1870 when once again the prairies and plains entered into a dry cycle. These years of drought, for whatever reasons, didn't show up in the tree-ring analysis. Nevertheless it was a drought. James C. Malin (1893-1963), past professor of history at the University of Kansas, Lawrence, wrote that "The year 1873 opened another period of prolonged severe drought, eight years of it, with only slight interruptions."[24]

On 22 November 1873, the Junction City, Kansas, *Union* reported that,

> Monday was the big prairie fire day all over the country. At Hays City the gale got up what is called in that region a 'sand storm,' rendering it almost impossible to discern objects, and while this was at its h[e]ight, a prairie fire made for the town . . . It was with the greatest difficulty that the people in face of the drifting, blinding sand, managed to keep the fire from entering and sweeping away the town.

National Oceanic and Atmosphereic Administration/
Department of Commerce, George E. Marsh album

Research into nineteenth century droughts indicates the dust storms of that era were just as impressive as this one photographed in Texas during the 1930s. Photos of nineteenth century storms are rare or nonexistant.

Newspaper articles and personal diaries suggest that 1874 was worse than 1860. Denver was experiencing much the same as eastern Kansas, and the *Monthly Weather Review*, commenting on the first months of 1879 reported "the most severe drought on record in the vicinity of Uvalde, Texas, where sheep and goats were dying of starvation and cold. In April, Dallas, Texas, reported the most severe drought in thirty years and three weeks of high, dry winds."[25]

Turning once again to Malin's articles, he writes that the "outstanding dust storm of March 1880, and probably of the whole year, or period, was that of 26-27 March, appearing in the Western plains 26 March and reaching the Mississippi river 27 March."

"Most violent wind storm for many years, dust gathered in drifts from 1 to 2 1/2 feet in depth" was reported at Howard, Nebraska, on the 27th.

The March 1880, issue of the *Monthly Weather Review* emphasized just how wide spread the "dust bowl" was by reporting wind and sand storms in Las Cruces, New Mexico; Omaha, Nebraska; Ft. Gibson, Indian Territory; Ft. Davis,

Texas; St. Louis, Missouri; Keokuk, Davenport, and Dubuque, Iowa; Milwaukee, Wisconsin; Knoxville, Tennessee; Louisville, Illinois; Morristown, Dakota Territory; Ashley, Missouri; Pierce City, Missouri; Geneva Nebraska; Wellington, Cedar Vale, and Lawrence, Kansas; and Ringgold, Ohio.

Judging from copy published in the 1 April 1880 issue of the *Saline County (Kansas) Journal)* conditions weren't improving very fast. The writer reported "Another windy, dusty, trying, headache-producing, vexatious, disgusting, terrific, upsetting, tearing, rearing, careening, bumping, sign-lifting, chimney absorbing, lung slaying, garment destroying, eye blinding, and rip-roaring storms, last Monday."

The attitude of residents subjected to these years of drought and wind were beginning to become a bit chaffed and raw but the weary folk tried hard to hold onto their humor. This, from *The Wichita (Kansas) City Eagle*, 15 April 1880, gives a hint of the stress that was lurking just beneath the humor.

> If there is a man, woman or child in Sedgwick county Kansas whose eyes are not filled with dust and their minds with disgust, he, she, or it must be an idiot or awful pious. From everlasting to everlasting this wind for a week has just sat down on its hind legs and howled and screeched and snorted until you couldn't tell your grandfather from a jackass rabbit . . . As for our poor women, weighted down with bar lead and trace-chains as their skirts are, their only protection from rude gaze is the dust, which fills up the eyes of the men so that they can't see a rod further than a blind mule.

An inkling of just how bad some people believed things had gotten for the livestock industry is illustrated by a letter from Hugo, in eastern Colorado, and published in the *Ellsworth (Kansas) Reporter*, 29 April 1880, "Kansas people would have us believe that the Great American Desert spoken of by geographers is a mythe but I am fully convinced of its existence and I think if any one who would stop here for a week would never doubt of its existence."[26]

The last drought to scorch the prairies and plains prior to the close of the century lasted for twelve years. It began in 1884 and kept the region dry and dusty through 1895.

The years 1885 to 1887 were extremely dry in some parts of Texas. "In May, the Colorado River went dry near Brady in McCulloch County, Texas." And "Ranchers in Baylor, Throckmorton, Archer, and Young counties of Texas were so frantic to find grass and water for their cattle that they simply turned the animals loose, allowing them to follow rivers and creeks down stream."

This caused considerable friction as "thirty thousand head of starved and thirsting stock began encroaching on the water supply and fields of Jack and Wise counties."

Once again the *Monthly Weather Review* provides a chronicle of drought conditions across the region. The following account is from July 1886.

> During July a very disastrous drought prevailed over Iowa, Illinois, Dakota, and Minnesota, as well as over the greater part of Wisconsin, Nebraska, Kansas and Texas. The dry weather commenced in May, and during June and July had become a severe drought, inflicting large losses on grain-growing interests in the Northwest and the cattlemen in Texas. During the first six days of the month very high temperatures occurred in the northern districts, especially in Dakota on the 6th, which added materially to the injurious effects of the dry weather.[27]

Commenting on the drought that was parching the nation's heartland during the last half of the 1880s, Malin wrote that the

> whole Trans-Mississippi West . . . reached its most extreme excesses, and the collapse in various degrees was in evidence before the end of the year. In historical perspective, it is evident that the turn occurred in 1886. The mute evidence of this was to be found in the cornerstones of many stone buildings bearing the date 1887 in towns west of the 100th meridian

in Kansas. Many buildings begun in 1887 stood for years unfinished, the stone finally being used for other purposes. Beginning in late 1886 the principal weather news was intense and prolonged drought.[28]

Perhaps no record of dust storms and wind erosion is more impressive than the report found in the *Monthly Weather Review* for January 1885. "This process of raising great clouds of dust, carrying them south and east and depositing the dust finally, either by reason of its own weight or in connection with rain and snow, is a process that must have begun in Montana on the 10th to be concluded in Ohio, Kentucky, Louisiana, and Texas on the 12th and 13th."[29]

Eolian activity and drought did not confine its devastation to Texas, Indian Territory, Kansas, and Nebraska but also wreaked havoc on the livestock industry in Montana. The timing couldn't have been worse; the drought came on the heels of the Big Die-Up. Granville Stuart, in his autobiography, wrote that

> The drouth continued and in July [1887] the short grass was dry and parched, streams and water holes drying up; but in spite of the drouth and short grass, cattle were being brought in from Washington and Oregon and the herds from the south were coming in undiminishing numbers and they were all thrown on the already over-stocked ranges of Montana.
> Added to the drouth was unprecedented heat. The thermometer stood at one hundred to one hundred and ten degrees in the shade for days at a time and then would come hot winds that licked up every drop of moisture and shriveled the grass.[30]

At Fort Maginnis, Montana Territory, in May 1887, events echoed Stuart's recollections where "at 9 p. m. of the 7th the air was filled with dense clouds of sand, rendering it almost impossible to face the wind. At 4 p. m. of the 10th the wind was blowing a gale and the air became so densely filled with sand that the sun appeared like a large ball."[31]

National Oceanic and Atmosphereic Administration/
Department of Commerce, George E. Marsh album

Dust storms buried farms and equipment, killed livestock and caused human death and misery during the Dust Bowl years. This image was made in the 1930s but would also have been representative of several droughts in the 1800s.

Out west of the 100th meridian even sunflowers and rattlesnakes have a devil of a time making a living. On this harsh range the tough old Texas Longhorns eat sunflowers and stomp rattlesnakes. But during these dry years, even the Longhorns succumbed to drought for they "could not rustle where there was nothing to rustle . . . at times they simply starved to death on their native ranges, the stomachs and intestines of some that died being found half-stuffed with sand and dirt they had taken in while chewing on stubble."[32]

Down south, many a Texas homesteader survived the drought of 1887 by "selling bones. Cattle died and their bones bleached with those of the buffalo. This new business was short lived, but many families were enabled to hold onto land they had bought by hauling bones to shipping points which they sold for enough money to buy food so they could hold on a little longer. Many would have literally starved to death with their cattle had there been no railroads crossing the plains of Texas."[33]

197

Elmer McCollum, in his autobiography, remembers the 1892 drought in Kansas.

> During the summer following my thirteenth birthday there was severe drought in our area. Our two ponds went dry, and the well at the house sank to a level of about two feet of water, which afforded only enough for household use . . . Fortunately we had a well in a low place in our south pasture that continued to supply water . . . Our neighbors were forced to drive cattle and horses to the river, some over a distance of three miles. One woman to the north of us drove her cows to the river three miles away, to prevent their dying of thirst . . .
>
> Since the pastures dried up, the cattle were starving and became so weak they could make the six-mile round-trip but three or four times a week.[34]

Four highly respected dictionaries which were consulted fail or refuse to recognize the word "dustfall." Rainfall and snowfall, however, are given respectful treatment; perhaps the compilers can be forgiven since one must experience drought to appreciate dustfall's reality.

According to the *Monthly Weather Review* the "dustfall" across Missouri in February 1895 was a major event.

"During the prevalence of the high northwesterly winds on the 6th and 7th, a considerable quantity of dust or fine black sand was deposited over the southwestern portion of the State, and as the ground for many miles to the westward was covered with sleet and snow to a considerable depth, it is believed that this dust was brought by the wind from the prairies of Kansas and Nebraska."[35]

The *Monthly Weather Review* reported that on 15 April [1895] "a terrible storm of sand and rain afflicted southern and western Kansas, Oklahoma, and the Panhandle of Texas. Egyptian darkness is said to have prevailed in western Oklahoma and the Panhandle. Showers of mud fell in Oklahoma, severe lightning occurred, and [?] were badly damaged. The number of cattle killed is extimated at 5,000, and a score of these were smothered. Drifts of sand 6 feet deep were reported along the railroad tracks in western Kansas."[36]

The *Johnson City (Kansas) Journal* issue of 13 April 1895, predicted that "Unless it rains soon many more [livestock] will perish, as the grass is so completely covered with the mud the stock can not eat it."

A single day in July 1895 removed all hope of harvesting a crop for the season in Nebraska. During the night of the 25th the south wind began to blow and by daybreak was howling a full gale across the plains. The temperature rose almost as steadily as the wind and by noon had topped the century mark. Omaha recorded a record-setting 106 degrees that afternoon.

"In that awful holocaust corn blades shriveled in the blast like grass in an oven. Nebraska farmers stood helpless while their harvest was swept away by the relentless breath of the devastating simoon. All remaining hopes for the season dissipated in a single day."[37]

##

"The wilderness and the solitary place shall be glad for them; and the desert shall rejoice, and blossom as the rose." So wrote the prophet Isaiah. Seeing the desert transformed into a garden paradise is a very, very old dream.

Water, everyone agrees, is the key.

So when Mother Nature altered her routine, or became bored with following the plow, man believed he could change the old gal's mind.

Newcomers to the prairies and plains had a long history of rainmaking experience to draw upon. "As long ago as the time of Plutarch it was 'a matter of current observation that unusually heavy rains fall after great battles,' and it is not impossible, according to the theory of the commingling of air currents, that such rains might have been produced by the great battles of ancient times."[38]

Napoleon shored up the theory when he confirmed that rain came on the heels of cannonading. Furthermore, veterans of both the Civil War and the Mexican War also avowed that rain followed battles in which heavy and prolonged artillery fire was present.

And, if desperate people needed further proof:

Senator Stanford, one of the builders of the Central Pacific Railway, informed me [Senator C. B. Farwell, of Illinois] lately that he was compelled to do a great deal of blasting through a part of the conuntry where rain had never been known to fall in any useful quantities and where it has never rained since, and that during the period of the blasting, which was nearly a year, it rained every day.[39]

It's not surprising then, when the rains failed and the dust blew, it brought rainmakers from as far away as Australia rushing to the drought-stricken prairies and plains. They made heaven and earth tremble with charges on the ground and charges carried aloft by balloons. Hour after hour the barrage continued and occasionally rain did follow.

Disappointingly, despite a few modest successes, the droughts continued unabated while the rainmakers departed with their fee and the farmers just departed—if they could.

Indians, too, had their rainmakers who pleaded with the spirits for rain when the grass browned and the dust blew. In 1832 artist George Catlin was among the Mandan Indians of the upper Missouri where he was privy to the rituals of such rainmakers.

Catlin records "two facts" that he wishes his readers to understand regarding these rainmakers.

"The first is, that when the Mandans undertake to make it rain, *they never fail to succeed*, for their ceremonies never stop until rain begins to fall. The second is equally true, and is this:—that he who has once *made it rain* never attempts it again; his medicine is undoubted."[40]

During the drought in the 1890s when the ground baked and sizzled out in the Nebraska Panhandle, back in eastern Nebraska "a Pawnee Indian promised a shower for ten dollars, a soaking rain for twenty. Someone gave him a jug of whiskey and the hail pounded the grass into the ground. It's a good story, told not without envy."[41] Drought sufferers were desperate enough to risk getting "hard water" over getting no water.

##

Porter D. Terry was a New York real estate speculator. Considering his profession, it isn't surprising that once promoters had transformed the Great American Desert into a veritable garden paradise, he was bitten by the frontier bug. Here was an opportunity for great financial gain and a chance to gain lasting fame. Terry resolved to build a town that would proudly bear his name for generations to come.

Thus inspired, Terry headed west in 1885 with considerable investment capital, tons of ambition, and boundless dreams. The region Terry chose for his embryonic metropolis of the plains was southwestern Kansas. Here in Finney County, about halfway between Garden City and Scott City, Terryton, Kansas, became a reality.

Once the town was on the map, rumor soon implied that several railroads would lay track to, and through Terryton. With the future practically assured, the new settlement experienced a boom as steam power promised to replace horsepower.

Within two years the town could boast of a grocery store, a real estate office, a livestock exchange, a general store, a hotel, a drug store, a livery stable, a lumber yard, and a newspaper office.

Until the rails actually reached Terryton, a stage station was located at the town to provide fresh teams for the stagecoaches that ran between Garden City and Scott City. The stage line was run by "Cannonball" Green a colorful character renowned for the speed of his coaches between frontier settlements.[42]

Terryton boasted of a superb baseball team and a big game was scheduled there almost every Saturday afternoon during the summer months. Just about everyone in the trade area turned out to cheer for their favorite teams and shop in Terryton.

Little by little the surrounding area attracted more newcomers who homesteaded on the seemingly endless plains where the prairie stretched unmarred to the distant horizon. Certain individuals found the unlimited space and vigorous climate nourishing to the body and soul.

Doctor Laban H. Johnson was a Yale educated physician who had practiced medicine in New York City for twenty-two years until he was suddenly struck blind while walking down Broadway. "A specialist whom he consulted recommended that he go west 'to the wide open spaces' for his health."[43]

It is feasible that both New Yorkers, Terry and Doctor Johnson, were acquaintances because Terry sold Doctor Johnson some land that lay about a half mile north of Terryton. Here the doctor had a twenty-two-room house built that eventually became known as the "Old Kentucky Home" or "The Castle on the Prairie" where he entertained many friends and colleagues from New York.

With a steady stream of wealthy easterners as potential investors, Terryton and community appeared as healthy and hearty as an eight-foot-tall Kansas sunflower.

##

"'We are the army of the great God,' said a locust, addressing Mohammed; 'we produce ninety-nine eggs; if the hundred were completed we should consume the whole earth, and all that is in it.'"[44]

Eastern myth? Yes.

Figurative? Yes.

Exaggeration? Perhaps not.

In 1877 Charles V. Riley, State Entomologist of Missouri and chief of the U.S. Entomological Commission, wrote in his treatise on the "Rocky Mountain Locust or so-called Grasshopper" that "no insect has ever occupied a larger share of public attention in North America, or more injuriously affected our greatest national interest, than the subject of this treatise. Especially during the past four years has it brought ruin and destitution to thousands of our Western farmers, and it constitutes to-day the greatest obstacle to the settlement of much of the fertile country between the Mississippi and the Rocky Mountains."[45]

The Rocky Mountain Locust is a species of grasshopper now considered extinct. These were the insects that comprised the huge swarms that converged on the prairies and plains during the nineteenth century. In fact, during that century, the Rocky Mountain Locust grabbed the attention of just about everyone between the Mississippi River and the Rocky Mountains. This was especially true for the state and territorial governors who were being besieged with requests for aid to the stricken regions.

The governor of Minnesota requested a special study of these insects when his state began suffering plagues of Biblical proportions. The 1876 governor's report began by stating that "at the present day it becomes necessary to know more . . . of an insect which has so seriously affected the welfare of some portion or other of the territory east of the Rocky Mountains almost every year for the last twelve years."

Actually, as the report goes on to show, grasshoppers had been a concern for more than the past twelve years and how frequent and how widely spread these ravages have been during the last half-century, is shown by the following list of times and places at which they occurred:

1818-19—Red River Settlement and Northwestern Minnesota.
1820—Western Missouri.
1845 and 1849—Texas.
1856—In diminished numbers in parts of Colorado, Utah, and Texas.
1856-57—Minnesota.
1857—Iowa and Texas.
1857-58—Manitoba.
1864-65—Manitoba, Minnesota, Southeastern Dakota, and Colorado.
1866—Kansas, Nebraska, Northeastern Texas and Western Missouri.
1867—The progeny of the preceding, and also a fresh invasion in the Mississippi Valley.
1868—The progeny of preceding invaders in Kansas, Missouri, and Iowa, (and a slight visitation Jackson County, Minnesota.)
1869—Dying out in Kansas, Missouri and Iowa.
1873—Colorado, Wyoming, Nebraska, Dakota, Minnesota and Iowa.
1874—Colorado, Wyoming, Nebraska, Dakota, Minnesota, Iowa, Missouri, New Mexico, Indian Territory and Texas.[46]

Grasshoppers and drought seem to go together like the proverbial horse and carriage or love and marriage. This apparent connection was noticed in the nineteenth century by entomologists studying the voracious insects. "The causes which impel huge swarms to issue forth upon their migrations are not fully known, but the summers of 1855 and 1874 were notably hot and dry, and so far as Minnesota is concerned, the same may be said of 1863 and 1864."[47]

Ironically during the dry years when scanty crops were badly needed for food and feed were the years the insects were most numerous. Eyewitness accounts penned during the nineteenth century droughts verify the frequent emergence of hoppers during the dry years and give ample testimony of their appetite.

Not only were the swarms innumerable but they were insatiable for "when driven by hunger the locust has been known to consume such substances as dry bark, wood, cotton, woolen, leather, tobacco, dead animals, and its disabled fellows . . . if driven by scarcity of food the Rocky Mountain Locust leaves no vegetation untouched."[48]

Traveling west of Topeka, Kansas, in 1858, Albert Richardson encountered a "countless army of grasshoppers darkening the air like great flakes of snow." He recounted that the grasshoppers were

> In a column one hundred and fifty miles wide and about one hundred deep . . . some farmers burn the prairies before them. This confounds the troublesome visitors; like human armies, finding their supplies cut off, they make forced marches. They strip to skeletons shining cottonwood leaves. They devour every shred of tomatoes and onions. They gorge themselves upon cabbages, reckless of the great truth that cabbages are indigestible. They roll the springing wheat as a sweet morsel under their tongues. They feast upon tender leaves and milky kernels of softest green corn. Witnesses aver that in some places they eat ripe corn, cob and all![49]

The following account tells of another grasshopper invasion in the Smoky Hill River Valley near Lindsborg, Kansas, and recorded in Emory Lindquist's *Vision for a Valley.*

> The Smoky Valley pioneers were confronted with great threats to their crops from the invasion of grasshoppers.

In August, 1874, on a clear Sunday afternoon, a large cloud suddenly appeared that shut out the sun. Adults stood outside their homes, awed by the spectacle that seemed to defy explanation. Mothers called their children from play and all hurried to the shelter of the house or dugout. The large, cloud-like formation was not a cyclone, or a hail or dust storm, but millions of grasshoppers that soon literally covered section after section of land. The McPherson Independent reported that crops disappeared in less than twenty-four hours. Gottfrid Magnuson and his hired man saw what was happening to their crops on their farm north of Lindsborg and hastened to cut some of the corn before it was all destroyed by the invaders. Before they had time to bring the bundles to the shelter of the barn, only the bare stalks remained of what had been luxuriant growth with dark green leaves. A peach orchard of 300 trees on the Magnuson farm had been growing steadily for three years. The orchard 'glistened in the sun like a forest of ivory' after devastation wrought by the grasshoppers. In one home, a partially open door permitted thousands of grasshoppers to enter where the curtains in two rooms were eaten to shreds and three loaves of newly baked bread were devoured on the kitchen table. A woman's sunbonnet was partially consumed while she was wearing it.[50]

During these major invasions, grasshoppers, i.e. locust, ate radishes and onions right out of the ground. Potatoes were too deep for them to get, but they quickly ate the plants.

When a cloud of locusts descended on Buffalo County, Nebraska in July 1874, residents remembered the sounds and sights and consequences of the invasion. "The water in the creeks, stained with the excrement of insects, assumed the color of strong coffee. The cattle refused to drink until compelled by extreme thirst. One writer reported that it was his daily task to climb down into the well and clear the hoppers out to keep them from polluting the water. Even the fish in the streams tasted like grasshoppers.[51]

Farmers, facing starvation and economic ruin, fought back with every ingenious, and not so ingenious, means available. They drug heavy ropes through the crops hoping to disturb and discourage the insects and thus make them move on—even if it was into the neighbor's field. Smudge fires of straw, manure, and green grass were set around a field hoping to dislodge the feeding hordes.

Willing to try anything, farmers in remote regions fired the prairies around their fields hoping to destroy the insects, to drive them away, or to destroy the eggs. Sometimes it worked; sometimes the fires did more damage than the hoppers.

Some tried to plough them under.

Some tried chemicals.

Some tried a salt solution.

Some tried capturing them in nets.

Some dug ditches around the field to trap the insects.

Some communities offered bounties for captured and destroyed locusts.

Some tried dragging a very large pan partially filled with kerosene through the field and when enough grasshoppers were collected in the pan it was emptied and the insects set on fire.

In the end it was a discouraging battle. If the hoppers were hatched from eggs laid the previous season "the young locust is to some degree under the control of the farmer, while the invading hordes are generally invincible."[52]

A swarm in 1875 was estimated to contain 3.5 trillion Rocky Mountain Locust. These innumerable hordes sometimes affected the frontier society in very bizarre ways. From Dakota Territory, Nebraska, and Kansas came stories of grasshoppers stopping trains. The tracks would become so oily and greasy from crushed hoppers that the drive wheels would spin and the train would stall until crews shoveled away the insects and sanded the rails.[53]

Legislators, pressed into acknowledging Nebraska's severe insect problem, "passed the Grasshopper Act in 1877, which placed the grasshopper in the category of a public enemy and required all able-bodied citizens to rally to fight the pest."[54]

Like the New Madrid earthquakes, the grasshopper invasion was a boon to religion and "to the mind of the clergy this great calamity proved to be a blessing in disguise. It made the individualistic frontiersman see how weak and helpless man was in the face of God's providence. He was humbled. The result was wonderful revivals."[55]

Other than revivals, could there possibly be a bright side to a grasshopper invasion? Perhaps, if humans can overcome two factors of "taste." During the years of high hopper population many farmers fattened hogs, turkeys, and chickens on grasshoppers. It was cheap feed but the downside was a very strong, disagreeable flavor to the meat from the butchered hogs and fowl.

Yet, it seems, some societies have acquired, or tolerated, a taste for the insects.

> From a very remote antiquity locusts have formed an article of food, not only in Africa and Asia, but even in ancient times in Europe. Sometimes they are smoked or salted, at others they are fried or ground or powdered and mixed with flour to make bread. This is not done only in times of famine, but also when there is no scarcity of other food, as the locusts are considered rather a delicacy than otherwise.
>
> From time immemorial the Digger Indians, in the desert country west of the Rocky Mountains, have also used locusts as articles of food.[56] [Great Basin Indian Tribes were called "Diggers."]

> Captain Ware, stationed at Fort Laramie, wrote about the swarms of grasshoppers that descended on the post in the summer of 1864.

> While we were there a flight of grasshoppers came, such as in after years on several occasions devastated the vegetation of the Western States. During August the air became filled with these insects, and they took the little garden of which I spoke and ate it up almost instantly. One of the officers of the Eleventh Ohio came to me to go out with him and take a look at that garden. The grasshoppers were bunched together in swarms like bees. I remember seeing upon a handle

of a spade a bunch of interwoven grasshoppers as big as a man's hat. The Indian women at the squaw camp were catching these grasshoppers, roasting them, drying them, and pounding them up into meal to make bread of during the winter. The Indians seemed to be anxious to utilize all the grasshoppers they could catch, and they made up a great many hundred pounds of them.[57]

A most difficult mental picture to overcome, before most present-day newcomers could develop a taste for grasshoppers is that "resembling in many respects the cockroach" they, in fact, belong "to the same order of insects."[58] Cockroach *de jour* isn't likely to be served at your local restaurant anytime soon— at least not intentionally.

##

Once newcomers actually inhabited this new Eden it didn't take long for them to notice a paradigm shift back toward the original Great American Desert. Many a "gardener" and his family became first discouraged and then destitute.

In fact, it came as a shock to some when rain failed to follow the plow. Thousands of settlers soon discovered that Mother Nature was still in charge. It was a discovery that others had already made long ago.

Severe droughts during the nineteenth century presented both Indian and newcomers with two options: flee or perish. They did both and some research reveals that "After a number of years in which optimistic agriculturalists flooded into the largely uncultivated margins of the frontier, the region experienced a net displacement of nearly three hundred thousand people. Many areas lost between half and three-quarters of their population. Several counties sustained near total depopulation."[59]

This depopulation produced a domino effect on newcomer communities as rural farmers moved away leaving unpaid bills at the local merchants. The merchants couldn't pay the banker and many times farmer, merchant, and banker all succumbed to bankruptcy. When these people fled it left fewer citizens and services to support the community which time and again resulted in a reoccurring round of failures.

National Oceanic and Atmosphereic Administration/
Department of Commerce, George E. Marsh album
During drought years grasshoppers could strip farmland, like this cornfield,
bare in a matter of hours.

As trade declined, businesses needed fewer employees. Job opportunities were almost nonexistent so the unemployed also joined the exodus. Sometimes, as the following quote shows, the end result was catastrophic for a community. "The Attorney General ruled that Wallace county [Kansas] was still organized under the law of 1868 although in the 'grasshopper year' of 1874 the entire population left the county and the records were lost. Wallace was attached to Ellis county for judicial purposes in 1875."[60]

Studies on the social impact of these nineteenth century droughts found that "nearly half of the population that had moved onto the plains in the 1880s moved out again in the 1890s."[61]

Then again, during the years of 1888 through 1892 "fully half of settlers in Kansas and Nebraska left the area."[62] As the drought deepened, two years later "in 1894, when as many as 90 percent of the settlers abandoned their farms in some areas. This same source argues that the history of the region and its flow of population in and out are closely linked to the incidence of drought."[63]

Western Nebraska was the destination of many thousands of hopeful newcomers during the decade of the 1880s. "Addison E. Sheldon estimated that 150,000 people settled in the western section between 1885 and 1890."[64] Unfortunately in some cases, after years of hard work, their dreams withered and died right along side the crops during the drought years of the early 1890s.

On 16 August 1894, The *Minden (Nebraska) Courier* reported that "Horses are being slaughtered in Hamilton county. There is no sale for common animals and they cannot even be given away. Two or three instances were chronicled where good work horses were killed and fed to hogs. A farmer who has a surplus of horse flesh cannot afford to winter them, as feed is very scarce."

The same issue carried a story headlined "Help Must Be Provided" stating "It is believed that thousands of families will either starve, emigrate or have to be fed by charity unless the people of the state as a whole provide employment or otherwise provide for them."

The drought lingered and,

> those immigrants who had dotted the tableland with their dwellings had for several years watched their crops wither when touched by that simoon of the southwind, until their hearts lost courage and like a defeated army the prairie-schooner was seen eastward-bound on every highway, and many continued their course until they crossed the Missouri and even the Mississippi. Just a few short years after the departure of the Indian, the soldier and the cattle, one following up the grass-grown but still well defined trail from Sidney to the hills, would see on either side as far as the eye could see, deserted and crumbling "soddies" as so many tombstones standing at the grave of buried hopes.[65]

Newcomers weren't the only ones to see their hopes buried in a parched, iron-hard earth. This trend of drought displacing Indians was observed as early as the 1830s when the Santa Fe Trail brought newcomers to, and through their land. Plains Indians struggled to keep their own hopes alive as drought and newcomers crowded them from their traditional buffalo hunting range which provided the major staple of their yearly food supply. This restricted range lessened the number of robes and hides that they could use to barter for items that were becoming more and more necessary to maintain their independence: corn and other vegetables to supplement their diet and firearms, powder, lead, and cartridges for hunting and self protection.

Equally serious for their lifestyle was losing much of their traditional summer ranges that provided nourishing grass to strengthen and sustain their horse herds during the season of hunting and warfare.

Even more devastating for the Plains Indians was the loss of their wintering sites along the sheltered rivers and streams of the central plains. An ever rising tide of newcomers traveled and camped along these riverine valleys where they chopped down trees for campfires and their animals grazed the grass into the ground.

Newcomers then began establishing way stations and road ranches along these thoroughfares. These permanent settlements quickly consumed more timber for cabins, corrals, and firewood. In a matter of just a few years following the Colorado gold strike in 1859, the Indians no longer had access to many of their vital wintering sites. And it was only a matter of time before their winter havens at the Big Timbers of the Republican River, the Big Timbers of the Smoky Hill River, and the Big Timbers of the Arkansas River were either destroyed or in the hands of newcomers.

Drought then became a deciding factor that further dislodged Indians out of, and off of, their traditional land and onto government reservations. They had fewer options than the newcomers; neither the newcomer communities nor the government rallied to ease their suffering.

During the nineteenth century the federal government was not accustomed to, or inclined to, nor prepared to, offer aid to settlers beset by drought and hoppers; not until the hue and cry reached a deafening roar.

The federal government was unwilling to help suffering Indians—period.

Many, if not most, newcomers had used their life savings or had borrowed money to homestead in the newly touted Garden of Eden. Unfortunately, the Great Plains' Garden of Eden wasn't any more forgiving than the original Garden and the "flaming sword" was perhaps hotter on the prairies and plains than it was at Eden's gate.

Desperate newcomers found themselves without food, clothing, transportation, or money to escape the reborn Great American Desert. An entry in the *Annals of Kansas* tells us that 1860 was "a very dry year. Large amounts of money and goods were sent from the North and East for the relief of Kansas, and were chiefly distributed by S. C. Pomeroy, at Atchison. The Legislature of New York appropriated $50,000; an appropriation was also made by the Wisconsin Legislature, and every Free State Contributed generously."[66] Government agencies did what they could but it was religious, social, and private generosity that succored most of the needy.

In the summer of the gold rush [to the Rockies] a vicious drought set in, and in some places virtually no rain fell between June 1859 and February 1861. . .

Relief efforts centered in Atchison, where the destitute were given navy beans, corn, dried apples, and salt pork, but there and elsewhere supplies eventually ran low . . . As far away as Connecticut, towns were plastered with broadsides calling for help:

> Forty thousand people are on the verge of Starvation.
>
> Families well supplied in the Fall are now destitute.
>
> Families have died from Starvation while the husband and father have gone to Atchison for food.
>
> A temporary hospital in Atchison for frozen Teamsters.
>
> Who among us has lost a meal?[67]

People and organizations responded generously and helped thousands. But it wasn't long before the cycle would repeat itself despite promoters' insistence that the prairies and plains were becoming wetter.

On 15 September 1874, Kansas Governor Thos. A. Osborn called a special session of the Legislature to assess the drought and grasshopper impact on rural Kansas residents. The governor's actions were prompted because "the total destruction of every green thing seemed imminent."

Photo by author

A dry bed is a reoccurring scene on the Platte River in drought years. This photo was taken at Columbus, Nebraska 14 October 2004. The riverbed is a popular place for ATV riders who ignore signs prohibiting such activity.

The swarms of grasshoppers that appear suddenly were enveloping the whole state and "starvation or emigration seemed inevitable unless aid should be furnished." Responding to the pressure, the governor informed the legislators that

> that portion of the State which has been almost entirely populated during the past eighteen months, will suffer for want of the necessaries of life unless provision is made for relief.
>
> . . . by reason of the great inflow of grasshoppers the corn crop has been very generally damaged, and in some localities, entirely destroyed. The new settlers in the western counties who have not yet got the soil ready for wheat were relying upon the usual crop of corn for their winter's subsistence, but this has been swept away, and many of them are left without means of support . . . That aid should be afforded these unfortunate people, all agree.

Wisely the governor insisted on further action and requested that the State Board of Agriculture survey the state and provide a summary of the conditions in each county. The preceeding and following excerpts are from the 1874 State Board of Agriculture's *Third Annual Report*. A citizen of Cloud County reported that "the most terrible calamity that has ever befallen northwestern Kansas has just swept over us like the devouring locust of Palestine. The land of Eden before them, and behind them a desolate wilderness . . . there will be considerable destitution and suffering among the farmers of the county."

Conditions in Decatur County were communicated to the governor by William P. Montgomery in a letter of 30 August 1874. The drought had destroyed the wheat, oats, barley and potatoes. The grasshoppers destroyed the corn. Assistance is requested for fifty-one families consisting of 189 persons.

Montgomery explained that "In August, 1873, there were probably 20 families in the entire county. There are now about 125 families. I would estimate the inhabitants of the county at 375. They came to secure homes . . . but the drouth and grasshoppers have taken their dependence, and they must leave or be aided. We ought to have from 75 to 100 stand of arms. With moderate aid, and arms for any emergency, our people will stay and battle the storms on the frontier. Without these we cannot do it."

From Norton County: "Crops entirely destroyed . . . Our reports state that the county has about 750 inhabitants, three-fourths of whom will need assistance, and that many of them, being actually destitute, need immediate aid."[68]

By 1886 West Texas was also teetering on the brink of total disaster due to drought. As relief supplies began to arrive it was "estimated that of the twenty-one counties represented in the meeting, there were thirty thousand individuals living in complete destitution."[69]

The *Chicago Daily Tribune*, 20 December 1890, reported on drought conditions affecting parts of the prairies and plains.

> Mr. George W. Williams, a lawyer . . . recently returned from a visit to Southern Dakota and Western Nebraska and Kansas, and he draws a sorrowful picture of the conditions of the people in those sections. There has

been a total failure of the crops there, and most of the farmers have nothing to feed either to their familes or stock, and no money with which to purchase clothing . . .

Mr. Williams attended a Sheriff's sale to satisfy a debt for farm machinery where good-sized pigs were sold for 12 cents each and cows for less than $10. At another sale the entire receipts were $11 and the legal costs $9. One of the special needs of the people is clothing . . .

Mr. Williams says that he will volunteer to see that any old clothing contributed will get into the hands and on the backs of deserving people there . . . Aid should be given promptly, for thousands are in imminent danger of dying from cold and hunger.

In Nebraska, especially western counties, the years 1890 and 1892-1894 were again grueling trials for settlers. In many cases the trials of dry-land farming gave way to the equally arduous trials of escaping the drought-stricken area with life and limb.

Along with all crops and vegetation, the drought had dried up any demand for agricultural farming equipment and livestock. Those determined souls who decided to stay and tough it out, or those that couldn't get out, eventually received some drought relief from the Nebraska Legislature which appropriated $100,000 to ease the suffering in its state. It was a start but it took the combined charity of churches, private citizens, and businesses from "back East" to provide adequate help to rescue those in desperate need.

When the drought had run its course it is believed that about one half of the farmers in Kansas and Nebraska headed back east, or in some cases headed "out west" to forget the nightmare of drought, dust, grasshoppers, hunger, disappointment, and poverty.

##

Mrs. Ball and her daughter Jennie learned first hand that the much-touted theory that "rain follows the plow" was a cruel lie. Ignorance and theory, however justified, doesn't "feed the bulldog" so to speak. Nor do they feed people. Nor did they feed Mrs. Ball and daughter Jennie.

Fortunately, the night that Jennie laid awake listening to her mother crying was the very night that "Father and brother were home with a load of groceries and vegetables."[70]

It was a happy ending to one drought crisis but it wasn't the last drought that the Ball family experienced. In 1885 the family moved to a farm near Caldwell, Kansas, not far from the Oklahoma line.

Jennie married E. X. Glover in 1890 and they began wedded life on a rented farm on the Kansas line. Here they made plans to stake a claim in the Cherokee Outlet, now part of Oklahoma Territory, that would open for settlement in 1893.

Once again Jennie experienced endless days without rain. She didn't write of the '93 drought perhaps because, unlike the episode in 1879, they didn't face the threat of starvation. Nonetheless there is ample evidence that she and her husband were living through a drought because

> all through that summer of 1893, rain had failed to moisten the earth. *The Beaver Advocate*, printed in the panhandle of Oklahoma Territory, published the U. S. Department of Agriculture's weather bulletin, which stated that 'rain is badly needed in the Cherokee outlet, on its borders are encamped many thousands awaiting the opening, all small streams are dry and the crowds have to go many miles for water . . . all the vegetation was dry as tinder . . . The weather took its toll on animals as well. Over 200 horses perished on the road between Guthrie and Orlando during the week prior to the run. Secretary Smith ordered railroads to haul car loads of water to various towns in the Outlet.[71]

Jennie and her husband, Ed, soon found that the drought was not the only foe awaiting in the Cherokee Outlet. During the run Ed was lucky enough to stake a good claim about five or six miles south of the Kansas line. However, when he went to the land office to file on the claim, someone had already filed.

216

The illegal claimant didn't want the land but rather wanted to be "bought out" for cash money.

A lawyer advised them to begin making improvements immediately. In a goodwill effort to prove up the claim Ed and Jennie moved a granary onto the claim. "We had saved up some money to build a small house . . . But we could not build, do fencing, plant trees and an orchard while this man had the filing."

Jennie recalls that after much worry and debate "we bought the man off for $350.00 and had enough left to make the shack more livable. You would be surprised how cozy it was, and we with our two-year-old son were settled on our own land."[72]

##

While Jennie and her husband were dreaming of a prosperous future in Oklahoma Territory, Terryton, Kansas, also nurtured dreams of a bright future. Fate smiled kindly on one dream only.

Mister Terry's dreams and his town languished and then died during the drought that scorched southwestern Kansas. By 1895 the dream was gone as were most of Terryton's residents. Terry was an easterner but he obviously developed a fine sense of pioneer humor as indicated by the following notice that he placed in the *Hatfield (Kansas) News*:

> For sale. A one-horse railroad boom, broken in the middle and without head or tail. It might be repaired to suit emergencies, as its constitution and plan were constructed with that end in view. A quit-claim deed will be given. Will be sold very low, as I wish to (or rather the people wish me to) give place to a more able man, and hie myself back to Yankee-dom where my real estate interests are. Porter D. Terry.[73]

##

A perennial crop of jokes and stories, partly truth and partly fiction, germinate and flourish in the West under the worst of trials. During the droughts and grasshopper visitations almost everyone was trying their hand at hard-luck humor. Where truth ends and fiction begins is oftentimes difficult to discern.

How hot did it get during the drought?

It was so hot that the chickens were laying hard boiled eggs. It was so hot that that corn popped on the stalk. It was so hot in the Texas Panhandle that they didn't need a fire to heat the branding irons. It was so hot that cats and dogs quit fighting and sat in the shade rolling dice to see who won.

How dry was it during the drought?

It was so dry that the cows were giving powdered milk. It was so dry that trees were chasing dogs. It was so dry you had to prime yourself to spit.

How hard did the wind blow during the drought?

The wind blew so hard that, depending on which way they were facing, chickens were sometimes laying the same egg two or three or four times. The wind blew so hard that landowners in Oklahoma had to go to North Dakota to pay taxes on their property.

How big were grasshoppers during the drought?

Grasshoppers were so big that if you were man enough to harness a pair you could plow forty acres in a single day. [A rule of thumb was that you could plow an acre a day per horse.] Grasshoppers were so big that occasionally father grasshoppers would steal whole railroad trains and take them back to the nest as toys for the young'uns.

Did grasshoppers really eat the hickory handles out of pitchforks? Eat the harness off of horses? Eat the uniforms off soldiers? Devour live cattle and horses' hoofs as well as pig's snouts? How about chomping up entire buggies?

Is the following "gospel" or just a windy told by an old-timer to impress a naive newspaper reporter? At a Kansas Day celebration in 1927 a pioneer who settled near Salina, Kansas, recalls the grasshopper plagues during the early years. "They talk about a grasshopper year,' he said. 'There were half a dozen, one almost as bad as the other. I remember one—not the famous one—when the grasshoppers clogged wheels of the stage so they stopped.'"[74]

There were only a couple of things that the independent-minded settlers hated worse than grasshoppers: lawyers and insurance companies. It isn't surprising that the three would end up in a windy hatched during a grasshopper plague.

One such story appeared in the May 11, 1875, issue of the *Leavenworth (Kansas) Daily Times.*

A gentleman who has just returned returned from Cherokee county, Kansas, is full with remarkable reminiscences of the grasshoppers infesting that vicinity. He will stand around for an hour, relating the hairbreadth escapes of the people whom the hoppers have completely overrun, and who are leaving their homes and fleeing from the fearful scourge. The traveler is inclined to think that many of the crimes attributed to the James boys are to be traced to the more hardened and dissolute grasshopper, many of whom, he says, are arming with shot-guns and organizing a sort of home guard [f]or offensive and defensive purposes.

One of his credible stories is to the effect that a few weeks ago, a woman dug up a panful of dirt in which to plant some flower seeds. She put the pan under the stove, and went out to see a neighbor. Upon her return, after an hour's absence, she found seven thousand bushels of grasshoppers generated by the heat, literally eating her out of house and home. They first attacked the green-shades on the windows, and then a green-painted dust-pan. A green Irish servant girl, asleep in one of the rooms, was the next victim, and not a vestige of her was left. The stove and stovepipe followed, and then the house was torn down so they could get at the chimney. Boards, joists, beams, plastering, clothing, nails, hinges, door-knobs, plates, tin-ware, everything, in fact, the house contained was eaten up, and when she arrived within a mile of the place, she saw two of the largest hoppers sitting up on end, and playing mumble-peg with the carving-knife, for which should have the cellar.

The way the matter leaked out was on a suit brought against the insurance company, which refused to pay the policy, on the ground that the building was not destroyed by fire; but the court rendered a verdict for the plaintiff, as she had proven that the grasshoppers were generated by the fire in the stove.

##

Despite man's efforts to conquer Mother Nature, she steadfastly refuses to be bossed. "Human domination over nature is quite simply an illusion, a passing dream by a naive species."[75]

Chapter Five notes

[1] Gwendoline and Paul Sanders, *The Sumner County Story* (North Newton, Kansas: The Mennonite Press, 1966), 44.

[2] Ibid., 44.

[3] Kevin Zachary Sweeney, "Wither the Fruited Plain: Nineteenth Century Droughts in the Southern Plains" (Ph.D. diss., Oklahoma State University, 2001), 17.

[4] L. Dean Bark, "History of American Droughts." in *North American Droughts.* edited by Norman J. Rosenberg (Boulder, CO: Westview Press, Inc., 1978), 9.

[5] Lyall Watson, *Heaven's Breath* (New York: William Morrow and Company, Inc., 1984), 41.

[6] Norman J. Rosenberg, "Climate of the Great Plains Region of the United States," *Great Plains Quarterly,* Winter 1987, 27.

[7] Richard E. Felch, "Drought: Characteristics and Assessment." in *North American Droughts.* edited by Norman J. Rosenberg (Boulder, CO: Westview Press, Inc., 1978), 26.

[8] Samuel Aughey, *Sketches of the Physical Geography and Geology of Nebraska* (Omaha: Daily Republican Book and Job Office, 1880), 44-45.

[9] Mrs. M. A. Humphrey, "The Sanitary Value of Plants and Trees," in *Kansas Horticultural Report, For the Year 1884* (Topeka: Kansas Publishing House: T. D. Thacher, State Printer, 1885), 8.

[10] John L. Allen, "The Garden-Desert Continuum: Competing views of the Great Plains in the Nineteenth Century," *Great Plains Quarterly,* Fall 1985, 208.

[11] L. Dean Bark, "History of American Droughts," in *North American Droughts.* Norman J. Rosenberg, ed., (Boulder, CO: Westview Press, Inc., 1978), 13.

[12] Connie A. Woodhouse and Jonathan T. Overpeck, "2000 Years of Drought Variability in the Central United States," *Bulletin of the American Meteorological Society (*December 1998): 2696-2697, http://www.ngdc.noaa.gov/paleo/amsdrought.pdf.

[13] Kevin Zachary Sweeney, "Wither the Fruited Plain: Nineteenth Century Droughts in the Southern Plains" (Ph.D. diss., Oklahoma State University, 2001), 85-86.

[14] Ibid., 117.

[15] Official Records: series 1, vol. 22, part 2, (Little Rock), http://ehistory.osu.edu/uscw/library/or/033/0572.cfm.

[16] Roy Sylvan Dunn, "Droughts." *The Handbook of Texas Online.* http://www.tsha.utexas.edu/handbook/online/articles/view/DD/ybd1.html.

[17] Lela Barnes, "Journal of Isaac McCoy For the Exploring Expedition of 1830," *Kansas Historical Quarterly,* November 1936, 364.

[18] Norman J. Rosenberg, "Climate of the Great Plains Region of the United States," *Great Plains Quarterly,* Winter 1987, 29, 30.

[19] Lela Barnes, "Journal of Isaac McCoy For the Exploring Expedition of 1830," *Kansas Historical Quarterly,* November 1936, 371.

[20] James C. Malin, "Dust Storms: Part Two, 1861-1880," *Kansas Historical Quarterly,* August 1946.

[21] Lettie Little Pabst, *Kansas Heritage* (New York: Vantage Press, 1956), 47.

[22] Elliott West, *The Contested Plains* (Lawrence, Kansas: University Press of Kansas, 1998), 253.

[23] "G. W. Martin Papers," in the manuscripts division of the Kansas State Historical Society. Quoted in "Dust Storms: Part One, 1850-1860, by James C. Malin," *Kansas Historical Quarterly*, May 1946, 138.

[24] James C. Malin, "Dust Storms: Part Two, 1861-1880," *Kansas Historical Quarterly*, August 1946, 270.

[25] Ibid., 276.

[26] Ibid., 294.

[27] Signal Office, U.S. War Department, *Monthly Weather Review*, July 1886 (Washington City, 1886), 198.

[28] James C. Malin, "Dust Storms: Part Three, 1881-1900," *Kansas Historical Quarterly*, November 1946, 400.

[29] Ibid., 404.

[30] Granville Stuart, *Forty Years on the Frontier,* edited by Paul C. Phillips (Cleveland, OH: The Arthur H. Clark Company, 1925), 2:230, 231.

[31] Signal Office, U.S. War Department, *Monthly Weather Review*, May 1887 (Washington City, 1886), 146.

[32] J. Frank Dobie, *The Longhorns* (Boston: Little, Brown and Company, 1941), 193,

[33] Lona Shawver, *Chuck Wagon Windies and True Stories* (San Antonio: The Naylor Company, 1950), 124.

[34] Elmer Verner McCollum, *From Kansas Farm Boy to Scientist* (Lawrence: University of Kansas Press, 1964), 61.

[35] Weather Bureau, U.S. Department of Agriculture, *Monthly Weather Review*, February 1895 (Washington, 1896), 53.

[36] Weather Bureau, U.S. Department of Agriculture, *Monthly Weather Review*, April 1895 (Washington, 1896), 130.

[37] Everett Dick, *Conquering the Great American Desert* (Lincoln: Nebraska State Historical Society, 1975), 345.

[38] Robert G. Dyrenforth and Simon Newcomb, "Can We Make It Rain?," *North American Review*, October 1891, 387.

[39] "The Artificial Production of Rain," *Scientific American*, 20 December 1890, 384.

[40] George Catlin, *North American Indians* (1844; reprint, Philadelphia: Leary, Stuart and Company, 1913), 1:139.

[41] Mari Sandoz, *Old Jules: Portrait of a Pioneer* (1935; reprint, New York: MJF Books, 1963), 149.

[42] Finney County Kansas Historical Society, *History of Finney County, Kansas* (North Newton, Kansas: Mennonite Press, Inc., 1976) 2:102.

[43] Lois Stringfield Harman, *Castle on the Prairie* (n.p.: n.d., most likely privately published, signed by author 5-28-76), 8.

[44] F. Buchanan White, "Locusts and Grasshoppers," *Frank Leslie's Popular Monthly*, April 1882.

[45] Charles V. Riley, *The Locust Plague in the United States* (Chicago: Rand, McNally & Co., 1877), 9.

[46] John C. Wise, Warren Smith, and Allen Whitman, comps., *The Grasshopper, or Rocky Mountain*

Locust, and its Ravages in Minnesota (Saint Paul: The Pioneer-Press Company, 1876), 6-7.

[47] Ibid., 22.

[48] Ibid., 29.

[49] Albert D. Richardson, *Beyond the Mississippi* (Hartford, CT: American Publishing Company, 1867), 552-553.

[50] Emory Lindquist, *Vision for a Valley* (Rock Island, IL: Augustana Historical Society, 1970), 85,86.

[51] Everett Dick, *The Sod-House Frontier 1854-1890* (Lincoln: Johnsen Publishing Company, 1954), 205.

[52] John C. Wise, Warren Smith, and Allen Whitman, comps., *The Grasshopper, or Rocky Mountain Locust, and its Ravages in Minnesota* (Saint Paul: The Pioneer-Press Company, 1876), 30.

[53] William John Meredith, "Old Plum Grove Colony in Jefferson County, 1854-1855," *The Kansas Historical Quarterly*, November 1938; Everett Dick, *The Sod-House Frontier 1854-1890* (Lincoln: Johnsen Publishing Company, 1954), 204.

[54] Everett Dick, *The Sod-House Frontier 1854-1890* (Lincoln: Johnsen Publishing Company, 1954), 211-212.

[55] Ibid., 206.

[56] F. Buchanan White, "Locusts and Grasshoppers," *Frank Leslie's Popular Monthly*, April 1882.

[57] Eugene F. Ware, *The Indian War of 1864* (Topeka, Kansas: Crane & Company, 1911), 275.

[58] F. Buchanan White, "Locusts and Grasshoppers," *Frank Leslie's Popular Monthly*, April 1882.

[59] Richard A. Warrick and Martyn J. Bowden, "The Changing Impacts of Droughts in the Great Plains," in *The Great Plains Perspectives and Prospects.* Edited by Merlin P. Lawson and Maurice E. Baker (Lincoln: Center for Great Plains Studies University of Nebraska-Lincoln, 1981), 126.

[60] Kirke Mechem, ed., *The Annals of Kansas 1886-1925* (Topeka: Kansas State Historical Society, 1972),1:18.

[61] John L. Allen, "The Garden-Desert Continuum: Competing views of the Great Plains in the Nineteenth Century," *Great Plains Quarterly*, Fall 1985, 217.

[62] L. Dean Bark, "History of American Droughts," in *North American Droughts,* Norman J. Rosenberg, ed. (Boulder, CO: Westview Press, Inc., 1978), 19.

[63] Norman J. Rosenberg, "Climate of the Great Plains Region of the United States," *Great Plains Quarterly*, Winter 1987, 29, 31.

[64] Everett Dick, *Conquering the Great American Desert* (Lincoln: Nebraska State Historical Society, 1975), 328.

[65] Grant L. Shumway, ed., *History of Western Nebraska and Its People* (Lincoln: The Western Publishing & Engraving Company, 1921) 2: 350.

[66] Daniel Webster Wilder, ed., *The Annals of Kansas* (n.d.; reprint, New York: Arno Press, 1975), 296.

[67] Elliott West, *The Contested Plains* (Lawrence, Kansas: University Press of Kansas, 1998), 327-328.

[68] State Board of Agriculture. *The Third Annual Report to the Legislature of Kansas. For the Year 1874.* Topeka, Kansas: State Printing Works: Geo. W. Martin, Public Printer, 1874. 14-27.

[69] Kevin Zachary Sweeney, "Wither the Fruited Plain: Nineteenth Century Droughts in the Southern Plains" (Ph.D. diss., Oklahoma State University, 2001), 139-140.

[70] Gwendoline and Paul Sanders, *The Sumner County Story* (North Newton, Kansas: The Mennonite Press, 1966), 44-45.

[71] Kevin Zachary Sweeney, "Wither the Fruited Plain: Nineteenth Century Droughts in the Southern Plains" (Ph.D. diss., Oklahoma State University, 2001), 171.

[72] Gwendoline and Paul Sanders, *The Sumner County Story* (North Newton, Kansas: The Mennonite Press, 1966), 47-48.

[73] Leola Howard Blanchard, *Conquest of Southwest Kansas* (Wichita: The Wichita Eagle Press, 1931), 183.

[74] "Some of the Experiences in 'The Sixties' as Told to the Society," *The Salina (Kansas) Journal*, 29 January, 1927.

[75] Donald Worster, *Under Western Skies* (New York: Oxford University Press, 1992), jacket copy.

Chapter Six

ELECTRIC SKY

In short, I doubt if there is any known region out of the tropics,
that can 'head' the great prairies in 'getting up' thunder-storms,
combining so many of the elements of the awful and sublime.
                    —Josiah Gregg, *Commerce of the Prairies*

Lieutenant George M. Bache and his two fishing companions began loading their gear into the Army ambulance as thunderheads piled up like dirty cotton in the afternoon sky. After the gear and day's catch were stowed away they climbed aboard and Bache headed the mule team toward San Antonio, Texas. It was May 10, 1868.

The fishermen were still several miles from home when the promise of a welcome shower began to appear more like the threat of a bad storm; lightning slashed and thunder vibrated across the plains. The mules grew restive under the restraint of tightly held lines. The air grew still and oppressive.

It became obvious to the men that the storm was closing in faster than they first anticipated. And unless they put on some speed, the storm would surely catch them before they reached home. Bache slapped the lines and set the mules at full gallop.

Within minutes the thunderheads slid over the sun, draping a curtain of gray across the landscape. As the men feared, the storm overtook the racing ambulance. Howling wind and driving rain forced Bache to rein the team off the road and put the storm at their backs. The incessant thunder, lightning, and rain mesmerized the men until something struck the side of the ambulance like a hit from a small artillery piece. The men looked at each other wondering but not comprehending. Then another, and another, and another projectile smashed into the ambulance.

This sound was joined by the dull thud of missiles impacting the mules. The team bolted. The men, fearing a wreck, jumped clear. It was a very bad idea; a life-threatening mistake.

Once clear of the ambulance they found themselves hammered by grapefruit-sized hailstones. The only shelter was to put their arms over their heads and seek the meager protection offered by mesquite bushes. The hail repeatedly knocked them down as they frantically sought some escape from the plummeting stones of ice.

##

Thunderheads, those beautiful, gigantic sculptures that tower majestically into the heavens, are really powerful energy engines. These engines, at full throttle, have inspired fear and trembling for as far back as mankind can remember. It's little wonder that thunder and lightning became part of ancient man's superstitions, myths, and religions.

For, the ancients reasoned, from within this awesome, terrifying heavenly display sounded the thunderous voice of the gods, from here blazed forth the flashing sword of the gods, from here emanated the deadly wrath of the gods.

Lightning, that brilliant, magical fire from above could be attributed to nothing less than the gods. Sometimes, depending on the time and place, it was Zeus, who the early Greeks believed used the lightning as a weapon of war. Thor was another god of mythology who used the lightning bolt as a weapon.

American Indians lived close to nature and their tribal mythologies, folk tales, and religion reflected this lifestyle.

> The thunderbird is a potent spirit in many Indian tribes, particularly in the Plains states, where summer thunderstorms are among the fiercest on the planet. A great winged creature often depicted as an eagle, the thunderbird has dominion over thunder, dark clouds, rain, and snow. Thunder resounds from the flapping of his enormous wings, lightning flashes from the winking of his eyes. He is a kind of Indian Zeus, and his yearly arrival in the first thunderstorm of spring is an occasion of great import.[1]

In the midst of this widespread myth and superstition there did occasionally arise a thinker/philosopher such as Socrates who believed lightning was due to natural phenomenon, not Zeus or any other god. Socrates, as hindsight proved, was on to something and after a few centuries of observation and experimentation some of the mysteries of a thunderstorm have begun to be unlocked.

A thunderstorm generally forms when an updraft of warm moist air (which provides the energy) rises into cold air. The resulting thundercloud—cumulonimbus—sometimes towers 13 miles above the earth. The base of such a cloud may be anything from 1/2 to 2 1/2 miles above the ground, and may cover an area of 100 or more square miles, and contain over a half a million tons of water.

The cloud base looks like a huge cauliflower or an enormous white anvil, topped by the 'cirrus umbrella' composed of countless millions of ice crystals. These giant cloud masses are cells of turbulent energy whose electrical potential is measured in millions of volts. A large thunderstorm releases as much energy as a megaton bomb.[2]

This colossal quantity of energy unleashed upon the open plains left very vivid impressions on newcomers. Colonel Dodge, writing in his *The Plains of the Great West,* describes the thunderstorm or "waterspout" of the high plains. The waterspout is, in his view, not your average rainfall experienced in a thunderstorm because the

rain, however, does not fall in drops, but in streams, as if poured from the strainer of a shower-bath.

As the myrids of streams are caught by the wind and deflected from their direct course, they present an appearance of sheets or waves of water, and form in the air thousands of mimic cascades of every conceivable variety; now falling in a smooth, unbroken, inclined sheet, now flying into an infinity of jets, down or up, or sideways . . .

> Nothing can be more beautiful or more disagreeable than these storms; and when the deluge of rain is, as is often the case, accompanied by huge rounded lumps and shapeless chunks of ice, they become really very serious.[3]

"Fear" and "terror" were additional adjectives Elizabeth Custer used to describe these thunderstorms. Whenever possible Libbie, as she was often called, accompanied her husband onto the prairies and plains during the years he was stationed in Kansas. Born in Monroe, Michigan, Mrs. Custer found the many thunderstorms that rumbled across the plains a new and extremely virulent species.

Following General Custer's demise at the Little Big Horn, Elizabeth Custer turned to writing as a means of supporting herself and perpetuating the hero status of her late husband. She penned a trilogy of books, *Boots and Saddles*, *Tenting on the Plains*, and *Following the Guidon*. Her impressions and experiences of a severe thunderstorm and the subsequent flood is included in two of the three works.

The incident took place on Big Creek, four miles south of the town of Walker, Kansas, which is approximately ten miles east of present-day Fort Hays, Kansas. This location was the site of the original fort.

Mrs. Custer didn't much like thunderstorms and wrote about how this storm in June 1867, affected her.

> Whatever Kansas did was with a rush; the lightning was more terrific than lightning elsewhere, the rain poured down in floods, and the wind blew hurricanes . . . we were always expecting some sudden announcement of Mother Nature, who did not propose to treat us to anything like a gentle shower, or a soft south wind that might be trying to "blow up rain." Everything came with a mighty "whew!" . . .
>
> . . . I was speechless with fear when the storm began . . . The lightning on the plains is omnipresent; it is such a continuous glare that the whole heavens seem a vast sheet of flame. I could not accustom myself to it, and as long as we lived out there each storm was a

new terror to me . . . To add to my terrors, immense hailstones pelted down on the cotton roof with such savage force that I believed no canvas could withstand their fury.[4]

Another account given in her book, *Tenting on the Plains*, reaffirms her terror of thunder and lightning.

One night we [Mrs. Custer and her colored maid] had retired, and were trying to believe that the thunder was but one of those peculiar menacing volleys of cloud-artillery that sometimes passed over harmlessly; but we could not sleep, the roar and roll of thunder was so alarming. There is no describing lightning on the Plains. While a storm lasts . . . there is no way of hiding from the blinding light . . . there seemed to be nothing for us to do but to lie quaking and terrified under the covers.[5]

Like all things in life, these storms were both good and bad, both a blessing and a curse. Without sufficient rainfall the area between the Mississippi River and the Rocky Mountains would soon live up to its early nineteenth century billing as the Great American Desert. Water is the life blood of this vast grassland.

So, bless the rain.

Unless you were traveling with team and wagon and the trail became a quagmire of bottomless mud that slowed or halted progress.

Unless your camp site was transformed into a soupy bog where mud pies were about the only entree at meal times.

Unless your tent suddenly imitated a sieve and passed more rainwater than it repelled.

A thunderstorm is also a lightning storm, although seldom called such. Yet, lightning is a most deadly component of the thunderstorm.

Around the world, at any one time, there are probably 1,800 thunderstorms in progress and a hundred lightning strikes every second . . .

> For such a common and impressive natural
> phenomenon, it has been extraordinarily hard to
> discover the exact mechanism of a lightning strike
> ... Even today there is heated debate over what exactly
> is going on.[6]

In a grossly over-simplified analogy it could be said that
lightning functions somewhat like the flash on a camera.
"The lightning causes a drop in the electrical charge in the
thundercloud. It recharges in about 20 seconds and it is then
ready for another flash."[7] As the charge rebuilds and approaches
the moment of another strike those near ground zero can feel the
charge building. The hair stands on end and physical elements
such as rocks and metal objects, begin to hiss or hum.

Thunder and lightning, indeed entire storm cells, are still
somewhat of a mystery but generally speaking the top of the
clouds are charged with a positive electrical charge and the
bottom with a negative charge. The earth normally maintains
a negative charge but by some phenomena the ground beneath
a thundercloud takes on a positive charge.

"On the earth directly below the cloud there is a buildup
of positive electricity, forming a 'mirror image' of the negative
charge above." This charge follows the storm like a shadow
building "Enormous differences of electrical potential between
earth and cloud." Leaders create a downward path of charged
particles that connects with a streamer creating an upward
path from the earth. When the two connect "the main lightning
stroke—a brilliant spear of light—soars *upward*," at speeds as
high as 87,000 miles per second. These strokes can carry up to
100 million volts of electricity.[8]

It is no wonder, then, that

> lightning, striking with a roar and a blinding flash,
> uprooting trees and fusing metal, bringing destruction
> and even death in its wake, has enjoyed a commanding
> and fearsome stature in the sight of men since the
> beginning of time. Depending upon our degree of
> culture and understanding, and even more upon our
> sensibility to the message of titanic forces, it has
> brooked no rivals as heaven-sent bogey man No. 1.

There is about thunder a strong suggestion of the day of wrath, and perhaps that should be accounted one of its benefits down through the ages—that it can so quickly and completely induce in careless mortals a sudden and perhaps forgotten respect for the Creator of the Universe. A man's conscience, which may have become too still and too small in daily practice, often assumes stentorian tones with the aid of thunder and lightning.[9]

The most controversial and awe-inspiring type of lightning is "ball lightning." Because of its elusive nature many scientists refuse to acknowledge its existence. Scientists may be skeptical but there are simply too many people who have recorded seeing ball lightning to discount its existence.

Here then, was another manifestation of Zeus, or Thor, or the Thunderbird. Sometimes these balls of fire would appear and disappear without a sound and without causing damage while other times they would cause serious damage; sometimes even death.

According to Frank W. Lane in his book *The Elements Rage* these controversial balls of lightning

> nearly always appear toward the end of a storm and vary in diameter from an inch to 40 feet. The average diameter is about 10 inches. They generally last for periods of from a second to three minutes . . . The color is usually lavender or pale red, but other colors have been reported. The appearance of a ball is often accompanied by a hissing noise. The balls sometimes follow air currents, sometimes move against the wind. Several observers have commented on a ball's rapid rotation compared with its slow progression— reminiscent of a spinning top.[10]

Anyone living on the prairies and plains has seen many types of lightning displays. A few of these individuals have been privileged to witness a display of ball lightning. With or without scientific sanction it remains one of the mysteries associated with lightning.

It took an eccentric Philadelphia printer with a strong intellectual curiosity and a kite to begin unlocking some of lightning's mysteries.

Benjamin Franklin, however, wasn't the only curious scientist investigating lightning's relationship with electricity. And he wasn't the first to draw electricity from a thunderstorm with a kite or other "laboratory" instrument. Three Frenchmen, using Franklin's sentry-box design, were successful in proving that lightning was electricity about a month before Franklin flew his famous kite.

Even so, Franklin is the most remembered name associated with lightning experiments and can rightfully be considered the father of lightning research. It's also fair to say that along with intellect and curiosity he had some good luck. Perhaps the most important bit of luck was that he lived through his experiments. Some didn't.

In 1753, in St. Petersburg, "Professor Georg Wilhelm Richmann, while performing a similar experiment with an insulated rod, was killed by a bolt of lightning."[11] The "similar experiment" was coaxing lightning out of the cloud via Franklin's aforementioned sentry box. The sentry box was a small edifice constructed atop a prominent hill or tower "big enough to contain a man and an electrical stand [insulating stool or table]. From the middle of the stand let an iron rod rise and pass bending out of the door, and then upright twenty or thirty feet . . . If the electrical stand be kept clean and dry, a man standing on it when such clouds are passing low might be electrified and afford spark, the rod drawing fire to him from a cloud."[12]

Although the Frenchmen successfully conducted the experiment without being electrocuted, it's probable that at this stage of experimentation Franklin didn't realize just how powerful and dangerous a lightning bolt could be.

Lightning fatalities were fairly common before, and even after, Franklin's invention of the lighting rod. The prairies and plains were especially vulnerable and there can be suggested two reasons why the region seemed to beg for lightning strikes. First, wrestling a living from the Great American Desert left most homesteaders strapped for money and time. Therefore

Frank Leslie's Illustrated Newspaper, *May 28, 1881; L. W. Macdonald*
A flash of lightning and the crash of thunder sent many a herd of Long-horns stampeding to parts unknown. It also was dangerous for the cowboys who on horseback were the highest objects on the prairie, making them tar- gets for the lightning. This storm broke over a herd near Kerrville, Texas.

few were in a position to equip their buildings with lightning rods which could have saved lives and property.

A second reason was that riding horseback, traveling in a horse-drawn vehicle, or even walking on the prairies and plains often made an individual the tallest object on the landscape for many miles around. Thus they became mobile lightning rods.

Diaries and journals from the period have preserved instances where lightning recognized and responded to these lightning rods. Quoted from Merrill J. Mattes' work is this excerpt from Amelia Knight's diary.

> May 17 [1853] we have a dreadful storm of rain and hail last night and very sharp lightning. It killed two oxen . . . We had just encamped in a large flat prairie, when the storm commenced in all its fury and in two minutes after the cattle were taken from the wagons every brute was gone out of sight . . . all gone before the storm like so many wild beasts . . . The wind was so high I thought it would tear the wagons to pieces.

Nothing but the stoutest covers could stand it. The rain beat into the wagons so that everything was wet, in less than 2 hours the water was a foot deep all over our camp grounds. As we could have no tents pitched, all had to crowd into the wagons and sleep in wet beds, with their wet clothes on, without supper.[13]

Wayne Gard in his book, *The Chisholm Trail*, writes that "Storms also took their toll. In 1868, lightning struck a trail camp north of Dallas, killing one man and burning three— one of them so badly that he had to quit. Two years later Ran Spencer and another trail hand, taking refuge under a tree during a thunderstorm, died from a single lightning bolt. In 1871, just south of the Red River, lightning killed a man in another outfit."[14]

As a result of such tragic incidents some cowboys were known to quit using "profanity during lightning storms, on the theory that cussing was disrespectful and therefore invited sudden destruction from the controller of the elements."[15]

Just in case it wasn't God throwing the thunderbolts, the cowboys did give Franklin some consideration as George W. Brock relates. In 1884 he was part of a crew that had just delivered a herd of Longhorns north of Julesburg Junction and on across the Platte River. Once the herd had forded the Platte, Brock was sent back to meet a following herd. He had only ridden a short ways south of the Platte when

about the middle of the evening, I met with something entirely different from anything I had ever before been up against. I thought up to this time that I knew what a Kansas storm was, but that evening I was shown that I had never been in one before. The lightning would strike the ground and set the grass on fire, then the rain would put it out. I got off my horse and tied the three [horses] together, took off my spurs, six-shooter and pocket knife, laid them down and moved away. After the storm was over the sun came out and it looked as though nothing had ever happened, so I moved on.[16]

Clearly not all cowboys or trail hands were big on superstition or religion. Cowhand Bruce Siberts recalls that religion was occasionally discussed around the campfire and some rather odd beliefs were held by a few of his companions.

> Once at a roundup we were arguing religion when a storm came up and lightning struck the cook's Dutch oven and scattered the pots and pans all around. This made the cook so mad he shook his fist toward the sky and said, "Raise your sights, you old bald-headed son of a bitch, if you want to get me." The other men were scared and ran all over the prairie. One said, "The Old Man will get him next crack. You will see. He shouldn't have said what he did." Some of these people spoke of "Old Johnny God" as a big bald man with whiskers who had quite a temper and might strike a man dead if he did wrong. Of course, with a few drinks in them, they didn't worry too much about it.[17]

Working cattle on horseback during a thunderstorm elevated the mobile lighting rod even higher. A crew trailing a herd through Kansas on their way to Wyoming reported that "a few days out of Dodge the crew passed the carcass of a horse killed by lightning and, next to the horse, the grave of its rider."

This wasn't an isolated incident and cowboys soon learned to dread the approaching thunderstorm with its deafening thunder and dazzling lightning. "Four men were killed and three seriously burned by lightning on the Chisholm Trail in three years. On the Salt Fork in Kansas a cowboy grimly recalled the lightning that 'would hit the side of those hills and gouge out great holes in the earth like a bomb had struck them, and it killed seven or eight cattle in the herd back of us.'"

Another cowboy trailing cattle up from Texas remembered an encounter with lightning.

> It first commenced like flash lightning, then came forked lighting, then chain lightning, followed by the peculiar blue lightning. After that show it rapidly developed into ball lightning, which rolled along the ground . . . then, most wonderful of all, it settled down

on us like a fog. The air smelled of burning sulphur; you could see it on the horns of the cattle, the ears of our horses and the brims of our hats. It grew so warm we thought we might burn up with it.

At such times, reported a young cowpoke named John Connor, "the horses stuck their heads between their knees and moaned and groaned till I decided the end of time had come. So I got down off my horse and lay flat on the ground and tried to die, but could not."[18]

##

It began as a trickle in the 1830s and 1840s, but by the 1850s the westward flow of newcomers had swelled into a tidal wave of humanity washing across the continent from east to west.

Toward the setting sun plodded the rich and poor, skilled and unskilled, devout and profane, young and old, male and female, smart and dumb, lucky and unlucky. To one traveler it looked as if "all mankind was adrift." Each one of these half-million-plus men, women, and children became a potential target for a lightning bolt.

Newcomers frequently waxed eloquent about the Great Platte River Road lauding it as "the greatest natural highway in the world." Perhaps it was, but it was also a turnpike of dying—sometimes by lightning.

Undoubtedly many knew of Franklin's experiment and recognized lightning's danger. But the traveling newcomer, totally exposed upon the naked plains, had little practical use for Franklin's discovery. Lightning was a hazard they lived with, and sometimes died with.

In 1847 Mary Saunders and husband were members of a company bound for Oregon "with one hundred wagons, more than three hundred men, half as many women, and it is hard to say how many children, as most of the families were large in those days."

They departed their home in Oskaloosa, Iowa, in May and crossed the Missouri River at St. Joseph. From her recollections we learn that "A few days later we experienced a severe storm, in which Mr. St. John (a member of our company) lost a son aged 12 years. He was killed by lightning."[19]

236

Harper's Weekly, *May 30, 1874; Frenzeny and Tavernier*

Kansas and wind are synonymous. In fact, that's what the name means— People of the Southwind. Newcomers to the prairies and plains quickly learned the winds add aggravation to any activity.

H. C. St. Clair was one of the many '49ers who kept a journal recording events along the Platte River Road. His impression of Fort Kearny was "a miscellaneous affair of adobes with dirt roofs. At this point the Big Platte was two miles wide. A wagon destroyed by lightning during a violent storm."[20]

H. Swearingen's letter of 14 June 1849, from Fort Laramie indicates that he understood some of the dynamics of lightning. The letter says that "During lightning storms Swearingen left the wagon for fear that the bolts might explode the gunpowder."[21]

And, wisely so, for a most extraordinary lightning death involved lightning and gunpowder. Young Lewis Shutterly left his wife and children in Pennsylvania and joined the countless argonauts headed for California in quest of the Golden Fleece.

Shutterly departed his home on 19 March 1849, and shoved off from Independence, Missouri, on 24 April. He and others arrived at the Platte River near Grand Island on 17 May.

Thunderstorms had been severe and frequent for several days and on 21 May, the party, wet and muddy, reached the vicinity of "fort childs [near Kearney, Nebraska]." Here, on the 22nd, he records two fatalities, "a man getting killed instantly by being run over with a wagon also of another being shot his gun being set off by lightning."[22] Unfortunately Shutterly doesn't provide additional details but it is a most unusual death by gunshot.

Livestock also frequently fell victim to lightning strikes. Just two accounts are included here but there were many more recorded, especially in the Platte River Valley.

In 1849, 20-year-old J. W. Gibson and two brothers were California bound along the Great Platte River Road. Their party "consisted of twenty men and boys, all from Buchanan County [Missouri]."

They crossed the South Platte about fifty miles "beyond the junction" and hit the North Platte at Ash Hollow. On the North Platte "A little beyond Chimney Rock we came to Scott's Bluff, which we reached late in the afternoon. We drove into a beautiful little valley and camped for the night. Just about dark the most terrific thunder storm I ever experienced in my life broke upon us. The whole valley seemed to be lit up in a blaze of fire and the thunder was deafening. Some three or four emigrant trains which we had overtaken were camped in this valley and next morning we counted fifteen cattle that had been killed by bolts of lightning. Fortunately none of them belonged to us."[23]

Another incident was recorded by George J. Kellogg who left Wisconsin in 1849 and headed west along the Great Platte River Road. By July he and others had reached Independence Rock where he noted "a cluster of '28 dead cattle from lightning.'"[24]

Since neither writer said, we don't know if these were milk cows, beef cattle, or oxen. Regardless of which it was, these killings represented a serious loss of food, investment, and/or motive power for these pioneers.

Sophia Lois Goodridge traveled the Mormon Trail in 1850. Her diary entry for 15 July records that "We traveled seven miles. Came to Fort Childs, formerly Fort Carney. A thundershower came up and William Ridge was struck by lightning and instantly killed. Three of his cattle were killed at the same time, and one of his children slightly injured. A number of people felt the shock."[25]

Mrs. Goodridge unintentionally confused the history of Fort Kearny. The first Fort Kearny was established in 1846 on the Missouri River about fifty miles below Omaha. The second Fort Kearny, or Fort Kearny II, was established in June 1848 on the south side of the Platte River about eight miles south of present Kearney, Nebraska.

This post was first called Post at Grand Island, then Fort Childs, and it officially became Fort Kearny on 30 December 1848.[26] Since Mrs. Goodridge passed Fort Kearny only a year and a half after its official designation as Fort Kearny it is possible that some still referred to the post as Fort Childs.

An 1851, traveler T. M. Barber, noted in his diary for Monday, May 26, that "Last night Mr. John M. Hurd from Hurricane, Grant County, was struck by lightening, while crossing the Elk Horn about eight oclock. He was struck on the right arm. Entered his body on right breast and passed entirely through to his ankles, where it passed from him, through his boots, leaving a hole in each boot about the size of a picayune. Of course death was instant. There were several men in the boat, all prostrated but one. We this day laid him out and consigned him to the grave." His entry for the 29th and 30th noted "there have been five deaths in and about this dirty stream within one week, four by drowning, and one by lightning."[27]

According to James H. Compton's diary, his journey began on a rather morbid note. He left Elkhart, Indiana, on 20 March 1853. After reaching Council Bluffs they "Built two boats to cross Missouri River, but could not cross until winds subside. While waiting witnessed the mob arrest, trial, and execution by hanging of a man for murder. Used their boats also to cross flooded Elkhorn River. A man drowned at Buffalo Creek, and two were killed by lightning at Wolf Creek, opposite Cedar Grove. Two women were crippled by a stampede and two others were kidnapped by Indians but managed to escape."[28] Despite this woe-begotten beginning Compton did reach California in September of the same year.

The following account took place along the Platte River in Nebraska Territory and is quoted from *The Indian War of 1864* by Captain Eugene F. Ware.

Before we reached the place a heavy storm was lowering. The air swirled around, and a cool wave descended. All at once a terrific storm broke in upon us from the southwest. We could hear it coming with continual resounding peals of thunder. Crash was following crash so loud, heavily and quickly that, fearful the horses would become terrified and break away, General Mitchell ordered the horses all to be taken down on the sand under the bank. Finally the General's horse, and the mules from the ambulance, and all were taken down under the bank. The storm at first went over our heads without rain, and furnished us a grand electrical display. The noise finally ceased for a little while, and there came a calm, and the boys got up on the edge of the bank above the horses, sitting down and holding their horses below them in the arroyo by the bridle-rein. We all thought the matter was about over, and were congratulating ourselves that we had not been soaked with a rain. We watched the electric storm roll over on the North Platte hills, when all at once came a flash of lightning and shock of thunder that knocked almost the entire company over. Several were stunned, several fell over the bank, and the balance jumped down. The lightning had struck one of the telegraph poles not far from us, and splintered the poles or damaged them for a great distance on each side. It was such an astonishing peal that it was a little while before anybody spoke. As we saw the wire lying on the ground, and the neighboring poles shattered, General Mitchell ordered two of the soldiers to go each way, and see how many poles were affected by that blow of lightning. The men reported that, taking the poles that were shattered or to some extent visibly damaged, there were thirty-three in number, which was nearly a half-mile on each side of us.[29]

##

Of course the Platte River Valley wasn't the only theater where Mother Nature performed act after act of "Death by Lightning" interrupted by intermittent light drama.

"Dunning D. McNair, recent appointee as Osage subagent [at Neosho River Agency], on June 2 [1831]. McNair was killed by a bolt of lighting while crossing a prairie. He was buried at Union Mission (Oklahoma.)."[30]

"It was 1858 when the settlement [Dragoon Creek, Kansas] first realized it needed a cemetery. A resident by the name of William Probasco was killed by lightning on the afternoon of 25 July 1858, during a shower and electrical storm. He was lying on a feather bed at the time. Other members of the family received electrical shocks but were uninjured."[31]

"Pvt. William W. Colburn, Co. I, 2nd Colorado Cavalry, and his horse were killed by lightning at Cow Creek on June 16, [1865]"[32]

A severe thunderstorm that rumbled across Kansas on the night of 10 July 1883, goes a long way to verifying that lightning does strike twice in the same place and that ball lightning is real.

Mr. J. Savage's account of lightning striking his home was published in the sixteenth annual meeting report of the secretary of the Kansas Academy of Science. Savage and his family had retired for the night when a strong storm struck the house and

> half asleep, we were suddenly aroused by a terrible shock. Springing to our feet, we found that lightning had struck one of the chimneys, which it had torn almost completely out . . .
>
> Finding the family had all escaped injury except being somewhat stunned, we now proceeded to examine as to the possibilities of fire. Entering another room in the chamber, and while near another chimney, we suddenly found ourselves sitting on the floor. Gathering up in an instant, we found this was now struck, brick and mortar flying all directions, and another charge of the sulphurous vapor.

Now fully convinced that lightning might strike in very nearly the same place, and that too within the space of five minutes, we at the instant made no further investigation . . . after another hour the storm had passed.

In the morning the night's work was examined carefully. The first chimney struck was on the east of the house. This was torn out half-way to the floor. The stoppers to the stovepipe holes, both in the chamber and in the dining-room below, had been driven in an exactly horizontal position across the rooms, fourteen feet, and breaking through the glass in the windows, were lodged in the blinds and just reversed in position.

A neighbor a short distance away, who was witnessing the storm and saw this chimney demolished, states that the lightning came down like a huge ball of fire. The second chimney was about in the predicament of the first. The lightning had descended to the kitchen stovepipe, then followed it across the room sixteen feet, and tearing it apart, jumped two feet into the brick lining of the house, thence into the guttering on the side of the house, melting it in three or four places, thence down the pipe, tearing off the corner-boards of the house, and made its exit in a barrel of water.

The family were troubled with a sort of lassitude for two or three days, and with myself were affected with a severe nausea for about a week.

This wonderful, invisible, subtle element which is so terribly sudden and potent in its operations, we now look upon with more mystery than ever.[33]

"Thursday, June 14th [1888] . . . This morning we heard that Ed. Burdick was struck by lightning and killed in his bed, at Beverly [Kansas] at about 2 o'clock. House considerably damaged."[34]

"May 31, 1890 - Lightning killed Neal Henney, near Severance [Kansas]."[35]

Where there's lightning there exists the possibility of hail. This offspring of a thunderstorm also found its way into the superstition and religion of ancient man. Because of its extremely destructive nature it was spoken of as the "White Plague."[36] This scourge "causes more monetary loss than any other type of thunderstorm-spawned severe weather."[37]

The threat prompted by gone civilizations to formulate specific rites and rituals in an effort to mitigate or prevent hailstorms. "The ancient Greeks used to sacrifice a lamb or pullet when hail threatened. In the Middle Ages peasants erected in their fields tall poles bearing strips of parchment inscribed with incantations against the hail god."[38]

Bell ringing to ward off thunderstorms and accompanying hail was an ancient practice that sometimes ended with tragic results; occasionally the bell ringer was killed by the very lightning he was trying to turn away.

One of the most published books in the world, the *Bible*, not only speaks of past hailstorms but goes one step further and prophesies of future hailstorms. The book of Exodus says, "and the fire ran along upon the ground . . . there was hail, and fire mingled with the hail, very grievous . . . And the hail smote all that was in the field, both man and beast; and the hail smote every herb of the field, and brake every tree of the field."[39] This sounds a lot like the description of nineteenth century ball lightning and hailstorms.

And that same *Bible* prophesied that in the future God will use hail to punish sinners. "And there fell upon men a great hail out of heaven, every stone about the weight of a talent: and men blasphemed God because of the plague of the hail; for the plague thereof was exceeding great."[40] Depending on the reference source, a talent weighs in at between seventy-five and ninety-seven pounds; that's the ultimate hailstorm.

Visions involving hailstorms aren't found only in the *Bible*. The famous Oglala Sioux, Crazy Horse, at about age fourteen had a vision that would govern his conduct for the rest of his life. In his vision Curley, as he was known at the time, watched a man on a horse ride directly toward his enemies while arrows and bullets fell thick around him but the rider was never injured or killed.

Behind the rider "a storm cloud rolled and thunder was in the air and on the man's cheek a little zigzag that seemed of lightning, and a few hail spots on his body . . . over him flew the small hawk with red on his back, making his killy-killy crying."[41]

After this vision his name was changed to Crazy Horse and this legendary man of the Oglalas derived his power from the hawk, thunder, lightning, and hail.

Without a doubt real hailstorms were a frequent event in Crazy Horse's lifetime. The prairies and plains where he lived was ideally suited for hailstorms because "the severest hailstorms occur in regions of great land masses and warm, though not tropical, climates."[42]

A severe hailstorm thrashed parts of Texas in 1885 and some supposedly educated folks refused to believe it really happened. When an article about the storm was submitted for publication, the editor of the *United States Monthly Weather Review* accused the author of having an "unusual capacity for exaggeration."

This incident, authored by Isaac Cline, took place before he received national recognition as the weatherman "on watch" when the infamous Galveston hurricane slammed ashore in 1900.

In 1885 Cline was transferred to a weather station at Fort Concho near San Angelo, Texas. He arrived in April and from then until mid-August not a drop of rain had fallen. Although the "prairies were brown and bleak" there continued to be good fishing in the Concho River which, as Cline wrote, "always received a good supply of water from some seemingly unknown source." It was while crossing a foot bridge over the Concho River that Cline encountered another mystery about the river.

Here's how he tells the story.

> I suddenly heard a roaring noise upstream. To my amazement there was a head of water some fifteen or twenty feet in height bulging down over the dry bed of the river. Some fifty yards above the foot bridge a man with two women was driving across the dry bed of the river where a cattle trail had worn down the banks. The head of water was traveling so rapidly that it caught them before they could get out of its way, and they were carried down stream and drowned.

The water rose rapidly and was soon nearly up to the footbridge and I hurried across to the San Angelo side of the river. When I reached the San Angelo bank I looked upstream and saw Mexicans and others taking large fish out of the water where it had spread out over the cattle trail. I was always interested in fishing and walked up to the cattle-crossing to find out how they were accomplishing the feat. A fish some two feet in length, unable to use its fins, drifted out to near where I was standing. I reached down to pick up the fish and lo and behold, my hand plunged into ice water! This icy water had chilled the fish until they could not swim and could be gathered in with the hands. No one there had seen anything of the kind, and all marveled that there should be a river of ice water in Texas in mid-summer. What caused the icy flood to come pouring down the dry river bed in summer? This was a question asked by everyone. There were several scholarly men in the community who theorized on the origin of the ice water, but none was correct. About ten days after the occurrence of the flood of ice water some people came down from Ben Ficklin, a place about 50 miles up the Concho River from San Angelo, and we learned all about the cause of the flood. They told us that a hail storm of great severity had visited that section and covered an extensive area. The hail stones, some of which were as large as ostrich eggs had killed hundreds of grown up cattle. So much hail fell that erosion gulches were filled and the hail was three feet deep on the level ground. This hail melting in 160 degree August sun caused a river of ice water in Texas that froze the fish till they could not swim so they could be gathered in with the hands.[43]

Cline's article was never printed.

John Lynch, in his book *The Weather*, writes that "Normal thunderstorms, despite being powerful enough to produce dramatic lightning shows, cannot form the deadly cocktail of grapefruit-sized hail . . . for this to happen something else is required: they need to last for hours . . . and to do that they need to be capped."[44]

Capping occurs when a layer of warm dry air flows over warm, moist air from the gulf. The layer of dry air is known as a temperature inversion and in effect works much like "the lid on a pressure cooker, with more energy building up beneath it" but not allowing any escape for the energy contained within a forming thunderstorm.

The thus contained system, if heated by sun-warmed surface air, finally breaks through the inversion creating a violent updraft that can rise upward into the path of high-level winds, sometimes even to the jet stream. This draws off some of the warm, moist air creating an increase in the updraft needed to replenish the loss. The energy engine is revving up toward full throttle.

The stage is now set for the super-cell thunderstorm capable of producing torrential rains, mega-hail, and F-5 tornadoes. These storms can last for hours and cut a swath miles wide and hundreds of miles long.

"As long as warm, moist air is being sucked up the cloud will grow until it creates the fabulous, towering columns of a nascent thundercloud. When it hits the top of the troposphere, higher level winds may spread the storm out, to form the famous 'anvil' shape of a thunderhead."

The updraft in one of these supercells keeps condensed water droplets suspended and when they reach the top of the system the air temperature can be as low as -70° F. Here begins the birthing process of hail. As the small ice particles rise and fall in the updrafts and downdrafts they grow in size until gravity overcomes the updraft and the ice falls to earth as hailstones.

The conditions and processes necessary to create hail are given in many books about the weather. This, from Lane's *The Elements Rage*, explains that

> a clue to a large hailstone's origin can be found by splitting it open. It generally consists of onionlike layers of ice built about a tiny central core, or nucleus, which is generally so tiny that it is invisible to the naked eye . . . A hail-bearing thundercloud sometimes towers over ten miles high, with air currents continuously rushing

Harper's Weekly, 21 *March 1874; Frenzeny and Tavernier*

Crude weather stations such as this one at Fort Gibson, Indian Territory, were some of the earliest outposts of the U.S. Army Signal Corp. The
weather service is now part of the National Oceanic and Atmospheric
Administration.

to the top. As these currents ascend they carry with
them water vapor and droplets which, in the higher
regions of the clouds, freeze on to a nucleus and gather
cloud droplets, forming coatings of ice.[45]

After riding the rising and falling air currents inside the
thunderstorm, these hailstones reach a weight sufficient to allow

them to fall to earth. How large they become before escaping the updrafts depends on the velocity of the rising air currents. Scientists estimate that the updraft wind speeds necessary to carry a hailstone with a "diameter of five inches requires an updraft of 157 m.p.h. in air with very little turbulence, and 278 m.p.h. in very turbulent air."[46]

The typical hailstone isn't typical. "Some are like pyramids with flattened bases, while others . . . resemble 'fruit jellies.' Still others may be covered with spikes from a quarter of an inch to almost an inch in length projecting from a central core. Some are in the form of a disk or lens."[47]

"Large hailstones," according to Lane, are "nearly as dense as pure ice, which are formed exclusively in severe thunderstorms during hot weather.

"Although ordinary hailstorms last for only a few minutes, severe ones sometimes last for several hours . . . Such storms may sweep across country at speeds up to 50 m.p.h., sometimes traveling 500 miles, but usually they travel slowly and are very local, rarely exceeding ten miles across."[48]

Lane goes on to explain that for many years "Most meteorologists accept that the largest authenticated hailstone fell on 6 July 1928, at Potter, Nebraska." A witness said that the 'monster chunks of ice . . . when they hit in plowed or soft ground completely buried themselves, and sank halfway in on prairie ground.'

"These monster stones—as large as grapefruit—fell from 10 to 15 feet apart. One was measured weighed and photographed immediately after falling: circumference 17 inches, diameter nearly 5 1/2 inches, weight 1 1/2 pounds."[49]

That record stood for forty-two years before it was eclipsed by a slightly larger stone. This hailstone was a 5.5-inch chunk of ice weighing 1.67 pounds that fell in Coffeyville, Kansas, in 1970."[50]

Yet, this record-setter was eclipsed in size by a hailstone measuring 7.0 inches in diameter with a circumference of 18.75 inches that plummeted to earth at Aurora, Nebraska, on 22 June 2003. It must, however, share the honors with the Coffeyville, Kansas, stone because the Aurora hailstone "struck a house roof in its descent and partially broke (survey by second author), an accurate weight of the hailstone was not possible." For that reason "the Coffeyville hailstone still retains the U.S. record for maximum hailstone weight."[51]

The NOAA authors who gathered the information on the Aurora hailstone are Jared L. Guyer, NOAA/NWS Storm Prediction Center and Rick Ewald, NOAA/NWS Hastings, Nebraska.

Of course it is very possible, and highly probable, that during the nineteenth century even larger hailstones fell on the prairies and plains but went unobserved and unauthenticated.

Today the National Weather Service uses the following descriptive words to estimate the size of hail:

- Pea = 1/4-inch diameter
- Marble/mothball = 1/2-inch diameter
- Dime/Penny = 3/4-inch diameter - hail of penny size or larger is considered severe
- Nickel = 7/8-inch diameter
- Quarter = 1-inch diameter
- Ping-Pong Ball = 1 1/2-inch diameter
- Golf Ball = 1 3/4-inch diameter
- Tennis Ball = 2 1/2-inch diameter
- Baseball = 2 3/4-inch diameter
- Tea Cup = 3-inch diameter
- Grapefruit = 4-inch diameter
- Softball = 4 1/2-inch diameter

That's where the National Weather Service stops. Apparently any hailstones larger than softball size can be called whatever seems appropriate.

Animals and man's handiwork suffer the most damage during a violent hailstorm. Yet, accounts in diaries, journals, and other nineteenth century sources verify that violent hailstorms posed a real threat to newcomers.

Mattes, in *The Great Platte River Road*, gives James Lyon's account of a severe hailstorm along the Platte: "All the wagon-covers looked as if they had been used during the Mexican War as a breastwork, or had received a shower of brickbats: and the men one would have thought had received a shower of Indian arrows, to have seen the blood streaming from their heads."[52]

A particularly sad episode was recorded by Elias Johnson Draper who was traveling from Indiana to California in 1853. A violent hailstorm raked the Platte River road and "caused one woman to have a miscarriage."[53]

Hailstorms and tornadoes are frequently generated by the same thunderstorm supercell such as the storm in June 1860: "Early thunderstorm activity had been noticed in the northwestern extremity of the Hawkeye State in the Sioux City area about 1400 [2 o'clock p.m.]. Severe hail storms, with stones estimated at six and seven inches in circumference, struck the Fort Dodge and Webster City area of Webster and Hamilton counties, some 65 miles northwest of Des Moines."[54]

Hailstorms normally aren't deadly to humans but Mother Nature isn't bound to normality as this report from St. Charles, Missouri, in 1863, shows.

> One of the most remarkable and violent storms ever known in the country occurred in St. Charles county Friday night last [11 September]. The fury of the storm was spent in about two miles square—four miles below St. Charles. The cornfields were completely stripped of the corn, leaving the stalks bare, and the corn having the appearance of being pounded in a mortar. One man was killed and others seriously injured by the hailstones. Pigs in numbers were killed, and the next day cartloads of ducks were taken from the Mauvais Temps Vlaire, killed by the hail. Fabulous stories were told about the size of the hail—a gentleman tells us that he saw one stone which, after being kept in an ice chest two and a half days, was still as large as a goose egg. The damage has been very great, as the storm occurred in a highly cultivated section of the country.[55]

James H. Cook was caught in a violent thunderstorm while trailing cattle from Texas to the railhead in Kansas. His account didn't give a specific date but is was sometime in the early 1870s. He said it "rained and poured, and then rained some more" from start to finish with a tornado and hailstorms thrown in for spicy variety.

Cook remembered that about noon one day the outfit was approaching the Canadian River when he

could see that we were in for a bad storm. I had never seen such queer looking clouds before . . .

I was on herd with the horses. Everybody but the cook and myself went to the cattle herd. I was herding the horses a short distance from the wagon . . . A few minutes later we were struck by a truly awful blast of wind, hailstones, and water. The horse herd was not hobbled. They stampeded, and I raced ahead of them, trying to check them. The air was now so thick with hail and water that I could not see ten feet ahead. The hail was hammering my head so fiercely that I seemed to see fire. I put one arm over my head until my hand and arm had been pelted as much as they could stand, and then changed to the other.

Suddenly we came to a gulch about fifteen feet deep . . . I could neither stop nor turn . . . Over we went! The horse herd all came over, tumbling about me . . . The hail was striking me in the face and on my hands, raising blood blisters. I could not hold my horse . . .

By this time the water was coming down the little gulch . . . I had to get out of the way quickly or be drowned, for, in a very few minutes, the water was seven or eight feet deep. When I crawled to the top of the bank I drifted with the storm, walking about a quarter of a mile out to a very level country. I was now in water and ice nearly to my knees. My head, face, and hands were one solid bruise, and I was played out. I made up my mind that my time had come, and that probably all the rest of the boys had been killed. The roar of the storm was awful. Every minute I expected some large hailstone to knock me senseless, and I knew that I should drown if knocked down. All I could do was to stand there, waiting for the end, praying one minute for the Lord to save me, and wondering the next if my body would ever be found.

Cook didn't die nor did any of the crew and they lost not a single head of cattle or horses. Later they discovered evidence that a tornado had passed scarcely a half mile from them. The aftermath of the storm left hail "in drifts three feet deep in low places. Thousands of prairie dogs and little prairie-dog owls, as well as rabbits and rattlesnakes, had been drowned out of their holes and chilled or beaten to death by the hail. Even the grass was smashed off at the roots and washed away in the drifts of hailstones."[56]

Unfortunately, the reporter and the newspaper are unknown in the following 1882 account.

> Probably the severest storm of rain and hail that ever prevailed in this section of the State [Kansas] occurred at Valley Falls about eleven o'clock on last Friday night . . .
>
> The storm came from the South, and was unaccompanied by any wind. The hail stones varied in size, but were mostly about the dimensions of a hen's egg, some few perhaps being larger . . .
>
> The falling hail penetrated the iron roofs like bullets, rebounded from the sidewalks and striking against the glass in show windows, shattering them into a thousand pieces . . . the roofs of the older houses, particularly, offering scarcely any resistance to the descending missiles.
>
> The people thought the crack of doom had come, and although the crash of broken glass was heard from nearly all the store buildings and churches, none dared venture forth, and many were overcome with terror and fainted away.

Thankfully, that storm didn't extend very far outside of Valley Falls and in the country "did little damage beyond killing a few sheep and young calves which were exposed."[57]

Any amount of hail, regardless of size, can inflict costly damage. Extensive crop damage is frequently the result of small hail driven by a strong wind. But don't discount the potential damage of large hail. On 20 August 1887, "Hailstones ten inches around caused $5,000 damage at Atchison [Kansas]."[58]

Under the dateline, "Atchison, Kan., August 20," are the details of the storm that was, according to the writer, the granddaddy of all hailstorms.

> The most terrific hail storm that ever occurred in this region swept over this city at 4 p. m. this afternoon. Hail measuring nine and ten inches in circumference fell . . . The storm appears to be general throughout northern Kansas. The cars on incoming trains of the Central branch of the Union Pacific, and Omaha extension of the Missouri Pacific had their windows on the north side broken by the hail . . . The immense hailstones came down at intervals and far apart, but with terrific violence, crashing through windows whenever they struck one like a cannon ball. H. C. Patchen . . . was struck by one of them and the bridge of his nose flattened. His injuries are very serious.[59]

Sometimes it was just the sheer volume of hail that was impressive, if not destructive. In Iowa's Adair and Union counties on 6 August 1890, hail was four inches deep on the level and "drifted into heaps six feet deep, where it remained, protected by debris, for twenty-six days." One gentleman visited the area several days after the storm and gathered "up enough hail to freeze a gallon of ice cream."[60]

South Dakota is another prime target for hailstorms and in Rapid City on 5 July 1891, "hail killed sixteen horses and injured others so seriously that they had to be shot. Some were even blinded. In other Iowa and Nebraska storms, cattle, horses, and smaller animals were reported killed, and people attempting to save the livestock sustained serious injuries, in some instances to the extent of broken bones."[61]

On 24 June 1897, in Topeka, Kansas, "horses were knocked down by hail, while others hitched to vehicles became panic-stricken and ran away."

"In Washington County, Iowa, on September 1, 1897, drifts of hailstones were six feet deep."

The "show me" state experienced a storm "in Nodaway County, Missouri, on September 5, 1898, in which hundreds of small animals were killed, chunks of ice went entirely through the roofs of houses . . . One man claimed he had to cut the ice out of his stovepipe before he could build a fire. In one locality it was impossible to get through a lane two weeks after the storm because of the depth of ice in it. Some of this hail remained for fifty-two days."[62]

This next account of hailstorm damage comes from Wayne Gard's *The Chisholm Trail* where he writes that "in hailstorms the stones occasionally were so big and struck with such force that they killed many of the cattle. In such a storm the cowhand had to take off his saddle and get his head and shoulders under it for protection."[63]

Horses and mules, more often than not, were terrified by hailstorms which caused even the best trained animals to bolt. A severe storm with hailstones the size of hen's eggs hit the Texas Panhandle town of Tascosa during its heyday in the 1880s. When the storm broke, a "Mexican called Trinidad was above town coming in with a load of roofing poles for building here, and his team took fright and ran, scattering his load, throwing him off and running the wagon over him, and at length broke loose from the wagon and came on to town. Trinidad received pretty severe injuries, and the beating of the hail alone was heavy enough to be dangerous. He was unable yesterday morning to be out of bed."

In the aftermath of the same hailstorm another "team came up to the lower town about dark, bringing the fore parts of a wagon. A horse was seen loose a few hundred yards above the river, wearing a buggy bridle. We have not heard if it was discovered who were the owners . . . and can only trust that nothing too serious may be developed. Doubtless many a little calf, and unlucky pig, or a poor chicken, had to turn its toes to the daisies."[64]

Today hailstorms are still so destructive that hail suppression research is being carried on around the globe. Researchers generally accepted that altering the path of a supercell, destroying it, or keeping it from forming is out of the question—-at least for man. So, the concept that has held out some hope of reducing hail damage is to create more hailstones of such small size that damage is minimized or eliminated.

The hope is that this can be accomplished by cloud seeding which introduces millions of tiny crystal particles into the thunderstorm. The theory is that around each of these tiny particles water droplets will begin to form and therefore "condense out so much of the available water as individual droplets . . . that no one crystal can find enough available water to grow to a large enough size to make hail."[65]

This hail suppression research, it would seem, has taken some strange turns. An old saying about pilots and thunderstorms states that there are two kinds of pilots: those that avoid thunderstorms and those that are dead. Now a third kind can be added: the pilot that flies an armored T-28 aircraft directly into thunderstorms.

The South Dakota School of Mines and Technology (SDSM&T), located at Rapid City, South Dakota,

> maintains and operates the only armored T-28 meteorological research airplane in the entire United States. The T-28 plane is specially equipped and modified to fly directly into hailstorms and to withstand damage from hailstones and lightning strikes.
>
> . . . the T-28 program has been conducting weather research nationally and internationally for almost thirty years-from the Dakotas to Texas to Canada and even Switzerland. The T-28 aircraft has flown into more than 900 hailstorms and thunderstorms to collect data on how hail stones develop.[66]

This program has "produced some tangible benefits" but, of course, hasn't eliminated hailstorms. It has, though, not only provided scientists "with an up close personal look at stormy weather, but also important meteorological data to better understand the mysterious forces of Mother Nature."

These "mysterious forces" have, for millennia, spawned some interesting legends and lore about thunderstorms and their associated thunder and lightning.

Washington Irving wrote down this legend just as he heard it in 1832 while on his tour of the prairies. Irving and his party experienced a "violent thunder-gust" somewhere northwest of Fort Gibson on Salt Fork.

Afterwards, he relates that sitting around the campfire "I drew from them some of the notions entertained on the subject by their Indian friends. The latter declared that extinguished thunderbolts are sometimes picked up by hunters on the prairies, who use them for the heads of arrows and lances, and that any warrior thus armed is invincible. Should a thunder-storm occur, however, during battle, he is liable to be carried away by the thunder, and never heard of more."[67]

Another story told was of a Konza Indian who was hunting on the prairie and during a storm was

> struck down senseless by the thunder. On recovering, he beheld the thunderbolt lying on the ground, and a horse standing beside it. Snatching up the bolt, he sprang upon the horse, but found, too late, that he was astride of the lightning. In an instant he was whisked away over the prairies and forests, and streams and desert, until he was flung senseless at the foot of the Rocky Mountains; whence, on recovering, it took him several months to return to his own people.[68]

On the trans-Mississippi frontier, especially during the Indian Wars, it was in the best interest of the newcomers to keep the telegraph wires up and humming. Consequently the military went to great lengths to convince Indians that telegraph wires were imbued with extraordinary powers linked to the spirit world. Special demonstrations of the "talking wire" succeeded in fooling many Indians into believing that the wire did, indeed, hold "big medicine."

Occasionally along would come a warrior who would have none of the medicine stories. During this time "A young Sioux Indian was determined to show that he had no faith in the Great Spirit's connection with the wires, so he set to work with his hatchet to cut down one of the telegraph poles. A severe thunderstorm was going on at a distance; a charge of electricity being taken by the wires, was passed to the pole which the Indian was cutting, and resulted in his instant death. After that the tribe never molested the telegraph again."[69]

As time passed, this respect eroded to the point where individual Indians again denounced the dreaded medicine and set out to destroy the talking wire. Captain Ware relates an incident told to him by a telegraph operator working the line along the Platte River Road in 1863.

> A party of Indian braves crossed the line up by O'Fallon's Bluffs, and one Indian who had been down in "The States," as it was called, and thought he understood it [telegraph], volunteered to show his gang that they must not be afraid of it, and it was a good thing to have the wire up in their village to lariat ponies to. So he chopped down a pole, severed the wire and began ripping it off from the poles . . . they cut off nearly a half-mile of wire, and all of the Indians in single file on horseback catching hold of the wire, proceeded to ride and pull the wire across the prairie towards their village.

While they were fleeing from the crime scene, an electrical storm unleashed a few lightning bolts and the results were predictable. "After they had gone several miles and were going over the ridge . . . by some means or other a bolt of lightning, so the story goes, knocked almost all of them off their horses and hurt some of them considerably. Thereupon they dropped the wire, and coming to the conclusion that it was punishment for their acts and that it was 'bad medicine,' they afterwards let it alone."[70]

##

The hailstorm near San Antonio, Texas that was hammering Lieutenant Bache and his fishing companions finally abated after twenty-two minutes; twenty-two minutes of violent punishment to the men, their mule team, and the town of San Antonio. Pouring rain flooded many buildings after the large hailstones had smashed all the windows and blinds on the north side of the structures.

San Antonio looked as if it had been subjected to thousands of shots fired at walls and roofs from point-blank range. Shingle roofs were destroyed by the hail; large stones cut holes through tin roofs and tin gutters. A few large hailstones smashed through the roofs and ceilings all the way to the floor. One hailstone punched a four-inch hole through both sides of a sheet-iron stove pipe.

Crops were beaten into the ground and trees and bushes were stripped of their leaves and small branches. Trees were stripped of bark like is seen "after cannonading in a forest."

At least one dog was killed by the hail and a woman had two ribs broken when she and her husband were caught in the storm while camping on the prairie.

What about Lieutenant Bache and his fishing party? Did they survive this assault by Mother Nature?

Just minutes after Lieutenant Bache and his fishing buddies jumped out of the run-away ambulance, they were beaten and battered nearly senseless.

The mules fared no better. The ferocity of the storm so disoriented the team that they circled back into the teeth of the rain and hail. The large hail stones' repeated blows to the animals' heads had so stunned and weakened the mules that the men were able to sprint to the ambulance and leap inside. In a few minutes the wheels of the vehicle became snagged on a rail fence and the exhausted mules didn't try to move any further.

The men put the ambulance seats over their heads and rode out the storm. The hailstones ripped the ambulance curtains to shreds and the poor mules were bruised and stunned. Nevertheless when the storm stopped, the team rallied and pulled the battered vehicle and its passengers back to San Antonio.

Lieutenant Bache and his friends arrived home, in his own words, "With black eyes, bloody heads, smashed hats, bruised arms, and torn and muddy clothes, we appeared as if we had just come from a free fight and had been very badly used."[71]

##

The number of fact-or-fiction stories related to thunderstorms rivals those associated with tornados.

Is it possible for hailstones to contain live fish?

How about live turtles?

And, perhaps, frogs?

*National Oceanic and Atmospheric Administration *
Department of Commerce, Herbert Campbell

Beauty and the beast. A thunderhead with a well-defined anvil like this one can sometimes tower thirteen miles above the Earth and contain a half million tons of water. They can release as much energy as a megaton bomb.

Lightning is credited with "melting holes in church bells, welding chains into iron bars, and blasting wooden sailboat masts into shavings."[72]

Lane included several accounts of freakish lightning stories in his work, *The Elements Rage.*

> Two ladies, quietly knitting, had their needles snatched out of their hands. A farmer's laborer was carrying a pitchfork over his shoulder when lightning hurled it 50 yards, twisting the tines into corkscrews. Lightning struck a room where a girl was sitting at her sewing machine, holding a pair of scissors. There was a brilliant flash of light, the scissors were spirited away and the girl found herself sitting *on* the sewing machine ...
>
> Occasionally, lightning makes marks on people's bodies which have been thought to be 'photographs'

on the tissues. The markings usually disappear in a few hours . . . a woman near a lightning flash had the likeness of a flower imprinted on the leg. A flower had stood in the route of the discharge and the image remained for the rest of her life.[73]

Lane, same source and same location, quoted the French astronomer Camille Flammarion who "says that there is a well-authenticated case of a landscape being 'photographed' on the inside of the skin of a sheep which had been struck by lightning."

Then there's the naked side of lightning. "Men struck by lightning have sometimes been found completely naked, their clothes scattered in fragments over a wide area. Two girls were standing by a reaping machine when lightning struck. The girls were stripped naked and their boots torn from their feet. They were unharmed—only embarrassed."

The explanation Frank Lane offered is that "The sudden intense heating of the air in the fabric causes it to expand so violently that cloths and footwear are blasted off."[74]

Lightning, it is told, struck a potato patch and turned the plants into cinders "but the potatoes underneath were cooked to a turn."

Birds, like airplanes, have been struck by lightning in mid-flight. Aircraft normally aren't killed and cooked, so to speak, but birds "have been seen to fall from the sky and when examined were found to be partly roasted."[75]

These stories are fascinating but the case of the "silver cat" has to be the undisputed champion fact-or-fiction lightning story. A period newspaper article in 1891 reported that lightning struck an old mansion at New Salem, Vermont, in which several revolutionary swords were displayed on the parlor wall. One of the swords was heavily plated with silver.

During an exceptionally violent thunderstorm, the family was stunned by a lightning bolt that entered the house through a half-dollar sized hole it melted through a parlor window. After recovering from the shock, the father and son discovered that laying on the parlor sofa was a silver cat with each hair and whisker as perfect as that of a real, live cat. Upon further examination of the room they discovered that the hilt and silver plate had vanished from the sword on the wall. It seems the family cat had been electroplated by lightning.[76]

##

In spite of sacrificial lambs, pealing church bells, and armored T-28s, Mother Nature is not impressed. She still rules supreme over her realm of thunder, lightning and hail.

THE DEADLIEST WOMAN IN THE WEST

Chapter Six notes

[1] David Laskin, *Braving the Elements* (New York: Doubleday, 1996), 36-37.

[2] Frank W. Lane, *The Elements Rage* (Philadelphia: Chilton Books, 1965), 119.

[3] Richard Irving Dodge, *The Plains of the Great West* (New York: G. P. Putnam's Sons, 1877), 81-82.

[4] Elizabeth B. Custer, *Following the Guidon* (New York: Harper & Brothers, 1890), 289-290.

[5] Elizabeth B. Custer, *Tenting on the Plains or General Custer in Kansas and Texas* (New York: Charles L. Webster & Company, 1887), 632-633.

[6] John Lynch, *The Weather* (Toronto: Firefly Books Ltd., 2002), 193.

[7] Frank W. Lane, *The Elements Rage* (Philadelphia: Chilton Books, 1965), 122.

[8] Ibid., 121.

[9] K. B. McEachron and Kenneth G. Patrick, *Playing with Lightning* (New York: Random House, 1940), 10-11.

[10] Frank W. Lane, *The Elements Rage* (Philadelphia: Chilton Books, 1965), 135.

[11] Peter E. Viemeister, *The Lightning Book* (Garden City, NY: Doubleday & Company, Inc., 1961), 41.

[12] Ibid., 39.

[13] Merrill J. Mattes, *The Great Platte River Road* (Lincoln: Nebraska State Historical Society, 1969), 94-95.

[14] Wayne Gard, *The Chisholm Trail* (Norman: University of Oklahoma Press, 1976), 126.

[15] William H. Forbis, *The Cowboys* (New York: Time-Life Books, 1973), 163.

[16] J. Marvin Hunter, comp. and ed., *The Trail Drivers of Texas* (San Antonio, TX: Jackson Printing Co., 1920-1923), 1:202.

[17] Bruce Siberts, *Nothing But Prairie and Sky*, comp. Walker D. Wyman (Norman: University of Oklahoma Press, 1954), 149.

[18] William H. Forbis, *The Cowboys* (New York: Time-Life Books, 1973), 162-163.

[19] Mary Saunders, *The Whitman Massacre* (n.d.; reprint, Fairfield, WA: Ye Galleon Press, 1977), 7.

[20] Merrill J. Mattes, *Platte River Road Narratives* (Urbana and Chicago: University of Illinois Press, 1988), 205. Taken from Mattes' summary of the MS.

[21] Ibid., 216. Taken from Mattes' summary of the MS.

[22] Lewis Shutterly, *The Diary of Lewis Shutterly 1849-1850* (Saratoga, WY: Saratoga Historical and Cultural Association, 1981), 8.

[23] J. W. (Watt) Gibson, *Recollections of a Pioneer* (1912; reprint, Independence, Missouri: Two Trails Publishing, 1999), 23-24.

[24] Merrill J. Mattes, *Platte River Road Narratives* (Urbana and Chicago: University of Illinois Press, 1988), 177. Taken from Mattes' summary of the MS.

[25] Kenneth L. Holmes, comp. and ed., *Covered Wagon Women : Diaries & Letters from the Western Trails 1850*, vol. 2 (1983; reprint, Lincoln: University of Nebraska Press, 1996), 217.

[26] Robert W. Frazer, *Forts of the West* (Norman: University of Oklahoma Press, 1966), 87.

[27] T. M. Barber Diary, RG 5127. Nebraska State Historical Society, Lincoln.

[28] Merrill J. Mattes, *Platte River Road Narratives* (Urbana and Chicago: University of Illinois Press, 1988), 406. Taken from Mattes' summary of the MS.

[29] Eugene F. Ware, *The Indian War of 1864* (Topeka, Kansas: Crane & Company, 1911), 250-251.

[30] Louise Barry, comp., "Kansas Before 1854: A Revised Annals" *Kansas Historical Quarterly*, Summer 1962, 186.

[31] Daniel Fitzgerald, *Ghost Towns of Kansas* Vol. I (n.p.: privately printed, 1976), 1:38.

[32] Daniel Fitzgerald, *Ghost Towns of Kansas* Vol. II (Holton, Kansas: The Gossip Printery, 1979), 2:141.

[33] J. Savage, "Some Lightning Freaks in 1883." in *Transactions of the Sixteenth and Seventeenth Annual Meeting of the Kansas Academy of Science, (1883-1884), with the Report of the Secretary* (Topeka: Kansas Publishing House, 1885), 9:41-42.

[34] Dr. J. W. Boyles diary, 14 June 1888. Typed transcript, "Dr. John W. Boyles' Diary." Salina, Kansas, Public Library, Campbell Room files, 32.

[35] Daniel Fitzgerald, *Ghost Towns of Kansas* Vol. II (Holton, Kansas: The Gossip Printery, 1979), 2:63.

[36] Frank W. Lane, *The Elements Rage* (Philadelphia: Chilton Books, 1965), 92.

[37] "Flash Floods and Hail: Property and Personal Devestation," http://ww2010.atmos.uiuc.edu/(Gh)/guides/mtr/svr/dngr/flood.rxml.

[38] Frank W. Lane, *The Elements Rage* (Philadelphia: Chilton Books, 1965), 94.

[39] Exodus 9:23-25

[40] Revelation 16:21

[41] Mari Sandoz, *Crazy Horse* (1942; reprint, Lincoln: University of Nebraska Press, 1961), 105.

[42] Frank W. Lane, *The Elements Rage* (Philadelphia: Chilton Books, 1965), 89.

[43] Isaac Monroe Cline, *Storms, Floods and Sunshine* (1945; reprint, Gretna, LA: Pelican Publishing Company, Inc., 2000), 51-52.

[44] John Lynch, *The Weather* (Toronto: Firefly Books Ltd., 2002), 65.

[45] Frank W. Lane, *The Elements Rage* (Philadelphia: Chilton Books, 1965), 82.

[46] Ibid., 84.

[47] Snowden D. Flora, *Hailstorms of the United States* (Norman: University of Oklahoma Press, 1956), 7.

[48] Frank W. Lane, *The Elements Rage* (Philadelphia: Chilton Books, 1965), 82.

[49] Ibid., 83-84.

[50] Richard Lipkin, "Weather's Fury," in *Nature on the Rampage,* with H. J. De Blij (Washington: Smithsonian Books, 1994), 45.

[51] Jared L. Guyer and Rick Ewald, "Record Hail Event—Examination of the Aurora, Nebraska Supercell of 22 June 2003," http://www.spec.noaa.gov/publications/guyer/aurora.pdf.

[52] Merrill J. Mattes, *The Great Platte River Road* (Lincoln: Nebraska State Historical Society, 1969), 96.

[53] Merrill J. Mattes, *Platte River Road Narratives* (Urbana and Chicago: University of Illinois Press, 1988), 408. Taken from Mattes' summary of the journal.

[54] David M. Ludlum, *Early American Tornadoes 1586-1870* (Boston: American Meteorological Society, 1970), 124.

[55] Ibid., 132; *St. Louis Republican,* 17 September 1863.

[56] James H. Cook, *Fifty Years on the Old Frontier as Cowboy, Hunter, Guide, Scout, and Ranchman* (New Haven: Yale University Press, 1923), 74-78.

[57] "Hurtling Hail: Valley Falls Visited by a Furious Storm on Friday Night." MPM, 22 April 1882. This clipping from an unknown newspaper, MPM, is in the Kansas State Historical Society files: 551.57R, Vol. 1, p. 59-70.

[58] Kirke Mechem, ed., *The Annals of Kansas 1886-1925* (Topeka: Kansas State Historical Society, 1972),1:41.

[59] "Atchinson Experiences the Most Terrific Hail Storm Ever Known." *Commonwealth* (Topeka, Kansas), 25 August 1887.

[60] Snowden D. Flora, *Hailstorms of the United States* (Norman: University of Oklahoma Press, 1956), 8.

[61] Ibid., 8-9.

[62] Ibid., 8-9.

[63] Wayne Gard, *The Chisholm Trail* (Norman: University of Oklahoma Press, 1976), 126.

[64] John L. McCarty, *Maverick Town* (Norman: University of Oklahoma Press, 1946), 207-208.

[65] John Lynch, *The Weather* (Toronto: Firefly Books Ltd., 2002), 212-213.

[66] "Armored Airplane Thunders Into Stormy Weather." *SDSM&T Quarterly*, 1998 Spring, http://www.hpcnet.org/sdsmt/SiteID=199437.

[67] Washington Irving, *A Tour on the Prairies* (Philadelphia: Carey, Lea, & Blanchard, 1835), 129.

[68] Ibid., 129-130.

[69] B. A. Botkin, ed., *A Treasury of Western Folklore* (New York: Bonanza Books, 1975), 184.

[70] Eugene F. Ware, *The Indian War of 1864* (Topeka, Kansas: Crane & Company, 1911), 111-112.

[71] House of Representatives. *Annual Report of the Board of Regents of the Smithsonian Institution, Showing the Operations, Expenditures, and Condition of the Institution for the Year 1870.* Lieutenant George M. Bache, U.S.A., "Account of a Hail-Storm in Texas." 42nd Congress, 1st Session, Ex. Doc. No. 20, 477-479. GPO 1871.

[72] Richard Lipkin, "Weather's Fury," in *Nature on the Rampage*, with H. J. De Blij (Washington: Smithsonian Books, 1994), 65.

[73] Frank W. Lane, *The Elements Rage* (Philadelphia: Chilton Books, 1965), 133.

[74] Ibid., 133.

[75] Ibid., 132-133.

[76] Peter E. Viemeister, *The Lightning Book* (Garden City, New York: Doubleday & Company, Inc., 1961), 267-268.

Chapter Seven

RIVERS OF DAMNS

Water is one of the most abundant and important substances in man's life—and one of his worst enemies.
                                    —Frank W. Lane, *The Elements Rage*

Heriet Seccombe labored as a faithful helpmate to her husband and his ministry for over thirty years. Under ideal conditions missionary work is never without trials. Going west with the gospel in the 1800s took the courage of King David, the strength of Sampson and the devotion of St. Paul— all coupled with faith to move mountains.

Mrs. Seccombe, her husband the Reverend Charles Seccombe, and their children would need all of the above attributes to face the terrifying "Perils of Waters" they encountered in 1881.

Both the Reverend and Mrs. Seccombe were born in Massachusetts where we assume they met and married. Records place them in St. Anthony, Minnesota Territory, (East Minneapolis, Minnesota) in 1853 where he helped organize and establish the First Congregational Church. Here he carried on his missionary work until 1866 when he was released as pastor.

The 1880 census places the Seccombe family in Cedar County, Nebraska, where Charles, age 62, is listed as a minister. Heriet is listed as a 51-year-old housewife. Their children residing at the same residence are listed as Hattie, age 21; Emma, age 19; Mary, age 16; and Charlie, age 12.

They plied their labor of love in the settlement of Green Island, Nebraska, "on the bottom land about one mile directly opposite Yankton, Dakota Territory."[1] By 1881 the village had approximately 100 residents and "two general stores, two blacksmith shops, one shoemaker, one hotel and restaurant, one Methodist Church, one Congregational Church, and one school house."

Apparently Reverend Seccombe and the Methodist minister were exceptionally effective in their work as the town had no saloons. "It was of course, unusual for a river town to have no saloon but the great majority of the citizens were opposed to it so they failed."[2]

The Seccombe family shared the same concern about flooding as the rest of the Nebraskans and South Dakotans who populated the river bottoms. Each spring the snow-melt and rains practically guaranteed flooding somewhere on the Big Muddy. But since the founding of Green Island in 1873, the town hadn't been molested by the river's boisterous spring freshets.

However, on Sunday night, 27 March 1881, Heriet Seccombe and family anxiously watched tiny lights, like fireflies, dancing on the rising waters of the Missouri River. These lights were lanterns in rescue boats as crewmen evacuated people from the extreme lowlands along the river. The Seccombes gave thanks that the water had only risen to their doorstep; when Monday morning dawned, the water was receding. Rejoicing was heard up and down the river as residents believed the threat was past.

The rejoicing was short lived.

At first light next morning the Seccombe family watches the river's muddy water quickly climbing the bank toward their home. Seven men rowed by in a skiff and one man shouted that Yankton had received a telegram warning that "a great rise in the river is headed downstream."

That night Mrs. Seccombe sees the skiff return about midnight and carry their neighbors to safety. The men manning the oars promise to return for Heriet and family in about a half hour.

In the interim the family gathers at the altar for prayer and then says their goodbyes to their work animals, their pets, and their home. The skiff is good to its word and soon the Seccombe family joins about forty others at a strong brick house located on higher ground. Food is short, accommodations crowded, and

Frank Leslie's Illustrated Newspaper, *16 April 1881*

The spring flood of 1881 brought great suffering and destruction along the Missouri River Valley from Pierre, Dakota Territory, to Sioux City, Iowa. In this newspaper illustration, residents of Vermillion, Dakota Territory, flee for their lives. Many settlers lost everything. Some even lost their lives.

the tobacco chewers and the swearers are unappreciated, but they rejoice in their deliverance.

Late that night they lie down, "one and another, upon the floor with quieted, trusting hearts. But faith and trust does not always bring sleep, especially when one has too many bones. So the night wears slowly away and the dawn delays to come. Wednesday morning, 30 March with the first eastern ray, we stand upon the door-step; and oh, the capricious water has crept up, up, to within a few feet of the door."[3]

Soon men begin to ask "Where is our God? I've lost my faith." Fear tries to gain a foothold in people's minds but Reverend Seccombe and his family lead them in singing hymns and encouraging them to trust God and keep the faith.

All the same, as time drags on and the river continues to stalk the house, some begin to talk of building a raft, fearful that they all shall drown if they remain.

With a roar like thunder, the whole river bottom shudders and groans. The ice gorge below town has broken. About noon the skiff returns and assures them that the ice will pass innocently with no harm suffered by anyone in the house. The rescuers then depart to check on another family on a lower part of Green Island.

Again the assurance of deliverance is short lived. "Hark! Do you not hear the distant roar? Look! Do you not see the on-coming of the mighty monsters? Like an army of wild, infuriated beasts these million-tonned ice cakes appear, threatening every minute to crunch everything between their icy jaws. See! The muddy water is coming rapidly up onto the long door step."[4]

A half hour later they watch spellbound as a cake of ice hits the Methodist Church and it drops to pieces.

The school house begins to float downstream.

The Bailey house drops.

The hotel disintegrates in the grinding ice.

The entire street of houses has vanished in a twinkling.

The big storehouse has set sail.

The Congregational Church sails slowly by and disappears. "The toiling missionary and wife had turned away, dizzy and heart sick. The precious sanctuary of labors, and tears, and the gifts within, organ, lamps, sofa, communion table, clock, carpet, Sunday school library, etc., from saints far away; all going—gone!"

The water has now reached the fifth step of the stairway to the second floor. Men salvage what lumber they can and begin building a raft. All seem to have abandoned hope and straining eyes see no rescue boat. Of course it would be impossible for the skiff to negotiate a river laden with deadly ice chunks.

Hope and faith evaporate.

Reverend Seccombe, still weak from a recent illness, instructs his wife to gather the family. Heartsick at the loss of their church and home, the family, eyes filled with tears, listen as he tells them, "dear mamma and dear children, I have thought it all over and with others think there is only about fifteen minutes at the longest between us and a watery grave."[5]

During the nineteenth century almost every major throughway from the Mississippi River to the Rocky Mountains followed a waterway. Therefore, river routes became the superhighways of the westward movement.

Primary among these river highways was the Mississippi and "Humans, dating back thousands of years to the first American Indians in the area, have always used the Mississippi River and its tributaries as major transportation routes. From the Mississippi River a boat can access over half of the United States."[6]

Some of the additional rivers that added cross-threads of travel throughout the mosaic of grasslands between the Mississippi and the Rockies were the Missouri, the Canadian, the Cimarron, the Arkansas, the Smoky Hill, the Saline, the Solomon, the Red, the Kansas, the Yellowstone, the Republican, the Platte, the Niobrara, and the Marais des Cygnes, or Osage.

There were others. In fact, thirty of the largest seventy U.S. Rivers are in the corridor between the Mississippi River and the Rocky Mountains. Including the Mississippi, their combined length is over 23,000 miles, or almost enough to circle the earth. Twenty-three thousand miles of potential flood plain.

The Deadliest Woman in the West

Will Rogers, commenting on floods in Oklahoma, said "When the Arkansas, Red River, Salt Fork, Verdigris, Caney, Cat Creek, Possum Creek, Dog Creek, and Skunk Branch all are up after a rain, we got more seacoast than Australia."[7]

Rogers' observation could well be said of every state between the Mississippi River and the Rocky Mountains. And along these flood plains sprang up the first newcomer settlements. This puzzled the Indians who learned long ago that river valleys and creek banks weren't flood-friendly sites and were not ideal locations for establishing permanent settlements.

Indians watching newcomers build homes and business in flood plains shook their heads in puzzlement and warned that floods would cover the valley with water from "hill to hill." The settlers and town fathers ignored such advice from unlearned savages.

And the floods came with water from "hill to hill."

"Floods," Dennis Flanagan writes in *Nature on the Rampage*, "are the most frequent rampages of nature."[8] These reoccurring rampages destroyed crops, livestock, and communities along with men, women, and children.

Water is the heart and soul of floods and "Water is heavy, which is why, en masse, it is so destructive. A cubic foot of water weighs about 62 pounds, the actual weight varying slightly with temperature and the amount of dissolved salts. A large bathful (a cubic yard) weighs three-quarters of a ton, and the water in a tank 30 x 25 x 20 feet (15,000 cubic feet—about the size of a six-room house) weighs over 450 tons."[9]

Where does that much water come from? "At any moment, some 2,000 storms are under way globally, adding up to about 16 million a year. A typical thunderstorm can spill 125 million gallons of water."[10] The other source for prodigious amounts of water is snowmelt.

##

As the century unfolded, nature's rampages appeared to be growing more destructive. "As the geologist and conservationist W. J. McGee observed in 1891, society seemed to have made great strides during the nineteenth century in taming four of its ancient adversaries—fire, famine, war, and pestilence—but

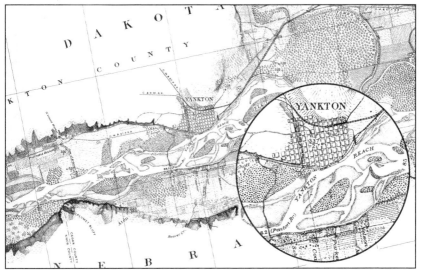

Author's collection

This is one of eighty-four pages mapping the entire Missouri River. It was created by Congress, produced by the Missouri River Commission and published in 1892-1895. The inset makes it clear that the town of Green Island, Nebraska, across the river from Yankton, Dakota Territory was literally "wiped off the face of the Earth" by the 1881 flood.

the fifth, floods, had, if anything, become more harmful than ever."[11]

What was responsible for this belief? There were several developments that contributed, not the least of which was the gathering and disseminating of news about floods.

News on the frontier traveled slowly. Until the telegraph web wired the country together, someone in California or New York might have been unaware of the death and destruction caused by a flood on the Missouri, Platte, or Canadian rivers. And unless the flood caused the death of a family member or close friend, or destroyed some of his personal property such a remote flood was of little concern. And the "weatherman" of the time didn't have radio or television by which he could inform millions of viewers about natural disasters as they happened.

TV today provides real-time footage of every flood in your community, your state, your country, and your planet—if they are destructive enough to be deemed newsworthy. The Red Cross, FEMA, and other emergency and relief programs swing into action soliciting funds for flood victims. Hence, it's difficult

271

to ignore floods in today's society. Does this mean that floods have been growing more frequent and more destructive?

The answer is set down succinctly in a passage from William B. Meyer's *Americans and Their Weather* showing that perception isn't always fact because

> there was little solid evidence that floods were any higher or more frequent than in former times. A bitter turn-of-the-century debate pitted forest conservationists against engineers, hydrologists, and meteorologists who assembled and analyzed long-term records of flooding and streamflow to show that increased extremes were not apparent even where much deforestation had taken place.[12]

Meyer then wrote "They might become so in the future, but times of extraordinarily high water in great river systems remained largely the work of the weather. The engineers understood better than the advocates of reforesting did the chief reason why damage was on the rise." He continues by quoting the following that documents stating that in 1909 some engineers understood what the Army Corp of Engineers is learning today.

> "Care should be taken," one of them observed, "not to ascribe to increasing flood heights or frequencies losses which are due to Man's operations in placing property in the way of floods." "It is true," another wrote to like effect, "that floods produce greater disaster and suffering than in years past, but this is due solely to the fact that the population in the overflow areas had increased, and many great industrial improvements have been built up directly in the face of the fact that the ground occupied was subject to serious overflow."[13]

In view of that, the argument can be made that the destruction caused by floods is, to a large degree, of human manufacture.

##

The Missouri River was the major tributary west of the Mississippi serving both Indians and newcomers as a highway of travel and commerce. Until the railroads traversed the trans-Mississippi West, its dirty water was the undisputed superhighway for river traffic into the prairies and plains—all 2,315 miles of it shifting course.

After the Little Bighorn battle in 1876, General Nelson A. Miles with six companies of troops were ordered to proceed by steamboat up the Missouri River from Fort Leavenworth to "the seat of war."

General Miles wrote about the trip in his personal recollections where he records a crew member's comments on the river.

> For ten days the great steamer ploughed its way up the Missouri, frequently coming upon a sand bank, owing to the constant changes in the channel of that turbulent river. When an accident of this kind occurred the great shafts in the bow of the boat were lowered, and with the engines the bow was partially lifted off, while the stern wheel was reversed and then another effort made to find the main current of the waters. At one time near the close of day the bow struck a sand bank. The weary roustabouts on board the vessel, impatient and tired as they were with the day's work were still inclined to be humorous, one of them remarking that "it had been said that the world was created in six days, but he did not believe that the Creator had yet made up his mind where he wanted the Missouri River."[14]

Even with its many faults, the Missouri River earned the reputation as being "the" river of the West. "When weighed in conjunction with its network of west-ward-reaching tributaries, the Missouri River was, for almost a century, the most important single means of entree into the whole wild and empty subcontinent that lay between the Mississippi and the Pacific Ocean."[15]

As early travelers rode its muddy waters they attempted to capture the river in words. "'A great spiral staircase to the

Rockies' was one 19th Century traveler's memorable metaphor for the Missouri."[16]

Another early traveler described it as "a little too thick to swim in, and not quite thick enough to walk on."

In 1857 journalist Albert Richardson wrote that "By daylight the broad current is unpoetic and repulsive—a stream of liquid brick-dust or flowing mud, studded with dead tree-trunks, broken by bars and islands of dreary sand, and inclosed by crumbling shores of naked soil."[17]

It could be other things.

In 1881 a heavy snowmelt bloated the Big Muddy into an ice-clad monster that went roaring down the Missouri River valley.

> Following the blizzards with unprecedented snowfall of the winter of 1880-1881, in March, as the result of Chinook winds in the Yellowstone country, the Missouri River ran like a wild sea down the entire valley from Pierre to Sioux City. Below Yankton settlers were driven out of the valley to Sioux City. Ice gorges in the river at Vermilion caused water to rise rapidly, destroying three quarters of Vermilion and sweeping the valley between Vermilion and Gayville clear of everything. The farmers of Clay County [present South Dakota] were left with nothing but the clothes upon their backs. Their houses, barns, fences, farming implements, and all their stock were swept away. One hundred and thirty-two buildings in Vermilion alone were totally destroyed.[18]

In Dakota Territory the 1881-1882 winter began in October with a serious blizzard and for the next five months one storm after another dropped the thermometer and prodigious amounts of snow.

The Missouri River was frozen over by 18 November and the ice reached a thickness of from four to six feet depending on the location of the report. When the ice breakup did come on Sunday, 27 March, the *[Ponca] Nebraska Journal Leader* reported "there was an ice gorge 12 miles long and extending across the river and far into Dakota."[19]

Frank Leslie's Illustrated Newspaper, *16 June 1877; T. G. Rowan*
This illustration captures the rescue effort to remove passengers from a
train stalled by floodwaters near Emporia, Kansas, in May 1877.

"Suddenly at about five o'clock on Tuesday evening, a
mountainous gorge formed a few miles below Yankton, and
a massive glacier of jagged cakes of ice built up all the way
westward to Springfield"[20] thirty river-miles upstream from
Yankton.

An inquisitive resident of Yankton, with a bent for figures,
calculated that one ice block he found at the foot of Capitol
Street "weighed ninety-seven and a half tons."[21]

It is impossible to portray the scene along the river better
than those who witnessed it. The following account, as observed
from the bluffs at Yankton, describes the river after the ice
gorge breakup on Wednesday.

> Looking south and east it was a solid river twenty
> miles wide and rolling a very bosom of destruction,
> cutting a swath of havoc and ruin which cannot be
> computed. Down the channel of the river swept hay-
> stacks, watertanks, live animals and the fragments of
> fences, houses, etc., which had been swept from God
> knows where up the river. Far over on the Nebraska
> bottoms could be seen clusters of cattle on every

knoll and as the water rose inch by inch, and the ice swept over and crushed them between its ponderous fragments, the struggles of the poor animals could be plainly seen. Great trees struck by the jagged chunks, whipped and shook as though jarred by a heavy wind, and finally would be cut clean off and tumbled into the seething hell of waters which roared about them. Here and there appeared the roof of a house, and alas! in too many instances, that roof held human beings, clinging to it in a desperate effort to save themselves from a watery grave. Women, and strong men, too, turned away from the awful sight, and refused to look upon it. No man ever wants to see the like again.[22]

The weather conditions, weeks and months prior, caused this flood and brought much suffering to newcomers unaccustomed and unprepared for a severe winter on the open plains. These newcomers relied upon railroads and steamboats for vital supplies such as food, clothing, heating coal, lamp oil, candles, and building supplies.

Railroads and steamboats depended on coal or cord wood to heat boilers to provide steam to deliver the goods. When any one of these links in the system broke, everyone had to tighten their belts and do with little, less, or none. Throw in Mother Nature and sometimes the entire web becomes unraveled. Deep snows stopped trains before they could deliver the winter's supply of coal to some settlements, and many trains spent the entire winter snowbound.

People got cold.

On those same trains was winter clothing.

People got colder.

Lamp oil and candles didn't arrive.

People spent the nights in darkness.

The floods destroyed railroad tracks. It was reported that "50 per cent of the railroad bridges in Nebraska had been washed out previous to 30 March, that year."[23]

More shortages in more communities.

In many cases, those driven from their homes by the flood waters spent some nights and days in temperatures ten to twelve degrees above zero.

More suffering.

Along the waterways wood cutters could no longer cut firewood. "About 10,000 woodchoppers who lived in the Bismarck territory were compelled to leave the lowland timbers and seek high land. The dwellings of these men were ruined. Several of the men were drowned. The loss of cord wood was tremendous."[24]

More people shivered through the days and nights.

People endured and improvised. "Late in December a Milwaukee engine leaving Yankton made the run to Elk Point using 50 bushels of ear-corn for fuel."[25]

People fed the hungry.

People took in the homeless.

People risked their lives to rescue neighbors and strangers.

People shared grief and sorrow.

People rebuilt their lives and communities.

Often, but not always.

Green Island, Nebraska was one community along the Missouri River that was literally "swept off the map" by the 1881 flood.

Other floods, on other rivers, in other years continually harassed Indians and newcomers alike. Mother Nature obviously didn't make any distinction between missionaries, settlers, soldiers, tramps, or Indians.

The white captive, John D. Hunter, no doubt encountered numerous floods during the ten to fifteen years he spent living among the Kickapoo, Pawnee, and Kansas Indian tribes. At least two of these floods left lasting impressions and were recorded in his memoirs. The years of their occurrences is difficult to establish from his account but they are sometime prior to 1816, which is the date that he left his life as an Indian and returned to the white man's world. The location is "in the central wilds of North America."

This first incident almost assuredly happened before the New Madrid earthquake of 1811, for Hunter mentions it in chronological order before that date.

> The squaw who had adopted me among her children, and who had treated me with great tenderness and affection, was accidentally drowned in attempting to

collect drift-wood during the prevalence of a flood. This circumstance was the cause of grief, apparently more poignant to be endured than is usually experienced in civilized life; because the customs of the Indians do not tolerate the same open expression of feelings, from the indulgence of which the acuteness of grief is relieved, and sooner subsides.[26]

It is important to distinguish the "Indian Territory" of the following account from the more familiar Indian Territory in Oklahoma. In the years between 1831 and 1833 the U.S. Congress, backed by the U.S. military, forced the Shawnee, the Delaware, the Miami, the Ottawa and other Indian tribes to relocate west of the Missouri River in what is now Kansas and Oklahoma. At this time the eastern half of Kansas was Indian Territory.

Other Indians suffered from floods. A letter dated "July 23, '44," written from the Shawnee Baptist Mission, Indian Territory, details the flood of 1844 and its injury to Indians along the Kansas River near present-day Kansas City, Kansas.

The letter was penned by Baptist Missionary, F. Barker, to Isaac B. Barker, Hanson, Massachusetts, and mailed at "Westport, Missouri, July 31, 1844."

Barker opens the letter by apologizing for not writing sooner and then mentions that the Indians "were determined to raise a crop. But alas, many of them are disappointed . . . They have spent much time in lamentation and wailing."

The cause of their distress began after

a mild winter and delightsome opening of Spring at the latter part of April the rains commenced falling in such torrents as to remind us of Noah's day when the fountains of the deep were broken up. The waters came up over the banks of the creeks and rivers so as to be in many places fifteen feet high where they were never known to come before. Fences were sweep (swept) away invariably, the newly planted crops destroyed, young orchards, &c., among the rest most of the buildings within several miles of the rivers or as far as the river bottoms extended, were swept away, corn cribs and all. Hogs were drowned, many horses and cattle also. Many persons barely escaped with their lives leaving all behind. Many have been drowned in the white settlements. I have not heard of any of the Inds. drownding . . .

The Ottawa Inds. located about 50 miles south of us were entirely, or almost so, washed out of their homes and every thing they had . . . Only a few days ago a company of his Inds., Brethren of the Ch. (Church) came in (families who were providing well for themselves) nearly in a state of starvation having lived for some time upon blackberries. Our Mission is several miles from the river bottom and of course has not suffered by the flood; but our crops have been very much injured by the continued rains as is universally the case throughout the region.[27]

Reverend Jotham Meeker was the missionary to the Ottawa Indians and his charges were the ones referred to in Missionary Baker's account. Meeker's diary verifies Baker's belief that the Ottawa Indians lost almost all their crops and livestock. Excerpts from Meeker's diary tells the story along with the drama of a near-drowning.

May 30—Never saw such a time of rain. It has fallen almost every day in the last three weeks. The river has overflown its banks; and the bottoms in many places have been inundated more or less for three weeks . . . There has been no plowing or planting . . . Many of the Indians fear that they will have no crops at all this year.

June 7—Rainy all day.

June 10—Rain falls all day . . .

June 11—The river rises higher than we have ever seen it. The water covers many of the Indians' fields and surrounds their houses. The Indians who live in the bottoms near by all fled to the hills.

June 12— . . . doubtless much of the Indians' stock and other property will be lost.

June 14—Last evening near night, our brother Oshosh, in coming from his house with a canoe load of his articles, ran against a tree. The canoe upset and all went down. He clung to a sapling and cried for help. We heard him but, having no canoe, we could render him no assistance, the tree bending and continually shaking terribly. He, after crying a long time for help and not being able to hear us for the noise of the water, gave up hopes of living through the night, sung in Ottawa the hymn commencing with "Father, I stretch my hands to Thee" and prayed for about an hour and we heard no more of him. Before morning we obtained a canoe and as soon as it was light, two of the brethren went, found him and brought him home, he having hung to the sapling all night with nothing but his shirt on.[28]

##

The U.S. Army's battle with Mother Nature during these ten decades was as tough, if not tougher, than battling the Plains Indians. Colonel Dodge spent more than thirty years of military service on the prairies and plains. His writings provide detailed eyewitness accounts of army life on the vast grasslands between the Mississippi River and the Rocky Mountains.

He said that "Almost all positions of the high plains are occasionally visited by most terrific rain-storms, so severe that they have the general name 'waterspouts.' The quantity of water poured from the clouds, and the effect produced, are so apparently incredible, that I would hesitate to describe them but that the facts are perfectly known to every plainsman."[29]

Colonel Dodge was at Fort Dodge, Kansas during one of these storms which he believed was "by no means as severe as several I have encountered, in which two and a half inches of rain fell in less than one hour."

It was his conviction that such rains can

> be more easily imagined than described. Depressions in the surface of the ground, scarcely noticeable in dry weather, become in a few moments raging torrent; ravines, ordinarily dry, become impassible rivers; and valleys, even though one or more miles in width, are

Photo courtesy of the South Dakota State Historical Society—State Archives
This ice chunk from the Missouri River flood of 1881 reportedly measured forty-four inches thick. It's weight was estimated at twenty-two tons. A raging river full of such battering rams could, and did, wreck just about anything in their path.

flooded to the depth of many feet. It took the railroad engineers some time to learn this phenomenon . . .

I have seen one such instance where the force of the water having broken the connection, the track, ties bound together with the rails, was swung off the break by the power of the current until the loose ends finally rested nearly a quarter of a mile from their proper position.[30]

Colonel Dodge includes, in his book, the following report written by a captain of Company F, 3rd U.S. Cavalry who's command was caught by a flash flood. The report is dated 9 June 1873 from Fort McPherson, Nebraska. We can be sure it was not a report the captain looked forward to writing.

> Sir, —I have the honour to report that, in accordance with instructions, I left Fort McPherson, Neb., May 27th, 1873, with one guide, one wagon-master, five teamsters, and fifty-five enlisted men of Company "F," 3rd Cavalry, for the purpose of patrolling the Republican Valley, as directed. . . . . May 31st, marched down to Blackwood about twelve miles, and went into camp. About 9 P.M. a terrible freshet, without any apparent cause, swept down the valley, carrying everything before it. Men, horses, tents, army-wagons, were swept along like corks. For five days previous we had no rain, and where this water came from so suddenly I cannot yet understand. The valley of Blackwood is about forty-five miles long, and about one mile to a mile and a half wide. This entire stretch of country was one raging torrent, at least from six to seven feet deep, how any man or horse escaped is marvellous.
>
> The only thing that prevented total destruction was the fact that my camp was surrounded by a belt of timber on three sides, and as the men were carried off by the current they were enabled to save themselves by catching the limbs of trees. When day broke on the morning of the 1st June, it showed almost all the men of my company on the tops of the trees, without any covering except remnants of underclothes, and beneath them the torrent still raging. After the lapse of a few hours the water began to fall, and a few men who could swim got to the hills. Afterwards the others, myself among the number, were got off with life-lines and various other means. Up to this time nothing was to be seen of what had been my camp, except the top

of an army-wagon, which had stuck to a log on the ground, and on this wagon were collected eleven men, who were thus saved from a watery grave. . . . . Six men of my company were drowned and twenty-six horses lost. I remained at the scene of disaster for four days, and recovered five of the bodies of the men.

The sixth body was apparently recovered later for there are six graves in the Fort McPherson National Cemetery where these men were laid to their final rest. There is also a stone for a soldier who drowned in the Laramie River and another who died in a ferry accident on the Platte River.

Colonel Dodge believed a flood of this magnitude was extremely rare and one which "Against such no human foresight or precaution can avail anything" but "care, knowledge, and fore-thought may fully protect a party" from lesser floods. [31]

Another flood put still more soldiers into the tree tops on 5 June 1867, when a violent thunderstorm broke loose near Fort Hays, Kansas. The original post was designated Fort Fletcher but the name was changed to Fort Hays in November 1866. The Fort was located on Big Creek about fifteen miles east of present-day Fort Hays.

One of those encamped on Big Creek at the time was Elizabeth Custer. She was terrified of thunderstorms but frequently had to endure them as she shadowed her famous husband whenever she could.

That night the flood waters came roaring into the campsite during the storm that Mrs. Custer admitted left her "quaking and terrified under the covers."

In a matter of minutes, she recalled, a guard was shouting for her and Eliza "to get up and make haste for our lives; the flood was already there!"[32]

Mrs. Custer writes in *Tenting on the Plains* that after struggling into wet clothing she and Eliza

crept through the opening, and, to our horror, the lightning revealed the creek—which we had last seen, the night before, a little rill in the bottom of the gully—now on the level with the high banks. The tops of good-sized trees, which fringed the stream, were barely visible, as the current swayed the branches in its onward sweep. The water had risen in that comparatively short time thirty-five feet . . . I believe no one attempted to account for those terrific rises in the streams, except as partly due to water-spouts, which were common in the early days of Kansas. I have seen the General hold his watch in his hand after the bursting of a rain-cloud, and keep reckoning for the soldier who was measuring with a stick at the stream's bed, and for a time it recorded an inch a minute.[33]

Spurred on by the rising water, Mrs. Custer and Eliza began lugging their belongings to higher ground

carrying burdens that we could not even have lifted in calmer moments, the lightning became more vivid and the whole arc above us seemed aflame. We were aghast at what the brilliant light revealed . . . The water had overflowed the banks of the stream above us, and swept across the slight depression that intervened between our ground and the hills. We were left on that narrow neck of land, and the water on either side of us, seen in the lightning's glare appeared like two boundless seas.

It was a grim night on Big Creek and the worst was yet to come. The water rose so suddenly that many of the soldiers at the post couldn't escape to high ground.

According to Mrs. Custer, she and Eliza rescued one soldier who was caught in the branches of a tree and was calling for help as the current threatened to dislodge him.

The memory of the flood was apparently so vivid and disquieting to Mrs. Custer that when writing the account she had Eliza tell the story in her words.

Miss Libbie, don't you mind when we took the clothes-line an' went near to him as we could get, he didn't seem to understan' what we was up to? We made a loop and showed it to him, when a big flash of lightnin' came and made a glare, and tried to call to him to put it

over his head. The noise of the water, and the crashin'
of the logs that was comin' down, beside the thunder,
drownded out our voices. Well, we worked half an hour
over that man. He thought you and me, Miss Libbie,
couldn't pull him in—that we wasn't strong enough
. . . Even then, he was so swept under that part of the
bank, and it was so dark, I didn't think we could get
him. I could hear him bubblin', bellowin', drownin' and
gaggin'. Well, we pulled him in at last.[34]

According to the report of Captain Sam B. Lauffer, assistant
quartermaster at Fort Hays, eight other men couldn't be
rescued. His report of 13 June 1867, listed the casualties as:
"five of General Smith's orderlies, two of the 38th Infantry,
and my principal herder, Eli Watson (civilian), who lost his life
trying to save the lives of several mules, he was an excellent
and trusty man."[35]

After newcomers' disease, drought, and the U.S. Army
laying to rest the Plains Indian problem, tens of thousands of
newcomers with unbridled ambition and unlimited ignorance
traveled over, and camped on very unfamiliar ground.

Newcomers were awed by the wide-open expanse of land,
which at times resembled the Great American Desert they'd
read or heard about. Stream beds could become bone dry during
the summer months and newcomers discovered too late, this
was one of Mother Nature's little white lies.

A flash flood surprised a family in Norton County, Kansas
during the summer of 1873. The family consisted of D. E.
Stevens, his wife and two daughters, Grace age five and Ada
age four. Son Edwin was thirteen months old. The Stevens'
claim was on Big Timber Creek about ten miles southeast of
Norton, Kansas.

Mrs. Stevens' brother, Alf Aplington had filed on a claim in
the extreme northeast corner of Norton County. The Stevens'
family had paid a visit to Aplington and were returning to their
claim on 31 July 1873. Aplington had decided to travel with
the family and about sundown as they approached the Stevens'
claim, a herd of buffalo was seen about a mile away. Aplington

shot one and returned to the wagon suggesting they go butcher out what they wanted.

Nightfall was now upon them and storm clouds began to roll in hiding the moon. Even though Stevens held a claim nearby, the country was still new to them and consequently they couldn't find the dead buffalo or their claim site. Realizing the storm was fast approaching and deciding the buffalo could wait, they drove to the timber along the creek and made camp.

The storm lasted most of the night and in the morning the creek had risen only slightly so they decided to remain at the same campsite. After breakfast the men began cutting timber to build a cabin on the Stevens' claim.

Toward evening storm clouds once again begin building in the west. Having weathered the previous storm, they gave little thought to this one. When it was time to retire for the night Mrs. Stevens and the children were dry and comfortable inside the wagon while Stevens and Aplington spread their bedrolls underneath.

At two o'clock it began to sprinkle and Stevens joined his family inside the wagon. The storm grew in intensity until Aplington noticed the rising water and shouted a warning to Stevens urging him get his wife and the children to safety. Mrs. Stevens passed the two older girls out to Aplington who grabbed them and headed for high ground.

Stevens helped his wife and baby out of the wagon just as rushing water broke around them and washed his wife under the wagon tongue. It took all Stevens' strength to pull her up but there was no avenue of escape from the rushing water. Their only hope was to climb back into the wagon and hope it wasn't carried away.

It was a false hope.

Almost immediately the water moved the wagon backwards into a small tree and it became obvious that the wagon was going to be swept away. Mrs. Stevens, clutching the child with one hand, grabbed a small limb with the other. Mr. Stevens wrapped his arm around the tree just as the wagon was torn out from under them.

For the next few hours they "clung to the tree, floating as a buoy. The water riffled over their faces and with difficulty they

Nebraska State Historical Society Photograph Collections

A Mormon wagon train fords the South Platte River near Fremont's Springs, close to the present town of Hershey, Nebraska. The water isn't deep but the river obviously is wide–two-to-three miles from bluff to bluff. This photo was taken in August 1866 by Charles R. Savidge.

kept from strangling. At times the wife thought the babe was dead. The rain had ceased and the water receded slowly. Just after day break he heard Alf calling; he was in a tree about 80 feet from them and had both girls."[36] All had miraculously survived.

It was a scene repeated again and again but not always with such a happy ending. In April 1885 an extremely heavy rain—what at the time was called a waterspout—fell near the headwaters of the Medicine Lodge River in Kiowa and Barber counties in south central Kansas. It caused the river to crest eight or ten feet higher than anyone had ever seen before.

"Those who saw the water coming up say that it came in a wave four or five feet high and with a velocity that swept almost everything before it." This wall of water passed Medicine Lodge, Kansas between four and five o'clock in the morning on Tuesday 20 April. About two hours later this rushing wall reached the town of Old Kiowa, Kansas about twenty miles downstream.

The Deadliest Woman in the West

"In the bottoms south of Medicine Lodge there was a company of movers camped. There were ten wagons in the company but the exact number of persons is not known, though supposed to be about forty."

It was a sorrowful day for many families; in some cases the entire family perished in the swirling waters that caught them sleeping in the predawn hours. By early afternoon ten bodies had been recovered by search parties. The toll would climb as the day advanced.

> The family of Jerry Gibbs, consisting of himself, daughter, and granddaughter, were all found. One family by the name of Maddox belonging to the company of movers contained 11 persons; of these six were drowned, the mother, three daughters and two sons . . . George W. Pattix's family, consisting of himself, wife and three children are supposed to be drowned. Frank Shepler's wife and baby were lost but he saved himself by catching a log. His house was swept away and torn to pieces in the torrent and it was impossible for him to aid them . . .
>
> The coming of the flood was so swift and unexpected that but few had time to escape and none to prepare.[37]

A month later on the evening of May 26, 1885, a party of seventeen newcomers were traveling across southwestern Nebraska on their way to stake homesteads in Hayes County.

The entourage consisted of four men, three women, and ten children. Their earthly belongings, with which they planned to build a new life, were stowed away in three wagons drawn by oxen.

At nightfall the party made camp in Richmond Canyon near the Republican River. Today the site is about half way between Bartley and Cambridge in Nebraska.

After the evening meal they retired for the night. About ten o'clock one of the men was awakened by the persistent barking of the family dog who had been tied to a wagon wheel. When the man climbed out of the wagon the water was already up to the wheel hubs. He grabbed a son and a daughter and took them to higher ground, then raced back to the wagon for his wife and two other children.

It was too late.

Just as he approached the wagon the raging water swept it and the rest of his family away. Another of the men tried to rescue his family and was swept away but managed to catch hold of some upper branches of a tree.

When morning finally came the wagons were gone, the oxen were gone, and three women and six children were gone. The man in the tree was rescued and when the water receded it was determined that his place of safety was twenty feet above the ground; a twenty-foot wall of water had surged through the canyon.

Rescuers and searchers from nearby towns combed the Republican River valley downstream for at least twenty miles. There grim findings confirmed that the missing women and children had perished. Eight of the nine bodies were recovered.

The community long remembered the flood and its victims for in May of 1924 some 1,500 people gathered to dedicate a monument to those who perished in the flood. It was placed in Richmond Canyon on a Sunday afternoon thirty-nine years after the tragedy.[38]

Another flood on another river in another year hastened the demise of Tascosa, Texas, located in the Texas Panhandle. The settlement had grown and prospered as a major trade center for trail herds being pushed North out of Texas.

When the XIT and other ranches began stringing hundreds of miles of barbed wire across the Panhandle it seriously limited access to the town and businesses began to close their doors. Some held on hoping that the proposed railroad route through the Panhandle would put Tascosa on the line.

The Canadian River made a great horseshoe bend that reached within a hundred yards of Tascosa's main street. Because of the town's close proximity to the river, some locals were concerned that a serious flood might do great damage to the community. In 1893 those concerns became a reality when

for three days the entire area was subjected to heavy, dashing rains. One old-timer remarked that it rained cats and dogs with pitchforks thrown in for good measure. The roof of one of the adobe buildings at the Frying Pan collapsed, pinning a number of cowboys underneath, but fortunately did not injure any of them . . . the Canadian River went on one of the worst rampages of its early-day history . . . Seventeen houses in Tascosa were washed away or collapsed from the onslaught of the flood and torrential rain . . .

When the flood abated and the bright sun shone again, the little town of Tascosa was in virtual ruins . . . The town presented a bedraggled and woebegone appearance . . . One span of the great Canadian River wagon bridge had been washed away and the entire bridge severely damaged . . .

The population of Tascosa dwindled in the succeeding days and weeks as large numbers of persons moved to Channing, Hartley, and Amarillo.[39]

##

Floods, mercifully, are not always deadly but they are always destructive in some measure. It isn't surprising then, that for centuries newcomers have sought ways to minimize this threat to life and property.

The fledgling Signal Service started issuing bulletins for farmers and "reports on river conditions and flood warnings" in 1873.[40] Although helpful in reducing some loss from slow-moving river floods, the Signal Service and its reports couldn't stop a flood any easier than they could stop a tornado. However it was a beginning.

John Bradbury, the Scottish born naturalist, was an early explorer of the trans-Mississippi West and left numerous writing about his travels. Bradbury, as you may recall, was on the Mississippi during the 1811 New Madrid earthquake. The flooding associated with the quake was an exceptional event but the Mississippi was, like other rivers, prone to periodic flooding without the encouragement of an earthquake.

The town of "St. Louis," Bradbury writes,

is very pleasantly situated on the Mississippi, about eighteen miles below the mouth of the Missouri

. . . It has a decided advantage over any of the other towns, on account of its being situated on a rock, but little elevated above the high floods of the river, and immediately on its border. Such situations are very rare, as the Mississippi is almost universally bounded either by high perpendicular rocks or loose alluvial soil; the latter of which is in continual danger of being washed away by the annual floods, to such an extent that a whole plantation, situated on the border of the river, has been known to have been swept away during one flood.[41]

For these reasons, flood prevention, in the minds of those living along the mighty Mississippi, had become mandatory. Nobody debated that reoccurring floods caused loss of life and property. There were however, a lot of citizens and government officials debating the best methods of minimizing this loss. William B. Meyer, in his book *Americans and Their Weather*, quotes from the *Congressional Record:* "The Mississippi would 'set at naught and laugh to scorn all efforts to confine or control it,' predicted one senator; 'excuse me,' said another, 'if I express a doubt whether the tinkering of man with that stream is going to do it any good.'"[42]

But, tinker they did.

Lane comments on just how much tinkering had been done by 1965 the year his book, *The Elements Rage*, was published.

Nowhere in the world has greater effort been given to flood control than on the lower Mississippi. A glance at a map and a rapid reading of its history show why— over 50 major floods in the 250 years of settlement. The first controls were begun soon after the founding of New Orleans in 1717. Ten years later the city was guarded by a levee 3 feet high, 18 feet wide and 5,400 feet long. Today there are about 1,700 miles of levees on the main Mississippi River, with an average height of 25 feet, a maximum of 40 feet. The base width is about ten times the height. Many have a 25-ft.-wide road at the crown. There are some 2,000 miles of levees on the tributaries. Many levees are sited a long distance away from the river—up to five miles in some places—to give additional area for excess water.

The Mississippi levee system is one of the greatest feats of American engineering; it is longer than even the Great Wall of China.[43]

But even levees weren't entirely successful.

Louisiana, Mississippi, and Arkansas maintained different standards on levee size and composition. By the late 1850s, the officials thought the 2,000 miles of levees constructed on both shores of the river at a cost of over $40 million would protect the lower Mississippi Valley from any future flooding. The flood of 1858-1859, the largest known to that date, temporarily destroyed their hopes at controlling the river as levees cracked and fell by the dozens.[44]

And, "Floods continued to destroy river-control efforts in Mississippi after the Civil War, with major overflows in 1874, 1882, 1883, 1884, 1890, and 1897 . . . (the levees held in the floods of 1886 and 1893)."[45]

For the next century this same pattern continued and the disastrous floods of 1993 prompted some officials to suggest that the "tinkering" stop, thus giving the Mississippi River back its freedom. "Frustrated by its 200-year-old tussle with the headstrong river, the federal government issued a report in May 1994, urging the Corps of Engineers to give up its preference for dams and flood control and instead evacuate flood plains, relocate farms and businesses, and restore the natural flood cycle."[46] Opinion, it seems, has come full circle. Only time will tell if policy follows.

Meanwhile the cycle of flooding along waterways continued unabated during the nineteenth century as the nation pushed relentlessly into and across the trans-Mississippi west.

The vast majority of these westbound newcomers had a brief flirtation with the Mississippi River. It was just one of the numerous rivers they had to cross, or it was the highway upon which they rode the steamboats to St. Louis and the Gateway to the West. From there, for most, it was more water-miles up the

Missouri River to the next gateway west or another destination farther up the river.

Without question the Missouri River was a major highway of the westward migration. Yet the Platte River was arguably the river that more newcomers spent more time close to than any other river.

The Platte was well known to the Indians and different tribes bestowed upon it names from their native tongue. The most recognizable is the Omaha's *Nebrathka* meaning Flat or Shallow Water.

To early newcomers it was *Rio Quivira, Rio Grande, Rio San Lorenzo, Riviere la Fourche, La Platte,* or *Belle Riviere.* All seemed to see it differently. It was to some the River of the Wolf, to others the Grand or Great River, still others saw it as the St. Lawrence. In addition there were those who called it the Forked River or the Beautiful River.[47] By any name, it was "the" river of the westward migration.

The North Platte is birthed high in the Colorado Rockies' North Park where the snow-melt begins its 900-mile journey eastward to the Missouri River.

The South Platte also begins its life in the Colorado Rockies about 100 miles, as the crow flies, south of the North Platte headwaters. After their initial solo journeys the two join and form the historic "flat and shallow" river just a few miles downstream from North Platte, Nebraska.[48]

> Old records indicate that in early spring, before snow melt, the river flow was low and occasionally ceased altogether in some reaches. Snow melt at the mountain headwaters then brought on a period of high flow beginning in April or May, reaching a peak in June, and usually receding in July. These high flows scoured the river channels and sandbars of vegetation and temporarily widened the river to the edges of its flood plain.
>
> ... after 1870, irrigation contributed to the frequent drying up of the river. After the year's first killing frost, vegetation died, irrigation ended, and flow was restored again, although the shallow river would often freeze to its bed during the coldest months of winter.

. . . Estimates from many explorers between 1813 and 1857 place the width of the river from 1/3-mile to three miles. Colonel Fremont, for example, in 1842, reported the channel immediately below the forks to be 5,350 feet—more than a mile. The Union Pacific Railroad survey of 1866 confirmed that figure.[49]

The Platte was never considered navigable although some trappers tried transporting their furs to market in shallow-draft bull boats—more often than not without success. And, there are unsubstantiated stories of a steamboat traveling upstream as far as Fort Kearney.

Occasionally, the Platte cooperated. In 1840 E. Willard Smith and six other men loaded "a craft thirty-six feet long and eight feet wide" with 700 buffalo robes and started down the South Platte for St. Louis. The South Platte was slow going due to low water but when they reached the forks in June, the "going was smooth for buffalo were plentiful and the rising river enabled them to make fifty miles per day." This rate of travel increased to eighty miles per day on the Missouri and they reached St. Louis on Independence Day.[50]

Newcomers found the Platte so different from other rivers that they constantly wrestled with words and phrases to capture its essence.

It was, they wrote, "a mile wide and an inch deep."

It was "a perfect curiosity, it is so very different from any of our streams that it is hard to realize that a river should be running so near the top of the ground without any timber, and no banks at all."

"It could not be ferried for lack of water and it could not be bridged for lack of timber."

"It was bad to ford, destitute of fish, too dirty to bathe in and too thick to drink."

"It drained one-fourth of a continent," but, one writer exclaimed, "an Indian canoe cannot float upon its broad waters."

It was universally damned except for a few settlers and travelers who believed it comparable to the Nile River and christened it the Nile of the Plains or Nebraska's Valley of the Nile.

Washington Irving reportedly quipped that the "Platte would be quite a river if you could stand it on edge."

Another was "impressed with its total uselessness and insignificance."

A correspondent from St. Louis wrote in 1855 that "In truth this Platte River is a humbug. It is about dry, and a person can cross it dry shod."[51]

Not always.

The second flood John Hunter mentions in his memoirs occurred on a return trip down the Platte River. He writes that

> Just before we arrived at the entrance of the La Platte into the Missouri, we experienced the most violent and long-continued rains, accompanied with heavy thunder, and the most vivid and incessant flashes of lightning, that I ever have before or since witnessed. Our engagements were now such as to render a constant exposure necessary; in consequence of which, our sufferings were great, and many of the party became sick. The river swelled into a devastating flood, covered the islands and alluvion grounds, and bore off whole herds of buffalo and forests of trees on its surface: the sight was so distressing and awful as to surpass my powers of description.[52]

John Dougherty was an individual of manifest talents and interests. A Kentuckian by birth, he traveled to St. Louis as a young man and spent six winters, 1809 to 1815, trapping on the Columbia River. During this time he learned to speak French plus several Indian dialects. Because of his skills as a linguist he traveled with Major Stephen H. Long's expedition as an interpreter.

Following his stint with Long's expedition, Dougherty served as an Indian agent from 1820 to 1837. He was a U. S. sutler and freighter and was elected to the Missouri State Legislature.

As Indian agent he was headquartered at Fort Leavenworth, Council Bluffs, and St. Louis. His letter book contains 153 letters, many of which are to William Clark, superintendent of Indian affairs at St. Louis.

His letter No. 46, written from Cantonment Leavenworth and dated 6 May 1828, informs Clark that he arrived at Leavenworth after an "indescribable trip of 20 days from St. Louis." Dougherty then expresses his concerns about an individual who is forty days overdue at the post. The delay was, according to the man's son, "that the high waters surpass any thing that has ever been known in the country, the grand river Platte is from 7 to 8 miles wide, that is, it extends from one bluff to the other; so that it and the Elkhorn together form but one river for the distance of 20 miles up from their junction."[53]

Francis A. Hardy traveled the Great Platte River Road in 1850. In his journal he notes that there were "Drownings at Upper Platte ferry more than could be counted."[54] According to D. Ray Wilson in his book *Fort Kearny on the Platte*, "There were several accidental drownings" in the Platte during 1864.[55] Make no mistake, there were times when *La Platte* was a mean piece of water.

##

Samuel Stearly wasn't scared of drowning and didn't mind getting wet in the Platte's muddy waters. He "enjoyed the fun and excitement of fording." The young man was, it seems, the perfect man for the job when he went to work for Charles Walker. It was Walker who held the government freight contract to haul supplies from the rail depot at Fort Kearny station across the Platte River to Fort Kearny, Nebraska. During the summer of 1869 Walker was hauling material to fence the government cemetery located near the Fort.

One afternoon a wedding party arrived at the crossing asking to be taken across the Platte River which "was very high at that time." The young couple bitten by the marriage bug lived on the Blue River southeast of Grand Island, Nebraska. Judge Patrick Walsh of Wood River Center was the nearest official with authority to tie the knot. So, because the river was running very high, the wedding party had traveled seventy-five miles to the ford at Fort Kearny. The party consisting of the bride and groom, John Martin and Miss Craig, the bride's mother, Mrs. Craig and her eighteen-month-old child.

Here they believed was a safe crossing, and it usually was. Two or three years later another Kearny resident desired to cross the Platte River when it was running high. This man, Francis O. Hamer describes his crossing.

> I was told that Charley Walker maintained a ferry boat and that I could easily cross the Platte river. I went to the place indicated as the point from which the boat would start. I found a driver and two steers. These steers took the place of paddles. The steers were hitched to the boat and proceeded to pull it along a channel and then across the ground between two small channels and then over the intervening channel and then into the main stream of the Platte river. It was a time of high water and occasionally the oxen swam but most of the time they waded and pulled the boat. When the oxen swam, they and the boat were carried down stream. It required about half a day to go across the river in this way, and while it looked as if there was danger of being upset, I was assured that the boat couldn't upset and that it was perfectly safe. When we finally reached the other side I paid the ferryman $1.50 for the trip and felt that I had the full worth of my money.[56]

Between the time Hamer crossed the river and the wedding party set sail, Walker had obviously made some improvements in his method and equipment for ferrying the Platte River.

The wedding party reached the crossing point about four o'clock in the afternoon, just in time to catch the last crossing for the day. To accommodate the wedding party, Stearly and the other employees put a wagon box on the wagon running gear and proceeded to "crib up the box with fence pickets to set their trunk and a roll of blankets on, so they would not get wet" because the river was running very high.

"There were ten yoke of oxen hitched to the wagon and two horseback riders, one on each side of the ox teams." Besides the wedding party, trunk, and blankets, there was a box of medicine and a box containing two prairie dogs. It fell to Stearly to safeguard the last two items.

Bracing himself in the wagon box, Stearly cradled the boxes of medicine and prairie dogs on his lap. The bull whips cracked and they moved out into the river. Stearly's regular job was to "keep the oxen on the lead of the team from swinging around the islands, or towheads as we called them."

To Stearly it seemed like just another crossing for about a quarter of a mile until they reached the deep channel. "Then the water went over the wagon box. Our load being light and the current so strong, it turned wagon, box and all upside down and the passengers all into the water."

When Stearly surfaced he saw young Martin helping his betrothed toward a wagon wheel. The next thing he saw was "Mrs. Craig come up with her child in her arms and the mother struggling for dear life."[57]

An old saying allows there are only two things a cowboy is afraid of: being afoot and being in the company of proper ladies. In all honesty there was a third thing that absolutely terrified some cowboys and that others just didn't much like.

Old West cowboys were land animals; their preferred domain was astride a good horse with four hooves firmly in touch with earth—most of the time. Few trail hands had any affinity for water, be it in a bathtub or a stream bed and they particularly hated the swift, deep water of a swollen river.

Horses and cattle were not unlike the cowboys—most just didn't like taking to the water. There were, however, some critters that didn't seem to mind. These were kept as lead swimmers and led many a herd across swollen streams. One such swimmer was a Jersey cow that helped pilot herds across the Arkansas River.

Then there was a team of oxen that, unyoked from the wagon, would plunge into any river, including the mighty Mississippi. Being much too valuable to sell for beef, they pulled the chuck wagon back to the home ranch after the herd was delivered. Here they lived a pampered life until the next herd was ready to trail to market.

Major rivers on the prairies and plains flow from west to east. Tributaries feed in from almost any direction. Conversely the Shawnee Trail, Chisholm Trail, Western Trail, and Goodnight-Loving Trail ran south to north. This lattice work of rivers and streams separated the real cowboys from the wannabes; sometimes it separated them from life itself.

Pushing a herd of cattle across a river during high water was a gamble with the river holding the high cards. J. Frank Dobie wrote about a herd of Texas Longhorns and the flooded Platte River. The year was 1879 when southern stock was being pushed from Texas to the northern range; the drovers were in a hurry to meet the delivery deadline. "Joseph P. Morris, after having crossed many rivers with his herd of 3014 big steers, arrived at the wide, wide Platte to find it bank-full."

Waiting for the Platte to recede was out of the question so "The herd was pointed in, and safely reached a sand bar about the middle of the channel. Here they stopped. They did not like the feel of the water coming down from the icy mountains. For eleven hours they refused to go on. Many of them were standing in shallow water, and it became a question of time before they would succumb to the numbing cold."

Finally Morris and his crew dislodged a few steers from the sand bar and the rest of the herd followed across. "A herd that attempted the same crossing the next day lost eight hundred in a mill that could not be broken."[58]

A mill occurred when the cattle began swimming around and around in a circle. A mill in midstream was a cowboy's worst nightmare; as the knot of cattle wound tighter and tighter as new swimmers were added to the circle, it pushed those at the center down under.

Occasionally an exceptionally devoted, or brave, or foolish young hand would solve the problem. A cowboy by the name of Foster related how he broke the mill during one high-water crossing of the Red River. "I stripped to my underclothes, mounted a big horse called Jack Moore, and went to them. I got off the horse and right on to the cattle. They were so jammed together that it was like walking on a raft of logs. When I got to the only real big steer in the bunch on the yon side, I mounted him and he pulled for the shore."[59]

With the mill broken, the herd was successfully pushed across the river. River crossings like this were the origin of the highest compliment that could be paid to a trail hand: "He'll do to ride the river with."

The Deadliest Woman in the West

Reverend Seccombe, surrounded by his family, calmly told them that he expected them all to perish in the ice-choked flood waters. He then led the entire group of men and women in prayer. Following the Amen they all joined in tearful goodbyes. "A boy," presumably twelve-year-old Charlie, tells his mother, "Mamma, dear, I will cling to the same piece of ice with you."

Just then a chunk of ice slammed into the house shaking it to the foundations. Another chunk follows, and then another until the house, trembling and groaning, threatens to collapse.

> Just now one of the men whispered to his wife, "See, the house is cracking. Let's get out of here!" So the word was gived to get out of the small window on to the roof—that steep roof. But bravely stepping out of that wet, coffin chamber, we ascended the heights— aged ones and children, stalwart men and trembling women, and for over two hours watched the moving ice, and eagerly looked for the life-saving skiff. Oh! how glad we were to sit, though astride this high ridge-pole, where we could see God's pure blue heavens, though all beneath makes us dizzy and sick, as we seem to be in the midst of one vast, moving lake.[60]

Divine intervention, or luck, favored the Seccombe family; the house withstood the river's onslaught. Now, however, there are forty-two men, women, and children clinging to the roof as the water and ice swirl about them. Then through the turbulent waters the skiff appears and heaves to at the roof. They are now faced with the painful decision of who will go and who will stay. The age-old "women and children first" prevails and the skiff departs.

After rescuing the first boatload, the skiff returns to the house but it's too late to attempt another run so all are forced to spend the night at the house.

On Thursday morning the rescue efforts continued until only a few souls, those too fearful to ride in the skiff, remain stranded on the roof. These decided to wait until the ice gorge froze solid allowing them to walk to the bluff on the Nebraska side.

Mrs. E. B. Custer Collection, Custer Battlefield Museum.
Lieutenant Colonel George Custer and wife Elizabeth dine in their tent at
Big Creek, Kansas, near Fort Hays. On 5 June 1867, a severe thunderstorm
and flash flood hit the fort, drowning eight men. Mrs. Custer and her maid,
Eliza, rescued one soldier from the flood.

All day long on Friday the men in skiffs and yawls risked
their lives to rescue people. About noon, according to Heriet
Seccombe's memory, two neighbors, Mister Morton and his
daughter Hannah, were elsewhere rescued from their floating
house after hanging on the rafters for six hours with the water
up to their waists.

By three o'clock on Saturday afternoon all of the Seccombe
family, along with the remaining refugees, were rescued and
landed safely at Yankton.

Heriet Seccombe, besides being a wife, mother, and
missionary also found time for art and literary work. The
information in the above account was taken primarily from a
small book she wrote and illustrated entitled *"Perils of Waters."*
It was published in 1883 at Springfield, Dakota, John Todd,
printer. Her stated purpose was to raise funds to help continue
their missionary work.

Samuel Stearly, struggling in the turbulent Platte River,
quickly realized that if Mrs. Craig and the child were to be

saved it was up to him to save them. Fortunately he was a good enough swimmer to reach mother and child and hold them until young Martin had insured the safety of his bride-to-be and then returned to aid in the rescue of Mrs. Craig and the baby.

The rest of the story is best told by Stearly himself.

> The trunk and blankets went down the river and one of the bullwhackers and myself were detailed to go after them. I want to tell you there was lively work for a while. When we got back with the trunk and blankets to the north bank of the river, the wedding party had all got ashore, and Mrs. Craig was sitting on the bank enjoying a good smoke out of a borrowed pipe. She thanked me very kindly for saving her, as she was going under the second time when I caught her. This delayed the wedding, as everything in the trunk and blankets got wet; and as the old lady's tobacco was wrapped up in the wedding dress, the dress was so stained it could not be used. Stores were not plenty in those days, and the party had to go to Grand Island, twenty-five miles east of Wood River Center, to buy another dress and make it. Some days later Patrick Walsh, justice of the peace married the happy couple, and they went on their way rejoicing. About three or four years after, I met Mrs. Craig in Grand Island. She called her little boy in off the street and introduced him to me and then told her son that I was the young man who had saved his and her life. She then said the only way she could pay me was to give me her last daughter, then about my age and a very beautiful girl.[61]

For whatever reasons, Stearly doesn't tell us whether or not he accepted the offered reward.

##

As with prairie fires, there didn't emerge many jokes or humor associated with floods. Occasionally though, a good story would come along.

Early in 1881, because of the unusually heavy winter snows, residents up and down the Big Muddy were concerned about the probability of spring floods. There had even been a prophet, actually a surveyor, who warned of a serious flood and even posted a warning in the Pierre, Dakota Territory post office.

Some did take heed. A banker, fearing his bank might be flooded or washed away, moved deposits of $11,000 to higher ground. "Then he enlisted the aid of eleven friends who guarded the money."

A lumber merchant "moved thousands of feet of lumber to the hills from his yard in the lowlands."[62]

The flood did come and after the water subsided, the lumber merchant tried to move his lumber back to his yard only to find an armed man, known as Scarface Joe, claiming the lumber was now his. Other merchants were being subjected to the same lawlessness.

"Realizing that the new town had nothing to gain by the presence of the hoodlums, a vigilante group was organized, the toughs rounded up, disarmed, a boat purchased and the entire outfit—14 men and one woman—were set afloat to seek their infamous fortunes elsewhere."[63]

Some newcomers were apparently not blessed with good sense, or maybe it was the endless miles and miles of prairies and plains that dislodged their common sense. Alfred Iverson (Babe) Moye from Kenedy, Texas encountered two such individuals, probably in 1872 or 1873. He was one of the hands trailing a herd north from Texas. Moye had been up the trail before but this time he said

> it seemed that we had more storms than usual. When we reached the Cimarron River in the Territory it was bankfull and we had to stay there several days before we could cross. While we were there two tramps came along who said they were going to swim the river. We tried to talk them out of the foolish undertaking, but they plunged in and when half way across they began yelling for us to come and help them out, but we could not get to them and they both drowned.[64]

The Deadliest Woman in the West

One of the legends of White Woman basin south of Scott City, Kansas, is attributed to a flash flood. The town of Friend and Shallow Water are located within the basin, about eight miles apart. During the early days a bachelor settled at Friend and a family with a beautiful daughter settled at Shallow Water.

A romance was born.

The story goes that the young lovers would rendezvous at a point halfway between their homes. This meeting site happened to be in the bed of a dry stream. One night the bachelor arrived before the girl and just as the young maiden came into view a flash flood came rushing down the stream bed and carried the man to his death in its raging torrent.

The girl was so distraught by what she had witnessed that she lost her mind and every night thereafter prowled the basin looking for her lost lover. "The wraith is seen there now, it is said, and those who in an older day met the white-robed 'something' presumed to be the spirit of the lady in search of her lover, christened it, 'the Valley of the White Woman.'"[65]

Following the devastating 1881 flood, "A Pierre resident often relates a brief yarn about the flood, but refuses to vouch for its authenticity. He tells of seeing about everything movable drifting with the current, but the most unusual spectacle was a musician clinging to a table as he floated by while his wife accompanied him on the piano."[66]

Just how far could a building float downriver amidst the raging water and grinding ice of the 1881 Missouri River flood? The "church and bell" story was found in many accounts and it varied somewhat with each telling. A composite story would read something like this: A small white church with the proper bell spire was swept away from the Santee Indian agency near Springfield. Still afloat it was seen by residents of Green Island as it bobbed along until disappearing behind a grove of trees. It was assumed to have sunk but some thirty miles down stream it was seen again, still afloat. According to witnesses along the way the bell tolled constantly as a "fitting requiem over the scene of destruction."

##

If she doesn't laugh, Mother Nature must at least chuckle at man's attempt to control her system of rivers and streams.

Chapter Seven notes

[1] J. Mike McCoy, *History of Cedar County Nebraska* (n.p.: n.p., 1937), 97.

[2] Ibid., 97.

[3] H. M. Seccombe, *"Perils of Waters"* (Springfield, Dakota Territory: John Todd, Printer, 1883), 6-7.

[4] Ibid., 9.

[5] Ibid., 12.

[6] Greg O'Brien, "Making the Mississippi Over Again: The Development of River Control in Mississippi." *Mississippi History Now,* March 2002, http://mshistory.k12.ms.us/features/feature25/msriver.html.

[7] Bette Roda Anderson, *Weather in the West* (Palo Alto, CA: American West Publishing Company, 1975), 158.

[8] Dennis Flanagan, "The Nature of Risk," in *Nature on the Rampage,* with H. J. De Blij (Washington: Smithsonian Books, 1994), 193.

[9] Frank W. Lane, *The Elements Rage* (Philadelphia: Chilton Books, 1965), 146.

[10] Richard Lipkin, "Weather's Fury," in *Nature on the Rampage,* with H. J. De Blij (Washington: Smithsonian Books, 1994), 30.

[11] William B. Meyer, *Americans and Their Weather* (New York: Oxford University Press, 2000), 102.

[12] Gordon B. Dodds, "The Stream-Flow Controversy: A Conservation Turning Point," *Journal of American History* 56 (1969), 59-69, quoted in William B. Meyer, *Americans and Their Weather* (New York: Oxford University Press, 2000), 103.

[13] H. M. Chittenden, in "Discussion: Forests, Resevoirs, and Stream Flow," *Transactions of the American Society of Civil Engineers* 62 (1909), 501, quoted in William B. Meyer, *Americans and Their Weather* (New York: Oxford University Press, 2000), 103.

[14] Nelson A. Miles, *Personal Recollections and Observations of General Nelson A. Miles* (reprint; Lincoln: University of Nebraska Press, 1992), 1:215.

[15] Paul O'Neil, *The Rivermen*, The Old West Series (Alexandria, VA: Time-Life Books, 1975), 17.

[16] Ibid., 7.

[17] Albert D. Richardson, *Beyond the Mississippi* (Hartford, CT: American Publishing Company, 1867), 19.

[18] Everett Dick, *The Sod-House Frontier 1854-1890* (Lincoln: Johnsen Publishing Company, 1954), 230-231.

[19] "Many Lives Lost In Flood of 1881," (Ponca) *Nebraska Journal Leader*, 24 June 1937.

[20] Robert F. Karolevitz, *Yankton: A Pioneer* Past (Aberdeen, SD: North Plains Press, 1972), 93.

[21] Ibid., 96. From Press and Dakotaian, 8 April 1881.

[22] Doane Robinson, *Encyclopedia of South Dakota* (Pierre: Privately published by author, 1925), 528.

[23] "The Flood of 1881," *Atchison* (Kansas) *Globe*, 1 July 1908.

[24] Ibid., 1 July 1908.

[25] Robert F. Karolevitz, *Yankton: A Pioneer* Past (Aberdeen, SD: North Plains Press, 1972), 91.

[26] John D. Hunter, *Memoirs of a Captivity Among the Indians of North America* (London: Longman, Hurst, Rees, Orme, Brown, and Green, 1824), 26.

[27] F. [Francis] Barker to Isaac B. Barker, Esqr., 23 July 1844, Barker Collection, Kansas State Historical Society.

[28] "The Floods of 1844," *Topeka* (Kansas) *Capital*, 3 June 1903. (Parts of Meeker's diary were published in the paper as a comparison to the 1903 floods.)

[29] Richard Irving Dodge, *The Plains of the Great West* (New York: Archer House, Inc., 1959), 81.

[30] Ibid., 82-83.

[31] Ibid., 87-88.

[32] Elizabeth B. Custer, *Tenting on the Plains or General Custer in Kansas and Texas* (New York: Charles L. Webster & Company, 1887), 636.

[33] Ibid., 636-637.

[34] Ibid., 638-643.

[35] Raymond L. Welty, "Floods Here Traced Back As Early As 1865," *Hays* (Kansas) *Daily News*, 12 June 1966.

[36] F. M. Lockard, *The History of the Early Settlement of Norton County, Kansas* (Norton, Kansas: Champion, [newspaper?], 1894), 46-47.

[37] "Waterspout in '86 Caused Great Loss of Lives, Property," *Kiowa* (Kansas) *Herald*, 23 April 1885.

[38] "1500 people Attend Monument Dedication," *Cambridge* (Nebraska) *Clarion*, 30 May 1924.

[39] John L. McCarty, *Maverick Town* (Norman: University of Oklahoma Press, 1946), 250-251.

[40] David Laskin, *Braving the Elements* (New York: Doubleday, 1996), 142-143.

[41] Reuben Gold Thwaites, ed., *Early Western Travels, 1748-1846*, vol. 5: *Bradbury's Travels in the Interior of America, 1809-1811* (1817; reprint, Cleveland, OH: Arthur H. Clark Company, 1904), 261-262.

[42] *Congressional Record*, 47th Congress, 1st session (1882), 3142, 3216, quoted in William B. Meyer, *Americans and Their Weather* (New York: Oxford University Press, 2000), 105.

[43] Frank W. Lane, *The Elements Rage* (Philadelphia: Chilton Books, 1965), 168-169. The length of the Great Wall depends to which time period and the method of measurement calculation (straight line east-to-west or actual length of structure). Lane seems to be referring to the east-to-west figure of 1,678 miles. See: Robert Sullivan, ed., "The Great Wall of China," *Life: The Seven Wonders of the World Yesterday, Today and Tomorrow* Vol. 3, No. 6, 15 December 2003.

[44] Greg O'Brien, "Making the Mississippi Over Again: The Development of River Control in Mississippi." *Mississippi History Now*, March 2002, http://mshistory.k12.ms.us/features/feature25/msriver.html.

[45] Ibid., March 2002,

[46] Richard Lipkin, "Weather's Fury," in *Nature on the Rampage,* with H. J. De Blij (Washington: Smithsonian Books, 1994), 72.

[47] "The Platte River," *Nebraska History and Record of Pioneer Days*, March 1918.

[48] Don Cunningham, "River Portraits: The Platte," *NEBRASKAland Magazine*, January-February 1983.

[49] Ibid., January-February 1983.

[50] Merrill J. Mattes, *Platte River Road Narratives* (Urbana and Chicago: University of Illinois Press, 1988), 38-39. Taken from Mattes' summary of Smith's journal.

[51] Merrill J. Mattes, *The Great Platte River Road* (Lincoln: Nebraska State Historical Society, 1969), 240.

[52] John D. Hunter, *Memoirs of a Captivity Among the Indians of North America* (London: Longman, Hurst, Rees, Orme, Brown, and Green, 1824), 86.

[53] John Dougherty to William Clark, May 6, 1828, Dougherty, John, Letter Book, 1826-1829 (C2292), State Historical Society of Missouri, Western Historical Manuscript Collection-Columbia.

[54] Merrill J. Mattes, *Platte River Road Narratives* (Urbana and Chicago: University of Illinois Press, 1988), 261. Taken from Mattes' summary of the journal.

[55] D. Ray Wilson, *Fort Kearny on the Platte* (n.p.: Crossroads Communications, 1980), 125.

[56] Judge Francis O. Hamer, "Old Fort Kearney: Historic and Consecrated Ground," *Kearney* (Nebraska) *Daily Hub*, 26 June 1909.

[57] Samuel Stearly, "Fording the Platte," *Publications of the Nebraska State Historical Society* Vol. 18, 1917 (Lincoln: The Nebraska State Historical Society, 1917), 194-195.

[58] J. Frank Dobie, *The Longhorns* (Boston: Little, Brown and Company, 1941), 82.

[59] Ibid., 82-83.

[60] H. M. Seccombe, *"Perils of Waters"* (Springfield, Dakota Territory: John Todd, Printer, 1883), 13-14.

[61] Samuel Stearly, "Fording the Platte," *Publications of the Nebraska State Historical Society* vol. 18, 1917 (Lincoln: The Nebraska State Historical Society, 1917), 195-196.

[62] "Recall Early Dakota Flood: Old Timers Reminded of Missouri River Rampage of 1881," No name, no date newspaper article from the South Dakota State Historical Society verticle file clippings under "Floods."

[63] Ibid., verticle file clippings under "Floods."

[64] J. Marvin Hunter, ed., *The Trail Drivers of Texas* (San Antonio, TX: Jackson Printing Co., 1920-1923), 1:414-415.

[65] Leola Howard Blanchard, *Conquest of Southwest Kansas* (Wichita: Wichita Eagle Press, 1931), 338-339.

[66] "Ohio Valley Flood Recalls South Dakota Disaster in 1881," No name, no date newspaper article from the South Dakota State Historical Society verticle file clippings under "Floods."

Chapter Eight

WAVES OF DYING

It would be better if a fog, thick, like a wall, should come up between the sea and the land that the latter might never see the crime of the former.
  —Colonel "Bill" Sterrett, *The Great Galveston Disaster*

Richard Hope Peek awakened early the morning of 8 September 1900. Three years as a cadet at the Virginia Military Institute had instilled a routine of rising before the sun. However, this morning it wasn't routine but worry that drove him from his bed.

Today's Galveston *News* was printing an interview in which he, as Galveston's city engineer, told the reporter macadam paving wasn't suitable for their city streets. Granted, it was cheaper than brick, and saving money made politicians look good, but he wasn't convinced it would hold up in Galveston's hot climate.

He dressed and left the house quietly. There was no indication that his wife or any of their six children were awake. Even the maid wasn't up at this hour.

With the pros and cons running through his head, he went to the stable behind the house and hitched a sorrel gelding to the shay and headed for his office. He wanted to review the facts one last time to insure he'd have a ready answer to anyone who challenged him on the issue.

Galveston was the fourth largest city in Texas and enjoyed a per capita wealth that surpassed all other Southwest cities. Thanks belonged to the deepwater port in Galveston Bay that brought a steady flow of goods and dollars to the city's doorstep.[1] Because of this burgeoning commerce, the city-on-a-sand-pile had electric lights, electric streetcars, telephone and telegraph service coupled with grand hotels, eloquent restaurants, and palatial residences. Its main thoroughfare, dubbed the Strand, boasted of more millionaires per mile than any other American city of its size with only one possible exception.

Churches of every persuasion, plus a synagogue, were an intricate part of the town, but this city was no prude. Rumor had it that the city could boast of 500 saloons plus brothels in necessary numbers. A frolic in the Gulf waters without the restrictive encumbrance of a bathing suit was occasionally enjoyed by bathers and gawkers alike—although some gawkers claimed to be "shocked" by such behavior.

But the flip-side of the coin was that the city government, despite the obvious commercial and personal affluence, was financially strapped which meant that cost was going to be a key factor in street paving contracts.

Richard Peek saw no lights in any residents of the new Denver Resurvey subdivision on the western edge of Galveston. He drove at a trot east on Avenue S to Bath Avenue where he turned north to Market Street and then east toward the city offices.

Sprinkled across the city a few lights punched yellow holes in the early morning darkness while the heavy air muffled the sounds and smells of a sleeping city. The odor of horse manure, mingled with other creature smells, hung in the oppressive air like languid fish in a quiet millpond. The flowering oleander bushes' fragrances stalked offending odors with a killer's intent and every revolution of the shay's wheels brought a changing blend of scents hitchhiking on an easy north wind.

A steamship whistle sounded along the wharf on the north side of the city which fronted Galveston Bay. Galveston's port vied with New Orleans as the leading cotton port in the country and was a solid third in wheat exports.

It was a few minutes after four o'clock when Richard let himself into his office in the city building on 20th Street. Gathering his files on street paving he began reviewing the street problems that plagued the city.

There was no consistency to the street surfaces, "some were paved with wood blocks brought in years earlier as ships' ballast. A few others were covered with shells, but the white shell caused such a glare that many persons had to close the shutters in midday. Many other streets were just sand, as nature had made them."[2]

In Richard's mind the issue was cost vs. durability and to an engineer's mind durability would always prevail. He hadn't recommended the material, macadam, because he believed the tar would liquefy under the hot summer sun. And, in some locations with a lot of stop-and-go traffic, he'd told the reporter that horses standing in one place for any length of time would make a depression in the paving which would soon become a hole. In his view this shortcoming must be overcome before macadam was utilized in the business portion of the city.

Macadam, he'd learned, was developed by Scottish civil engineer, John Loudon McAdams, in the early 1800s. McAdams was involved in the tar business and hit upon the idea of binding together layers of compacted broken stone with tar to use as a street and roadway pavement. It became known as the tar-McAdams method, or tarmacadams, and finally "tarmac."

However, neither the British Isles nor Europe experienced the prolonged blistering heat that is normal for the southern United States and Peek doubted that the surface would hold up in Galveston's high temperatures.

All that aside, he did acknowledge to the newspaper reporter that macadam could be had "for about $1 per square yard, which is about eighty cents per yard cheaper than brick paving." Yet it was a considerable savings and after reviewing his notes Richard wondered if it could be used to good effect on some of the residential streets. Perhaps here was a compromise that would satisfy all parties.

Leaning back in his chair he checked his pocket watch which agreed with his stomach; it was past six o'clock and past breakfast time. He decided to eat at a downtown cafe and inside the eatery he picked a solitary table where he could think and scribble notes.

Lingering over a last cup of coffee he overheard talk of a powerful storm somewhere in the Gulf. Once back on the street he looked to the roof of the Levy Building and saw a square red flag with a square black center topped by a white pennant. He knew the red and black flag indicated "a storm of marked violence" was approaching. The white pennant meant the winds were now from the northwest. He made a mental note to check the flags often; if the weathermen replaced the white pennant with another red and black flag it would mean a tropical hurricane was expected.

Obeying a sudden impulse he drove down to the beach. The tide was already flooding some low parts of the city making for slow travel. It was just after sunrise when Richard reached the beach but the sun only winked periodically through the broken cloud cover.

Reining the sorrel to a stop Richard sat and watched the high waves break far past the normal shoreline. The streetcar trestle was now surrounded by water and provided a theater where the waves could take center stage. They surged over the rails and crashed against the pilings sending plumes of white spray soaring high into the air.

Richard had never seen them so powerful. As he watched, the Gulf water seemed to rise like the bosom of a sleeping woman and then slowly fall as if she were exhaling. It followed a slower rhythm, independent of the waves but as this rise broke on the shore it could be felt as well as heard.

Even at this early hour, scores of residents were streaming to the beach to watch the high breakers roll in from the Gulf; their festive mood reminded Richard of a holiday celebration. Spotting Isaac Cline's hack parked further down the beach Richard drove there and reined in beside him.

"Good morning, Doctor Cline."

The man didn't respond but continued looking down at his hand and then out to the Gulf. Richard saw he held a watch and was obviously timing the waves.

"Hello, Captain." Cline said dropping the watch back into his vest pocked. "Hope you haven't come for a swim unless you like rough seas."

"No. I saw the storm flags and was just down for a look. What's your professional opinion?"

"Officially, right now, the Weather Bureau predicts a strong tropical storm."

"Anything to worry about?" Richard asked as he watched each wave break just a little further in than the last one.

"Captain Peek, I'll be honest. I believe those living within three blocks of the beach would be well advised to move to higher parts of the city. And I plan to tell any people I meet from the mainland to return immediately."

"Doctor Cline, you seem to be of two persuasions, your personal belief and your official capacity. Should I take this as an indication to worry?"

"I don't want to alarm anyone but there is a real threat of serious island flooding and very high winds. You shouldn't worry, I'm sure you made certain that your new house is well built and it should withstand any storm. And, you are more than three blocks back from the beach." Cline retrieved his watch and Richard realized the conversation was over.

Photo courtesy Virginia Military Institute
Richard Hope Peek as a cadet at Virginia Military Institute. Peek was city engineer for Galveston, Texas, when a hurricane wrecked the island city in 1900.

"Thanks," he said as he flicked the lines along the horse's back and drove toward his office. He was now concerned; reassured but concerned. Richard knew that hurricanes visited Galveston on a recurring, but unpredictable, schedule. Like the other Galvestonians, Richard and his family went about life much as all people do who intellectually know that they are at risk. If you dwell on it, it either drives you crazy or drives you away.

And every part of the country had its own set of frightening possibilities—earthquakes, tornadoes, droughts, blizzards, or floods. He'd made Galveston his home for better or worse and they would ride out this storm as others had ridden out storms before. Still, as he thought back on the scene at the beach he could feel a little gathering of nerves in the pit of his stomach.

Back at his office Richard recalculated costs, figuring the numbers of blocks of sand streets, shell paved streets, and streets with wooden blocks. But by eleven o'clock he could no longer concentrate on street problems so he stacked the papers on his desk and left for home. Outside he felt the wind's increased velocity and noticed the clouds were lower and darker.

A light rain had begun falling so Richard put the shay's top up before leaving the livery. Once on the street the wind tore at the top threatening to rip it from the vehicle. When he turned west on Market Street, water was running curb deep and, in what seemed comic irony, the wooden paving blocks were beginning to float and ride the current like giant corks in a mill race.

The rushing water and floating debris forced the gelding to pick its way slowly. Richard pulled his hat down and listened to the wind and the pounding from the beach as the lady of the Gulf exhaled.

He didn't reach his house at 5408 Ave. S. until half past one and was very thankful to find his family safe. They were bubbling with stories of the grand sites at the beach. His family, like the others at the beach, found it exhilarating; the maid, Ida Schultz, a fourteen year old girl from Germany, wasn't a lover of the sea.

Richard listened to their stories while eating a quick lunch before going outside to unharness and stable the horse. He noticed that water was flooding the low places; the wind had again gained in velocity and the clouds had grown darker. If his watch hadn't told him it was only half past three he'd have guessed it was sundown.

After securing anything that the wind could pilfer he went inside and told Alice that he was going to walk to the beach and that she and the children were not to leave the house.

He didn't have to walk the entire five blocks because the beach was coming to meet him. Frequently a bucket, or a board, or some other item came bobbing along on the water that was now knee deep. After he passed the last house he stopped and tried to peer through the wind-driven rain and spray. It was

Photo by author

Ben Peek, grand-nephew of Richard Hope Peek. Bottom: Grave marker at the Peek family plot in Galveston Memorial Park Cemetery, Hitchcock, Texas.

difficult to see out into the Gulf but he could tell the waves were exceptionally high with overhanging crests covered with white foam. Wind whipped the foam into spindrift as the lady of the Gulf breathed deeply.

While Richard shielded his eyes against the driving rain he saw a great gray wall moving toward shore. He wasn't sure if it was a very high wave or some very low clouds. Suddenly he had an urgent need to be far away from the sea.

But he had faith in the strength of his home; if any dwelling could weather the storm he believed the Peek house could. On the trip back the water got deeper by the minute. Slate shingles, ripped from the roofs, were splashing down around him. Richard found it discomforting to know that it required almost hurricane velocity winds to dislodge slate shingles from a new roof.

Struggling through waist-deep water he finally reached home where he fought to keep the wind from tearing the front door from his grasp. Before he could get the door closed and latched the wind had blown over a lamp and sent a picture and frame crashing to the floor.

He finally wrestled the door shut and when he turned around his family was gathered before him in the foyer and their faces told him he needed to remain calm and reassure them they would be safe.

First he instructed the maid to get the candles and oil lamps that had been stored in the pantry for use if the electricity ever failed. He then told his family to all dress in warm clothing and to make sure they had on hat and shoes. Finally he asked Alice and their oldest son to gather any rope they could find in the house.

At approximately 5:45 p.m. Richard noticed a marked increase in the wind's fury and the tide rose four feet in "one bound" bringing water into the Peek home. Just before sundown 12x12-inch beams from a wrecked Fort Crockett, carried by the raging waves, began to assault the Peek home.

Galveston Island is a sand island some thirty miles long and a half-mile to three miles wide. The island parallels the Texas coast on a southwest to northeast alignment. In 1900 the wharfs and business district of the city were located toward the east end of the island and on the north, or mainland, side much as they are today. The island is separated from the mainland coast by two miles of water known as West Bay. Across this bay and inland for many miles the mainland is level and low, being in some locations lower than Galveston Island.

At the turn of the twentieth century Galvestonians were well aware that their fair city was in harm's way. Hurricanes were certainly no stranger to Galveston. During the nineteenth century tropical storms or hurricanes struck Galveston in 1818, 1837, 1842, 1854, 1867, twice in 1871, 1875, 1886, and 1900.[3]

In its natural state the island could muster only about 4.5 to 8.7 feet of elevation above sea level. For this reason citizens and city officials occasionally flirted with the idea of building a protective sea wall but it would be costly and, besides, there was "evidence" that a devastating hurricane could never strike the city.

Evidence aside, a hurricane in 1886 completely destroyed Galveston's rival, Indianola, Texas, situated just a few miles down the coast. Once again Galveston's citizens focused on their vulnerability but the lesson wasn't learned.

Following Indianola's demise, a letter published in the *Galveston Daily News* argued that "Galveston could never suffer like Indianola because it only happened where the storm surge hit a solid object like the mainland. The bay would absorb the shock for Galveston."

And if that wasn't enough "proof" to calm any nerves the city had about hurricanes, "Matthew F. Maury, a national authority famous for navigational observations, stated that Galveston was exempt from the force of destructive hurricanes. It was located in a 'cove of safety,' protected by shallow water and sandbars running parallel to the shore. Inhabitants need not be apprehensive, he said, because the storm waves could never reach the shore in full force."[4]

Some were not persuaded.

Engineer James B. Eads, designer of the Eads Bridge at St. Louis, took a look at Galveston and came to a very different conclusion. In retrospect it was easy for survivors of the 1900 storm to admit that "When Captain James B. Eads said we must raise Galveston island eight feet and build a sea wall, spoke he more wisely than we know."[5]

Arthur E. Stilwell was another skeptic. However he didn't arrive at his judgment from an engineering analysis but, according to him, from a much higher source.

Stilwell was born at Rochester, New York, on 21 October 1859 and died in the same city on 26 September 1928. His brief flirtation with Galveston Island and the 1900 hurricane is explained by him in his book, *I Had a Hunch.*

> All my life, even when a child, I have received messages from the spirit world and they have greatly influenced my life. When I was 15 years of age my life's companion was selected for me by this choir invisible, and I was told that I would marry her when I was 19 years old, which I did. The wisdom of their selection and my appreciation of it has been the paramount factor in strengthening my faith in these leadings.
>
> From the plans and advice received in this way I have been able to build five western railroads, 2,500 miles altogether—more than any other living man has constructed. By this means I have founded forty-odd cities and villages with a combined population of more than 125,000. I was warned by my nightly advisers not to make Galveston the terminal of the Kansas City Southern Road because that city was destined to be destroyed by a tidal wave, which prediction was fulfilled, tragically, four years later. Thereupon, I constructed the City of Port Arthur, Texas, and built the Port Arthur Ship Canal and Harbor under the same guidance, not deviating from the plans revealed to me in any way.[6]

Whether or not Stilwell tried to warn the city of Galveston of its prophesied doom isn't known. Understandably, if the city disregarded Stilwell's warning, it must be remembered that he received the warning four years prior to 1900. People do grow complacent; both prophet and hearers frequently say "enough" and forget the whole unpopular business. Of more value would have been a warning just prior to 8 September 1900, that a hurricane was flailing about somewhere in the Gulf of Mexico.

There is evidence that many Galveston residents knew of an approaching storm well in advance of that fateful day. The 11 September issue of the *Houston Daily Post* in an article datelined, Galveston, Texas, 10 September said, "The center of the West Indian hurricane, which had been predicted here for several days, struck here at 9 o'clock Saturday morning."

Someone, perhaps the editor who nursed a philosophical, religious, and self-righteous viewpoint informed the readers of the *Wichita (Kansas) Daily Eagle* on Tuesday, 11 September that "Galveston had a warning of two thousand years standing in the Bible in regard to the man who built his house upon the sands."

Although it would be years before the age of radar and satellite imaging, this hurricane was, so to speak, on the U. S. Weather Bureau's "radar" for several days. A special "Galveston Disaster Edition" of the *Southern Industrial and Lumber Review* issued on 22 September 1900, ran copy previously published in the *Galveston News*.

The newspaper published this itinerary of the storm's approach.

> The first message of the storm was received at the weather office at Galveston at 4 p. m. on the 4th instant. It was then moving northward over Cuba. Each day thereafter until the West India hurricane struck Galveston bulletins were posted by the United States weather bureau officials giving the progressive movements of the disturbance. On the 6th . . . over southern Florida . . . off the Louisiana coast on the morning of the 7th when northwest storm warnings were ordered up for Galveston. On the morning of the 8th the storm had increased in energy and was still moving westward and at 10:10 a.m. the northwest storm warnings were changed to the northeast. Then was when the entire island was in apparent danger. The telephone at the United States weather bureau office was busy until the wires went down . . . people came to the office in droves inquiring about the weather. About the following information was given to all alike: 'The tropical storm is now in the gulf southeast of us: the winds will shift to the northeast, east and probably to the southeast by morning, increasing in energy. If you live in low parts of city move to high grounds.'[7]

Isaac M. Cline, local forecast official and section director of the Galveston office of the U. S. Weather Bureau filed a special report on the Galveston hurricane on 23 September 1900. In this report to the Washington office he notes that "Storm warnings were timely and received a wide distribution not only in Galveston but throughout the coast region. Warning messages were received from the Central Office at Washington on September 4, 5, 6, 7, and 8."

In his autobiography Cline added that

> A tropical cyclone made its appearance early in September and was north of Cuba on the 3rd, passed through the Florida Straits on the 4th and 5th and traveled in a northwesterly direction through the Gulf of Mexico. It was centered about 200 miles south of the Mississippi River at 8 a. m. on September 7th . . . the storm center at that time being about 400 miles from Galveston . . . The cyclone was advancing towards the Texas coast with a speed of about 12 miles per hour while the winds near the center of the cyclone were of hurricane force and probably exceeded 100 miles per hour.[8]

The storm was expected.

The hurricane-force winds were suspected.

The devastation was neither.

According to the 1900 U.S. Census there were 37,789 residents on the island.[9] After assessing the storm damage, Texas Governor Joseph D. Sayers stated his belief that the loss of life was 12,000.

Other reports place the number at "six thousand in the city, one thousand on the island, and one thousand on the mainland."[10]

No one will ever know for sure, but there were roughly thirty thousand survivors; each with a story of deliverance. And there were roughly 8,000 to 12,000 tragic stories of death. Most of these stories will never be known.

Yet, there are thousands of recorded incidents showing why the 1900 Galveston Storm reigns as the most deadly natural disaster in U.S. history. No matter where the survivors looked, or went, they were constantly reminded of the dead. In sunlight,

During the 1900 Galveston hurricane, many residents took to the rooftops to escape the raging waters. Unfortunately, for many people it provided only a short reprieve from their ultimate fate.

reminded by sight; in starlight, reminded by loss; in both day and night, reminded by stench.

According to the period's phraseology the scene that greeted survivors on Sunday morning "beggared description." On 10 September, Henry Decherd, a medical student, wrote to his mother saying "I shall not try to describe in words the horrible picture of desolation here—that would be useless." A few accounts, as Decherd said, "will give you some idea."

The following story was published in the 21 September 1900, edition of the *Alvin (Texas) Sun*.

> Burniss Ward, of Alvin, who was working on the Santa Fe drawbridge, narrowly escaped with his life. He succeeded in reaching Virginia Point and with others began the work of rescue. Mr. Ward went to a small house to rescue a woman and child. On one arm she carried her child and in the other hand she held $500. Before Mr. Ward could reach her she dropped the money, and in her attempt to get it dropped her child, and the fury of the storm swept both money and child away. Mr. Ward succeeded in rescuing the mother.

Another incident from near Virginia Point tells that "On Monday a brakeman of the Galveston, Houston and Northern [railroad] left Virginia Point and started to walk toward Texas City. He found a little child, which he picked up and carried for miles. On his way he discovered the bodies of nine women. These he covered with grass to protect them from the vultures until some arrangements could be made for their interment."[11]

Most, if not all, the homes at Virginia Point were destroyed. From the *Houston Daily Post*, Tuesday Morning, 11 September 1900, comes a report from near Virginia Point. Thankfully, under the headline "Some Grewsome Sights" is included a paragraph of less gruesome content. "At Virginia Point an entire train of merchandise was demolished, some of the cars being carried in the interior for a distance of several miles and overturned, among which was a car of beer upon which the crowd quenched their thirst. The beverage was somewhat warm, but served as a good substitute for water, none being found until late in the evening."

It is possible that some of the alcoholic beverage was consumed for reasons other than thirst. In all too many cases, identifying bodies was difficult at best and frequently impossible. Nonetheless great effort was made to mark graves and provide whatever identifying details that the burial parties could provide. These lists were then published in many of the area newspapers.

Considering lists like the following, perhaps a train car of beer was not an excessive amount.

- Woman, about 55 years old, five feet six inches, grey hair and one tooth in upper jaw; checked waist brown sack, shirt of green cast; checked apron and white stockings.
- Boy about 4 years old, three feet two inches, light hair; nude.
- Woman, about 25 years, about five feet nine inches, brown hair, corset and underwear, kid shoes, black stockings, scapula worn around the neck.
- Girl baby, flaxen hair, about 4 years old, two feet eleven inches; naked.

- Woman, about five feet five inches, black hair, about 23 years old.
- Girl, about 9 years old.
- Woman, about 25 years old, curly, dark brown hair, white button corset, black stocking, low quarter shoes, about five feet eight inches.
- Woman, about 35 years, blue shirt waist, mark on back between hips, rather stout; gold ring on little finger left hand inlaid with silver and gold, with green flying bird with leaves and wreath; not initials in ring; light hair.
- Girl, about 19 nineteen years old; black stockings and button shoes, brown hair, black cashmere shirt.
- Girl baby, red hair, about 2 years old.

The loss of life was tragic but the living faced their own grim trials just to stay alive. Summing up the destruction and plight of the survivors, Joel Chandler Harris, author of the Uncle Remus stories, believed "the condition of thousands of those who have been spared is far more pitiable than that of the dead. Their resources have been swept away by wind and tide, and they are desolate in the midst of desolation."[12]

##

In their book, *Atlantic Hurricanes*, Gordon E. Dunn and Banner I. Miller write that "because man's most boastful efforts at destruction, and these include the H-bomb, cannot begin to match the fury of nature on the loose . . . That leaves the hurricane as the most spectacular and the most destructive of the 'Unchained Goddesses.'"[13]

The word hurricane has its roots in the Spanish word *huracan*, which probably was borrowed from the Caribbean Indians. The now nearly extinct Taino tribe of the Bahamas, especially of Haiti, also used the word *huracan* for a hurricane—it meant evil spirit. "The Galibi Indians of Dutch and French Guiana used the word *hyoracan*, or devil, the Quiche of southern Guatemala spoke of 'Hurakan' the thunder and lightning god. Other Carib Indians words for hurricane were *aracan*, *urican*, and *huiranvucan* which have been translated as 'Big Wind,' and similar terms."[14]

Any, and all, would be appropriate since these powerful storms definitely contain extraordinary winds and their curriculum vitae reads like it was penned by a darksome deity.

The National Oceanic & Atmospheric Administration's (NOAA) web site explains that a "hurricane is a type of tropical cyclone, which is a generic term for a low pressure system that generally forms in the tropics. The cyclone is accompanied by thunderstorms and, in the Northern Hemisphere, a counterclockwise circulation of winds near the earth's surface."

Today there are two sets of nomenclature used to describe the evolution of a hurricane. The beast is born as a tropical depression and reaches its full stature as a category 5 major hurricane.

The first set of classifications are,

> **Tropical Depression:** An organized system of clouds and thunderstorms with a defined surface circulation and maximum sustained winds* of 38 mph (33 kt**) or less.
>
> **Tropical Storm:** An organized system of strong thunderstorms with a defined surface circulation and maximum sustained winds of 39-73 mph (34-63 kt).
>
> **Hurricane:** An intense tropical weather system of strong thunderstorms with a well-defined surface circulation and maximum sustained winds of 74 mph (64 kt) or higher.
>
> *Sustained winds are defined as a 1-minute average wind measured at about 33 ft (10 meters) above the surface.
> ** 1 knot = 1 nautical mile per hour or 1.15 statute miles per hour. Abbreviated as "kt".[15]

Once the storm has reached hurricane status it is further defined by the Saffir/Simpson Hurricane Scale formulated in 1969.

> **Category 1:** Winds: 74-95 mph (64-82 kt) No real damage to building structures. Damage primarily to

unanchored mobile homes, shrubbery, and trees. Also, some coastal flooding and minor pier damage.

Category 2: Winds: 96-110 mph (83-95 kt) Some roofing material, door, and window damage. Considerable damage to vegetation, mobile homes, etc. Flooding damages piers and small craft in unprotected moorings may break their moorings.

Category 3: Winds: 111-130 mph (96-113 kt) Some structural damage to small residences and utility buildings, with minor amount of curtainwall failures. Mobile homes are destroyed. Flooding near the coast destroys smaller structures with larger structures damaged by floating debris. Terrain may be flooded well inland.

Category 4: Winds: 131-155 mph (114-135 kt) More extensive curtainwall failures with some complete roof structure failure on small residences. Major erosion of beach areas. Terrain may be flooded well inland.

Category 5: Winds: 155+ mph (135+ kt) Complete roof failure on many residences and industrial buildings. Some complete building failures with small utility buildings blown over or away. Flooding causes major damage to lower floors of all structures near the shoreline. Massive evacuation of residential areas may be required.

Note: A "major" hurricane is classified as Category 3 or greater.[16]

The ingredients that Mother Nature folds into the atmosphere to create a hurricane are warm tropical oceans, moisture, and light winds aloft. To be more specific "the sea needs to have a surface temperature of at least 80°F (27°C) and be warm to a depth of 230 feet (70 meters)."[17] Given these conditions and enough time, a hurricane can be conceived.

Atlantic hurricanes begin their gestation somewhere off the west coast of Africa when a line of thunderstorms coalesce into a spiral configuration caused by the earth's rotation. This constitutes the beginning stages of what may eventually become a hurricane.

Of the approximately 100 tropical depressions that form in the Atlantic Ocean off the African coast, only nine or ten will grow into a tropical storm. Of these tropical storms only about five will become full-blown hurricanes. This is on the average; some years will have a greater number while some years will have a lesser number. Mother Nature, no doubt wanting to keep man humble and to keep him guessing, birthed not a single Atlantic hurricane in 1914.

Once the infant storm begins to wind itself around a low-pressure core it has all the potential of becoming a hurricane if conditions remain favorable. Richard Lipkin in *Nature on the Rampage* describes the maturing system.

> The tubular core, or eye, remains calm, a place where exhausted dry air spills back to the sea. Around the eye a wall of wind, or eyewall, spins fastest, often above 100 miles per hour. Driven by the low-pressure center, the storm sucks humid air up from the sea, cools it, then dumps dry air and rain back down. This organized condensing of sea mist keeps a cyclone spinning, the warm sea water serving as metaphorical steam for the atmosphere's spinning turbine.[18]

These powerful turbines can extend to an average width of "340 miles (550 kilometers) across—approximately the length of Scotland. The eye in the middle is an area of 12-30 miles (20-50 kilometers) diameter."

The amount of moisture required to sustain such a huge engine is incredible, almost impossible to grasp. A large hurricane lifts a quarter of a million tons of water vapor a second. This being the case, torrential rains that often accompany a hurricane can be better understood.[19] "It was estimated that in the 1900 Galveston hurricane, two thousand million tons of rain a day came down."[20]

The eye of a hurricane can extend upwards to nine miles and the winds often exceed 125 miles per hour. A mature hurricane is "a hundred times larger than a thunderstorm and a thousand times more powerful than a tornado. An ordinary summer thunderstorm can have the power of three nuclear bombs; a hurricane has twenty-five thousand times that power, and if it remains over warm ocean water it can be fueled for days."[21]

An illustration used in *The Complete Story of the Galveston Horror* hints at the terror and tragedy that befell the ten sisters and ninety-three children at St. Mary's Orphanage. Only three children survived.

In fact, "some cover half a million square miles and last three weeks."[22]

The 1900 Galveston Storm was about eleven days old when it hit the island. Not an exceptionally old hurricane. In width it was probably not above average. And experts have only given it an after-the-fact Category 4 rating. This wasn't the biggest or baddest hurricane to ever churn the waters of the Atlantic Ocean and the Gulf of Mexico.

Why, then, was it so deadly?

A simple layman's answer is realizing that both wind and water are responsible for hurricane damage. However, water in the form of a storm surge causes the greater destruction. Dunn and Miller explains one factor that determines the height of a storm surge and a clue to why this hurricane was so destructive.

> The angle the hurricane track makes with the coast line. As a rule in order for the maximum hurricane surge to be produced, the center of the storm must approach the coast so that the angle between the coast and the right side of the track is 90° or less. If the storm approaches the coast at an angle of considerably

less than 90° and if the coast line is such that the shortest distance between the coast and the hurricane is growing rapidly less, such as occurred in the Galveston hurricane of 1900, extreme surge heights may be reached.[23]

They go on to write

A storm of hurricane intensity moving toward or crossing a coast line will always be accompanied by tides above normal, particularly near and to the right of the center. The surge may be as little as three or four feet or less if only a few of the factors are making their maximum possible contribution, and fifteen to twenty feet or more if all factors are making the maximum possible contribution to the total elevation of the sea surface. Due probably in part to the concavity of the coast line, hurricanes in the Gulf of Mexico are usually attended by abnormally high storm tides and occasionally devastating surges.[24]

These exceptionally high tides and storm surges translate into an unfathomable amount of water and, as mentioned earlier, water is heavy. It weighs in at about three-fourths of a ton per cubic yard. Add to this tree trunks, railroad ties, heavy timbers, and other wreckage debris moving up to sixty miles per hour and you have a monster capable of wrecking almost any man-made object.[25]

Another factor attributing to a high storm surge is low barometric pressure. The approach of a hurricane precipitates a falling barometer and the lowest readings occur in, or near, the eye.

Normal barometric pressure is about 29.92 inches which fluctuates a few points during normal weather changes. However, during a hurricane the bottom seemingly falls out of the instrument. Years later NOAA scientists published that the lowest barometric pressure reached during the Galveston storm was 27.64 inches.[26]

"Such differences may seem very little, but for every inch drop in pressure about 70 pounds is lifted off every square foot of surface. Thus a drop in barometric pressure from 29.92 to 27.92 inches, removes a load of some two million tons from each square mile."[27]

The consequence of such a pressure reduction amplifies the storm surge by causing the water near the eye to rise into a mound. An over-simplification is that the low pressure acts like suction in a straw and the lower pressure allows the water to rise within the eye. This dome along with the water piled up by the high winds can create a storm surge of fifteen feet, eighteen feet, or even higher and send it crashing ashore with deadly force.

This surge of water is like a relentless, tireless, miles-long bulldozer leveling everything in its path. There isn't just one storm surge but there can be as many as 600 waves per hour hammering ashore. Their speed doesn't approach that of the wind but they can travel in excess of thirty miles per hour. Their destructive force is off the charts—literally. Marine engineers have devised ways to measure the force of wave action and the results are astonishing. French engineers performed some tests in 1963 which yielded a force of "6.6 tons per square foot at a point just above the base of the [sea] wall."

That's the extreme, yet your garden-variety storm waves have plenty of power potential. "When heavy waves crash against vertical obstacles, water sometimes shoots upwards at 200 m.p.h., reaching 200 feet, with spray flying 20 to 30 feet higher. Tons of water fall with such force that 12-inch timbers are broken like the proverbial matchsticks."[28]

In 1900 marine engineers and meteorologists didn't have the technology that is available today, however there were some indicators that were recognized as foreshadowing a hurricane. The slow, heavy waves that began to roll ashore at Galveston on Friday afternoon were warning of an approaching hurricane.

Isaac Cline did recognize these heavy swells but it is unclear just what action he took in the following hours. Perhaps, because these swells can reach land 400 or 500 miles before the actual hurricane, as time went by and no hurricane materialized, Cline assumed he'd misread the signs.

In his book, *The Elements Rage*, Lane describes these waves, or swells, as having "a slower beat than ordinary waves: roughly four to the minute instead of seven or more. They pound against the shore with a roar that is sometimes heard for several miles inland. In the New England hurricane of September 1938, the trembling of the earth as the seas fell on the shore was recorded on seismographs in Alaska, 3,000 miles away. So, when slow heavy waves start crashing on the beach—'ware hurricane!"[29]

At the outbreak of the Spanish-American War in 1898, Willis L. Moore of the U. S. Weather Bureau went to President William McKinley and "pointed out that throughout history more ships had been sunk by weather than by war. After examining the evidence McKinley said: 'I am more afraid of a West Indian hurricane than I am of the entire Spanish Navy. Get this [hurricane warning] service inaugurated at the earliest possible moment.'"[30]

##

The horrific death and destruction experienced on Galveston Island has been the subject of thousands of newspaper articles, hundreds of magazine articles, and scores of books.

Yet, the hurricane didn't wear itself out on the island. After the storm crushed Galveston, the beast roared inland. In its path scores of villages and towns were hammered by the storm, sweeping some completely out of existence.

Texas Governor Joseph D. Sayers' executive message to the Senate and House of Representatives following the 1900 Galveston Storm is preserved in the *Senate Journal*. His message read, in part,

> On the 8th day of September last a storm broke upon the portion of the Texas coast, embracing the counties of Galveston and Brazoria and extending into the interior, that for destructiveness was without precedent on the North American Continent.
>
> It is believed that fully eight thousand lives were lost, and that property aggregating many millions of dollars in value was destroyed.
>
> Its severity fell most heavily upon the counties of Galveston, Brazoria, Fort Bend and Waller, and upon portions of Harris, Matagorda, Wharton, Washington, Austin, Grimes and Montgomery.[31]

In Temple, Texas, the editor of the *Temple Times*, 14 September 1900, included a reminder to its readers that, even though Galveston suffered greatly and rendering aid was certainly appropriate, "it should not be forgotten by any one that human suffering is not all concentrated in Galveston. The entire coast country is suffering . . . A poor working man in a little village can suffer just as acutely as the most unfortunate man in the city."

Thousands did.

After passing the Florida Keys, the storm tracked northwest across the Gulf until the eye made landfall thirty miles down the coast from Galveston Island. After landfall it continued inland, still on a northwesterly heading, until somewhere near Temple, Texas, it began to curve northward after which it passed through central Oklahoma, eastern Kansas and central Iowa. Here it began strengthening and zeroing in on Chicago, Illinois. It had now scribed a parabolic path through the central United States and was headed east, northeast, across the Great Lakes and eastern Canada before exiting the continent.

What lay strewn in its path was enduring grist for newspapers, large and small, worldwide. In addition to providing news of the 1900 Galveston Storm to its readership then, these newspapers, in archives or on microfilm, provide part of the storm's record for us today

Because of its path and the concave shape of the Gulf coast, the storm began to brush the Texas coast well east of Galveston. As it maintained this northwesterly course the more severe the damage became. "Dateline Beaumont, Texas, September 10— Sabine Pass is still isolated, though, it is expected the wires will be working into this city tomorrow morning . . . the storm did but little damage at that point, and there was no loss of life."

However, further west "There are reports that many thousand head of cattle have been drowned in the lower part of Chambers county and on Bolivar peninsula." It was on this peninsula that the storm also began to turn deadly for humans.

A lighthouse stood on the tip of the peninsula where some 200 people, along with the keeper H. C. Claiborne, rode out the storm. A passenger train was caught at the end of the track near the lighthouse where, fortunately, five passengers sought refuge in the lighthouse. Unfortunately the remaining eighty-five passengers who chose to remain on the train all perished.

Northwest across Galveston Bay from Bolivar Point stood the towns of Morgan Point and Seabrook located on the west shore of the bay. Reports told of "The Terrible Experience of Houstonians at Morgan Point and Seabrook. Some of Them Found a Watery Grave."

About seven miles west of Galveston City on a point of land jutting out from the mainland stood the town of Virginia Point. Its location was roughly where the present causeway from Galveston Island meets the mainland. A Santa Fe Railroad agent made a survey of the line from Hitchcock to Virginia Point. He reported that

> Twelve miles of track and bridges are gone south of Hitchcock. I walked, waded and swam from Hitchcock to Virginia Point, and nothing could be seen in all of that country but death and desolation. The prairies are covered with water, and I do not think I exaggerate when I say that not less than 5,000 horses and cattle are to be seen along the line of the tracks south of Hitchcock.
>
> The little towns along the railway are all swept away, and the sight is the most terrible that I have ever witnessed. When I reached a point about two miles north of Virginia Point I saw some bodies floating on the prairie, and from that point until Virginia Point was reached dead bodies could be seen from the railroad track, floating about the prairie.
>
> At Virginia Point nothing is left. About 100 cars of loaded merchandise that reached Virginia Point on the International and Great Northern and the Missouri, Kansas and Texas on the night of the storm are scattered over the prairie, and their contents will no doubt prove a total loss.[32]

The situation at Hitchcock was equally grim.

Author's collection

Scenes from the 8 September 1900, hurricane that destroyed 3,600 Galveston homes. Sixty-seven blocks of the island city were devastated and 75 percent of businesses were wrecked beyond repair.

The damage at Hitchcock was not less than $100,000, but the news from there was disheartening. A bulletin from a reliable source, dated September 15, said: "Country districts are strewn with corpses. The prairies around Hitchcock are dotted with the bodies of the dead. Scores are unburied, as the bodies are too badly decomposed to handle and the water too deep to admit of burial.

A pestilence is feared from the decomposing animal matter lying everywhere. The stench is something awful. Disinfecting material is badly needed."[33]

The town of Angleton, Texas "was nearly wrecked; the storm took the town twice, once from the north and once from the south. Two Deaths Are Known. Others Reported. Property Destroyed."

About halfway between Galveston Island and Houston, and a little west, lies the town of Alvin. R. W. King went to Alvin to investigate the situation following the storm. He arrived on 15 September and reported

I arrived in Alvin from Dallas and was astonished and bewildered by the sight of devastation on every side. Ninety-five per cent of the houses in this vicinity are in ruins, leaving 6,000 people without adequate shelter and destitute of the necessaries of life, and with no means whatever to procure them. Everything in the way of crops is destroyed, and unless there is speedy relief there will be exceedingly great suffering.

The people need and must have assistance . . . Clothing is badly needed . . . Only fourteen houses in the Town of Alvin are standing, and they are badly damaged.[34]

Alvin residents, themselves reeling from the tragedy, opened their hearts and homes to thousands who were even less fortunate. The town could boast a population of approximately 2,000 souls before the storm. Two weeks after the storm the local paper printed that "About 7000 people are being fed from Alvin."

Prior to the storm some small farmers near Alvin Texas were experimenting with fig trees as a cash crop. Perhaps it was one of these trees that saved the life of a young woman and her brother. A letter written by the woman's daughters is preserved in the vertical files at the Rosenberg Library in Galveston and gives just a bit of the story. "At age 17, our mother and her parents survived that disaster [the 1900 hurricane] while living in Alvin, Texas, a few miles inland from Galveston . . . Our mother didn't talk about this experience very often but we remember that she told about spending the night hanging on to a fig tree, holding her younger brother, and that her mother's eventual death resulted from the back injury received during the storm."

Moving northward from Alvin, the storm's next big target was Houston some fifty miles inland from the Gulf coast. Houston native, John Ephraim Thomas Milsaps, "was born in the 'village of Houston' in 1852 and spent the next twenty-five years either in the city or very close to it."[35] One of the close locations where he lived was Galveston Island.

In 1877, at age twenty-five, Milsaps left his native Texas for the gold fields of the Black Hills in Dakota Territory. His fortune and future wasn't to be found in the Black Hills. By the time the 1900 hurricane changed Galveston, Milsaps' life had experienced change on a matching scale.

He was now a Major in the Salvation Army and editor of the organization's publication the *War Cry*. His duties took him to many parts of the globe but he visited Texas at every opportunity and kept up a correspondence with many from his home town.

Milsaps left a voluminous collection of seventy-three volumes of his personal diaries. He was in San Francisco when the 1900 hurricane devastated Galveston. His diary contained his personal beliefs on Galveston as a townsite plus excerpts from a letter from Houston.

His diary entry for Friday, 14 September notes that he

Read a letter from Mrs. Eliza Milsaps, Houston, Texas, September 10th. She says: "Our house is completely ruined. We stayed in it until it went off the blocks then we went to a neighbor's house until morning and we will have to stay there until we can get our own house built. The Lord only knows when that will be. There was only four houses in our neighborhood that was not hurt by the storm. Galveston is suppose to be gone. There has been nothing heard from there since 5 o'clock Saturday. Thank God we were not hurt during the storm. It was the worst I ever [saw] in all my life."[36]

Houston, Tex., Sept. 10—"There is no doubt that the cotton crop has been seriously injured throughout southern and central Texas. Owing to the excessive rains this year the cotton has grown to weed more than ever known and in some fields it ranges from six to ten feet high and is very rank with leaf." Taken from the *Topeka (Kansas) State Journal,* 10 September 1900.

The story at other communities sounded like a broken record on a slow turntable. Southwest of Houston at Missouri City, resident C. C. Robinson told the governor's investigative committee that,

we need something to feed our stock on. We have no feed, and have not much to eat ourselves. We have received two carloads of cotton seed and one car of corn. I got ten bushels of cotton seed and enough corn to plant thirty acres with. I don't know whether any of our people have made application [for relief] or not. Our barns were all blown down. I had six mules mortgaged from last year and I brought them to town (Richmond) today and turned them over because I could not raise the mortgage.[37]

T. L. Smith, also of Fort Bend County, reported to the committee that "I don't know of a large plantation immediately around Columbia that has not been abandoned. There were fifty families of Italians and there are only two left. I think that twenty-five per cent. of the land will be cultivated this year that was cultivated last year."

In 1900 Richmond and Rosenberg were two communities some thirty miles southwest of Houston. Here "Eight Lives

Reported Lost In the Town and in the Vicinity of Richmond."
And, "Eighteen people are reported killed near Richmond; the
town is almost wrecked."

From Rosenberg: "Three Were Killed By Debris. Much
Damage Done in the Town of Rosenberg."

The town of Wharton located on Texas's Colorado River
reported "Great damage was done at Wharton and the lives of
several negroes were lost on adjoining plantations."

Nearly sixty miles almost due north of Wharton is Hempstead,
Texas, where "An immense amount of damage was done on
the plantations near Hempstead; several negroes are reported
killed." Hempstead is 100 miles inland from Galveston.

A newspaper article datelined "Independence, Washington
County, Texas., Sept. 9," reads

> At 9 o'clock Saturday night there were indications of
> a storm. At that hour the wind came from due north;
> as it veered to the east about 2 o'clock it increased to
> a hurricane and spread devastation in its path. Four
> stores were utterly wrecked, two of them were leveled
> to the foundation. Nearly every residence was badly
> damaged, most of them unroofed, barns and other
> outhouses converted into splinters. Buggies, wagons,
> and farming implements were crushed. Fences, fruit
> trees, ornamental shrubbery and forests were swept
> away, and cotton was swept clean from the fields, but
> no human life, so far as heard from was lost . . . Such
> a storm never visited this part of the state. A number
> of families are homeless and in need.[38]

It was in Washington County, Texas, that a historic family
name and a grand old mansion came face-to-face with the
storm. The name survived unscathed but the home wasn't as
durable.

The enormous four-story stone house, five stories if you
include the drive-in cellar, with a hall ninety feet long was
constructed by Nestor Clay and his brother Tacitus. Nestor Clay
began to build the house after obtaining a Mexican land grant
in March 1831. Nestor died in 1835 after being wounded in an
Indian raid. "Following the death of Nestor Clay, his younger

brother, Tacitus, not only completed the mansion but developed the extensive acreage owned by the Clays into one of the finest cotton plantations in the county. The first cotton 'planted and raised in Washington County was at Clay Farm.'"[39]

The Clay's named their home "Ingleside" and exactly how big "Ingleside" was is open for debate, but tales of a hallway ninety feet long probably isn't an exaggeration. A floor plan in Betty Plummer's book, *Historic Homes of Washington County 1821-1860*, places the probable dimensions as seventy-five by ninety-six feet. That's 7,200 square feet per level, or 36,000 square feet of floor space.

Equally impressive is the fact that "All woodwork inside the house, including the floors, was of cedar construction. The prevalence of cedar at Independence in the early decades of colonization permitted an extensive use of cedar lumber."

That's the pedigree of the house; the family's pedigree is even more notable. "The name of Clay has been associated with American history since the early 1600's, when Sir John Clay immigrated from Wales. The first American-born Clay, Charles, was 'a soldier in Bacon's Rebellion.' During the years of the American Revolution, Thomas Clay served as a captain in the Virginia militia. His cousin, Henry Clay, later made history as the silver-tongued orator of the American Congress."

Ingleside was an oasis on the Texas landscape where travelers, neighbors, and strangers all received gracious southern hospitality. For over half a century the home stood like an indestructible haven for family and community.

But it was no match for Mother Nature and "The massive four-story structure, built in 1836, remained in good condition until the Galveston storms of 1900 and 1915 caused irreparable damage to this 'showplace of Washington County.'"

Temple, Texas, northwest of Washington County, is 200 miles inland and at this point the storm was 200 miles wide and making a turn toward the north.

An article in the 14 September 1900, newspaper, the *Temple (Texas) Times*, gives an accounting of the damage at Temple, Texas. "No lives were lost and no one seriously hurt." But, "Windows were blown in, houses unroofed, outbuildings tumbled over, and trees broken, twisted, split and sprawled all over town. The morning came but no cessation or abatement of the storm, hour succeed hour and yet the wind blew a hurricane. Corn was flattened, cotton tangled, twisted and whipped; the bolls were beaten off as likewise forms and blooms. There is no estimating the damage to cotton and corn."

North of Temple at Waco the cotton crop suffered and the newspapers reporting on the damage noted that "It Has Been Very Heavy in Central Texas. Negroes Declare that There is Nothing Left in the Fields About Waco."

The storm is now moving mostly north and hits Denton where it blows "trees down, cotton crop injured, and telephone service knocked out by falling trees." At Paris, Texas, not far from the Texas-Oklahoma border there was reported "considerable damage to crops and fruit trees."

After the storm waltzed across Texas, the beast still had plenty of life left. From the *Wichita (Kansas) Daily Eagle* datelined "Washington, Sept. 10—Prof. Willis Moore, chief of the weather bureau said today the West Indies storm which developed into a hurricane after reaching the United States and did such appalling damage in Texas was central in Oklahoma today and was rapidly losing its destructive character, the wind at Oklahoma City being reported as blowing thirty miles and hour."

From the *Topeka (Kansas) State Journal*, dateline "St. Paul, Minn., Sept. 11—The tail end of the West Indian storm which devastated Galveston struck this city last night and today, making itself apparent in the heaviest rainfall ever recorded in the local weather office. In sixteen hours there was a precipitation of 4.23 inches, most of which fell between 11:30 last night and 7:00 this morning. The rains caused several bad washouts on the Northern Pacific in the northern part of the state."

A continuing report on the storm's progress appeared in the 12 September edition of the *Houston Daily Post*.

Dateline: Washington, September 11—The West Indian storm which has passed from Texas to Iowa since Sunday, has increased greatly during the last twenty-four hours. From Iowa it will move northeastward and cause severe gales over Lake Michigan tonight and over Lakes Huron and Eastern Superior late Tuesday and Wednesday. The storm is also likely to cause severe thunder storms and squalls from Eastern Iowa and Eastern Missouri over Illinois, Indiana, Southern Wisconsin, Lower Michigan, Northern Ohio and Lakes Ontario and Erie.

From the *Wichita (Kansas) Daily Eagle*, Wednesday morning, dateline "Chicago Sept. 11—The storm of today was one of the severest that has visited Chicago in years. At one time the wind reached a velocity of 72 miles an hour and at no time during the day was the velocity less than 50 miles an hour. Two people lost their lives as a result of the gale and a number were injured."

From the windy city its path eastward included Toronto where it smashed windows, toppled trees and telegraph wires and played havoc with marine craft.

Orchards in the Niagara Peninsula suffered as at least half the crop was harvested by the winds. Paris, Ontario, had three fourths of its business district destroyed by a fire that the storm's winds whipped out of control.

Two ships were lost in Lake Erie. Eleven drowned when the steamer *John B. Lyon* foundered five miles off Conneaut, Ohio. Two additional lives were lost when the schooner *Dundee* sank 15 miles from Cleveland.

Again from the *Topeka (Kansas) State Journal*, dateline: "Cleveland, O., Sept. 12—As a result of the furious gale which swept over the lake region last night telegraph and telephone lines were prostrated in all directions from this city today. During the height of the storm the wind reached a velocity of 60 miles an hour. Today the storm is subsiding. Up to noon today the big passenger steamers City of Erie and the Northwest, which left Buffalo last evening for this port and State of Ohio from Toledo, have not been heard from. They were due here at 6 o'clock this morning."

From *The Topeka (Kansas) Daily Capital*, 13 September 1900, another dateline from Cleveland on 12 September:

A telegram from Erie, Pa., says the steamer *R. Lyons* [perhaps the same craft as the *John B. Lyon*] foundered off Girard, Pa., in the big gale of last night and it is believed fourteen persons went down with her.

At 5 p.m. today a telegram was received at J. C. Gilchrist's office here stating that a wrecked steamer, believed to be the *Lyons*, had been sighted five miles off Conneaut and that with the aid of glasses a dozen or fifteen men could be seen clinging to the rigging.

Tugs have been ordered sent out from Conneaut to the assistance of those on the wrecked steamer.

"Canadian hurricane" sounds like it should rank right up near the top of the oxymoron list.

Not so.

Atlantic hurricanes frequently reach as far north as Canada, Nova Scotia, or Newfoundland. However, having one reach these locations from the Gulf of Mexico with enough punch left to cause extensive property damage and loss of life is not common.

Canadian author John D. Reid, in his article "The Great 1900 Galveston Hurricane in Canada," writes that this storm "caused more US fatalities than the legendary Chicago Fire, San Francisco Earthquake, and the Johnstown Flood combined."

North of the border the fatalities "while only one hundredth those in Texas, still meant more deaths than from hurricane Hazel in 1954, which killed 84. And more than the 1998 Ice Storm, 2000 Pine Lake and 1988 Edmonton tornadoes combined."[40]

When the beast began to tread on Canadian soil it still remained a newsworthy event. From the *Topeka (Kansas) State Journal,* datelined

Buffalo, N.Y., Sept. 12—Reports from Crystal Beach, a summer resort on the Canadian side of Lake Erie, say that every dock has been destroyed by the terrific wind storm of last night, and all the boats of the Buffalo club and many sea yachts anchored there were completely wrecked. The damage there has been very heavy. The wind here attained a velocity of 72 miles an hour, but beyond the blowing down of a number of trees, the wrecking of awnings and chimneys and the destruction of a tower of one of the Pan-American buildings in course of erection, no serious damage has been reported.

Picking up the track again in Reid's article: The storm visited Montreal on the 12th and then "Passing through Gaspe and northern New Brunswick the system regained energy . . . By 8 p.m. on Wednesday the 12th the storm centre lay offshore of Port aux Basques."

Most damage and loss of life was at sea:

- Perce—30 boats and six men lost.
- New Brunswick—eight fishing schooners, 38 *Acadian* crew members drowned.
- Prince Edward Island—35 ton *Reality* wrecked, crew of four drowned.
- Newfoundland—82 schooners ashore or foundered and 100 more seriously damaged. Reported at least 50 lives lost. Another 25 feared lost.
- St. Pierre et Miquelon—"Nine schooners and 120 men were reported lost leaving 50 children without fathers."[41]

Finally remnants of the deadly 1900 Galveston Storm then churned out into the north Atlantic and it assumedly lies in an unmarked grave somewhere in Siberia's cold, cold wasteland.

The beast's reign of terror finally ended far from the prairies and plains but not before leaving an unprecedented legacy of death and destruction through some 3,000 miles of the North American continent.

##

Human nature's dark side never takes a holiday, even in the wake of disaster. The water had barely begun to recede before the lawless element took to the streets looting and robbing. Roaming thieves viewed unguarded homes, businesses, and dead bodies as easy targets.

Moving quickly to establish law and order, the mayor ordered all saloons closed until further notice and local authorities declared martial law on Monday. That same day police, deputies, and local milita were augmented by surviving soldiers from the artillery regulars at the forts. Order began to be established in the city after these forces were sworn in but it required some harsh lessons before the point was finally made.

A Houston publication, quoting from the *Galveston News* reported that

> Monday the city was practically placed under martial law. Soldiers and hundreds of special officers were placed on guard. The citizens' committee sequestered all food supplies and ordered that no able-bodied man should be allowed to eat unless he worked. Men were impressed at the point of the bayonet to do the work that must be done.
>
> Quite a number of negroes were killed for looting. No one was allowed in certain parts of the city without a pass, nor anywhere after 9 o'clock at night without a permit from the authorities.[42]

This same newspaper goes on to describe the situation that teetered on the brink of anarchy throughout the prostrate city. The "thin blue line" was almost overwhelmed when

> several times on Monday and on Tuesday there were riots caused by the impressments of men to do the public work. But by Tuesday evening there was better organization all around; the law officers had a firmer grip on the city and authority was better respected. Still the situation was grave. The stench arising from human bodies, dead animals, damaged goods and wreckage of all kinds was terrible. The need of disinfectants in enormous quantities was keenly realized and appeals went out for help of this kind.

Later in this article the writer pleaded with the public telling them "the people of the state will do Galveston a great kindness in keeping sightseers away from Galveston at this terrible time."[43]

Many publications apparently overstated the frequency, and number, of looters being shot. Yet, enough remaining letters and diaries do mention the killings, making it impossible to disregard all published accounts as fabrications.

One such story is found in a letter written by Mrs. John Focke who was the wife of a Galveston merchant. Two of the Focke's daughters were spending the summer studying in Germany and Mrs. Focke wrote them a letter dated 11 September 1900, plus another dated 14 September.

In the first letter the mother assures the daughters the family members living at home on Galveston Island are safe but "We have lost everything, though our house still stands without roof or windows." She then explains that the sister's oldest brother, John, didn't come home during the night of the storm. But, he is now safe and "Since that time he sleeps by day and at night, and heavily armed, he guards our store against the large band of thieves looting the town. We are under martial law and the few soldiers who were not drowned are simply shooting down all idlers; last night they shot seventeen."[44]

Another personal correspondence, this time from a son, Henry Decherd, to his mother mentions the problem of looting. Henry was a medical student and involved in rescuing the patients from the Sealy Hospital "in 8 feet of water and a hurricane of 100 miles an hour." On Sunday afternoon he made a tour of the town and mentions the hundreds of dead people and animals. He tells his mother that the "doctors say burn up the city; the council says no, something may be saved."

Decherd goes on to describe the incredible destruction and how busy he was helping care for the sick and injured. Then he writes that "eleven negroes shot through the head for cutting off fingers and wrists for rings & bracelets. I made my way to town last night; I was challenged 21 times by pickets. Of course town is under martial law."[45]

In his autobiography, Isaac Cline remembers the lawlessness as being very widespread. He wrote that

> Martial law was declared to protect the living from thieves and the dead from ghouls. The low criminal element, both white and colored, would cut the heads off the dead to get their necklaces and the fingers from their hands to get their rings. A large number of responsible citizens were sworn in as guards, and

they were instructed to shoot on sight any ghoul seen mutilating the dead. One of the guards told me that he shot twelve men in the act of robbing bodies, and that more than one thousand ghouls were shot before body robbing could be checked.[46]

For some reason Cline, an extremely well educated man, felt compelled to overstate the facts. Overstated or not, these grisly stories made good newspaper copy because of people's fascination with disaster of any kind. The Galveston Storm combined natural disaster with human atrocities to make irresistible "news" that ran for days in almost every newspaper around the world.

Before the era of radios and television, these newspaper stories provided the grist for endless conversations, or gossip. On 16 September the *Topeka (Kansas) Daily Capital* ran a story picked up from the *Wellington (Kansas) Mail*.

Last night at the postoffice some one expressed a doubt about the truth of the newspaper report of a soldier at Galveston killing five men at five shots. Then Sheriff Shawver told a five-shot story that left no more room for doubt. The story was of the old cowboy days in Barber county, when Charley and his partner had just come into camp from the roundup and found neither water nor anything to eat but dice [rice?]. He started to hunt water and his partner took a gun with only five shells and went hunting for something to eat. He fired five shells and killed an antelope, a jackrabbit two ducks and a rattlesnake.

A counterbalance to all the sensationalism is a book titled *Galveston in Nineteen Hundred* which was edited by Clarence Ousley and published in 1900. Governor Sayers gave his official approval to this work.

As we know, martial law was established on Monday, 10 September and this book explains that

Sunday and Monday there was some looting. In every community there are ghoulish natures. Galveston had her share, perhaps, but no more. The remedy was swift and effective, as the situation required. The local militia had been employed to preserve order and these, with the police and sheriff's forces, held the lawless in check without the delay of formal complaint and arrest. Current reports at the time represented that as many as seventy-five ghouls were shot in their tracks. Diligent inquiry fails to discover conclusive proof of one-tenth the number. It may be safely put down that if any were killed the number will not exceed a half-dozen. At any rate the reports and display of force served a good purpose.[47]

Not everyone with inclinations to profit from this disaster had the stomach to rob from the dead. But some weren't above indulging in less grisly profiteering.

In March 1901 a "Joint Committee, appointed by virtue of House Concurrent Resolution No. 2, providing for investigation into the condition of the people residing in the district damaged by the storm of 8 September 1900, and to investigate the method and manner of distribution of relief funds received by various committees in said section."

Their report submitted to the Texas Legislature was, in most part, a positive one that documented a remarkable effort to aid the suffering.

This six-man investigative committee did note some exceptions. Complaints were voiced that many large property owners on the mainland who were "able to take care of themselves" received "liberal donations" while the truly needy received very little. The investigators also "found that some of the committee [to distribute funds] made this a means of collecting some debts from the suffering and destitute people of that place."

In Brazoria County they believe that "the distributing committee were very liberal with themselves." One enterprising, or greedy, individual from Alvin contracted with sufferers to obtain relief for them for a fee of 10 percent.

The legislative committee left Alvin on 28 February and traveled to Galveston. Their report from Galveston documented that "On the first day that we were in Galveston we received something in the neighborhood of three thousand applications in shape of affidavits. We made a personal inquiry into the condition of each individual making such application. We found that at least 95 per cent of the applications presented to us upon that day were without merit."

Notwithstanding, the committee, overall, could report that much suffering had been alleviated and much good done as a result of the relief effort of the state. In the conclusion, or resume, of the report the committee found it necessary to mention the dark side of human nature.

Your committee further reports that it was the intention of the committee to carefully look out and select the needy and destitute people of the section visited by us, but as we have heretofore stated, that the imposition of the greedy horde of undeserving applicants was so great that it made it impossible for your committee to segregate and select from the mass of applications the names of the very needy, which fact we very much regret, and therefore we are unable to suggest to this Legislature the granting of relief to those needy and deserving people. We also found that there was a general disposition, frequently unwarranted, to complain of the distribution made by the distributing committees. In many cases the duties of these committees were so large and so extensive and arduous the only wonder is that there were not more acts of theirs to be complained of.[48]

The committee reported some specific acts that drew complaints: selling or stealing donated relief items. Mister Kehler, of Galveston County, voiced his displeasure when he told the committee that "a great many of provisions that were sent here were sold, when the people needed them. There were lots of groceries sold. I understand there were carloads of them sold."

Kehler referred to a notice published by P. A. Lang who made the accusation that "A car of barreled apples intended for the poor was sold by the relief committee to a peddler, who brags he made $100 on the purchase. Why was the car of apples not given to the needy?"

Kehler went on to testify that carloads of hay donated as livestock feed "was sold." And, "About a car of Waukesha water was sent here. The man that sent it here came here afterwards, and heard that it had been sold. He was very much disappointed at the action of the committee."[49]

D. S. Hooker, of Galveston, was employed as a merchant's night watchman. Referring to the commissary where the relief supplies were stored, he testified before the governor's relief committee investigators that "My business is to watch the stores at night. I had occasion to be around the commissary of the relief supplies a great deal at night. I never saw such stealing in all hours of the night as I saw there."[50]

Despite any real or imagined improprieties, thousands of private individuals, businesses, municipalities, and foreign countries sent aid.

Browsing through the thousands of letters and telegrams in the files of Governor Joseph D. Sayers[51] validates the generosity of Americans from every station in life. Many handwritten letters addressed to Governor Sayers, some in an almost illegible scrawl, stated they wanted to help with their small "mite." Five dollar mites came from Marlin, Texas, from Ashland, Kentucky, and from Boston, Massachusetts, just to mention three of thousands.

An individual in Troy, Texas, sent $10.

Someone sent $100 from Chicago, Illinois, and the Omaha Musical Festival also contributed $100. A telegram from Portland, Oregon, advised the Governor that $831 was on its way.

From Davenport, Iowa, came a donation of $500 with another $500 from St. Louis, Missouri. St. Louis added an additional $1,000 which was mentioned in another correspondence.

Philadelphia, Pennsylvania, was forthcoming with a check for $5,000 from the city of brotherly love.

According to the *Senate Journal*, the amount of aid received by the governor's office totaled $1,948,414.03. The same journal goes on to state that it must not be supposed, however, that the foregoing statement embraces all the contributions that reached the flood stricken district. Not only from many counties in the State, but also from other localities, supplies were forwarded direct, of which no account has been rendered to the Executive Office. An official report, however, has been received of one hundred and nineteen cars of such freight passing through Houston for Galveston. The statement, also, does not include donations by the Red Cross and secret societies, by benevolent organizations, by churches and by many individuals, nor does it include the fifty thousand government rations sent from San Antonio.[52]

Many of the letters and telegrams are from corporations and companies that donated their services "without charge." And the Governor then reported

nor were measures of relief confined to our own country. Funds were forwarded from British Columbia, Canada, Cuba, England, Switzerland, France, Germany, Hawaii, the West Indies, and the Congress of the Mexican Republic voted an appropriation of $30,000 from its treasury in addition to subscriptions by individuals.

Contributions were also made by the Chinese and Costa Rican Ministers, and expressions of sympathy came from the governments of Great Britain, Germany, France, Mexico, Spain, Peru, Chili, Uruguay and Haiti through their representatives at Washington, and also from the Governor of Porto Rico and the mayor of San Juan.[53]

Others offered aid of a different nature such as a telegram from Bastrop, Texas, dated 11 September 1900 which read: "The members of Sayers Rifles if needed hereby cheerfully tender their services in behalf of the Galveston Sufferers."

Another telegram dated 11 September advised the governor that "40,000 pounds of provisions started tonight." That from the "New York World."

Everyone tried to help but sometimes the heart was right even if the contribution wasn't. A telegram "From: Houston, Tex. Sept. 17, 1900. To: Gov. J. D. Sayers, Austin, Texas. Two car loads ice here consigned Galveston they dont want it there what shall we do with it."[54]

The fate of the ice hasn't been learned. But it's a sure bet the ice didn't last long in the Texas heat. Even though it was September the temperature was, according to one report, "hotter than July."

And hot weather was not what the ravished communities needed. Cleaning up the city and countryside was a daunting task made almost unbearable by the relentless heat. The heat, working on the dead bodies, made cleanup detail a task workers could endure only a short time without some relief.

Although the saloons were ordered closed, strong drink was made available to the cleanup crews. John Edward Weems in his book, *A Weekend in September*, shows just what kind of relief was made available.

> When few men volunteered for the job of handling the dead, troops and temporary officers put men to work at gun point. But the longer they worked the more bodies they found.
>
> 'It soon became so that the men could not handle those bodies without stimulants,' Father James Kirwin said. 'I am a strong temperance man. I pledge the children to total abstinence at communion, but I went to the men who were handling those bodies, and I gave them whisky.'
>
> Young Henry Ketchum saw the laborers drinking, at intervals, during this work.
>
> 'There was a barrel of whisky, with tin cups, in the barge,' Ketchum recalls. 'Every time a worker made a trip down into the barge he took a drink.'[55]

Even with 2,000 to 4,000 working it quickly became apparent that burying on the island and burying at sea was too slow. The city government agreed that burning the dead, both humans and animals, was the only way to protect the health of the living.

350

Mrs. Winifred Black, special correspondent to the *New York Journal*, was the first woman reporter to file a story from Galveston. Black's account is extremely dramatic making it ideal as a tool to help raise funds for the storm's survivors. Her graphic story no doubt moved many people to reach for their pocketbooks.

> We sat on the deck of the little steamer . . . along the line of the shore there rose a great leaping column of blood-red flame.
>
> "What a terrible fire." I said. "Some of the large buildings must be burning."
>
> A man who was passing on the deck behind my chair heard me. He stopped, put his hand on the bulwark and turned down and looked into my face, his face like the face of a dead man; but he laughed.
>
> "Buildings!" he said. "Don't you know what is burning over there? It is my wife and children—such little children! Why, the tallest was not as high as this"—he laid his hand on the bulwark—"and the little one was just learning to talk. She called my name the other day, and now they are burning over there—they and the mother who bore them . . ."
>
> "That's right," said the U.S. Marshal of Southern Texas, taking off his broad hat and letting the starlight shine on his strong face. "That's right. We've had to do it. We've burned over 1,000 people to-day, and to-morrow we shall burn as many more."[56]

So it was throughout the city. Day and night for weeks the funeral pyres burned. In the Denver Resurvey subdivision where Richard Peek had built his new home there were funeral fires burning every 300 feet for many blocks.

##

What exactly happened at the Richard Hope Peek home on that fateful day will never be known but a few clues have survived. The first mention of their fate appeared in the *Galveston News* issue of 9 September 1900, in its list of dead is "Peek, Capt. R. H., wife and 5 children."

Quoting from John Edward Weems, "R. H. Peek, the city engineer . . . was drowned, along with his wife and six children. Peek had tied his family together with a long rope; he probably thought he could save them if the house fell. But when it collapsed all eight members of the family were drowned together."[57]

In *Through a Night of Horrors,* by Casey Edwards Greene and Shelly Henley Kelly, we find another account. "Everyone looked to the west where their neighbors' [Peek's] home had stood. Not a plank nor brick remained. Not even a trace of the foundation. Richard Peek, his wife, eight children, and two servants were gone. To this day their bodies have never been found."[58]

From the *Houston Daily Post*: Tuesday Morning, 11 September 1900. "The house of Charles Vedder is the only one left in the Denver Resurvey." Also from that paper, "The home of Captain Peek in the Denver Resurvey was seen to overturn when the captain was on it, and he has not been seen since."

Such discrepancies in these accounts can no doubt be attributed to the trauma and confusion following the storm. Family records show there were six children at the Peek home that day. Living relatives of the Richard Hope Peek family provided some additional information. Paul Keene, a distant relative, related that family lore says Richard Peek's body was identified by his Virginia Military Institute (VMI) ring. Supporting evidence is found in Ida Smith Austin's memoir found in *Through a Night of Horrors*: "Captain Richard Hope Peek, a graduate of the V.M.I. who will be pleasantly remembered . . . his wife and six children perished. Their bodies were found several days afterwards all tied together and Captain Peek was identified by his class ring."[59]

Ben Peek, grandson of Charles Peek who was Richard's brother, said it was a family belief that the bodies were found and Mrs. Peek was identified by her wedding ring.

The family's final resting place remains unknown and an obituary was never found. If there is one filed away in some still undiscovered source it would perhaps read something like this:

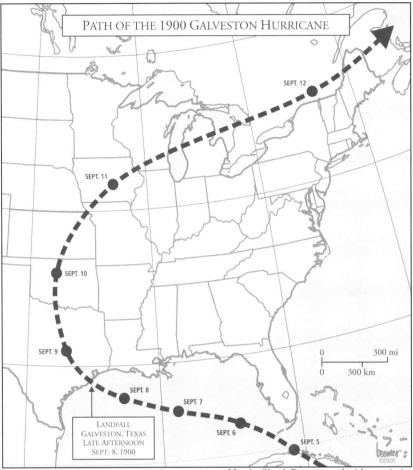

PATH OF THE 1900 GALVESTON HURRICANE

SEPT. 12

SEPT. 11

SEPT. 10

SEPT. 9

SEPT. 8

SEPT. 7

SEPT. 6

SEPT. 5

LANDFALL
GALVESTON, TEXAS
LATE AFTERNOON
SEPT. 8, 1900

0   300 mi
0   300 km

Map by Chuck Beemer; used with permission

The 1900 Galveston hurricane remains the deadliest natural disaster to ever strike the United States. After demolishing the Texas port city, the hurricane continued to inflict death and destruction through several other states and Canada.

The entire Richard Hope Peek family of Galveston, Texas, perished in the storm that struck that city on September 8, 1900.

Richard Hope Peek, age 43, was born November 15, 1856, in Hampton, Virginia. In 1872 he attended Randolph-Macon College in Ashland, Virginia. He was accepted at the Virginia Military Institute in 1875 and graduated from that school in 1878.

Mr. Peek was a civil engineer and had been employed by the City of Galveston for some years. He was the construction engineer in charge of the pipe line for fresh water from Alta Loma to the city of Galveston in 1895.

He then served as superintendent of water works for the city until 1899 when he also filled the position of city engineer. From February 1900 until his death he was city engineer for the city of Galveston, Texas.

His wife, Alice Virginia Peek, age 39, was born Alice Virginia Jones in Mississippi in July 1861. The couple exchanged wedding vows on 28 March, 1883, in Columbus, Mississippi, in the St. Paul Episcopal Church. The Rev. Wm. Munford officiating. The couple was married seventeen years and remained together in death.

Joining them in departing this life were:

Son, John S., age 16, born in April of 1884, in Alabama.

Daughter, Alice Virginia, age 15, born in June of 1885, in Alabama.

Son, Walter H., age 13, born in May of 1887, in Alabama.

Son, Charles S., age 8, born in April of 1892, in Galveston, Texas.

Son, Richard H., age 4, born in December of 1895, in Galveston, Texas.

Son, George M., age 2, born in December of 1897, in Galveston, Texas.

The family was preceded in death by a son, Richard H., who died in 1887 at age 16 months.

The family's maid, Ida Schultz, a fourteen year old girl from Germany, also perished with the Peek family.[60]

As a note of clarity it is important to point out that the Peek family traditionally uses family names many times and the son Richard H., who died in 1887, was given the exact same name as son Richard H., age 4; both were named Richard Hope Peek, Jr.

It is probable that the family was buried in some unmarked grave or burned in one of the many funeral pyres. However, the Lakeview Cemetery on Galveston Island and the Galveston Memorial Park Cemetery at Hitchcock, Texas, both have monuments to the Richard Hope Peek family although there is no evidence that their bodies are interred at either location.

Family tradition holds that the son Richard H. who died in 1887 was buried in the Galveston's Lakeview Cemetery which is the reason a family monument is located in that cemetery. Death and burial records confirms the tradition.[61]

The Peek family plot in the Hitchcock cemetery was purchased by Richard Hope Peek's brother, Charles S. Peek, who rode out the storm in his downtown office building. His grandson, Ben Peek of Hitchcock, Texas, said his grandfather knew that many of the graves on Galveston Island were washed open by the 1900 storm. Consequently, Ben's grandfather decided he didn't want to be buried on the island. Ben said that after the 1900 storm many other Galvestonians felt the same as his grandfather did. These citizens then established the Galveston Memorial Park Cemetery in 1925 in Hitchcock, Texas. Hitchcock is located on the mainland about twenty miles northwest of downtown Galveston.

It is possible that some of the first bodies to be buried at the cemetery location were bodies that had been washed inland from Galveston to Hitchcock during the 1900 Storm.

Only one hurricane related joke was found.

It seems that a man living along the coast where hurricanes are a possibility went to the store and purchased a barometer. While hanging the instrument he noticed that the reading was extremely low and indicating "Hurricane" so he pounded on it and turned it every way possible but still the low reading and "Hurricane" warning remained. Disgusted with such an inferior product he sat down and wrote the manufacturer a lengthy and angry letter. He then went into town to mail the letter and when he returned a hurricane had destroyed his house.

As with all the great natural disasters, animals suffer right along side humans. In the *Alvin (Texas) Sun*, Friday, 5 October, is a short note wondering where all the sparrows have gone. Apparently many of the townspeople recognized their absence and remarked "we hated them when they were here, but now that they are gone we miss them and wish them back again. The question of their being entirely swept away can be answered only by 'He who marks the sparrow's fall.'"

The 1900 storm killed countless animals both wild and domestic but, as documented in other disasters, animals have a remarkable intuition that where humans are safe, they too will be safe. A story from the west end of Galveston Island tells of a man who

> swam out to the barn to release his horse, two cows and a calf, and give them a chance for life. The horse came out immediately and swam after the man to the back steps, which held, and walked right into the kitchen. The two cows and the calf followed directly after the horse into the kitchen.
>
> A family horse not only came into the house when the door was opened, but, as the water rose, went up the stairs to the second story, where, at last accounts, he was still lodged, afraid to come down.
>
> Another man said his cow managed to get upon the veranda. During the storm the veranda gave way, except one section about eighteen inches wide, whereon the cow contrived to stand all night and was found there, ten feet above the ground, in the morning.[62]

The hurricane spawned some interesting tales of survivor's ingenuity, like the story of a "recluse living in a shanty at the far western end of the island" who had seen many a storm come and go without concern. This storm came, but didn't go as the others did. When the recluse decided it was time for action the water had risen until it was inside his dwelling. Searching for some way to ride out the storm he "found a pair of large empty water jugs . . . He stoppered them tightly and bound them on either side of his body with rope." When the storm surge wrecked his shanty "He rode the Gulf like a cork in a torrent, eventually landing inland some eight miles away."[63]

A fact-or-fiction curiosity associated with hurricanes in general is aircraft pilots reporting "flocks of birds that had become caught in the eye of a hurricane as it formed, now unable to fly out to where they had intended to travel. Instead they were forced to journey the ocean inside a huge natural cage until the storm finally faded and released them."[64]

Dunn and Miller in their book, *Atlantic Hurricanes*, wrote that "It is well known that birds tend to 'ride with the wind,' and often many thousands of birds are blown into the center of the storm. Exhausted birds will sometimes completely cover the deck of a ship which has found its way into the center of the hurricane. Hurricanes kill many birds, but apparently some can travel long distances in these storms, since tropical or semitropical birds have been found in New England following the passage of a hurricane."[65]

In a few rare hurricanes the wind is estimated to have reached 200 miles per hour. During this level of severity the wind-driven sand has sandblasted the bark from trees, the paint from houses, and "persons were literally sandblasted to death and found with no skin and no clothes except for belt and shoes. During the height of the storm, electro-statical discharges were emitted from wind-driven sand, appearing like millions and millions of fireflies."[66]

One incident during the 1900 Galveston Storm is reminiscent of an extraordinary event that occurred during the St. Louis tornado.

> At seven o'clock First Mate Ledden of the *Comino*, which was tied up at a wharf, noted that the ship's barometer read 28.30 inches. He also wrote in the log:
> "Wind blowing terrific, and steamer bombarded with large pieces of timber, shells, and all manner of flying debris from the surrounding buildings."
> The bombardment made a floating wreck of the *Comino*. While the crew huddled below deck hoping they would live to see England again, a board four feet long and six inches wide was blown through one of the inch-thick iron plates.[67]

Another fact-or-fiction report claimed

the wind and waves played strange freaks with many houses that are interesting and amusing. Mr. Sol Bromberg lived in a raised cottage on Sealy Avenue, between Twenty-fifth and Twenty-sixth street. This cottage was twelve feet above the ground. It was lifted from its foundations and set upon the center of the lot adjoining. It rests perfectly plump, even with the street; not a pane of glass was broken or a bottle upset. Every window and door will open and shut. The family were in it at the time, and only experienced a slight jar.[68]

There's also the story about a Galveston family who returned to their home and found their fine crystal in the china cabinet "still standing up. Not a single piece had been broken because the water had risen and fallen and, when it fell, it left all the silt and dirt and sand in the glasses. That material had weighted them down and kept them from breaking."[69]

At Angleton, Texas, "William Ficklin was found dead in a street, he appeared to be unmarked. Closer examination revealed a hurricane fired nail had struck him in the temple like a bullet."[70]

There is some disagreement about the number of homes that survived the 1900 Galveston Storm in the newly developed Denver Resurvey subdivision west of Galveston. Some accounts say only the Vedder house remained while others state that three homes survived. Either way, most of these houses, including the Peek house, disappeared without a trace.

However, it was recorded that in the new development there remained part of a "brick storeroom on whose shelf sat in defiance of wind and wave, a lone bottle of beer and a can of sardines."[71]

Sunday morning after the water had receded, a family set out to see if other family members and friends had survived the storm. The streets were impassable so they went to the beach where walking was at least possible. They came upon a bicycle partly embedded upright in the sand. Astride the bike was a dead Negro man still wearing a derby hat on his head and having a cigar clenched between his teeth.

Another individual reported seeing a soldier from one of the Forts on Galveston Island riding the crest of the huge waves on a dead mule.

As the water receded from the central business district there was seen in the middle of the street a drowned horse still hitched to a gig with the driver still seated on the seat with lines in hand. The driver had also drowned.[72]

Perhaps the record for the longest ride was the man who said he rode a door for fifty miles inland before reaching safety.

Then there was the case of "any pot in the storm" when a man saved himself by riding an outhouse through the waves to safety.

Impossible?

Improbable?

Unbelievable?

Who's to say!

During the nineteenth century Mother Nature shook Indians and newcomers with earthquakes, froze them with blizzards, crushed them with tornadoes, burned them with prairie fires, scorched them with drought, washed them away with floods, and drowned them with hurricanes.

But their spirit proved indomitable.

So after a century of courting, the love affair remained passionate but prairies and plains dwellers learned what all lovers eventually learn: You can never really change your lover, only accept their faults as well as their virtues.

-End-

Chapter Eight notes

[1] John Edward Weems, *A Weekend In September* (New York: Henry Holt and Company, 1957), 18.

[2] Ibid., 25.

[3] Clarence Ousley, ed., *Galveston in Nineteen Hundred* (1900; reprint, La Crosse, WI: Brookhaven Press, 2000), 64.

[4] David G. McComb, *Galveston: A History* (Austin: University of Texas Press, 1997), 31.

[5] Murat Halstead, *Galveston: The Horrors of a Stricken City* (Chicago[?]: American Publishers' Association, 1900), 225.

[6] Arthur E. Stilwell and James R. Crowell, foreword to *I Had a Hunch: The Amazing Story of the Last of America's Great Empire Builders.* Port Arthur, TX: The Port Arthur Historical Society, 1977, xviii-xix.

[7] *Southern Industrial and Lumber Review* (Houston, TX), 22 September 1900. Galveston Disaster Edition; From *Galveston News.*

[8] Isaac Monroe Cline, *Storms, Floods and Sunshine* (1945; reprint, Gretna, LA: Pelican Publishing Company, 2000), 92.

[9] David G. McComb, *Galveston: A History* (Austin: University of Texas Press, 1997), 122.

[10] Clarence Ousley, ed., *Galveston in Nineteen Hundred* (Atlanta: William C. Chase, 1900), 265.

[11] John Coulter, ed., *The Complete Story of the Galveston Horror* (n. p.: United Publishers of America, 1900), 148.

[12] John Edward Weems, *A Weekend In September* (New York: Henry Holt and Company, 1957), 152.

[13] Gordon E. Dunn and Banner I. Miller, *Atlantic Hurricanes* (Baton Rouge: Louisiana State University Press, 1960), 206.

[14] Ibid., 7.

[15] NOAA, "Hurricane Basics," http://hurricanes.noaa.gov/prepare/title_basics.htm.

[16] NOAA, "The Saffir/Simpson Hurricane Scale," http://hurricanes.noaa.gov/prepare/categories.htm.

[17] John Lynch, *The Weather* (Toronto: Firefly Books Ltd., 2002), 42.

[18] Richard Lipkin, "Weather's Fury," in *Nature on the Rampage,* with H. J. De Blij (Washington: Smithsonian Books, 1994), 39.

[19] Frank W. Lane, *The Elements Rage* (Philadelphia: Chilton Books, 1965), 21.

[20] Ibid., 22.

[21] John Lynch, *The Weather* (Toronto: Firefly Books Ltd., 2002), 46-47.

[22] Frank W. Lane, *The Elements Rage* (Philadelphia: Chilton Books, 1965), 2.

[23] Gordon E. Dunn and Banner I. Miller, *Atlantic Hurricanes* (Baton Rouge: Louisiana State University Press, 1960), 210.

[24] Ibid., 212.

[25] Ibid., 221.

[26] Jerry D. Jarrell, Max Mayfield, and Edward N. Rappaport, "The Deadliest, Costliest, and Most Intense United States," Hurricanes From 1900-2000." NOAA Technical Memorandum NWS TPC-1.

Miami: NOAA/NWS/ Tropical Prediciton Center, http://www.nhc.noaa.gov/pastint.shtml.

[27] Frank W. Lane, *The Elements Rage* (Philadelphia: Chilton Books, 1965), 9.

[28] Ibid., 24.

[29] Ibid., 6.

[30] Ibid., 31.

[31] State of Texas, *Senate Journal*, 27th Legislature, 29 January, 1901, 116-118.

[32] John Coulter, ed., *The Complete Story of the Galveston Horror* (n.p.: United Publishers of America, 1900), 155-156.

[33] Ibid., 150.

[34] Ibid., 150.

[35] Charles Orson Cook, "John Milsaps's Houston: 1910" *The Houston Review: History and Culture of the Gulf Coast*, vol. 1, no. 1, Spring 1979.

[36] John Milsaps Diaries, Houston Public Library, Texas Local History, Salvation Army Archives roll #2 vol. 12.

[37] State of Texas, *House Journal*, 27th Legislature, 23 March 1901, 883.

[38] This article was found in the vertical files located in the Texas Local History Room at the Houston Public Library-Houston Metropolitan Research Center, Houston, Texas. Unfortunately it was only a tear sheet from an unnamed newspaper.

[39] Johnnie Lockhart Wallis, ed., *Sixty Years on the Brazos*, 180, quoted in Betty Plummer, *Historic Homes of Washington County 1821-1860* (San Marcos, Texas: Rio Fresco Books, Inc., 1971), 46.

[40] John D. Reid, "The Great 1900 Galveston Hurricane in Canada," http://www.magma.ca/~jdreid/great_1900_hurricane.htm.

[41] Ibid., "The Great 1900 Galveston Hurricane in Canada,"

[42] *Southern Industrial and Lumber Review* (Houston, TX), 22 September 1900. Galveston Disaster Edition.

[43] Ibid., 22 September, 1900. Galveston Disaster Edition.

[44] W. Maury Darst, ed., "September 8, 1900: An Account by a Mother to Her Daughters," *Southwestern Historical Quarterly* 73, (1969-1970), 56-66.

[45] Henry Benjamin Decherd to Mary Elizabeth Decherd, 10 September 1900, Galveston, Texas, Decherd (Mary Elizabeth) Papers, Family Correspondences and History, 2D54, Center for American History, University of Texas at Austin.

[46] Isaac Monroe Cline, *Storms, Floods and Sunshine* (1945; reprint, Gretna, LA: Pelican Publishing Company, Inc., 2000), 100-101.

[47] Clarence Ousley, ed., *Galveston in Nineteen Hundred* (Atlanta: William C. Chase, 1900), 37-38.

[48] State of Texas, *House Journal,* 27th Legislature, 23 March 1901, 856.

[49] Ibid., 881.

[50] Ibid., 877.

[51] Papers, Governor Joseph D. Sayers, Box 301-184, Correspondence 11 September 1900. Texas State Library and Archives Commission: Austin, TX.

[52] State of Texas, *Senate Journal*, 27th Legislature, 29 January, 1901, 116-118.

[53] Ibid., 116-118.

[54] Papers, Governor Joseph D. Sayers, Box 301-184, Correspondence 11 September 1900. Texas State Library and Archives Commission: Austin, TX.

[55] John Edward Weems, *A Weekend In September* (New York: Henry Holt and Company, 1957), 144,145.

[56] Paul Lester, *The Great Galveston Disaster* (1900; reprint, Gretna, LA, Pelican Publishing Company, 2000), 296.

[57] John Edward Weems, *A Weekend In September* (New York: Henry Holt and Company, 1957), 152.

[58] Casey Edwards Greene and Shelly Henley Kelly, ed., *Through a Night of Horrors* (College Station, TX: Texas A&M University Press, 2000), 183; Quoted from Katherine Vedder Pauls oral history in an interview on 3 February 1970.

[59] Casey Edwards Greene and Shelly Henley Kelly, ed., *Through a Night of Horrors* (College Station, TX: Texas A&M University Press, 2000), 71.

[60] 1900 U. S. Census, Galveston County, TX. Additional information for the obituary was taken from several sources including: Cadet records at VMI Archives at Preston Library, Lexington, VA; Letters from Richard Hope Peek's brother, Charles S. Peek, to VMI administration, VMI archives; Letters from Richard's brothers to Charles S. Peek, Rosenberg Library vertical files.

[61] Galveston City Death and Burial Records, MSS# 86-0005.

[62] Murat Halstead, *Galveston: The Horrors of a Stricken City* (Chicago[?]: American Publishers' Association, 1900), 155.

[63] Herbert Molloy Mason, Jr., *Death from the Sea* (New York: The Dial Press, 1972), 168.

[64] John Lynch, *The Weather* (Toronto: Firefly Books Ltd., 2002), 47.

[65] Gordon E. Dunn and Banner I. Miller, *Atlantic Hurricanes* (Baton Rouge: Louisiana State University Press, 1960), 82.

[66] Ibid., 216.

[67] John Edward Weems, *A Weekend In September* (New York: Henry Holt and Company, 1957), 101, 102.

[68] Clarence Ousley, ed., *Galveston in Nineteen Hundred* (Atlanta: William C. Chase, 1900), 289.

[69] "Echoes of The Storm," *Houston Chronicle* (Special Report), 3 September 2000.

[70] Ibid., 3 September 2000.

[71] Casey Edwards Greene and Shelly Henley Kelly, ed., *Through a Night of Horrors* (College Station, TX: Texas A&M University Press, 2000), 182.

[72] John Edward Weems, *A Weekend In September* (New York: Henry Holt and Company, 1957), 137.

The Author

Rod Beemer is a freelance writer whose work includes several books, magazine and newspaper articles, plus anthologies. Born and reared on a livestock and grain farm near Abilene, Kansas, he has spent more than six decades enjoying, and enduring Mother Nature on the prairies and plains.

Rod and his wife Dawn have been married for thirty-eight years and have three sons and one granddaughter. They make their home in Bennington, Kansas.

BIBLIOGRAPHY

Books

Anderson, Bette Roda. *Weather in the West: From the Midcontinent to the Pacific.* Palo Alto, California: American West Publishing Company, 1975.

Atherton, Lewis. *The Cattle Kings.* Lincoln: University of Nebraska Press, 1961.

Aughey, Samuel. *Sketches of the Physical Geography and Geology of Nebraska.* Omaha: Daily Republican Book and Job Office, 1880.

Bang, Roy C. *Heroes Without Medals: A Pioneer History of Kearney County Mebraska.* Minden, Nebraska: Warp Publishing Company, 1952.

Barclay & Co. *The St. Louis Disaster, or Broken Hearts and Homes.* Cincinnati: Barclay & Co., n.d.

Bark, L. Dean. "History of American Droughts." in *North American Droughts.* edited by Norman J. Rosenberg. Boulder, CO: Westview Press, Inc., 1978.

Barry, Louise, comp. *The Beginning of the West: Annals of the Kansas Gateway to the American West 1540-1854.* Topeka: Kansas State Historical Society, 1972.

Blanchard, Leola Howard. *Conquest of Southwest Kansas.* Wichita: The Wichita Eagle Press, 1931.

Bluestein, Howard B. *Tornado Alley: Monster Storms of the Great Plains.* New York: Oxford University Press, 1999.

Botkin, B. A. *A Treasury of Western Folklore.* New York: Bonanza Books, 1975.

Brown, Lauren. *Grasslands.* New York: Alfred A. Knopf, n.d.

Catlin, George. *North American Indians: Being Letters and Notes on Their Manners, Customs, and Conditions, Written During Eight Years' Travel Amongst the Wildest Tribes of Indians in North America, 1832-1839,* 2 vols. 1844; reprint, Philadelphia: Leary, Stuart and Company, 1913.

Cline, Isaac Monroe. *Storms, Floods and Sunshine.* 1945; reprint, Gretna, Louisiana: Pelican Publishing Company, Inc., 2000.

Cook, James H. *Fifty Years on the Old Frontier as Cowboy, Hunter, Guide, Scout, and Ranchman.* New Haven: Yale University Press, 1923.

Coues, Elliott, ed. *New Light on the Early History of the Greater Nortwest: The Manuscript Journals of Alexander Henry, Fur Trader of the Northwest Company and of David Thompson, Official Geographer and Explorer of the Same Company 1799-1814; Exploration and Adventure among the Indians on the Red, Saskatchewan, Missouri, and Columbia Rivers.* 3 vols. New York: Francis P. Harper, 1897.

Coulter, John, ed. *The Complete Story of the Galveston Horror: Written by the Survivors.* N.P.: United Publishers of America, 1900.

Cramer, Zadok. *The Navigator.* 1814; reprint, Utica, Kentucky.: McDowell Publications, 1979.

Curzon, Julian. *The Great Cyclone at St. Louis and East St. Louis, May 27, 1896. Being a Full History of the Most Terrifying and Destructive Tornado in the History of the World, with Numerous Thrilling and Pathetic Incidents and Personal Experiences of Those Who Were in the Track of the Storm. Also An Account of the Wonderful Manifestations of Sympathy for the Afflicted in all Parts of the World.* St. Louis: The Cyclone Publishing Company, 1896.

Custer, Elizabeth B. *Following the Guidon.* New York: Harper & Brothers, 1890.

—. *Tenting on the Plains or General Custer in Kansas and Texas.* New York: Charles L. Webster & Company, 1887.

Dale, Edward Everett. *The Range Cattle Industry: Ranching on the Great Plains from 1865 to 1925.* Norman: University of Oklahoma Press, 1960.

Dary, David A. *The Buffalo Book: The Full Saga of the American Animal.* Chicago: The Swallow Press Inc., 1974.

Davis, William Morris. *Whirlwinds, Cyclones and Tornadoes.* Boston: Lothrop, Lee & Shepard Co., 1884.

366

BIBLIOGRAPHY

Dick, Everett. *Conquering the Great American Desert: Nebraska.* Lincoln: Nebraska State Historical Society, 1975.

—. *The Sod-House Frontier 1854-1890: A Social History of the Northern Plains from the Creation of Kansas & Nebraska to the Admission of the Dakotas.* Lincoln: Johnsen Publishing Company, 1954.

Dixon, Olive K. *Life of "Billy" Dixon: Plainsman, Scout and Pioneer.* Austin: 1927, reprint; State House Press, 1987.

Dobie, J. Frank. *The Longhorns.* Boston: Little, Brown and Company, 1941.

Dodge, Richard Irving. *The Plains of the Great West and Their Inhabitants Being A Description of the Plains, Game, Indians, &c.of the Great North American Desert.* New York: 1877, reprint; Archer House, Inc., 1958.

Dow, Lorenzo. *History of Cosmopolite; or, the Four Volumes of Lorenzo Dow's Journal,* 4th ed. Wheeling, VA: Joshua Martin, 1848.

Duke, Cordia Sloan and Joe B. Frantz. *6,000 Miles of Fence: Life on the XIT Ranch of Texas.* Austin: University of Texas Press, 1975.

Dunn, Gordon E. and Banner I. Miller. *Atlantic Hurricanes.* Baton Rouge: Louisiana State University Press, 1960.

Echert, Allan W. *A Sorrow in Our Heart: The Life of Tecumseh.* New York: Bantam Books, 1992.

Editors. *The American Indians: Tribes of the Southern Plains.* Alexandria: Time-Life Books, 1995.

Ellet, Charles, Jr. *The Mississippi and Ohio Rivers: Containing Plans for the Protection of the Delta from Inundation.* Philadelphia: Lippincott, Grambo, and Co., 1853.

Felch, Richard E. "Drought: Characteristics and Assessment." in *North American Droughts.* edited by Norman J. Rosenberg. Boulder, CO: Westview Press, Inc., 1978.

Finley, John P. *Character of Six Hundred Tornadoes.* Washington: Signal Office, 1884.

Finley, J. [John] P. *Report of the Tornadoes of May 29 and 30, 1879.* Washington: Government Printing Office, 1881.

Finney County Kansas Historical Society. *History of Finney County, Kansas,* Vol. 2. North Newton, Kansas: Mennonite Press, Inc., 1976.

[Fiske ?, M.] *A Visit to Texas.* 1834; reprint, Ann Arbor: University Microfilms, Inc., 1966.

Fitzgerald, Daniel. *Ghost Towns of Kansas,* vol. 1. n.p.: privately printed, 1976.

—. *Ghost Towns of Kansas,* vol. 2. Holton, Kansas; The Gossip Printery, 1979.

—. *Ghost Towns of Kansas,* vol. 3. Holton, Kansas; Bell Graphics, 1982.

Flanagan, Dennis. "The Nature of Risk," in *Nature on the Rampage,* with H. J. De Blij. Washington: Smithsonian Books, 1994.

Fletcher, Robert H. *Free Grass to Fences: The Montana Cattle Range Story.* New York: University Publishers Incorporated, 1960.

Flora, Snowden D. *Hailstorms of the United States.* Norman: University of Oklahoma Press, 1956.

—. *Tornadoes of the United States.* Norman: University of Oklahoma Press, 1953.

Forbis, William H. *The Cowboys.* New York: Time-Life Books, 1973.

Frankenfield, H. C. *The Tornado of May 27, 1896, at Saint Louis, Missouri.* Washington: Weather Bureau, 1896.

Frazer, Robert W. *Forts of the West: Military Forts and Presidios and Posts Commonly Called Forts West of the Mississippi River to 1898.* Norman: University of Oklahoma Press, 1966.

Frink, Maurice. *Cow Country Cavalcade: Eighty Years of the Wyoming Stock Growers Association.* Denver: The Old West Publishing Co., 1954.

Fuller, Myron L. *The New Madrid Earthquake.* 1912; reprint, Gape Girardeau, MO: Ramfre Press, n.d. Originally published as United States Geological Survey *Bulletin 494.*

Gard, Wayne. *The Chisholm Trail.* Norman: University of Oklahoma Press, 1976.

—. *The Great Buffalo Hunt.* New York: Alfred A. Knopf, 1959.

Gibson, J. W. (Watt). *Recollections of a Pioneer.* 1912; reprint, Independence, Missouri: Two Trails Publishing, 1999.

Gilbert, Bill. *The Trailblazers.* New York: Time-Life Books, 1973.

BIBLIOGRAPHY

Gilbert, Miles. *Getting a Stand*. Tempe, AZ.: Hal Green Printing, 1986.

Grazulis, Thomas P. *Significant Tornadoes 1680-1991*. St. Johnsbury, Vermont: Environmental Films, 1993.

—. *Significant Tornadoes, 1880-1989 Volume I: Discussion and Analysis*. St. Johnsbury, Vermont: Enviromental Films, 1991.

—. *The Tornado: Nature's Ultimate Windstorm*. Norman: University of Oklahoma Press, 2001.

Green, Martin. *The Great Tornado at St. Louis*. St. Louis: Graf Engraving Co., 1896.

Greene, Casey Edwards and Shelly Henley Kelly, eds. *Through a Night of Horrors: Voices from the 1900 Galveston Storm*. College Station, Texas: Texas A&M University Press, 2000.

Halstead, Murat. *Galveston: The Horrors of a Stricken City: Portraying by Pen and Picture the Awful Calamity that Befell the Queen City on the Gulf and the Terrible Scenes that Followed the Disaster*. Chicago [?]: American Publishers' Association, 1900.

Harman, Lois Stringfield. *Castle on the Prairie: Memories of the Old Kentucky Home Ranch*. n.p.: n.d.

Hill, Douglas. *The Opening of the Canadian West: Where Strong Men Gather*. New York: The John Day Company, 1967.

History of Southeast Missouri. Chicago: Goodspeed Publishing, 1888), 307, quoted in James Lal Penick, Jr., *The New Madrid Earthquakes,* rev. ed. Columbia: University of Missouri Press, 1981.

Holmes, Kenneth L., ed. *Covered Wagon Women: Diaries & Letters from the Western Trails 1850*, vol. 2. 1983; reprint, Lincoln: University of Nebraska Press, 1996.

Hunter, J. Marvin, comp. and ed. *The Trail Drivers of Texas: Interesting Sketches of Early Cowboys and Their Experiences on the Range and on the Trail During the Days that Tried Men's Souls-- True Narratives Related by Real Cow-Punchers and Men who Fathered the Cattle Industry in Texas*. 2 vols. San Antonio, Texas: Jackson Printing Co., 1920-1923.

Hunter, John D. *Memoirs of a Captivity Among the Indians of North America*. London: Longman, Hurst, Rees, Orme, Brown, and Green, 1824.

Hyde, George E. *Life of George Bent Written from His Letters.* Norman: University of Oklahoma Press, 1983.

Irving, Washington. *A Tour on the Prairies.* Philadelphia: Carey, Lea, & Blanchard, 1835.

Karolevitz, Robert F. *Yankton: A Pioneer Past.* Aberdeen, South Dakota: North Plains Press, 1972.

Krech, Shepard, III. *The Ecological Indian: Myth and History.* New York: W. W. Norton & Company, 1999.

Lane, Frank W. *The Elements Rage.* Philadelphia: Chilton Books, 1965.

Laskin, David. *Braving the Elements: The Stormy History of American Weather.* New York: Doubleday, 1996.

Latrobe, J.H.B. *The First Steamboat Voyage on the Western Waters.* Baltimore: Maryland Historical Society, 1871.

Lester, Paul. *The Great Galveston Disaster.* 1900; reprint, Gretna, Louisiana, Pelican Publishing Company, 2000.

Lewis, Meriwether and William Clark. *The Journals of Lewis and Clark*, abridged by Anthony Brandt. Washington: National Geographic Society, 2002.

Lewis, Willie Newbury. *Tapadero: The Making of a Cowboy.* Austin: University of Texas Press, 1972.

Lindquist, Emory. *Vision for a Valley: Olof Olsson and the Early History of Lindsborg.* Rock Island, Illinois: Augustana Historical Society, 1970.

Lipkin, Richard. "Weather's Fury," in *Nature on the Rampage,* with H. J. De Blij. Washington: Smithsonian Books, 1994.

Lloyd, James T. *Lloyd's Steamboat Directory and Disasters on the Western Waters.* Cincinnati: James T. Lloyd & Co., 1856.

Lockard, F. M. *The History of the Early Settlement of Norton County, Kansas.* Norton, Kansas: Champion [newspaper?], 1894.

Lowe, Percival G. *Five Years a Dragoon ('49 to '54) and Other Adventures on the Great Plains.* Kansas City, Missouri: The Franklin Hudson Publishing Co., 1906.

Lucas, Henry S., ed. *Dutch Immigrant Memoirs and Related Writings, vol. 2.* Assen, Netherlands: Van Gorcum & Comp. N.V. - G. A. Hak & Dr. H. J. Prakke, 1955.

Ludlum, David M. *Early American Tornadoes 1586-1870.* Boston: American Meteorological Society, 1970.

—. *The History of American Weather: Early American Winters II 1821-1870.* Boston: American Meteorological Society, 1968.

Lynch, John. *The Weather.* Toronto: Firefly Books Ltd., 2002.

Malcolm, Andrew H. *Mississippi Currents: Journeys Through Time and a Valley.* New York: William Morrow and Company, Inc., 1996.

Marcy, Randolph B. *The Prairie Traveler: A Hand-Book for Overland Expeditions. With Maps, Illustrations, and Itineraries of the Principal Routes Between the Mississippi and the Pacific.* New York: Harper & Brothers, Publishers, 1859.

Martin, Geo. W., ed. *Transactions of the Kansas State Historical Society, 1907-1908,* vol. 10. Topeka: State Printing office, 1908.

Mason, Herbert Molloy, Jr. *Death from the Sea: Our Greatest Natural Disaster the Galveston Hurricane of 1900.* New York: The Dial Press, 1972.

Mattes, Merrill J. *The Great Platte River Road: The Covered Wagon Mainline Via Fort Kearny to Fort Laramie.* Lincoln: Nebraska State Historical Society, 1969.

—. *Platte River Road Narratives.* Urbana and Chicago: University of Illinois Press, 1988.

McCallum, Henry D. and Frances T. *The Wire That Fenced the West.* Norman: University of Oklahoma Press, 1969.

McCarty, John L. *Maverick Town: The Story of Old Tascosa.* Norman: University of Oklahoma Press, 1946.

McCollum, Elmer Verner. *From Kansas Farm Boy to Scientist.* Lawrence: University of Kansas Press, 1964.

McComb, David G. *Galveston: A History.* Austin: University of Texas Press, 1997.

McCoy, J. Mike. *History of Cedar County Nebraska.* n.p.: n.p., 1937.

McCoy, Joseph G. *Historic Sketches of the Cattle Trade of the West and Southwest.* Kansas City, Missouri: Ramsey, Millett & Hudson, 1874.

McDowell, Bart. *The American Cowboy in Life and Legend.* Washington: National Geographic Society, 1972.

McEachron, K. B. and Kenneth G. Patrick. *Playing with Lightning.* New York: Random House, 1940.

McMurtrie, Henry. *Sketches of Louisville and Its Environs.* Louisville: S. Penn [printer], 1819.

Mechem, Kirke, ed. *The Annals of Kansas 1886-1925.* Topeka: Kansas State Historical Society, 1972.

Meyer, William B. *Americans and Their Weather.* New York: Oxford University Press, 2000.

Miles, Nelson A. *Personal Recollections and Observations of General Nelson A. Miles,* 2 vols. Reprint; Lincoln: University of Nebraska Press, 1992.

Nordyke, Lewis. *Cattle Empire: The Fabulous Story of the 3,000,000 Acre XIT.* New York: William Morrow and Company, 1950.

—. *Great Roundup: The Story of Texas and Southwestern Cowmen.* 1955; reprint, Edison, NJ.: Castle Books, 2001.

O'Neil, Paul. *The Rivermen, The Old West Series.* Alexandria, Virginia: Time-Life Books, 1975.

Orpen, Mrs. *Memories of the Old Emigrant Days in Kansas, 1862-1865: Also of a Visit to Paris in 1867,* New York: Harper & Brothers, Publishers, 1928.

Ousley, Clarence, ed. *Galveston in Nineteen Hundred.* 1900; reprint, La Crosse, Wisconsin: Brookhaven Press, 2000.

Pabst, Lettie Little. *Kansas Heritage.* New York: Vantage Press, 1956.

Penick, James Lal, Jr. *The New Madrid Earthquakes,* rev. ed. Columbia: University of Missouri Press, 1981. Previously published as: *The New Madrid Earthquakes of 1811-1812.* 1976.

Rath, Ida Ellen. *The Rath Trail.* Wichita: McCormick-Armstrong Co., Inc. 1961.

Richardson, Albert D. *Beyond the Mississippi: From the Great River to the Great Ocean. Life and Adventure on the Prairies, Mountains, and Pacific Coast; With more than Two Hundred illustrations, from Photographs and Original Sketches, of the Prairies, Deserts, Mountains, Rivers, Mines, Cities, Indians, Trappers, Pioneers, and Great Natural Curiosities of the New States and Territories 1857-1867.* Hartford, Connecticut: American Publishing Company, 1867.

Bibliography

Riley, Charles V. *The Locust Plague in the United States: Being More Particularly a Treatise on the Rocky Mountain Locust or so-called Grasshopper, as it Occures East of the Rocky Mountains, with Practical Recommendations for its Destruction.* Chicago: Rand, McNally & Co., 1877.

Robinson, Doane. *Encyclopedia of South Dakota.* Pierre: Pivately Published, 1925.

Robinson, Elwyn B. *History of North Dakota.* Lincoln: University of Nebraska Press, 1969.

Roosevelt, Theodore. *Ranch Life and the Hunting-Trail.* 1888; reprint, New York: Winchester Press, 1969.

Sanders, Gwendoline and Paul. *The Sumner County Story.* North Newton, Kansas: The Mennonite Press, 1966.

Sandoz, Mari. *The Buffalo Hunters: The Story of the Hide Men.* 1954; reprint, Lincoln: University of Nebraska Press, 1954.

—. *Crazy Horse: The Strange Man of the Oglalas.* 1942; reprint, Lincoln: University of Nebraska Press, 1961.

—. *Old Jules: Portrait of a Pioneer.* 1935, 1963; reprint, New York: MJF Books, 1985.

Saunders, Mary. *The Whitman Massacre: A True Story by a Survivor of This Terrible Tragedy Which Took Place in Oregon in 1847.* n.d.: reprint, Fairfield, Washington: Ye Galleon Press, 1977.

Seccombe, H. M. *"Perils of Waters."* Springfield, Dakota: John Todd, Printer, 1883.

Shawver, Lona. *Chuck Wagon Windies and True Stories.* San Antonio: The Naylor Company, 1950.

Shumway, Grant L. *History of Western Nebraska and Its People*, 2. Lincoln: Western Publishing & Engraving Co., 1921.

Siberts, Bruce. *Nothing But Prairie and Sky: Life on the Dakota Range in the Early Days*, comp. Walker D. Wyman. Norman: University of Oklahoma Press, 1954.

Simmons, Marc. *"The Santa Fe Trail . . . Highway of Commerce,"* in *Trails West,* ed. Gilbert M. Grosvenor. Washington: National Geographic Society, 1979.

Spokesfield, Walter E. *The History of Wells County, North Dakota, and its Pioneers:With a Sketch of North Dakota History and the Oregin [sic] of the Place Names.* Valley City, North Dakota, 1929.

Stewart, David and Ray Knox. *The Earthquake America Forgot: 2,000 Temblors in Five Months . . . And it Will Happen Again.* Maple Hill, Missouri: Gutenberg-Richter Publications, 1995.

Stilwell, Arthur E. and James R. Crowell. *I Had a Hunch: The Amazing Story of the Last of America's Great Empire Builders.* Port Arthur, Texas: The Port Arthur Historical Society, 1977.

Stuart, Granville. *Forty Years on the Frontier as seen in the Journals and Reminiscences of Granville Stuart Gold-Miner, Trader, Merchant, Rancher and Politician.* Edited by Paul C. Phillips. 2 vols. Cleveland, Ohio: The Arthur H. Clark Company, 1925.

Tanner, Ogden. *The Old West: The Ranchers.* Alexandria: Time-Life Books, 1985.

Thwaites, Reuben Gold, ed. *Early Western Travels, 1748-1846*, vol. 5: *Bradbury's Travels in the Interior of America, 1809-1811.* 1817; reprint, Cleveland, Ohio: Arthur H. Clark Company, 1904.

Vauck, Henry. *Blizzards: Reunion and Fiftieth Anniversary 1888-1938.* Clay Center, Nebraska: John M. Fisher, printer, 1938.

Viemeister, Peter E. *The Lightning Book.* Garden City, New York: Doubleday & Company, Inc., 1961.

Wallis, Johnnie Lockhart, ed. *Sixty Years on the Brazos.* Quoted in Betty Plummer, *Historic Homes of Washington County 1821-1860.* San Marcos, Texas: Rio Fresco Books, 1971.

Ware, Eugene F. *The Indian War of 1864.* 1911; reprint, New York: St. Martin's Press, 1960.

------. *The Indian War of 1864: Being a Fragment of the Early History of Kansas, Nebraska, Colorado, and Wyoming.* Topeka: Crane & Company, 1911.

Warrick, Richard A. and Martyn J. Bowden, "The Changing Impacts of Droughts in the Great Plains," quoted in *The Great Plains Perspectives and Prospects.* Edited by Merlin P. Lawson and Maurice E. Baker. Lincoln: Center for Great Plains Studies University of Nebraska-Lincoln, 1981.

Watson, Lyall. *Heaven's Breath: A Natural History of the Wind.* New York: William Morrow and Company, Inc., 1984.

Webb, Walter Prescott. *The Great Plains.* Waltham, Massachusetts: Blaisdell Publishing Company, 1959.

Weems, John Edward. *A Weekend In September.* New York: Henry Holt and Company, 1957.

West, Elliott. *The Contested Plains: Indians, Goldseekers, & the Rush to Colorado.* Lawrence, Kansas: University Press of Kansas, 1998.

—. *The Way to the West: Essays on the Central Plains.* Albuquerque: University of New Mexico Press, 1997.

Wilder, Daniel Webster. *The Annals of Kansas.* n.d.; reprint, New York: Arno Press, 1975.

Wilson, D. Ray. *Fort Kearny on the Platte.* Dundee, Ill: Crossroads Communications, 1980.

Wise, John C., Warren Smith, and Allen Whitman, comps. *The Grasshopper, or Rocky Mountain Locust, and its Ravages in Minnesota: A Special Report to the Hon. C. K. Davis Governor of Minnesota.* Saint Paul: The Pioneer-Press Company, 1876.

Wollaston, Percy. *Homesteading.* New York: Penguin Books, 1999.

Worster, Donald. *A River Running West: The Life of John Wesley Powell.* New York: Oxford Universtity Press, 2001.

—. *Under Western Skies: Nature and History in the American West.* New York: Oxford University Press, 1992.

Manuscript Collections

Barber, T. M., Diary, RG 5127. Nebraska State Historical Society, Lincoln.

Barker, F. [Francis] to Isaac B. Barker, Esqr., 23 July 1844, Barker Collection, Kansas State Historical Society.

Boyles, J. W. Diary, 14 June 1888. Typed transcript, "Dr. John W. Boyles' Diary." Salina, Kansas, Public Library, Campbell Room files, 32.

Decherd, (Mary Elizabeth). Papers. Henry Benjamine Decherd to Mary Elizabeth Decherd, 10 September 1900, Galveston, Texas. Family Correspondences and History, 2D54, Center for American History, University of Texas, Austin.

Dougherty, John to William Clark, 6 May 1828, Dougherty, John, Letter Book, 1826-1829 (C2292), State Historical Society of Missouri, Western Historical Manuscript Collection-Columbia.

Irvine, Esther Hulpieu. *Histories of the Jelly Family and the Hulpiau [sic] Family* (n.p. n.d.) Paper at Kansas State Historical Society, Topeka, Kansas. (There is a typo in the paper's title. The author signed "Esther Hulpieu Irvine." The paper was signed in 1951.

Marshall, H. J. "Pioneer Days in North Dakota." MS 20053, Small Manuscripts Collection. State Historical Society of North Dakota, Bismarck, ND.

Milsaps, John. Diaries. Texas Local History Room. Houston Public Library, Houston.

Peek, Richard Hope, Papers. Virginia Military Institute Archives. Preston Library, Lexington, VA.

Sayers, Governor Joseph D., Papers. Texas State Library and Archives Commission, Austin.

Shutterly, Lewis. Diary. Wyoming Historical and Cultural Association, Saratoga.

Sweeney, Kevin Zachary. "Wither the Fruited Plain: Nineteenth Century Droughts in the Southern Plains" (Ph.D. diss., Oklahoma State University, 2001).

VMI Archives. Cadet records. Prestion Library, Lexington, VA.

Public Documents

Academy of Science. *Transactions of the Sixteenth and Seventeenth Annual Meeting of the Kansas Academy of Science, (1883-1884), with the Report of the Secretary.* J. Savage, "Some Lightning Freaks in 1883." Topeka, Kansas: Kansas Publishing House, 1885.

Congressional Record, 47th Congress, 1st session (1882), 3142, 3216. Quoted in William B. Meyer, *Americans and Their Weather.* New York: Oxford University Press, 2000.

First Annual Report of Montana Bureau of Agriculture, Labor and Industry, 272-276, quoted in Edward Everett Dale, *The Range Cattle Industry: Ranching on the Great Plains from 1865-1925.* Norman: University of Oklahoma Press, 1960.

BIBLIOGRAPHY

Galveston City Death and Burial Records, MSS# 86-0005.
   Rosenburg Library: Richard Peek d. May 23, 1887, at 6 pm on
   Ave M 1/2 between 12 & 13, 16 months old, born in Alabama, d.
   of congestion of the brain. Buried in the Lakeview Cemetery on
   May 24, 1887.

House of Representatives. *Annual Report of the Board of Regents
   of the Smithsonian Institution, Showing the Operations,
   Expenduitures, and Condition of the Institution for the Year
   1870.* Lieutenant George M. Bache, U.S.A., "Account of a Hail-
   Storm in Texas." 42nd Congress, 1st Session, Ex. Doc. No. 20.
   Washington, DC: GPO, 1871.

—. *Annual Report of the Board of Regents of the Smithsonian
   Institution, Showing the Operations, Expenditures, and
   Condition of the Institution for the Year 1858.* Timothy Dudley,
   "The Earthquake of 1811 at New Madrid, Missouri." 35th
   Congress, 2d Session, Mis. Doc. No. 57. Washington, DC: GPO
   1859.

Kansas Horticultural Report, For the Year 1884. Mrs. M. A.
   Humphrey, "The Sanitary Value of Plants and Trees." Topeka,
   Kansas: Kansas Publishing House. T. D. Thacher, State Printer,
   1885.

Martin, G. W. Papers. Manuscripts division of the Kansas State
   Historical Society. Quoted in "Dust Storms: Part One, 1850-1860,
   by James C. Malin," *Kansas Historical Quarterly*, May 1946.

Secretary of War. *Annual Report of the Chief Signal-Officer to the
   Secretary of War for the Year 1872.* I. A. Lapham, "The Great
   Fires of 1871 in the Northwest." (Washington, DC: GPO, 1872).

Signal Office. U.S. War Department, *Monthly Weather Review.*

State Board of Agriculture. *The Third Annual Report to the
   Legislature of Kansas. For the Year 1874.* Topeka, Kansas: State
   Printing Works, Geo. W. Martin, Public Printer, 1874.

State of Texas. *House Journal*, 27th Legislature, 23 March 1901.
   Center for American History, University of Texas at Austin.

—. *Senate Journal*, 27th Legislature, 29 January, 1901. Center for
   American History, University of Texas at Austin.

U.S. Census 1900. Galveston County, Texas.

U.S. Secretary of War. *The War of the Rebellion: A Compilation of the Official Records of the Union and Confederate Armies.* Washington: Government Printing Office, 1893-1922.

Weather Bureau. U.S. Department of Agriculture, *Monthly Weather Review,* 1896.

Journals

"Artificial Production of Rain," *Scientific American,* 20 December 1890.

Allen, John L. "Garden-Desert Continuum: Competing views of the Great Plains in the Nineteenth Century." *Great Plains Quarterly* (Fall 1985).

Barnes, Lela. "Journal of Isaac McCoy For the Exploring Expedition of 1830." *The Kansas Historical Quarterly,* November 1936.

Barry, Louise, comp. "Kansas Before 1854: A Revised Annals." *The Kansas Historical Quarterly* (Summer 1962).

Darst, W. Maury, ed. "September 8, 1900: An Account by a Mother to Her Daughters." *Southwestern Historical Quarterly* 73 (1969-1970).

Davis, R. Bruce. "Tornado of 1840 Hits Mississippi." *Journal of Mississippi History* 36, no. 1 (February 1974).

Dyrenforth, Robert G. and Simon Newcomb, "Can We make It Rain?" *North American Review.* October 1891.

Malin, James C. "Dust Storms: Part One, 1850-1860." *The Kansas Historical Quarterly* (May 1946).

—. "Dust Storms: Part Three, 1881-1980." *The Kansas Historical Quarterly* (November 1946).

—. "Dust Storms: Part Two, 1861-1880." *The Kansas Historical Quarterly* (August 1946).

Meredith, William John. "Old Plum Grove Colony in Jefferson County, 1854-1855." *The Kansas Historical Quarterly* (November 1938).

Rosenberg, Norman J. "Climate of the Great Plains Region of the United States." *Great Plains Quarterly* (Winter 1987).

Bibliography

Magazines

Chittenden, H. M. "Discussion: Forests, Reservoirs, and Stream Flow." *Transactions of the American Society of Civil Engineers* 62 (1909), quoted in William B. Meyer, *Americans and Their Weather*. New York: Oxford University Press, 2000.

Cook, Charles Orson. "John Milsaps's Houston: 1910." *The Houston Review: History and Culture of the Gulf Coast* 1, no. 1 (Spring 1979).

Cunningham, Don. "River Portraits: The Platte." *NEBRASKAland Magazine*, January-February 1983.

Dodds, Gordon B. "Stream-Flow Controversy: A Conservation Turning Point." *Journal of American History* 56 (1969), 59-69, quoted in William B. Meyer, *Americans and Their Weather*. New York: Oxford University Press, 2000.

Grundy, Frederick. "Cyclones and Tornadoes," *Frank Leslie's Popular Monthly* 15, no. 3 (March 1883).

"Platte River" *Nebraska History and Record of Pioneer* Days 1, no. 2 (March 1918).

Stearly, Samuel. "Fording the Platte." *Publications of the Nebraska State Historical Society* 18 (1917).

Sullivan, Robert, ed. "Great Wall of China." *Life: The Seven Wonders of the World Yesterday, Today and Tomorrow* 3, no. 6 (2003).

White, F. Buchanan. "Locusts and Grasshoppers." *Frank Leslie's Popular Monthly*, April 1882.

Databases

American Meteorological Society "Glossary of Meteorology." http://amsglossary.allenpress.com/glossary; Atlantic Oceanographic and Meteorological Laboratory, Hurricane Research Division, "Frequently Asked Questions." http://www.aoml.noaa.gov/hrd/tcfaq/A1.html.

"Armored Airplane Thunders Into Stormy Weather." *SDSM&T Quarterly,* Spring 1998. http://www.hpcnet.org/sdsmt/SiteID=199437

Barkley, Roy R. "Blue Norther." *The Handbook of Texas Online.* http://www.tsha.utexas.edu/handbook/online/articles/view/BB/ybb1.html.

Dunn, Roy Sylvan. "Droughts." *The Handbook of Texas Online.* http://www.tsha.utexas.edu/handbook/online/articles/view/DD/ybd1.html.

"Flash Floods and Hail." http://ww2010.atmos.uiuc.edu/(Gh)/guides/mtr/sur/dngr/flood.rxml.

Guyer, Jared L. and Rick Ewald, "Record Hail Event--Examination of the Aurora, Nebraska Supercell of 22 June 2003." http://www.spec.noaa.gov/publications/guyer/aurora.pdf.

Jarrell, Jerry D., Max Mayfield, and Edward N. Rappaport, "The Deadliest, Costliest, and Most Intense United States *Hurricanes From 1900-2000." NOAA Technical Memorandum NWS TPC-1.* Miami: NOAA/NWS/ Tropical Prediction Center. http://www.nhc.noaa.gov/pastint.shtml.

National Weather Service Forecast Office, Tulsa, Oklahoma, "The Fujita Scale." http://www.srh.noaa.gov/tsa/wcm/fujita.html.

NOAA. "Hurricane Basics." http://hurricanes.noaa.gov/prepare/title_basics.htm.

—. "The Saffir/Simpson Hurricane Scale." http://hurricanes.noaa.gov/prepare/categories.htm.

O'Brien, Greg. "Making the Mississippi Over Again: The Development of River Control in Mississippi." *Mississippi History Now* (March 2002). http://mshistory.k12.ms.us/features/feature25/msriver.html.

Official Records: series 1, vol. 22, part 2, (Little Rock), http://ehistory.osu.edu/uscw/library/or/033/0572.cfm.

Reid, John D. "The Great 1900 Galveston Hurricane in Canada." http://www.magma.ca/~jdreid/great_1900_hurricane.htm.

Turekian, Karl K. and Barbra L. Narendra, "The Origins and Early History of Earth Sciences at Yale." *Science at Yale*, S. Altman, ed. New Haven: Yale University, 2002. http://www.yale.edu/geology/graduate/history.html.

U.S. Secretary of War. *The War of the Rebellion: A Compilation of the Official Records of the Union and Confederate Armies.* Washington: GPO. http://ehistory.osu.edu/uscw/library/or/index.cfm.

Woodhouse, Connie A. and Jonathan T. Overpeck, "2000 Years of Drought Variability in the Central United States." *Bulletin of the American Meteorological Society*, December 1998. www.ngdc. noaa.gov/paleo/amsdrought.pdf.

Newspapers

Atchison (Kansas) *Globe.* "The Flood of 1881." 1 July 1908.

Beatrice (Nebraska) *Express.* "The Saline County Prairie Fire Slaughter."

Cambridge (Nebraska) *Clarion.* "1500 People Attend Monument Dedication." May 30, 1924.

Chicago Daily Tribune. "Are Destitute and Suffering." 20 December 1890.

Commonwealth (Topeka, Kansas), "Atchinson Experiences the Most Terrific Hail Storm Ever Known." 25 August 1887.

Fletcher, James. "Earthquake." *Pittsburgh* (Pennsylvania) *Gazette*, 14 February 1812.

Hamer [rb], Francis O. "Old Fort Kearney: Historic and Consecrated Ground." *Kearney* (Nebraska) *Daily Hub*, 26 June 1909.

Hill City (Kansas) *Times*, "Trials That Harassed the Settlers," May 22, 1980.

Houston Chronicle, "Echoes of The Storm," 3 September 2000, Special Report.

Johnson City (Kansas) *Journal*, 13 April 1895.

Kiowa (Kansas) *Herald*, "Waterspout in '86 Caused Great Loss of Lives, Property," 23 April 1886 (1885?).

Leavenworth (Kansas) *Daily Times,* 11 May 1875.

Minden (Nebraska) *Courier*, "Over the State," 16 August 1894.

MPM [unknown newspaper], "Hurtling Hail: Valley Falls Visited by a Furious Storm on Friday Night." 22 April 1882.

(New Orleans) *Louisiana Gazette and Daily Advertiser.* 21 December 1811.

Nebraska City (N.T.) *News*, "Prairies on Fire," 4 December 1858.

"Ohio Valley Flood Recalls South Dakota Disaster in 1881," No name, no date newspaper article from the South Dakota State Historical Society verticle file clippings under "Floods." This clipping was donated to the Society with no identification as to paper of origin. The dateline reads "Pierre, Feb. 3."

(Philadelphia) *Pennsylvania Gazette*, 15 April 1812.

(Philadelphia) *Pennsylvania Gazette*, 26 February 1812.

(Philadelphia) *Pennsylvania Gazette*, 11 March 1812.

Pierce, William Leigh. "The Earthquake." *New York Evening Post*, 11 February 1812.

Pittsburgh (Pennsylvania) *Gazette*, "The Earthquake." 14 February 1812.

(Ponca) *Nebraska Journal Leader*, "Many Lives Lost In Flood of 1881," 24 June 1937.

"Recall Early Dakota Flood: Old Timers Reminded of Missouri River Rampage of 1881." No name, no date newspaper article from the South Dakota State Historical Society verticle file clippings under "Floods." This clipping was donated to the Society with no identification as to paper of origin. The dateline reads "Pierre, S. D. — Special."

Salina (Kansas) *Journal*, "Some of the Experiences in 'The Sixties' as Told to the Society," 29 January, 1927.

Southern Industrial and Lumber Review, (Houston, Texas), 22 September 1900. Galveston Disaster Edition.

Speed, Mathias M. "Earthquake." (Philadelphia) *Pennsylvania Gazette*, 15 April 1812.

(St. Louis) *Louisiana Gazette.* 15 February 1812.

St. Louis Republican, 17 September 1863.

Topeka (Kansas) *Capital*, "The Floods of 1844," 3 June 1903.

Unnamed newspaper. Vertical files. Texas Local History Room, Houston Public Library-Houston Metropolitan Research Center, Houston, Texas.

Welty, Raymond L. "Floods Here Traced Back As Early As 1865." *Hays* (Kansas) *Daily News*, 12 June 1966.

Western Cyclone (Nicodemus, Kansas), "A Big Fire," 14 April 1887.

Wichita (Kansas) *City Eagle*, 15 April 1880.

ACKNOWLEDGMENT OF PERMISSIONS

Grateful acknowledgment is made to the following university presses, historical societies, and individuals for permission to reprint excerpts from their material:

From *Platte River Road Narratives*. Copyright 1988 by the Board of Trustees of the University of Illinois. Used with permission of the University of Illinois Press.

Reprinted by permission of Louisiana State University Press from *Atlantic Hurricanes* by Gordon E. Dunn and Banner I. Miller. Copyright © 1960, 1964 by Louisiana State University Press.

From *Tornadoes of the United States*, by Snowden D. Flora. Copyright © 1953, 1954 by the University of Oklahoma Press, Norman. Reprinted by permission of the publisher. All rights reserved.

From *6,000 Miles of Fence: Life on the XIT Ranch of Texas*, by Cordia Sloan and Joe B. Frantz. Copyright © 1961. Reprinted by permission of University of Texas Press, Austin, publishers.

The Earthquake America Forgot, by David Stewart & Ray Knox, Copyright © 1995. Reprinted by permission of Gutenberg-Richter Publications, Marble Hill, Missouri.

Significant Tornadoes 1680-1991, by Thomas P. Grazulis. Copyright © 1993. Reprinted by permission of Environmental Films, Johnsbury, Vermont.

Significant Tornadoes, 1880-1989 Volume I: Discussion and Analysis, by Thomas P. Grazulis. Copyright © 1991. Reprinted by permission of Environmental Films, Johnsbury, Vermont.

"The Great 1900 Galveston Hurricane in Canada," by John D. Reid. Copyright © 2001. Reprinted from website with permission. http://www.magma.ca/~jdreid/great_1900_hurricane.htm

INDEX

INDEX

INDEX

INDEX

For a free catalog of Caxton titles write to:

CAXTON PRESS
312 Main Street
Caldwell, Idaho 83605-3299

or

Visit our Internet web site:

www.caxtonpress.com

Caxton Press is a division of THE CAXTON PRINTERS, Ltd.